PYTHON PRESS

Peter Cowman
The Sheltermaker's Manual
Volume 1

Peter Cowman is an architect, eco-builder, writer and teacher delivering Courses & Workshops internationally on the subject of Living Architecture. He was born and educated in Dublin, Ireland, graduating from the School of Architecture, University College Dublin in 1976. Apart from his work as an architect, at various points of his nomadic life Peter has worked as a salesman, an art gallery director, a handyman and as a full-time parent. He began teaching people how to design their own homes in 1989, a task which he still pursues as director of the Living Architecture Centre. Never having had a mortgage himself, Peter has a special interest in the creation of affordable, low-impact, mortgage-free buildings and has developed a unique timber framing system for cost-conscious self-builders. Originator of the 'Sheltermaker' and 'Living Architecture' concepts Peter's work has been widely publicised in both print as well as broadcast media, worldwide.

The Sheltermaker's Manual

Volume 1

Peter Cowman

PYTHON PRESS

For sheltermakers everywhere ...

Special thanks to: Siãn Cowman, Johnny Gogan, Gerard Greene, John Long, Mary Dineen-Long, Brendan Lyons, Alanna Moore, Sharon Ray, Bairbre Madden-Reddy, Jim O'Donnell, Leo Regan, Deirdre Stephens, Leitrim Co. Enterprise Board, Sligo-Leitrim VEC, Tommy Waters

♥PYTHON
♀PRESS

© Peter Cowman 2013

First published as 'The Handbook of House Design & Construction Volume 1' ISBN 0 9519365 0 6

Printed on acid free paper by Lightning Source
Lightning Source Inc., an Ingram Content Group Inc. company, is committed to manufacturing books in a manner that both respects the environment and helps preserve the world's natural resources.

ISBN 978-0-9757782-6-5

Published by:
Python Press
P.O. Box 929
Castlemaine
Victoria 3450
Australia

EMail:
pythonpress@gmail.com

Web:
pythonpress.com

Design & Illustration
Peter Cowman

Cover: Sharo's Studio
Photo by Peter Cowman

A Note from the Publisher

When Peter Cowman dreamed up his groundbreaking 'Be Your Own Architect' concept in 1989 he quickly discovered that his university education had neglected to teach him the rudiments of house design! Realising that people had for millenia designed and built their homes he set out to revive this vernacular architecture tradition, reawakening what he called our 'sheltermaker genes'.

As a student working in America, its radical sub-culture and anti-war movement were an inspiration to Peter, especially the idea of *conscientious objection*. After graduating from University in his native Ireland an itinerant lifestyle, escaping the tyrannies of professional practice and mortgage debt, left him well qualified for an unconventional return to the world of architecture.

Peter worked at various jobs across Europe, from salesman to small builder, from art gallery owner to fulltime parent. Architectural practice, he found, had little relevance to the real world. Living revealed that the invisible realms were an essential component of a meaningful and fulfilling life.

In 1992 the first volume of architect Peter's 'Be Your Own Architect' Handbook appeared, inspired by the courses he was regularly delivering on the subject. This book was taken up to such an extent that he was drawn into many exciting projects, uncovering many secrets of what he described as 'living architecture' - working with real people on real projects in real time. His building site experiences, that thread through *The Sheltermaker's Manual,* highlighted the shortcomings of the desk-bound training he had received and revealed the strong psychological dimension of designing one's own home.

With a passion for small-scale, mortgage-free sheltermaking, Peter initiated *The EconoSpace Project* in 1997, developing practical solutions to issues of designing and constructing low-cost, low-impact buildings, empowering others to practice eco-construction in their own backyards!

He went on to become a well known figure in Ireland, his work featuring on Irish television in the documentary *'Building On the Edge'* and the highly popular *Nationwide* show. Along with numerous magazine and newspaper articles his reputation as an innovative architect and originator of the 'living architecture' concept was set.

Visiting Australia in 2007 led to the exportation of his ideas and a widening of their influence. From there Peter watched the collapse of the Irish property market - which he had long predicted. Freed from the gravity of his native land, the Australian landscape captivated him, while his freely given ideas fell on fertile ground.

Drawing upon the Irish-Australian spirit of larrikanism*, his irreverent approach to architecture was well nurtured. Aboriginal traditions of the Dreamtime also inspired a deepening of his exploration into what he termed 'invisible architecture'. As this most ancient of cultures is not focussed on the material world, it's architecture is ephemeral. As a consequence, it's social fabric is rich with hidden meaning.

Teaching his 'living architecture' in Asia has since allowed Peter's innovative and exciting concepts to discover their roots in India's *Vastu Shastra* and Chinese *Feng-Shui*. These ancient traditions are based on balancing the life force of buildings and empowering their occupants in the quest for harmonious and fulfilling lives.

Today Ireland's 'Celtic Tiger' is dead, austerity rules and the credit that once fuelled 'mac-mansions' and 'ghost estates' nationally and globally has mostly evaporated. Republication of the 'Be Your Own Architect' Handbook as *'The Sheltermaker's Manual'* could not be more timely. With over 600 pages of practical information, these two volumes present a unique and proven sheltermaking methodology that turns conventional architectural practice on its head. Revealing the hidden aspects of how buildings affect peoples' lives and the life of the planet, the *Manual* offers the opportunity to not only be one's own architect, but also to reclaim time and space lost to an economy that has ruthlessly exploited the need for shelter.

Of universal relevance, this is a book for everywhere and everyone.

Alanna Moore
Python Press

*larrikin: an Australian expression which means 'a fundamentally good person that tests the boundaries of dubious rules'

Contents

Surveying 137

Structure 175

Environment 204

Heating & Ventilation 214

Appendices 271

Introduction

The desire to create shelter is an expression of the human will to survive. For thousands of years people have created shelter without recourse to professional architects. The style of buildings produced in this way is known as vernacular architecture *figs 1-2*. Vernacular styles of building exist all over the world. These styles are characterised by their simplicity, by their use of local materials and by the ease with which they can be constructed. The knowledge required for the creation of such buildings was long regarded as being common knowledge and freely available to all.

The decline of the vernacular tradition with its simple forms and its accessibility to people has resulted in the loss of the knowledge and skills needed to design and construct small buildings, especially the buildings in which people live – their homes. This loss has resulted in the involvement of professional architects and other building designers in the housing field. It has also resulted in the application of a more formal approach to the creation of such buildings than was previously the case with the vernacular tradition. The widespread frustration that has resulted from this is now so common that it has become the accepted state of affairs.

Professional architects are currently the only people who are trained to design buildings. This academic training is based on a formal approach to architecture and is very much biased in favour of large and complex projects that take little account of people or of individual need. Because house design is so closely related to people and to their day to day needs, the application of this formal approach has failed to produce houses that satisfy people in the way their vernacular counterparts did in the past.

Formal architecture is characterised by its scale and grandeur and is quite different from the simple forms of the vernacular tradition. Where the vernacular style is an expression of the human instinct to survive, the formal tradition is more expressive of the will to triumph *figs 3-4*.

fig. 1: *Traditional Irish thatched cottage.*

fig. 2: *Traditional farmhouse.*

fig. 3: *World Trade Centre, New York.*

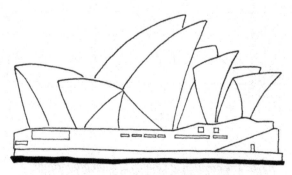

fig. 4: *Sydney Opera House.*

1

Historically, architects were craftsmen themselves and the word 'architect' is derived from the Greek for 'chief carpenter'. The early professional architects were in fact craftsmen and were directly involved in the creation of buildings. In contrast, the modern professional architect is academically trained and does not create buildings directly but rather creates designs in an office environment and relies on others to realise their construction. The practice of formal architecture has always existed alongside the vernacular tradition and concerned itself mainly with the creation of large formal buildings.

Where the vernacular architectural tradition can be seen to have been available to all, the formal architectural tradition is characterised by secrecy. This tradition stretches back to Ancient Egypt and to Greece, where priests applied their secret knowledge of proportion and form to the design of sacred buildings *figs 5-7*. In the Middle Ages, knowledge of building form and technique was passed down through the Crafts Guilds, especially the Stonemasons Guild. Such knowledge was regarded as being secret knowledge. This was in contrast to the vernacular tradition where the information needed to build was freely available to all.

fig. 5: The Pyramids of Egypt.

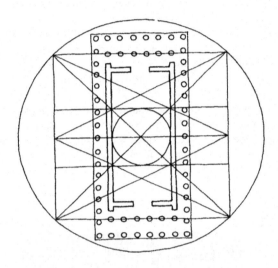

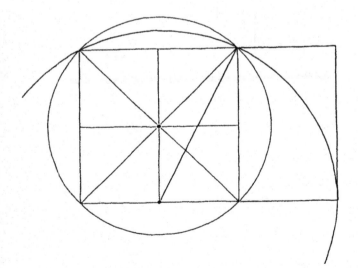

fig. 6: The creation of Golden Section proportions based on the use of the circle and the square.

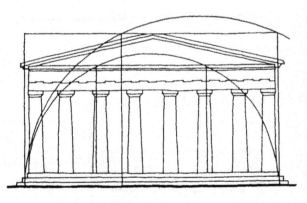

fig. 7: The Parthenon of Athens. This building is constructed in accordance with Golden Proportions, mathematical relationships based on spiritual values.

The modern professional architect, being academically trained, is very much removed from the actuality of making buildings. This contrasts with his historical counterpart who was a craftsman *figs 8-9*. This detachment has had a severe effect on the quality of all professionally designed buildings. Where at one time the architect was a carpenter or a stonemason and so could be relied upon to have an intimate knowledge of his materials and the actuality of their use, the modern professional is neither a carpenter nor a stonemason but an academically trained person. Despite this obvious limitation, architects control the design process, select materials and direct their assembly by the building team. The shortcomings of this approach to building design and construction results in regular conflicts between architects and the builders who must follow their directions. It has also resulted in the creation of buildings very much lacking the qualities of their earlier counterparts, both in terms of space as well as craftsmanship. This is a direct result of the relinquishment by the 'architect' of his tools, and his insistence on leading the construction team despite the limitations of a purely academic training.

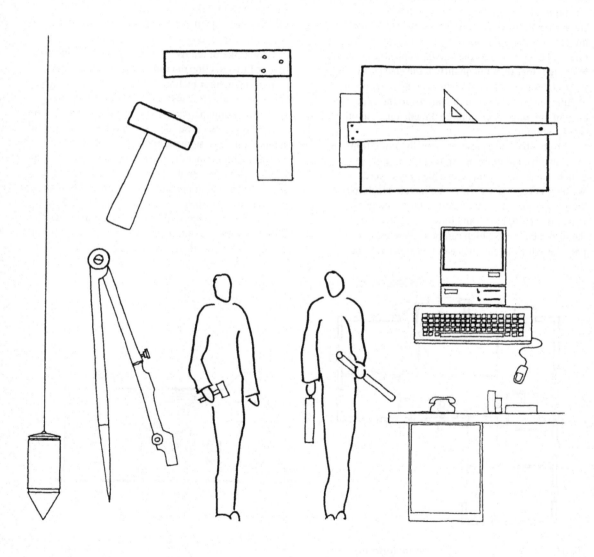

fig. 8: Craftsman's tools.

fig. 9: Architects' tools.

All modern building design involves the use of drawings that communicate ideas and information to those involved in the construction process. The limitation of drawings in illustrating space are very severe in that only two dimensions can be displayed in relationship to each other at any one time. What can actually be drawn on paper are the flat surfaces of walls and floors *fig 10*. The nature of the space – the architecture – formed by these surfaces cannot be seen on paper. Instead, the spaces so formed must be imagined in three dimensions and it is not until the spaces within the design are actually constructed that they can be experienced. The effect of this limitation of drawing technique has been to emphasise flat surfaces at the expense of highlighting space and it has caused the meaning of 'architecture' to be redefined as the outward appearance of a building rather than the quality of the spaces within it *fig 11*. A reliance on drawings in the creation of architecture is very much in contrast to the experience of creating space in three dimensions – in other words, building.

From a building point of view, the limitations of two-dimensional drawings in representing three-dimensional objects and space are very severe. While it is very easy to draw a concrete block in two dimensions on paper, the reality of a concrete block is that it is cold, heavy and unwieldy. Similarly, damproof courses, which can be represented on paper as a line and as such can be expected to pre-

vent water penetration, are in reality rolls of plastic which are difficult to insert into any construction. Concrete, which again is easy to draw, is in fact a heavy, wet and cumbersome material to use *fig 12*. From the building operatives point of view these materials are very different from the architect's perception of them.

While two-dimensional drawings are a very necessary means of communication between architect and builder, the idea that what is shown on paper is a reflection of three-dimensional reality, is false. This fallacy is the basis of the architectural style usually referred to as the 'modern movement'. This style is characterised by flatness and a lack of decorative effect, a consequence of the belief that two-dimensional drawings allow one to see what something will look like in reality. A reliance on drawings has also led to a decline in craftsmanship and a restriction of the natural inclination of craftsmen to embellish their work. Because such decoration is essentially three-dimensional, it is difficult to represent on paper *fig 13*. Because of this, it has been eliminated from building design and the appearance of the resulting flat surfaces has been promoted as being a 'style'. A failure on the part of professional architects to properly appreciate the realities of the building operative's world and to value, utilise and encourage craftsmanship has engendered resentment, suspicion and mistrust and has led to an unfortunate decline in standards of workmanship.

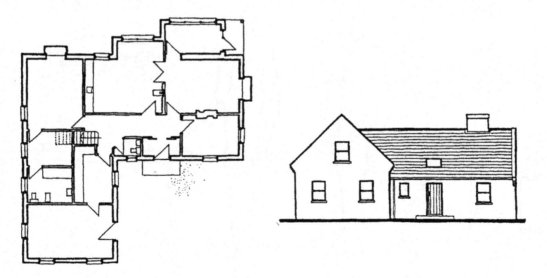

fig. 10: The limitations of drawings in illustrating space are very severe. What can actually be drawn on paper are the flat surfaces of walls and floors.

4

fig. 11: The word 'architecture' has been redefined to mean the outward appearance of a building, rather than to describe the quality of the spaces within it.

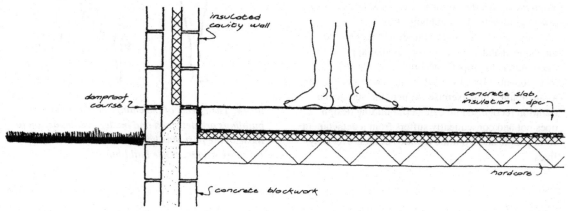

fig. 12: Concrete blocks, dampproof courses and a concrete slab as represented by drawing. The reality of these materials is very different to their appearance on paper.

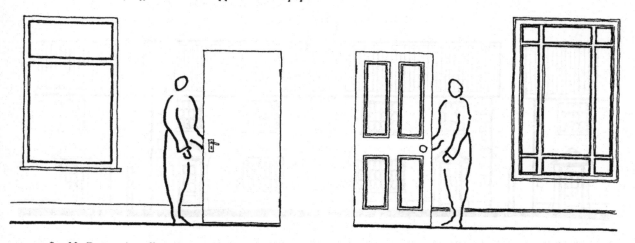

fig. 13: Decorative effects are very difficult to represent on paper. For this reason, the use of decoration has been eliminated from building design.

The effects of the changes in how modern buildings are designed and made, in comparison to those of the past, has had very serious consequences for those who most use buildings – people *fig 14.* Modern buildings are often described as being soulless or dehumanised. Both these observations are consequences of the modern formal approach to architecture. Surprising as it might seem, people are rarely taken into account in building design. Nowhere has this been more evident than in the field of housing. The professional, academically trained architect learns to balance and resolve complex issues that do not involve people at all. While this approach might be justified in the design of large impersonal buildings, when it is applied to the design of a person's home it is simply unworkable. Formal architectural practice makes no room for the individual, but only for the notional 'standard' human being that might use the finished building.

In essence a house is a building based on individual need and so requires a particular approach if the design is to properly accommodate the needs of its occupants. Because of this, the house stands apart as an architectural exercise. Where the vernacular tradition recognised this, modern building design does not and consequently suffers from a detachment from people and from the realities of their everyday lives.

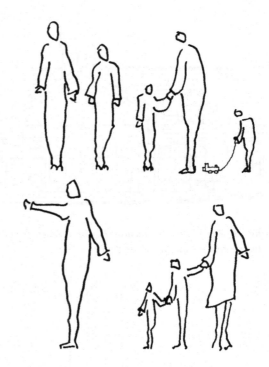

fig.14: The effects of the changes in how modern buildings are designed and made, in comparison to those of the past, has had very serious consequences for those who most use buildings – people.

fig. 15: People's very real need for shelter is only too often exploited by unscrupulous persons, to the detriment of good value and design.

Because professional architects are the only persons actually trained to design buildings, their failure to provide reasonable house design solutions is very serious. Where other building designers have sought to fill this void, the formal approach has also been employed and the results have been equally disappointing. In reality, no one is designing houses, or indeed buildings, with real people in mind. All sorts of other questions take precedence over people, and the very real need for shelter is only too often exploited by unscrupulous persons, to the detriment of good value and design *fig 15*. The loss of the vernacular tradition with its simple approach to the provision of shelter has, until now, left little alternative to the use of the formal architecture approach.

Professional architects have, in large part, abandoned the housing field, particularly their involvement with individual house designs. The main reason for this are the difficulties encountered in dealing with people on such a personal level and an inability to integrate individual needs in the design proceedings. Normally such proceedings create frustration for client and architect alike and rarely are design solutions produced that embody the kind of individuality that people desire from their homes. This failure must be seen to be not only a shortcoming of the formal academic approach but also an indicator of the extreme difficulty of the task of house design itself. Notwithstanding the limitations of the formal architectural approach, to ask a professional architect to design your home is to ask for the services of a lifestyle analyst as well as a building designer *fig 16*. Normally, an architect is not trained to engage people in this very personal way.

Pattern books now predominate as a source of house design solutions. Such designs, created as they are in isolation from people's real needs, fail to provide a satisfactory answer to the housing question *fig 17*.

While it has been recognised that the vernacular tradition can provide some answers in making modern buildings more sensitive to people, it is the mere outward appearance of the vernacular style that has been borrowed to to this. Inwardly, modern buildings continue to be flat and two-dimensional and require that people adapt themselves to their forms. Properly, it is the building form that should conform to the needs of the occupants.

In part, the failure of modern house design solutions are a result of the impossibility of developing design solutions that are relevant to all people in all situations. Where vernacular house designs were usually the repetition of a basic plan and were well suited to the lifestyles of those inhabiting them, the complexity of modern life and technology requires more varied and flexible design solutions. In other words, it is simply not enough to retreat to the vernacular tradition, with its simple forms, and transplant it into the present expecting it to function as it did in the past. What is required are new solutions suited to the realities of modern life and lifestyles.

In truth, the responsibility for providing shelter rests within us all and it is by accepting this responsibility that buildings can be created that are sensitive to people, their needs and their lifestyles. The development of a method of house design that directly involves people has long been necessary. When the need for people to take more direct responsibility for their housing needs is recognised, the failure of modern house designs can be recognised for what it is. That is, it is both a failure of the formal architectural approach to the problem as well as a failure to recognise the diverse nature of human life and individuality.

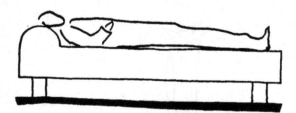

fig. 16: To ask a professional architect to design your home is to ask for the services of a lifestyle analyst as well as a building designer.

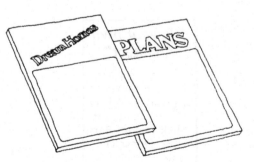

fig. 17: Pattern books now predominate as a source of house design solutions.

At present, many people undertake the design and even the construction of their own homes. In many cases people are drawn to restore and extend vernacular buildings – farmhouses, cottages, barns and so on. Also, many choose to employ pattern book solutions. While such activity can be seen to be an effort to circumvent the shortcomings of modern building design, the close involvement of people in the creation of their own homes springs not only from frustration but also from the recognition that to take responsibility for this task is to take responsibility for the reality of their lives.

While many people have recognised that it is necessary to undertake the creation of their own homes, the lack of information and technique to do so has been a major frustration. Despite this, creative and satisfactory buildings have been created by people using the limited resources available to them. In doing so, a new tradition, a modern vernacular, is being created. Such activity is a positive response to the basic question of shelter as faced by humanity at all times during its presence on the planet.

As an architect, the realisation that people should become directly involved in the design and even the construction of their own homes resulted from a steady flow of people seeking advice and information on house design. While it was clear that these people had rejected modern design solutions and were frustrated with 'architecture' as commonly practiced, the energy that fuelled their creativity was clearly not negative but positive – the energy result-

ing from the taking of responsibility for sheltering themselves from the world.

This understanding, and the very clear demand for information, led to the initiation of the Be Your Own Architect Courses in 1989. These Courses were conceived as a way of providing people with the information and skills they needed to properly evolve designs for their homes. The Courses met with a very positive response and drew people from all walks of life.

Inevitably, time was given over in the Courses to the voicing of complaint and frustration with modern buildings. At the same time, it was recognised that the power to initiate change lay in people's hands and that such change could be brought about through positive action and by the clear articulation of the demand for change.

Because the formal tradition had clearly failed to produce adequate design solutions, and the vernacular tradition, suited as it was to its time, was not flexible enough to satisfy the realities of modern life, an entirely new way of designing houses had to be evolved for these Courses. The design strategy that emerged from this process is both simple and comprehensive, allowing the designer to consider each aspect of the project in turn and to harmonise these in a properly balanced design. The direct involvement of people in the development of this strategy has ensured its relevance to the needs of the individual and to the task of creating homes suited to the times in which we live.

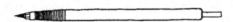

The assembly of coherent information on proper methods of Heating and Ventilation proved to be the most difficult task in evolving this new building design strategy. The profound influence that Heating and Ventilation systems have on most other aspects of building – the materials, the construction system, the orientation, the layout and the internal environment – make it extremely important to consider Heating and Ventilation at an early stage of the design process. The recognition of the vital nature of Heating and Ventilation in the creation of proper and healthy living environments will, more than any other aspect of the Be Your Own Architect approach, allow the designer to create a building that is beneficent not only to its occupants but to the wider world of which it is recognisably a part.

The evaluation of what sort of building one actually wants and how much one can afford to pay for it is the foundation of this new approach. A further aspect is the use of a simple technique for the preparation of scaled drawings. This technique eliminates the traditional T-square and drawing board, allowing accurate scaled drawings to be made on any flat work surface. These drawings are used to prepare simple scale models, allowing the spaces created by the flat surfaces of walls and floors to be seen and examined in model form. In this way, the architecture of the design is made real and visible. The models produced in this way are entirely different from the normal architectural model. Rather than striving for dolls-house accuracy, the design model is a cre-

ative tool which can be modified and adapted, in conjunction with two-dimensional drawings, to refine and develop the building design.

By this process of drawing and model making, the building design is allowed to grow outwards from the interior spaces that are being created. Heating and Ventilation systems, orientation, siting, materials, exterior and interior wall construction, building structure, plumbing and electrical services, drainage, planning regulations, design style and costing are then considered, and the design is allowed to develop naturally by taking all aspects of the building into consideration. It is only when the vital aspects of the project have been carefully considered and properly related to each other that the building layout is finally created. Houses and small buildings are relatively simple structures that can be easily understood by anyone. The approach stresses this, while providing the student with a straightforward design strategy that can be applied to any building project.

If it is nothing else, this new approach is a way of saving you frustration and, almost certainly, money. By devoting one's own time to a house design project, savings can quite obviously be made. By allowing choices to be made in terms of the size, quality and finish of the various elements that go together to make a building, savings can also be achieved in construction. These choices are choices that you yourself, as house designer, make and so the overall cost of the project remains firmly in your hands.

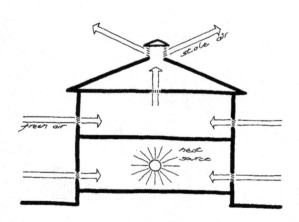

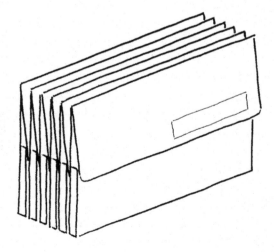

Because the design process remains within the control of the individual, clear choices can be made in terms of cost, appearance, size and style. For example, a method of construction might be chosen to allow for a large element of self-building. Or a small scale starter house might be designed to be expanded as need demanded. A person might choose to create a design that would allow for a business to be operated from the home. Also, a designer might choose to remain without a mortgage and to build strictly according to their means.

The implications of this breakthrough in the process of house design are very great, allowing the general dissatisfaction with modern houses to be relieved. The response to the Be Your Own Architect approach, since its inception, has clearly shown the widespread desire that people have to regain control of their living environments and to take responsibility for their house designs. To keep pace with this emerging trend, there is a clear need for the building industry to acknowledge the obvious demand for a change in its construction practices. This is especially true of the 'concrete block and slab' mentality, which urgently needs to be revised. A reappraisal of traditional materials, skills and techniques is also clearly necessary to restore faith in the house building sector of the industry. Similarly, the Planning Authorities must act positively in response to imaginative and sensitive design solutions, rather than impose generalisations and limitations that frustrate the individual designer. If such positive steps are taken, the creation of houses sensitive to both people and to the wider environment can become the norm.

Taking responsibility for the design of your own home will deeply satisfy the strong urge we all share to provide shelter for ourselves and for our families. We all have in us the desire to build. We express this most directly when we are children. By creating model buildings the exciting world of

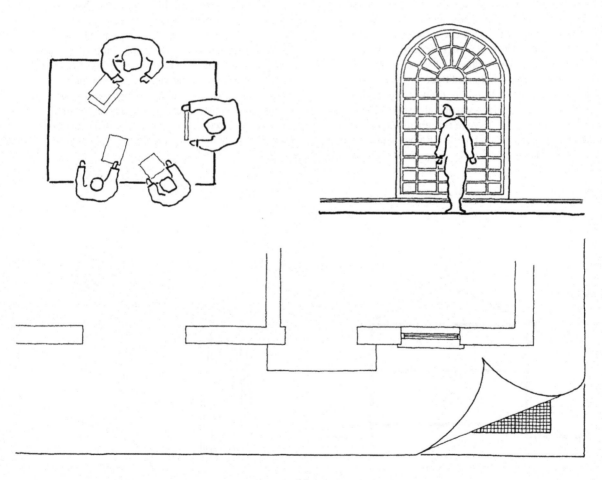

architecture can be explored and the pleasure of creating space enjoyed by adults. You can literally create your own home in miniature. This will allow you to become familiar with your home before it is even built. The advantages of this are very great. It is oftentimes a shock for architects to see their buildings erected. This is because, when only drawings are made of a design, the shape of it is not seen in three dimensions until it is built! Models have many creative uses and are a simple way of examining space. Space is architecture. It is very easy to forget this, because space is so difficult to see!

The approach is not without its pitfalls. Even the design of a small building is a time consuming job. A reasonable degree of commitment is therefore needed to complete a design. It can also happen that questions about lifestyle, values, relationships and all sorts of other topics will surface as the design evolves. These can often lead to conflicts between those involved in the design exercise. These, however, are merely the questions that we all must ask ourselves about our lives. Designing a house will allow you to answer many of them. It is important, therefore, to give yourself time to answer these questions and to see the project through to its natural conclusion.

While this book has been primarily written to allow for the development of individual house designs, many other types of buildings can be designed using these principles. Information on surveying and extending existing buildings has also been included.

The process of teaching and writing on the subject of Be Your Own Architect has been a very satisfying one for me. I have learned a great deal from my students, especially about being an architect. This work would not have been possible without their genuine response to the idea of being *their* own architects.

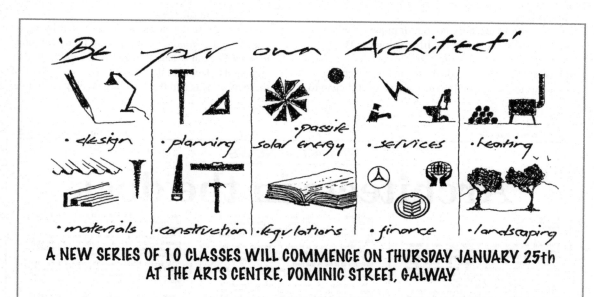

Advertising poster, *circa* 1989

Introduction to Volume 2
(2000)

When *Volume 1* of this *Handbook* was published in 1992 I thought that my work was about to get much easier. The plan was simple - publish *Volume 1*, generate income from sales, pay for the print run out of this income and use part of it subsidise the completion of *Volume 2*.

Clutching fresh books, overlooking the wild reaches of Roaringwater Bay in West Cork, I watched these assumptions be devoured by storms. While newspaper reviewers welcomed my book and trumpeted my efforts, I trudged to the Unemployment Office to sign on!

Ousted from my subsidised office by skittish local functionaries, I was brought face to face with a grim reality. The *Be Your Own Architect Studio* was suddenly gone! I was adrift, resourceless, my energies focussed on the day-to-day tasks of survival rather than on the niceties of self-promotion, selling books and the completion of *Volume 2*.

Borrowing money to finance this drama was simply not an option. *Life* and *Business* Plans were at odds. It was time to lay low and to focus on survival!

I tell this story not out of pique or anger but because it illustrates the life of an idea. These depressing events gave me pause to wonder if being a *Writer/Publisher* was the best way of presenting my ideas to the world. Inevitably, *Life* itself began to provide answers to this question and, in the end, a clear way forward.

This process began by abandoning the wild beauty of West Cork to plunge into the wild excess of Dublin. This homecoming was no *Easy Street!* Issues repressed since childhood, adolescence and my early professional life clustered around me like hungry children.

Throughout this unfolding, positive feedback from readers of *Volume 1* lightened my load and lit my way. In effect, what was happening was that the original idea behind the *Handbook* was being realised - the translation of the *Be Your Own Architect* Course format into a practical 'how to' manual. What I had not reckoned on was how much I was part of the *Handbook* and how much the *Handbook* was a part of me. Readers were quick to understand this however! Apart from endless enquiries about when *Volume 2* would 'be ready', I was slowly drawn into projects based on the *Volume 1* material. This 'real world' interaction with readers spurred the development of *Worksheets* and a *Be Your Own Architect Design Programme* - aids to best utilising the *Handbook* information and optimising a students' time commitment to their design - and it began to have a profound influence on the content of '*Volume 2*'.

These developments imparted a 'living' quality to the *Handbook* and fostered the evolution of what I began to call '*Living Architecture*'. It also signalled a deeper reality - that I was the *Teacher* of these new ideas and that I had to develop a suitable

---

EVENING PRESS Supplement

HOME STYLE, 7 October, 1992   3

Property News

Architects in the dock

Con Power
Property Editor

Currrent house design methods have come under heavy fire, with the architectural profession slammed for failing to adapt to modern lifestyles.

"Professional architects have, in large part, abandoned the housing field, particularly their involvement with individual house designs," Skibbereen-based architect Peter Cowman states in a radical new publication on house design.

Mr Cowman claims that architects have largely failed to integrate individual needs in the design process.

"Because professional architects are the only persons actually trained to design buildings, their failure to provide reasonable house design solutions is very serious," he says.

The West Cork architect begins from the premise that people have created shelter without recourse to professional designers for thousands of years.

This resulted in highly effective vernacular styles of building - characterised by their simplicity, use of local materials and ease of construction.

This tradition has, however, been replaced by a formal architectural approach based on academic rather than populist principles.

"Where vernacular house designs were usually the repetition of a basic plan and were well suited to the lifestyles of those inhabiting them, the complexity of modern life and technology requires more varied and flexible design solutions," Mr Cowman continues.

"In other words, it is simply not enough to retreat to the vernacular tradition, with its simple forms, and transplant it into the present expecting it to function as it did in the past.

"What is required are new solutions suited to the realities of modern life and lifestyles."

In response to constant demands for more personalised designs, Mr Cowman decided to break through conventional moulds and launched his own "Be Your Own Architect" courses in 1989.

People from all walks of life have since attended these courses in West Cork. The architect has now published a detailed (240 page) house/design handbook setting forth his alternative approach.

This involves replacing conventional two-dimensional plans with three-dimensional scale models, highlighting the crucial spatial aspects of modern living.

Mr Cowman claims that the average home owner can thus effectively assume responsibility for the design of a house specifically geared to his/her particular needs.

"Because the design process remains within the control of the individual, clear choices can be made in terms of cost, appearance, size and style," he comments.

"For example, a method of construction might be chosen to allow for a large element of self-building. Or a small scale starter house might be designed to be expanded as need demanded.

"A person might choose to create a design that would allow for a business to be operated from the home. Also, a designer might choose to remain without a mortgage and to build strictly according to their means."

This new participative "school" is a welcome departure from the mass production practices all too prevalent nowadays. But this provocative new publication nevertheless looks certain to prove highly controversial.

The new national building regulations have made architects and others more conscious than ever of the need for professionalism in the construction sphere.

■ "Be Your Own Architect," published by Peter Cowman, is available from the Business Development Centre, North treet, Skibbereen, west Cork. Design courses for non-architects are also presented regularly at the centre.

vehicle - other than just books - in which to deliver this '*sheltermaking information*'!

It is within the context of the *Course in Sustainable House Design & Construction* that *Volumes 1 & 2* of the *Handbook* now reside, the key components in an evolving framework of *Sheltermaking Information* that allows for the creation of shelter based on our sense of survival and on our conscious and positive participation in *Life*.

Underpinning all of this *Sheltermaking Information* is the notion of 'living architecture'. Because it is so apposite in identifying a *feeling* it is difficult to define in words exactly what *Living*

Architecture is. One way to imagine it is to think of the very fabric of your home being part of your *vital existence,* to think of walls, floor, roof, light, colour, air and smell as being an intimate part of your own *life,* as lived by you, within your home. Even rejection of this idea highlights how we feel about our homes - we simply do not imagine living in them as being a sensuous experience! Another way to imagine *Living Architecture* is to think of your home as an 'outer layer' of your own *Self.* By designing your home in this awareness you actually 'live' your 'architecture' and create a 'living' building.

Cork Examiner, Monday, September 21, 1992   Page 11

Your home could be all your own design

WHY is it that the vast majority of architects who design kitchens for women are men?

Why do people building their own home rely totally on the expertise of an architect, without accepting that they too have ideas of their own?

Peter Cowman, B.Arch, has written a book which will surely be a boon for those who have ideas about design but are reticent about putting it into practice.

Entitled *Be Your Own Architect - The Handbook of House Design and Construction* it has just been published and is a radical rethink of house design.

One of the unique features of the book is that Peter Cowman, an architect himself, thinks that the designs of homes are best undertaken by the people who actually use them.

Peter is in favour of low-cost, self-build construction techniques and explores the idea of healthy, breathable house construction. He especially advocates the use of wood.

I can almost see architects shaking their heads in dismay and conjuring up all kinds of mistakes that the layman/woman could make.

Possibly so — but take a drive towards Killarney or Galway and have a look at the ghastly, 'Southfork' monstrosities that litter the countryside, complete with false pillars, arches, red brick and garden designs far removed from the local environment. These are architect built constructions and I have a strong feeling that the novice couldn't do worse!

Peter has taught his Be Your Own Architect course since 1989 and has recently completed Summer Workshops which attracted people from all over the country as well as from abroad.

MAUREEN FOX ON MONDAY

One of the surprising aspects of the courses and seminars was that people never questioned that they could design their own homes. What Peter had thought of as radical was not radical at all to people themselves.

He found people highly receptive and capable of undertaking the designs of their own homes. He found that the women who took the course were on the whole more receptive to new ideas and had thought a great deal about how houses should work.

The *Handbook* is a result of three years of research and on Peter's part a complete rethinking of everything he had been taught as a university trained architect. He approached the subject completely new — as if he didn't know anything.

Peter will be going on a nationwide tour to publicise his book and by undertaking a lecture tour hopes to convey the excitement of this idea to a larger audience.

The tour will visit all parts of the country and interested groups or organisations who wish to hear Peter talk on this topical subject can contact him in Skibbereen — telephone number 028-22408.

13

These discoveries, made in the classroom, on building sites and within the resultant finished buildings, not only emphasise the need for thoughtful house design but also highlight the need to select and use sheltermaking materials sensitively. They also highlight the way in which materials are put together - the 'workmanship' - as being a vital part of creating shelter that *feels* good. They further reveal how critical the healthiness of a home is, both to its inhabitants as well as to the environment of which it is an integral part. On a deeper level, taking responsibility for your '*Self*' allows for the making of a 'home' that respects your individuality and nourishes your personal development.

Designing and building homes in this way has revealed to me the hidden psychological aspects of housing and made it clear that when a person designs a home for their specific needs, the very nature of their *life* is embodied in their design! *Life* itself, and, *life* as people wish to live it, physically and emotionally, is really a vital and integral part of the design and construction process! This, I now realise, is what underpinned the original *Be Your Own Architect* idea!

While these ideas have been developed in an Irish context, this fact, oddly enough, has ensured the usefulness of the material in a wider geographical context. Because house design in Ireland is so bad, all aspects of *sheltermaking* had to be examined and, creative, workable solutions had to be found to the minutiae of the design and construction process. The curiously intact state of Irish *intuition* lent further assistance to this development simply because Irish people have such an innate sense of the importance of *life* itself.

Replacing the rational-based decision making of conventional architecture with a process that relies on intuition and on how we *feel* about our shelter triggers a cascade of change that appears to offer an opportunity to resolve many predicaments that bedevil the world.

By changing the way in which we look at the subject of human shelter we gain the potential to change our lives. It is this key factor - the incorporation within a home of the natural ability to change and adapt - that offers the power to change not only ourselves but, in consequence, the world. It is the need for such change that characterises all proposed solutions to the problems of global warming, pollution, toxic waste, food contamination, etc.

The reason that house design wields such power is simple. Settled life is the basis of civilisation as we know it. Houses are the cornerstone of settled life, and, in consequence, underpin all the civilised values we revere. By thinking in new ways about how we design, construct, pay for and live in our shelter, we can change ourselves and the world of which we are all a part.

This vital role that housing plays in civilised life is clearly reflected in the economic structure of the world where special status is ascribed to houses. Where virtually all other commodities fall in value after purchase, the opposite is true of houses which normally increase in value over the course of their lifetimes. This trick of accounting is a key component of the the market led economic system that now shrouds the globe.

The special status that houses and property enjoy is forged by linking the work we do to the shelter we need to survive. By treating our working time as a commodity the economic value of our labour over a specified period - say, over 20 years - can be quantified. By allowing one to borrow against the projected value of this work and to use these borrowings to invest in a place to live, the 'worker' is tied to his or her job because he or she must repay from it the cost of the shelter that is essential to their survival.

The work/shelter cycle, as long as it satisfies people and their desire to live, is a miracle of progress. However when this cycle grows to depend on factors that are beyond the needs of people they become hostages to economic forces that have nothing to do with them or the life of the planet. This is the situation in the developed world at the present time. Economic growth is everything. This favours increased consumption and the application of market-driven solutions to the resultant woes. Because business is normally bottom-line driven and head-centred, the consequences of unbridled economic growth is often threatening to *life* on the planet. Solving these problems in a market led economy will, it is imagined, further assist economic growth!

Because houses form a vital part of economic systems, which are normally wholly focussed on commercial values, any change in the established work/shelter cycle is strongly resisted. That such a situation can prevail is easy to understand. Because houses are essential to human survival, fear that we will not survive is never far

Peter Cowman

■ An artist's impression of Peter's first home.

my first home

■ Architect **Peter Cowman**

Peter Cowman - author of the controversial new book "Be Your Own Architect" — believes convention should take a back seat when it comes to choosing a home.

"What might have been my first home is probably worth a fortune today — a red bricked terraced house in the Liberties of Dublin," the West-Cork based architect relates. "But as a young man with a curiosity about the world, the solid immobile quality of a fixed abode and the dread sounding 'mortgage' shied me away.

Dead money

"Instead, the freedom to change, to move, to get bored and to actually be able to do something about it seemed to me to be the exact opposite of the 'dead money' that people associated with paying rent. To me, the real dead money was mortgage money. The very word sounded of it!

"In any event, I did finally become the owner of a home — paying cash for it on the spot. An estate agent might have described it as being 'compact and full of character.' At best, it could be said to have had two rooms — a tiny 'sitting room' and a bedroom/livingroom/kitch en. Oh, and an outdoor toilet.

"We moved in the very day we looked at it — after first having a quick nip around the canals of Amsterdam where it was located. This home was, in fact, an old VW bus which the previous owner had carefully furnished with a fitted kitchen, a generous folding bed, a dining table and built-in units.

Irrestible

"Sitting there gracefully on the cobbled quayside, it was irrestible. We just had to have it. The deal done, we drove our house away in a combination of excitement and trepidation, stocking up as we went with kitchen supplies and food. It seemed like the best posible combination of two worlds — a desire to move and a desire to have a home.

"In all, there was around 35 square feet of floor space, extended when necessary by opening the sliding door to the outside 'terrace'. Its major drawback was the fact that one could not stand upright inside it and its major plus was that it could move."

The Cowman moving 'house' went by the name of 'La Philomel.' coined from the gentle twirping song she sang as she slowly droned along.

"La Philomel gradually absorbed our character as we covered the walls with paintings and tapestries, filled the shelves with books, stashed our

Property

Con Power

belongings and enjoyed the wild comfort of parking, eating and sleeping wherever we felt like it," Peter recalls.

"Like all homes, this one had its idiosyncrasies — like the bed that was impossibly difficult to open/close and the gear shift that refused to stay properly in place, requiring two people to manipulate it. But this only added to the charm of a new relationship, a new home and a new life.

"We lived in our home for about a year travelling through Holland, Belgium, France, Spain, Portugal, Yugoslavia, Greece, and Italy — living in some of the most beautiful places imaginable.

"The most memorable occasion was riding on the open deck of an Aegean ferry with the sliding door ajar and the table sumptuously laid with feta, retsina and fine Greek bread. Alas, shortly afterwards, La Philomel was struck by cardiac failure and had to be laid to rest in an 'auto cemetario'.

Low cost

"My sense of freedom has yet to desert me since those days as a prospective buyer of a Dublin artisans dwelling. Since then, I have lived in about 30 rented homes in a variety of places and countries. If a home cannot bring one freedom, then there is something wrong indeed.

"My feelings about mortgages have not changed and now that I am about ready to create a family home, it will be a low cost one, built from income and inspired by the freedom it can offer us — to work, to dream, to travel and to further expand our world."

AUCTIONS

The following properties will be put up for auction next week:

Wednesday: Extensive premises, Bunclody, Co. Wexford (Thomas M. B Byrne & Son); 4 and 5 Michael Street, Wexford (Halley Grace & Co. Ltd.

Thursday: 56/57 Capel Street, Dublin 1 (Keane Mahony Smith)

away in any consideration of our lives or of where we are to live. This fear is a mighty beast that we mostly avoid rather than confront because it goes by that fearful name - *death*. Where we do not acknowledge such fears openly or consciously we are hostages to these fears and to global economic forces which have their own agenda for us.

Changing our relationship to the work/shelter cycle and to the economic forces of the world demands that we confront our fear of not surviving. This brings us face to face with our own mortality. By openly acknowledging our fear of not surviving - *dying !* - we can embrace our desire to *live* and to nurture all life on the planet. Such desires are decidedly heart-centred and find expression in that part of our selves we call our *intuition*.

The mysterious world of our intuition, when brought to the sheltermaking process, invests design with life-sensitivity. This propels us deep into the world of spirit and mystery and imparts these qualities to the living spaces which we create. If we succumb to this allure it lends new perspective to the world as we perceive it, infused as it is with the joy of being alive. This is in contrast to the *rationale* which normally drives the design process, investing space with qualities that have little to do with the primacy of *life* and have nothing at all to do with spirit! This is the origin of the *soullessness* so often referred to when speaking of modern houses.

Changing our homes begins by changing ourselves. Learning to trust our intuition, becoming canny at using 'market forces' for our own purposes, clearly articulating our wants and needs, grasping the idea that *there is* such a thing as choice when it comes to where, and, in what, we live. All such actions favour the adherent of the *Be Your Own Architect* concept. That is not to say that being different is all that easy. However, knowing that you want something different is all that is required to set yourself in the right direction.

It is undoubtedly by *sheltermakers* joining forces that major changes favouring people can be enacted within the world of housing. Such alliances are at the very heart of the reality that we need each other to further the life we share on the planet. The lobbying of the legislature, the pressuring of lending institutions, the exploitation of inherent freedoms within the Planning Laws, the offering of mutual support, the sharing of resources and the clear articulation of demands for practical changes in house design and construction practices, can all facilitate the changes that every heart centred person knows are overdue. The key to securing such change will hinge not on expressed opposition to the norm, as is currently the case, but on the bringing forward of practical, realisable solutions that benefit all.

The entire *Be Your Own Architect* concept can be summarise in a very straightforward way - it is a way of taking responsibility for our lives. This simple fact roots our sheltermaking firmly within the cycle of our existence on the planet. It is from here that the broad outpicturing of our commitments to life spring forth. All other considerations are subsidiary to this ethos of survival and, what I call, *thrival*. Thrival is survival with a flourish!

In the realisation of any creative endeavour the contribution of helpmates is often taken for granted. I have been more than fortunate with benefactors, moral supporters, friends and associates, have been the recipient of much encouragement, praise and help and I know that I have not always shown the gratitude that such generosity warranted. Even those who have reacted strongly to my ideas or who, for one reason or another, blocked my progress, have made their contribution. Please accept my sincere thanks for all your help.

In Short

• Settled life is the basis of civilisation as we know it.

• Houses are the cornerstone of settled life.

• When a person borrows against the projected value of their work to pay for their house, the (unspoken) promise is that they will survive and that their property will continually rise in value.

• Modern economies are based on the special status ascribed to property - while other material goods can be expected to depreciate in value as soon as purchased, property, it is said, always appreciates in value.

• Continuous growth, the mantra of modern economics, is underpinned by the Establishment continuously striving to ensure that property values steadily rise - and constantly exhorting people to work hard and to consume as many material goods as possible.

• Because mortgaging - borrowing to pay for a home - is central to national economic systems, solutions to housing problems that help people avoid mortgages are instinctively opposed.

• Any proposed change to the established 'Settle/Work/Mortgage/Shelter/Consume/Waste' cycle is seen as a threat to civilised life and is stirred by fears that one cannot survive outside of this 'system'.

• Planning Laws are used to ensure the primacy of mortgaged shelter in market economies.

• Remember, *Live Your Own Architecture!*

Peter Cowman
March 2000

Introduction to the CD-ROM edition of the Course In Sustainable House Design & Construction with Design Programme *(2005)*

The journey that I embarked upon with the first *'Be Your Own Architect'* Course has so far taken 16 years. One of the most interesting discoveries along the way has been the fact that our homes engage us on a physical as well as on an emotional level. This is a function of the architecture which acts to separate the inside from the outside. This delineation of 'inner' and 'outer' allows us to engage outwardly with the physical 'outer world' and inwardly with our emotional, or, 'inner world'.

By including both 'inner' and 'outer' worlds in the design equation one activates what I refer to as *'the sheltermaking gene'*. This stimulates both our rational as well as our intuitive faculties, allowing for the balancing of physical/material considerations with emotional/psychological need, nourishing both aspects of our lives. This offers one the opportunity to live more deeply and harmoniously, the essence of a sustainable life.

The doctrine of 'sustainability' and its working document, UN Local Agenda 21, encourages change in the mechanism of our survival activity in order to sustain life and to safeguard the choice mechanisms of future generations. This demands a radical restructuring of our current way of life. Sustainable house design is critical to the realisation of this, facilitating, as it does, profound lifestyle choices.

Traditionally, information on house design was drawn from the body of freely available common knowledge. Reference to the mystery of life was invariably included in this, borne in myth across the threshold separating 'inner' and 'outer' worlds. In the move away from an agrarian way of life to a job-focussed one, the design of basic shelter changed from the traditional 'cottage' to what we now refer to as 'the modern home'. Because the industrial age work ethic demanded the surrender of a person's time in exchange for a wage, a reliance was placed on third parties to undertake this sheltermaking activity. These new dwelling types made no reference whatsoever in their design or construction to a deeper reality. Emotional nourishment had to be sought elsewhere, done without, or, ersatz satisfaction sought through material consumption.

The loss of cultural identity suffered in the rural to urban shift, reflected in the lifeless architecture of the modern home, was compounded by a downgrading in the role of the home as the foundation of survival activity. The transference of this function to a time consuming 'job' effectively consigned male territorial identity to the shopfloor. With women naturally assuming control of the home, previously shared with the man, the displaced male was consigned to battle for territory with other men in the workplace, the new pivot of survival activity. The fact that men continue to be the prime creators of homes, while at the same time being marginalised in regards to the occupation of the home territory, has had a profound negative effect on house design and construction activity

The deeper implications of the changes wrought by the shift from an agrarian economy to an industrialised one are now being felt on a vast scale within all developed countries. While the loss of emotional connectivity resulting from this can seemingly be endured, the present threats to physical survival are less easy to bear. This has prompted a search for deeper meaning, a process that stimulates strong emotions with the potential to reunite the separated strands of our 'inner' and 'outer' worlds. This is the desire for a natural and sustainable life, nourished within a secure and healthy home territory. The power to create such a 'living architecture' is within us all, rooted in our essence and carried forward by our sheltermaking instincts.

It must be borne in mind that the changes inherent in a move towards sustainable living run counter to the mechanism of the global economy. This exploits the necessity to be housed in order to satisfy its greed. Mortgage Credit is the primary instrument of this indenture, staining the recipient with the pallid bloom of modernity and shackling them to a life-threatening cycle of consumption and waste from which it can be difficult to escape. With its emphasis entirely focussed on the material, the 'real' world offers no comfort for the anguish inherent in the struggle to transcend this destructive cycle in the search for a more satisfying life.

Where 'vernacular' sheltermakers could draw on common knowledge to assist them, their modern counterparts must rely on the compilation of new knowledge and the free circulation of this in order to achieve their objectives. This 'sheltermaking information' must acknowledge the inner connections which make us whole as well as the external connections which tether the modern home to the outside world. These facilitate the inward flow of necessities and allow people to engage with the world. The fossil fuel derived energy that sustains this activity now threatens its vitality. Contemporary house designs must acknowledge this reality.

The *Course In Sustainable House Design & Construction* has evolved from the original *'Be Your Own Architect'* Courses, first staged in 1989. This 16 year evolution has required a deep exploration of the physical and psychological aspects of sheltermaking. In the process, 'house design' has revealed itself as the articulation of who we are, where we are going and how we intend getting there. The journey inherent in such a quest is deeply personal, human, life-affirming, liberating and satisfying.

The present Course information, made up of a *Design Programme*, the *Handbook of House Design & Construction* plus supporting *Worksheet*, can be viewed as the 'map' on which you plan your unique journey towards your desired objectives.

We all have ideas about how houses should be designed, about their style, construction, layout and so on. All this knowledge will prove invaluable as you develop a unique design. However, it is important to

commit yourself to the map this *Design Programme* sets out for you - this has been created after much thought and effort and in consultation with those who have already followed this path. By adhering to this you will avoid many of the pitfalls that house designers are normally prey to.

The *Design Programme* is set out as a series of *Steps* which allow you to follow the design process easily. This facilitates the creation of a properly balanced design that takes full account of your desired objectives, harmonising these with the larger world. The step-by-step approach allows you to make the best possible use of your time and energy.

When the process of planning, investigating, learning and decision-making has been completed, only then will you be putting the plan of a building together. This is in contrast to normal design practice where the plan is the first thing that is created. This can lead to insurmountable problems, as can be witnessed in many professionally designed homes. It is important that you accept the common sense of the *Design Programme* at this point and to trust that it will lead you safely to your objective. When you do this your creative energies will be freed to tackle the real work in hand.

It is a good idea to spend some time on your project every day. This will keep everything fresh in your mind and will keep the project moving. Your greatest ally will be the good feeling and excitement generated by the creative process. There will be moments when it might all seem too much for you to do. This is why it is important to focus on the work in hand, confident of how it fits into the overall picture. Work steadily and enjoy yourself. Try to work at a table or desk rather than sitting in an easy chair. As you progress keep your equipment, books, files and so on where you can reach them easily, so that when you decide to work you can begin with the minimum of fuss.

Individual students can decide how 'deep' they wish to enter into the Course material. This can range from 'Fastrack' to 'Full Immersion'. A 'Fastrack' approach would require 40 hours part-time work, spread over a period of two or three months. 'Full Immersion' naturally requires more time input, spread over a six month period. The 'spread' of input to the Course is important because it allows time for for contemplation and reflection which contribute greatly to the design process.

It can be useful to work in groups, either family groups or groups formed around a common interest in sustainable shelter and living. Group energy can be a great motivator, though it is best that individual design solutions are developed rather than everyone trying to agree on a single one.

Peter Cowman
June 2005

Introduction to The Sheltermaker's Manual
(2013)

Our ability to create shelter emerges from our survival instincts and acts as a stimulus for the development of culture and identity. The activities associated with sheltermaking puts people in touch with nature and expose them in an active way to its processes, cycles, likes, dislikes, preferences and possibilities which nurtures people's sense of aliveness.

The practice of vernacular architecture largely died out with the advent of industrialisation. In this new world drudgery and uncertainty were to be replaced by surety. Instead of spending time producing ones own food and building ones own home, people used the proceeds from paid employment to provide for their needs on the open market. Fossil-fuels and technology replaced what heretofore people had provided for themselves either by their own energies or assisted by natural or animal power.

The industrial-era home was a utilitarian box within which people could partake of food, rest and procreation. Forged out of obeisance to the new gods of power and money, these 'homes' provided none of the natural connectivity which the traditional shelter offered

Those consigned to live in the new industry-based, job-focussed world would also witness the disintegration of 'the family' as a survival unit. Superceded by fossil fuels, a family's labour no longer needed to be co-ordinated and directly focussed on survival activities liberating people from the obligations and responsibilities inherent within the traditional survival structure of family+community.

While domestic-scale food production did not entirely cease as a result of this new way of life, the practice of building ones own home did. Because vernacular architecture traditions were oral and perpetuated by practical example when this activity ceased vital sheltermaking knowledge was forgotten. In this new world sheltermaking activity became the responsibility of a building 'industry' controlled by self-interested third parties motivated by profit. In this way the home was commodified and turned into yet another product of the machine age.

Apart from the disturbance to the continuity of the vernacular house design tradition another pernicious influence imposed itself on the housing market - debt. Acquiring a home now involved engagement with lending institutions locking people into a cycle of work and credit obligations in order to survive. As a consequence, culture and identity, which spontaneously emerge from the traditional food and sheltermaking cycles of activity, were replaced by idealisations exclusively available through the new matrix of survival activity - the market economy.

It is certain that the traditional family+community lifestyle was readily abandoned in exchange for the promises of the machine age. However, as has been amply demonstrated in the past two hundred years, the disconnection from the natural world which results can have the effect of starving people of the stimulus which a life lived closer to nature delivers. While it is perhaps understandable, even necessary, that the world changed in this way, no one realised that the conflagration of the past would consume a sense of who we were before we had quite figured out who we had become.

Back in 1989, the piecing together of this sheltermaking story greatly assisted my understanding of what I was embarking upon in my 'Be Your Own Architect' Course. I was attempting to revive a dormant tradition! Because of the oral nature of that tradition information on how to actually practice this sheltermaking activity was nowhere to be found! In a world awash with information on various types of building, knowledge of the sheltermaking process itself was completely absent. While there were many books which detailed aspects of house design, instruction on how to utilise this wealth of information to create meaningful, practical and affordable buildings was non-existent. Neither could I find a dedicated school of house design or a body of experts conversant with the house design process. So, I set out to write a book on the subject, based on the experience of teaching my eager students. This manual, and its associated material, is the result.

The creation of architecture is inexorably tied to the shift from a hunter-gatherer to a settled agriculture-based lifestyle with its demands for territory and security. The impulse to build arises directly from our survival instincts, driven by the desire to maintain our aliveness and perpetuate our genes. This requires air; water; light; food; social interaction and the security of a place to rest and reproduce - the home.

Essentially all human beings have the same basic needs which must be fulfilled in order to survive. Those who accumulate surpluses beyond their immediate needs increase the chances of maintaining their aliveness, thereby enhancing their status and their desirability as potential mates. This fosters - competitiveness, inter-male aggression, territoriality, hierarchy and leads to the creation of large homes strategically placed to signal the high status of their occupants.

Apart from satisfying their physical needs humans also have a need for emotional nourishment. This feeding of the 'inner self' allows people to engage with the invisible aspects of their aliveness - with their imaginations and with their dreams which is essential to the development of a sense of identity and purpose in life.

The inside and outside of buildings consist of the same thing - space. The process of creating the walls, floors and roof of a building act to separate this space into distinct parts, for example 'outside space' is separated from 'inside space'. Space is not actually created in this process but is simply hived off from the pre-existing and infinite space of the Universe - space that existed before the building was made and space which will continue to exist after the building has disappeared. This mysterious aspect of architecture is often overlooked – largely because space is invisible and is therefore impossible to see. As a result undue emphasis is normally placed on the parts of buildings that are readily visible - the building body or fabric. This way of looking at

buildings is so common that people believe that this is what architecture is.

The bounding of a portion of infinite space in the construction process has the effect of scaling down the Universe to manageable proportions, that is, it reduces the vastness of infinity to a human scale. As a result, the space enclosed within a building enables people to engage with a portion of the Universe without being overwhelmed in the process. This allows the architecture to be experienced as 'the world in microcosm', a concept that is evident in all indigenous sheltermaking traditions.

The fact that architecture is made up of two essential parts - the building fabric and the inside space - makes buildings very much like people. People have physical bodies and an invisible interior world made up of their emotions, imaginations, dreams, their instincts, their unconscious, their ego, personality and sense of self. This interior world, or inner space, is invisible and just like its architectural counterpart it allows people to engage with a portion of infinite space without being overwhelmed in the process. It is the similarity between buildings and people that makes architecture such a powerful tool in our quest to survive.

Space is invisible and consists of 3 dimensions - length, breath and height. Normally we orient ourselves to the sun which allows us to confer directions on space - up/down (height); front/back (breadth); left/right; (length).

Orientation to the sun creates an awareness of a 4th dimension - time. We perceive time by virtue of the fact that the sun 'comes and goes' at predictable intervals as the earth rotates on its axis. This daily 'rhythm' allows for the calibration of cycles of change - days; months; seasons; years; decades; centuries; millenia; etc. In essence, time is a measure of the changes that naturally occur within space.

In effect, space and time are inseparable. Together they are referred to as 'space-time' which is another name for the Universe. This consists of energy and matter which are one and the same thing in different forms. Energy can be imagined as a vibration which, if it is vibrating very intensely, produces a sensation of solidity which is called 'matter'.

Because architecture is all about space it is also about time and therefore all about space-time, energy-matter and the Universe. The energy which animates matter, thereby creating 'aliveness' is referred to as the '*lifeforce*'. In eastern cultures this is called '*chi*' or '*prana*'. As maintaining aliveness is the driving force behind sheltermaking a focus on spacetime is required in order to create shelter that fully connects to the Universe and to life.

Within the vernacular tradition attunement to these invisible aspects of space and time served to orient people within the world by fostering the development of ritual and myth celebrating the mysteries of life; by nurturing artistic expression through storytelling, poetry, music, dance and art. The loss of such traditional sheltermaking activities has resulted in a disconnection from the invisible but vital aspects of life. Such disconnection has now become a dominant characteristic of the modern world.

While shelters' role in providing for peoples' physical needs is well understood, its role in providing emotional sustenance is less obvious. The inner space of a shelter is where people live out their emotional lives protected physically and emotionally from the outer world by the physical fabric of the building.

By including both inner and outer worlds in the house design and construction process, our innate sheltermaking faculties are activated. This stimulates both our rational as well as our intuitive abilities, allowing for the balancing of the head with the heart, thereby fostering the opportunity to live harmoniously within the natural world.

The modern world devalues the intangible realm of life and along with it the instincts and emotions which allow us to interpret it. The discreditation of the heart as an essential and innate design tool has emphasised material values over emotional satisfaction, defining shelter as a purely material phenomenon. This has led to a situation whereby any discussion of architecture or houses is limited to their physical aspects - what they are made from, how much floor area they enclose and the address of their location. The invisible or intangible aspects of buildings - the space they enclose, how they make people feel, whether or not they foster creativity and dream - never play a part in any architectural discussion. Generally, this has had the effect of deadening buildings, and, as a consequence the deadening of the people who inhabit them.

Sheltermaking is the modern practice of vernacular architecture. This keys people into the survival instinct itself, bringing people face to face with nature and with the unknown. This stimulates awareness, self-expression, ritual, art, music, poetry, dance and inquiry into the intangible realms of life.

This invisible realm is accessed mainly through dreams. Dreaming impels us to pursue our own distinctiveness, which is a process of 'individuation'. This is a modern trend - an evolutionary development arising from the industrialisation process. The family as 'unit' is replaced by collections of individuals.

The liberation of the individual however has been turned by the market into an indulgence fetish feeding on people's desires to maintain their aliveness at any cost. Ignoring the deeper psychological implications that individuality suggests, the market creates illusions and mouths promises that lure the unwary into a false sense of security. Harried to sell their time, cajoled to borrow as much as possible and encouraged to lard their grandiose homes with a surplus of belongings, property owners have been ensnared in a complex web that resists all efforts to escape.

This is the antithesis of the 'maternal womb' that, according to Karl Jung, the Swiss psychologist and psychiatrist, we discover when we surrender to the 'individuation process'. Jung believed that our lives could be understood as a 'process of becoming what was intended from the beginning' if we paid attention to our dreams. He himself used architecture as a means of accessing his inner world - by playing house and designing and constructing his own home.

A clear link can be detected here between exploring ones 'inner world' and creating one's 'dream home'. At the heart of this idea of is the notion of a space where one can truly be oneself. This allows us to think of sheltermaking as a nutrient for our self-development - a place into which we can literally plant our selves so that we might grow into selfhood.

The disconnection from the immediacy of survival activity that a job-focussed industry-based culture creates removes one from the minutiae of day-to-day survival and from the rhythm of life. Natural rhythm is calibrated in days, months, seasons and years. The sense of timelessness which this engenders accords with our body rhythms and allows us to harmonise with the pace of the natural world.

The rhythm of the clock is the rhythm of the machine - explosive and intense - a consequence of igniting the pent-up energy contained within fossil fuels. Formed over millions of years but released almost instantly, this explosive force lays down a beat to which everyone must march. It is the role of the clock to broadcast this rhythm which it does with robotic efficiency, policing our days and our nights.

Apart from the physical consequences of this, because machines are inanimate, soulless, tireless and without emotion, the prevalence of machines in human life has resulted in a dulling of the natural emotions which we all enjoy as human beings. This distancing from natural rhythms has further removed us from a sense of who we are and where we are going.

The deeper implications of the changes wrought by the shift from an agrarian economy to an industrialised one are now being felt on a vast scale within all developed countries. While the loss of emotional connectivity resulting from this can seemingly be endured, the present threats to physical survival are less easy to bear. This has prompted a search for deeper meaning, a process that stimulates strong emotions with the potential to reunite the separated strands of our inner and outer worlds.

Economics is the system whereby people gain access the necessities of life - air; water; light; food; social interaction and the security of a place to rest and reproduce - the home. Money is the medium which the economic system uses to facilitate the production and trade of the goods and services required to satisfy peoples' desire to maintain their aliveness.

Originally money, in the form of coinage and bank notes, were tokens representing tangible goods of a certain worth held securely in 'banks' for security and convenience. This early banking system developed to allow for the creation of more tokens than there were tangible goods to 'secure' them. These tokens were distributed as 'loans' to borrowers with interest accruing which steadily increased the amount to be repaid by the borrower. Such loans, in turn, had other loans issued against them on the strength of the promises of repayment made by the original borrowers.

With the onset of the Industrial Revolution time became convertible into money thereby ensuring a seemingly endless supply. Where time is eternal it was assumed that money was also eternal. This is the illusion which stimulates the demand for endless growth which drains the world of vitality.

The conversion of time into money is a seemingly simple affair. However, the reality is quite different! Because time is all that a person comes into the world with - their 'lifetime' - and because of the deep connections which time allows people to forge with the intangible realms of life, the commercial exploitation of people's time has been destructive to people and planet alike.

Because money is a human construct when it is said to 'grow' such growth is unlike the growth seen in nature. The growth of money is reliant on new money continuously being created. This is unlike natural growth which is fuelled by solar energy. Money growth is derived from people converting their time into money through paid employment and by creating debts to provide themselves with a place to live. This requires that the homes such loans are secured against continuously grow in value - while all other consumer goods continuously fall in value as soon as they are purchased. In order to maintain continuous growth economies rely not only on the creation of debt but also on the use of machines to optimism work activity and to maximise productivity.

The use of the home as 'security' for borrowings has tied people to the success and failure of the global economy and to strategies for economic growth. Where the home also provides emotional security for its occupants, people have become emotionally enmeshed in these strategies as well.

Market economies use the repayment commitments made by mortgagees, the notional values of the properties attached to them and projections of consumer spending as the basis of new loans, securities and other financial 'instruments'. The elaborate paper structure which results is supported by the commitments made by mortgagees and by people spending money to acquire the basics of life on the open market.

When this system falters the vast paper structure that is the world economy begins to collapse. This results in a decline in property values, a loss of consumer confidence, negative growth and the devaluation of the financial instruments constructed on the strength of mortgage debt repayment commitments.

The economic meltdown of 2008, triggered by the sub-prime mortgage crisis, has now proven beyond doubt that mortgage debt plays a vital role in fuelling economic growth and perpetuates the endless cycle of exploitation and destruction that bedevils the world.

The move towards a sustainable life is first and foremost a survival strategy. This is as much about awareness and consciousness-raising as it is about how we live physically. Firstly, one has to accept that sustainability is not something one can buy. This is it's greatest challenge as well as its greatest safeguard. A sustainable life must be lived, acknowledging our physical and emotional selves and celebrating our wholeness.

Where the home is critical to people's physical and emotional wellbeing the move towards a sustainable life must by facilitated by buildings that nurture all aspects of human life. Such buildings will largely determine how well we will survive in a post-Oil Peak, climate-changed world. Such designs will emerge from the lives people have to live, a process of merging 'inner' qualities with those of the 'outer' world to form a 'living' architecture which will contribute to and compliment a 'sustainable' culture founded on a deep commitment to life.

Fresh, imaginative and cost-effective sheltermaking solutions will be required to achieve a truly sustainably way of life. Clearly these must be created and financed on a scale and in a manner which allows a degree of independence from the global economy. Where this is hardly going to promote economic growth those drawn to live sustainably will find themselves open to challenge and even ridicule as a consequence of their life choices.

Understanding the puzzle of our selves and of modern life is an integral part of repossessing the sheltermaking process - identifying who we are, where we are going and how we plan to get there. This begins by acknowledging the intangibles qualities of life that are so critical to the process of harmonisation with nature. These are invisible and mysterious, residing within our deeper selves.

When we articulate our desires about how we wish to live it stimulates these parts of ourselves that long for a deeper connection to life. This signals the beginning of a painful but necessary evaluation of our values, beliefs, ideals, aspirations and dreams. Such a perspective invites us to reclaim our time and our space, to alter our consciousness and our entire way of life. The dynamics of such a consciousness shift are as much cultural as they are personal allowing us to embark on a process of renewal, the forging of a new cultural paradigm. From here we can begin to recapture the sheltermaking imperative, re-occupying our time and our space, reforming our homes and our selves.

Because a sustainable life is an emotional as well as a physical one, it is vital that buildings designed for sustainable living take this into account from the outset. While such an approach might appear to be overwhelming, this is merely a consequence of including an 'inner' dimension in the design. This tracks right to the heart of our deepest fears concerning our survival. The potential onslaught from such encounters are indeed challenging, however, the strength derived from facing such fears will comfortably carry one through such ordeals. This is due to the response of one's sheltermaking 'gene' which, if it's call is honoured, will prove to be a steadfast ally. It is from this vantage that one 'lives one's architecture', in the process reclaiming identity and contributing vitally to a culture of sustainability. It must be understood that the power to initiate such change lies within us - it can never belong to governments nor their agencies despite their claims to be arbiters of 'sustainability'.

The *Sheltermaker Design Programme* which follows this *Introduction* offers the safest route through this *Manual*. It would be wise to follow this path on your sheltermaking journey. Also, bear in mind that the *Programme* not only facilitates the design and construction of sustainable shelter but also functions as a self-developmental tool allowing a person to create a paper-based design which can assist inquiry into a person's life journey. The *Programme* also supports the insertion of external supporting material which should be introduced at the relevant *Steps*.

Peter Cowman
February 2013

The Sheltermaker Design Programme (SDP)

We all have ideas about how houses should be designed, about their style, construction, layout and so on. All this knowledge will prove invaluable as you develop a unique design. At this stage, it is important to commit yourself to the route this *Sheltermaker Design Programme* sets out for you - this has been created after much thought and effort and in consultation with those who have already followed this path. When you do this your creative energies will be freed to tackle the real work in hand, allowing you to make the best possible use of your time and energy. The *Programme* is set out as a series of *Steps* which facilitate the creation of a properly balanced design that takes full account of your desired objectives, harmonising these with the larger world. Supporting *Worksheets* can be downloaded from: livingarchitecturecentre.com

1 Sheltermaker Design Programme
Starting Off

Like all creative projects, starting off can be the most difficult thing of all. Reading the *Introduction* will have given you a sense of what is involved. Something to watch out for is the idea that architecture in general, and particularly the architecture of the home, embraces 'living' qualities that connect us intimately to life and to our deeper selves.

The *Manual* has been in evolution since 1989. Some of the exercises it describes are now supported with *Worksheets*. These can be downloaded free from livingarchitecturecentre.com

The practical use to which the Manual information has been put during its 21+ year life has revealed that some of the exercises described have been discovered to be less critical than was at first thought. All of these developments and discoveries are detailed at each relevant item in the *Design Programme*. Think of this as your companion and guide. Tackle each item in turn and allow the careful structure to direct you on your way. It is easy to feel overwhelmed that there is so much to learn and do, but if you follow the step-by-step approach this is unlikely to happen. Remember, house design is not just about 'bricks 'n mortar,' it's about life and our deep connection to its mysterious processes.

Use the *Progress Worksheet* (available free from livingarchitecturecentre.com) to mark off completed items as you move through the *Sheltermaker Design Programme* .

2 Sheltermaker Design Programme
Drawing Up A List Of Spaces

Read pages 26 & 27 of *The Brief*. Bear in mind that much of the work of drawing up lists and analysing space will be largely confined to you entering preferences onto the pre-formatted *Worksheets*.

The prevalence of computers should not be a temptation to those wishing to shy away from the task of completing *Worksheets* by hand. Handwriting is a certain way to activate our innate sheltermaking instincts. The benefits of such engagement can easily by lost if a computer is used.

Print the *List of Spaces Worksheet*. This is divided into numbered sections. Within these sections each *Space* also has an individual number. Mark off on the *Worksheet* the *Spaces* that you wish to have in your design. Now, this is easily said and relatively easily done, but lots of questions will arise as you do this ...

Sheltermaker Design Programme
List Of Spaces Worksheet
© Peter Cowman 2011

4.9 [ ] Sunspace •
4.10 [ ]
4.11 [ ]

5. Work & Play

5.1 [ ] Office/s •   (No.   )
5.2 [ ] Waiting Area •
5.3 [ ] Hobby/Craft Room •
5.4 [ ] Workshop/Studio •

8.5 [ ] Staircase/s • (No.   )
8.6 [ ] Cloakroom •
8.7 [ ]
8.8 [ ]

9. Indoor / Outdoor

9.1 [ ] Verandah/s • (No.   )
9.2 [ ] Covered Areas •
9.3 [ ]

Can I afford all of this? Should I have a home office? What if my mother came to live with us? That difficult questions arise is normal and indicative of what the design exercise is all about - articulating your needs then refining these answers as a means of developing a satisfactory solution to all the issues that arise from this enquiry. So, if you accept that you do not have all the answers but are in the process of finding them, the filling in of the *List of Spaces Worksheet* takes on a different perspective. It is a *draft* of what it is you want, or think that you want. As such it will be subject to much adjustment before being finalised.

Take your time with this exercise and be as generous to yourself as you want - there will be plenty of opportunity to downsize when this becomes necessary. This might not involve 'losing' a *Space* but might mean that all proposed *Spaces* are provided with multi-functional capacity to allow them to cater for a variety of activities.

What is most important now is that you cater for the entire range of activities that you would like your building to host, particularly leisure, pleasure, relaxation, creativity, food production and storage, plus, the possibly of catering for work and business related activities. Think in terms of what your building can do for you. If a *Space* you want to include is not listed on the *Worksheet* write the name of this against a number in the appropriate *Worksheet* section. Print fresh copies of the *List of Spaces Worksheet* as you need them. Each version should carry a *Draft Number* inserted into the box on the bottom right of the *Worksheet*.

If you are planning an extension to an existing building mark off both the existing as well as the additional *Spaces* required on the *List of Spaces Worksheet*. You may need to be a little versatile in naming the existing *Spaces* where they are destined to change as part of the design. For example an existing *Sitting Room* that is to become part of an enlarged *Kitchen/Dining/Living* area might be titled '*Existing Sitting Room/New Kitchen/Dining/Living Room*', or some variation on this.

The exercise of writing things down is intended to extract things out of your imagination and to place them in front of you in tangible form so that you can develop and refine them. They will not be perfect in the form that they emerge! The whole process of design is, in fact, the process of refinement of these emerging ideas. This has to take place in the physical world as opposed to in your imagination where anything seems possible! This work will become the foundation of the entire house design. This makes it crucial that you not only take your time but that you give plenty of thought to what you want your building to encompass.

You can choose to use the designated numbers, as displayed on the *Worksheet* for your chosen *Spaces* or you might prefer to simply call each *Space* by its own name.

As you complete these exercise print the *Progress Worksheet* and mark off on this the items you have completed.

Next, each *Space* will be subject to further analysis. It is these probing exercises which will prompt changes in the *List of Spaces Worksheet*.

Next: SDP3 - Assembling Design & Style Information, page 28

The Brief

The first step in the process of designing your own home is to set down in words the sort of house you wish to create. This is the foundation of the design and so requires careful consideration. Nothing more than pencil, paper and thought are needed to begin. It is best to use plain sheets of A4 paper for writing things down *fig. 1.*

Use the pre-formatted Worksheets for these exercises - available free from livingarchitecturecentre.com

Fig. 1: Nothing more than pencil, paper and thought are needed to begin your house design. It is best to use plain sheets of A4 paper for writing things down.

As the design process unfolds, all manner of things will be considered and written down, allowing you to gain an objective view of the job you are undertaking. This written information, considered as a whole, is known as The Brief for the project. This, in effect, will comprise of files of written information describing all aspects of the building. Each individual file will be dedicated to a particular aspect of the project, for example a Heating File, a Drainage File, a Materials File.

Buildings are made by following the directions set out in words and drawings. These drawings are made by following the directions set out in the words of the Brief. This makes the Brief a very critical document in the design process.

Whether you are designing a new building or an extension to an existing one the initial approach is the same – a clear Brief must be formulated allowing you to articulate your objectives. Essentially, the Brief is a seed that will grow into a complete building.

The Brief is a written description of the building you wish to design. It is a word picture that covers all aspects of the building, from the sense of space you wish to create, to location, orientation, size, cost, heating, insulation, construction and so on. A Brief allows you to see all these things individually as well as in relationship to each other. Balancing the various considerations that you express in your Brief is the process of design.

The creation of a building such as a house can be a very rapid process – a matter of weeks in fact. Organisation is the key to building quickly and efficiently. A clear Brief will allow you to get organised so that you can design the building you want in as short a time as possible. Building a building should always be about just that – building. If critical design decisions have to be made as the building work progresses the construction process will become muddled and the work will drag on. A Brief allows the building process to be examined beforehand, it allows potential problems to be uncovered, it allows advice to be sought and choices to be made. In short, it allows you to plan out the sort of house you want and decide how best to get it.

Starting A Brief

Start with a simple list of all the spaces you want to have in your building *fig. 2.* Include everything you can think of including circulation and storage space. This list can be more generous or ambitious than you need or can afford but that does not matter. The Brief is a working document. You will be adding to it and changing things as you go along. What is important is to write things down, to look at them, think about them, make decisions and to keep the project moving. As long as you are working with paper and pen you can easily change your mind about any aspect of the design by crossing things out or adding things in.

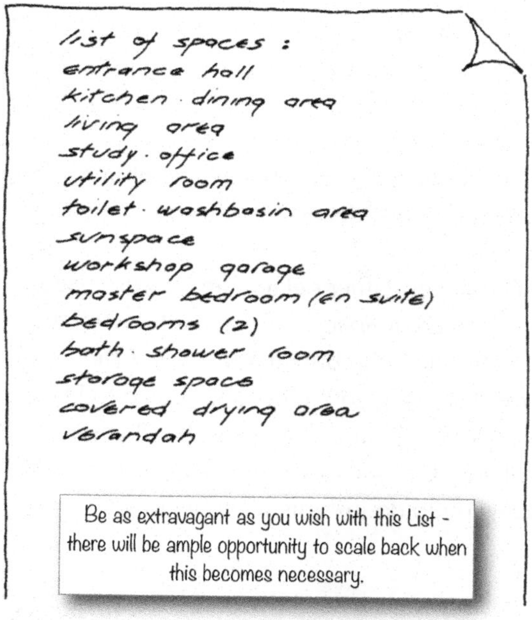

```
list of spaces :
entrance hall
kitchen · dining area
living area
study · office
utility room
toilet · washbasin area
sunspace
workshop garage
master bedroom (en suite)
bedrooms (2)
bath · shower room
storage space
covered drying area
verandah
```

Be as extravagant as you wish with this List – there will be ample opportunity to scale back when this becomes necessary.

Fig. 2: Start your Brief with a simple list of all the spaces you wish to include in your design.

Spaces

Your list of spaces will contain some of the following: *Front porch. Front Entrance Hall. Cloakroom. Kitchen. Dining Area. Living Area. Kitchen/Dining Area. Pantry. Scullery. Study/Office. Toilet with washbasin. Utility Room. Back Porch. Sitting Room. TV Room. Music Room. Library. Workshop. Garage. Fuel Store. Boiler Room. Conservatory. Sunspace. Bedrooms. Bathroom. Shower Room. Hot Press. Storage Space. Circulation Space. Sauna. Snooker Room. Games Room. Granny Flat. Swimming Pool. Wine Cellar. Verandah Space. Outdoor Space. Gazebo. Summer House.*

The consideration of how much and what type of workspace you include in your design is very important. Workspace can be provided in the form of a Study/Office or it can be in the form of a general Workshop Space. Providing these types of spaces in a house will provide options to the occupants about how they might spend some of their free time or how they might earn a portion or all of their living by carrying on a home based business. This type of flexibility within a design can make owning a house a very economical proposition.

A Sunspace can be used to grow plants, vegetables and fruit as well as contributing to the heating of the building by gathering and storing solar heat. Circulation space is the space which connects the individual rooms together and is itself connected to the outside. This space can also provide easily accessible storage space within the house.

It is important at this stage of the design exercise to include everything you can think of in terms of spaces and rooms. It does not matter if this list gets too long. You can easily rationalise it by combining several activities in a single space. For example, if you put down on your list a Garage and a Workshop space you might in the end decide that to provide a single space to cater for both activities might be the most economical solution. What is important at this stage is to think what your house can do for you in terms of freedom, for example, making a house that you can work as well as live in.

Any future needs that you can envision should be considered at this stage also. If you can foresee a need for extra accommodation at some stage in the future put this down on your list. This extra accommodation will have to form part of the overall design. When the initial building project is undertaken this extra space will not be built, but any provisions necessary to make the future building work easy to carry out might be completed. For example, drains or foundations for the future extension might be installed initially to allow the future building work to be easier and less disruptive to carry out.

Any accommodation that is required which is likely to be external to the main house should be included in your list of spaces. A separate garage or workshop, for example, a greenhouse, a gazebo, a folly or any other construction that would be located away from the main building needs to be made part of the overall design.

If the building you are designing is something other than a house, for example a workshop, a studio or a playhouse for the children, the procedure is the same – you make a list of the space or spaces that will be contained within your building and proceed from there in the same way as you would for a house design. Proper regard should be paid to any buildings already existing on the site to which your design should relate.

If you are designing an extension to an existing house you should make a list of all the existing spaces in the house and add to this the additional spaces you wish to make.

3 Sheltermaker Design Programme
Assembling Design & Style Information

In order to help you visualise the type of building that you wish to create begin assembling photographs of rooms, facades, windows, doors, furniture, floors, decorative effects, kitchen units and so on, that appeal to you.

Magazines will prove to be the greatest source of such images. Either detach the relevant page or make a photocopy of the image, noting the relevant *Space* or *Spaces* referred to by writing the name/number of the *Space* on it. This exercise will assist you in bringing into focus the general style you are aiming to achieve. It will also quickly bring your emerging design to life and, of course, raise many more questions! This, you will realise at this stage, is the 'rhythm' of the design process - lots of questions arising that all need satisfactory answers. The *Sheltermaker Design Programme* is structured to allow you to do just this without going crazy in the process.

4 Sheltermaker Design Programme
Analysing Your Chosen Spaces

You are now going to expand the initial *Brief* as represented by the draft *List of Spaces Worksheet*. This exercise is described in *'Expanding The Brief'* on page 30. As before, much of the drudgery has been taken out of these exercises by the pre-formatted *Space Analysis Sheets*. There is one of these for each *Space* marked with an asterisk* on the *List of Spaces Worksheet*.

Print *Analysis Sheets* relevant to the *Spaces* you have listed. If no pre-formatted *Sheet* exists use an *Analysis Sheet Blank*, writing the relevant name/number on top. If you are planning an extension to an existing building print *Analysis Sheets* for the existing and the proposed *Spaces* as set out on your *List of Spaces*.

As you will see each *Analysis Sheet* deals with *Activities; Furniture & Equipment; Abstract; Location; Surfaces; Furniture & Equipment Measurements* and *Floor Area/Volume*. The significance of the first five of these headings is described on pages 30 and 31 and it is these same five headings that will be the focus of your attention now. The portion of the *Sheets* devoted to *Furniture & Equipment Measurements* and *Floor Area/Volume* you will be leaving blank for the moment.

The completion of the *Analysis Sheets* is going to breathe life into the emerging design. Remember - it is easier to write something down and then to change it, rather than spend hours trying to come up with a perfect description of what it is you want. You can create as many versions of each *Analysis Worksheet* as you wish. Either discard the earlier versions or number each new one.

Pages 32 - 54 set out *Ideas for Spaces* along with *Sample Analysis* to guide you. It is a good idea to begin the process of filling in your *Analysis Sheets* with a selection of these, where they are similar to your own *Spaces*. The following *Spaces* are analysed in this way:

Your *Design & Style* information will now prove of great assistance in helping you focus on what it is you want to achieve particularly in regard to *'Surfaces'*. It will be these surfaces - floors, walls and ceilings - that will eventually enclose each *Space* in the building. Where a

Front Doors/Porches Page 32

Hallways Page 34

Cloakrooms Page 35

Kitchen/Dining Areas Page 36

Living Areas Page 38

Study/Offices Page 39

Toilet/washbasin Areas Page 40

Utility Rooms Page 41

Workshop/Studios Page 42

Garages Page 43

Sunspaces Page 44

Bedrooms Page 45

Bathrooms Page 46

Hot Presses Page 48

Storage Space Page 48

Circulation Space Page 49

Verandah Space Page 49

Outdoor Space Page 50

Fuel Stores Page 52

Boiler Rooms Page 53

Back Porches Page 54

Coldrooms Page 54

Design & Style image is relevant to a particular *Space* attach it to that *Analysis Sheet*. This will help develop a strong sense of what a *Space* will feel like in reality. In the case of designing an extension to an existing building you should note existing *Surfaces* and any change you wish to make to any of these.

Work your way through the analysis exercises slowly but steadily, otherwise you will become overwhelmed. Remember that you cannot possibly come up with all the right answers from a standing start. However even a wrong answer provides a person something that can be changed, as opposed to a blank that conveys nothing. Work on the *Analysis Sheets* will be ongoing, continuing in parallel with other design exercises. However it is critical that you plunge in as deeply as possible right from the start, rather than waiting for some sudden revelation that will clarify everything for you. Refining the analysis information is the revelation!

Also, as you go about your daily business, keep your eyes open and look at the various buildings you experience. Above all, allow yourself to dream and imagine creating beautiful and welcoming *Spaces* - read *'Looking At Spaces'* on page 55.

Next: SDP5 - Analysing Regular Household Activities, page 56

Expanding The Brief

The next stage of the design process is to expand the initial Brief. This is done by analysing each space individually under several headings. These headings are – *Activities; Furniture & Equipment; Abstract Qualities; Location and Surfaces.* This work should be done on A4 plain paper. Each page should carry the name of the space to which it refers and the relevant headings. For example, the page containing information on the Activities that will be carried on in the Utility Room should be headed *'Utility Room – Activities'.* Similarly, the page or pages containing information on the Furniture & Equipment for the Living Area should be headed *'Living Area – Furniture & Equipment'.* This level of organisation will make the job of filing and retrieving information very straightforward. Individual files for each space in your building should be created to store this information.

Activities are the things that will normally happen in a space. For the Kitchen these would be cooking, possibly eating and perhaps baking or preserving. For a Studio/Office they might be operating a computer, a telephone and a fax machine, meeting clients, writing, typing and so on. For a Bedroom the activities would be sleeping and also maybe studying, reading and relaxing *fig. 3.*

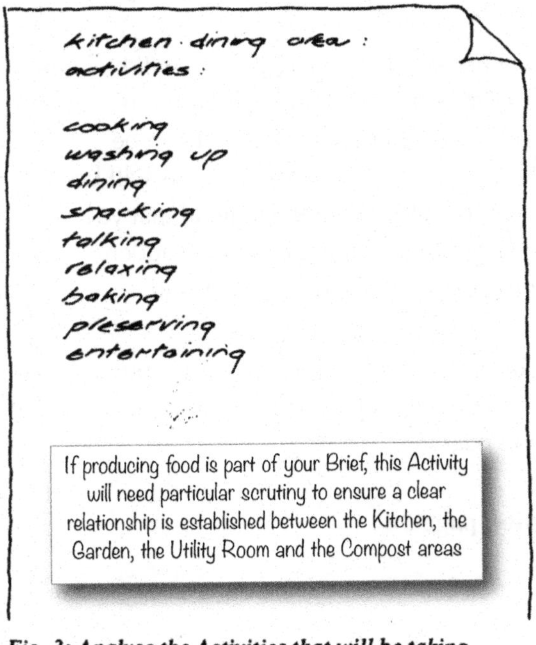

kitchen · dining area :
activities :

cooking
washing up
dining
snacking
talking
relaxing
baking
preserving
entertaining

If producing food is part of your Brief, this Activity will need particular scrutiny to ensure a clear relationship is established between the Kitchen, the Garden, the Utility Room and the Compost areas

Fig. 3: Analyse the Activities that will be taking place in the various spaces in your design.

Furniture & Equipment is literally everything you want to put into the spaces you are going to design. For a Bedroom this might be a bed, a bedside table, a study desk and chair, bookshelves, clothes storage and general storage space. For the Utility Room it might be a washing machine, worktop space and shelving. For a Living Area you might include sofa, armchairs, coffee tables, TV/video, a music centre as well as any other furniture, paintings or art objects in your possession *fig. 4.*

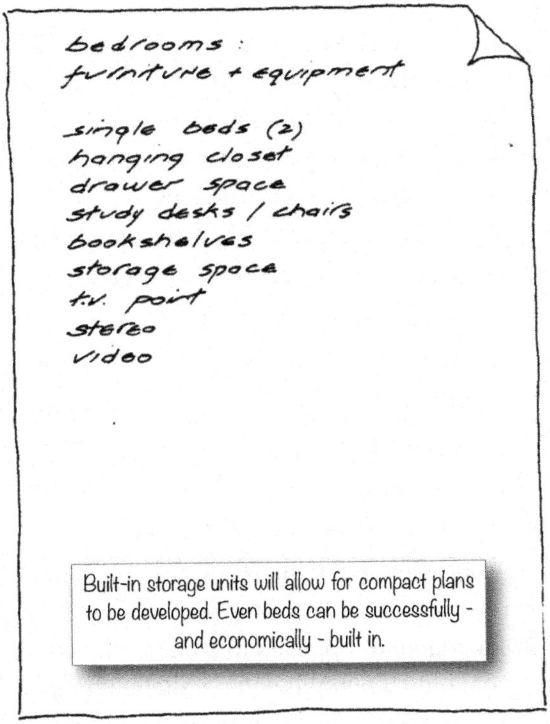

bedrooms :
furniture + equipment

single beds (2)
hanging closet
drawer space
study desks / chairs
bookshelves
storage space
t.v. point
stereo
video

Built-in storage units will allow for compact plans to be developed. Even beds can be successfully - and economically - built in.

Fig. 4: List the Furniture & Equipment you intend to have in each of the spaces in your design.

The Abstract Qualities of the spaces you wish to design are very important to think about at an early stage. Light is a critical one of these. For a Living Area one might consider evening light desirable while in a Kitchen you might want to enjoy the sun whenever it shines. Morning or evening sun is pleasant in bedrooms. All rooms should get sunshine at some time of the day. Other abstract qualities you might like to write down are things like spaciousness, warmth, peacefulness, security and healthiness *fig. 5.*

```
obstract qualities
master bedroom:

cosy
warm
spacious
comfortable
secure
relaxing
sunny in morning
```

> Carefully and sensitively enumerating the Abstract Qualities that are desired in a space is what gives a space its 'feel'.

Fig. 5: List the Abstract Qualities you wish the spaces in your design to be endowed with.

Location has to do with where you want any particular space to be in relation to any other space in the house. For example you might want the Utility Room to be very close to the Kitchen, or the Study/Office to be beside the Front Entrance. You might want to provide a Toilet and Washbasin near to the Living Areas and you might want to locate your Bedroom away from any source of noise that might irritate or disturb you on a regular basis *fig. 6*.

```
study. office
location:

close to front door
off main hallway
close to toilet whb area
near kitchen
```

> Location information will have a large bearing on how a plan eventually 'shapes up' - be sure to carefully articulate how your outdoor spaces will relate to your indoor spaces, particularly where a kitchen garden or outdoor work areas are to be established.

Fig. 6: Consider the relationships you wish to create between the various spaces in your design.

Consideration of the Surfaces enclosing these spaces will cause one to think what you want walls, floors and ceilings to look like when the building is complete. If you intend to hang things such as paintings or posters on your walls this should be noted in the Brief. In some rooms you might want timber panelling, in others, tiling or just plain painted walls. Timber floors might be wanted in Living Areas, Bedrooms, in the Study/Office and in the Circulation Spaces. You might want high ceilings over living spaces and lower ones over the bedrooms. In some areas you might want to apply decorative plaster mouldings to the ceilings. Alternatively, plain painted ceilings might be more to your taste *fig. 7*.

```
living area.
surfaces:

wood floor
loose rugs
paintings on walls
plain colours
high ceiling
```

> A careful and sensitive choice of surface materials is what gives a space its character.

Fig. 7: Consider how you want the various internal surfaces in your design to look when the building is complete.

By looking at these aspects of the spaces that are to be contained within your building, a word picture is gradually built up of what you want these spaces to be like. It is this type of information that guides you in making your design decisions. The more information that is available about any particular space, the more likely you are to achieve your design objectives in the finished building.

If you are working on the design for a house extension, you should analyse any existing space that is to be altered or modified, as well as the new spaces that you wish to create.

Ideas For Front Door/Porches

➤ The front door and the space immediately inside it – the front porch – are very important in any building, especially a home. At the threshold the private world of the dwelling and the outside world meet. Beyond the threshold the householders are undisputed rulers of their territory.

The use of the word 'threshold' is derived from the layout of old farmhouses, where the threshing floor had first to be crossed before the dwelling proper was reached. Nowadays, there being no use for a threshing floor, no space is allocated for use as a 'threshing area' – a place where the outside world and the privacy of the dwelling can be considered to overlap. The advantage of such a space lies in the fact that it can offer the householder a place to briefly entertain callers that normally would not need to be invited further within the building – bill collectors, salesmen, officials and ticket vendors to name but a few – people that you might prefer to entertain in the front porch rather than in the living room or kitchen.

A further advantage of a reasonably sized front porch lies in the fact that it can act as a 'draught lobby' for the remainder of the building – protecting the main part of the dwelling from cold air that might rush in when the front door is opened. On a day-to-day basis a front porch can function as the place where coats, shoes, keys, umbrellas, the dog's lead and so on are kept.

➤ As far as furniture and equipment is concerned, a small table or built-in writing desk with a mirror above it is very useful to have in the front porch. A chair, stool or bench will come in handy for all sorts of things, like sitting down to change your shoes. Good storage for outdoor wear will be critical in this area – sufficient and accessible coat hanging facilities. This can be done using hangers on a rail or simply using old-fashioned hooks or pegs. Whichever you choose, remember that outdoor clothes are oftentimes wet when brought home. Some form of open storage is better for drying damp or wet clothes than an enclosed hanging closet. Other items such as hats, gloves, umbrellas and bags can be accommodated on shelves or in drawers. Outdoor shoes should invariably be taken off in the front porch and replaced by lighter indoor footwear. A low level shelf/bench arrangement can be organised for this. A floor mat for wiping wet shoes should also be considered. A 600mm wide zone along one side of a porch could be dedicated for a built-in unit containing a writing desk, shoe storage/bench, hanging facilities, shelves and drawers.

A clock is useful to have in the front porch as might be a barometer. A pinboard for putting up timetables, a calendar and that type of thing will also be found useful. Some form of knocker or bell will be needed outside to allow visitors to summon you to the door. The door itself can be solid, glazed or a combination of both. If you always want to be able to see who is at the door, you will have to have a glazed panel either in the door or to one side of it. A reasonable amount of overhead cover should be provided immediately outside the front door to protect a caller from the rain.

The size of your porch will need to be gauged in relation to the use it is likely to get and the amount of storage that you need in it. The more people that are likely to use it at any one time, the more floor space you will need in it. If you are generous in allocating space to this area and the space is used to deal with clothes, accessory and shoe storage, it will indeed be space that proves itself useful.

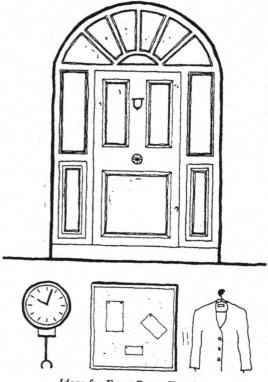

Ideas for Front Doors/Porches

➤ In abstract terms, a front porch should be sunny and welcoming. This will require that the space be reasonably large and be oriented to the south or west. A tall ceiling will give the porch dignity and might allow a fanlight to be provided above the entrance door. Neat storage arrangements for clothes will assist in making the porch presentable to visitors as well as easy to use on a day to day basis. When thinking about entrance porches it should be remembered that a back porch can provide an efficient means of dealing with the everyday human traffic to and from the house, leaving the front door to be used only on more formal occasions.

➤ As far as location is concerned, the front door/porch will be the link between the outside world and the interior space of the home. Because of this, the position of the front door will to a certain extent be dictated by the connection of the actual site to the wider world. This connection will be in the form of a path or driveway connected to the public road. It is on such a path or driveway that occupants and visitors alike will approach the building, so the front door should be clearly visible from these. If you plan to use the front door to handle the daily comings and goings, you will need to have parking space nearby outside, which means that the driveway will have to arrive at or near the front door.

Within the building the front porch will connect the circulation space and the individual spaces together. Circulation space can be anything from a corridor to a formal hallway. Usually, the front porch should join the circulation space close to the kitchen and living areas of the home. It is to these spaces that visitors and occupants alike will most likely be heading when they come through the front door. If you are considering running any kind of home business you might also have business callers arriving at the front door. This will require that your office, study or studio is located nearby. An alternative worth considering is the provision of a separate door to such accommodation.

➤ The surfaces in a front porch should be hardwearing and cleanable. A tiled floor with a matwell will serve well in this regard. Some of the denser softwoods or a hardwood such as oak would also make a durable and warm floor. Built-in units should preferably be of timber construction. Exposed wall areas and the ceiling can be plain painted, tiled or timber sheeted.

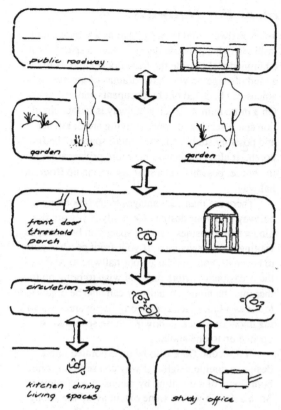

Ideas for Front Doors/Porches

Sample Front Door/Porch Analysis

Activities: Coming and going. Visitors, arrival. Threshold crossing! Waiting for door to be opened! 'A holding area!'.

Furniture & Equipment: Door – solid wood with glass side panels and fanlight over it if possible. Floor mat for wiping feet. Mirror on wall? Shelf/drawer for keys etc.?

Abstract: Welcoming. Sunny. Uncluttered/roomy. Large enough to speak to occasional visitors in, so that they do not have to be brought inside the house. Front porch is transition space between the house and the outside world. It should also act as a draught lobby.

Location: Near to Kitchen/Living areas. Close to Office. The front door should be visible from front gate.

Surfaces: Tiled floor with mat set into it. Easily cleanable/hardwearing. Plain painted walls or wood panelling? White ceiling.

33

Ideas For Hallways

➤ A hallway might be regarded as a somewhat old fashioned idea in house design. Such a space, located immediately inside the front door/porch, is in fact a kind of stage on which the dramas of greeting and adieus can be acted out by occupants and visitors. On a more humble level, a hallway is in fact circulation space serving to connect living areas, kitchen and possibly study/office or studio space to the front porch. It also connects to the more private areas of the house, possibly via a staircase rising up from the hallway.

There are many advantages to incorporating a hallway into your design. Certainly if you are running a home business, such a space can be useful as a waiting area for visitors. If your front porch is going to be small, you could use your hallway to deal with the occasional visitors that you wish to bring no further into the home. A hallway can also be organised to act as a link space connecting living areas via sliding doors or screens, allowing these spaces to be opened up to one another.

If a second floor is to be incorporated into a design, a double height hallway can serve to connect both floors of a dwelling by means of a balcony. Such a device will to some extent avoid the strong separation that can often exist between floors in two storey buildings.

➤ The furniture and equipment for hallways can range from tables and chairs to grandfather clocks, standard lamps, sculptures and so on. It is not rec-ommended that coats, shoes and such everyday items should be kept in a hallway space. It should be remembered that this space will contain the doors or sliding screens to the various ground floor spaces of the house and that the primary function of the hallway is to provide for the circulation needs of the building. In this regard, very little furniture should be placed in the space.

➤ A dignified feeling should exist within a hallway and the space should receive a reasonable amount of sunlight. Because it will be bordered with the living areas and the front porch it can sometimes be difficult to put a window into a single storey hallway. With a double height space this problem can be overcome by using high level windows to bring in natural light.

➤ Hallways should immediately connect the front door with the major living areas of the home. If a second floor is to be used in the design, the stairs to this should also open off the hallway. A toilet and washbasin is also an area that should be installed close to a hallway.

➤ Wood, tiles, rugs or carpet are all acceptable floor finishes for hallways. Wall finishes can be anything from painted smooth plaster to wallpaper or timber panelling. A hallway, especially a double height one, can be a very useful area in which to display artworks, especially paintings. If this is to be the case, a neutral wall finish will be needed and careful regard will need to be paid to lighting arrangements.

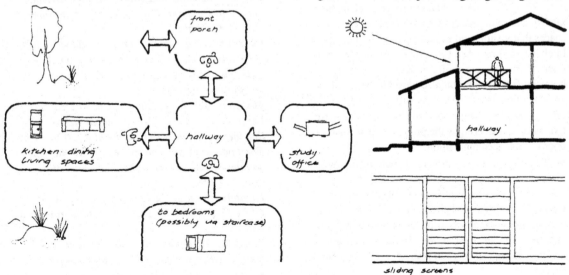

Ideas For Hallways

34

Sample Hallway Analysis

Activities: *Circulation from room to room. Circulation from outside the house to inside. Telephoning? Visitors waiting to come into office.*
Furniture & Equipment: *Chairs and table. Clock? Barometer on wall. Mirror? Shelf/drawer for keys?*
Abstract: *Light/airy. Sunny. Well proportioned. Avoid "corridor" feeling.*
Location: *Connecting outside and inside. Connecting cloakroom/living areas/kitchen/toilet/office. Also connects with circulation space for bedrooms.*
Surfaces: *Wood floor with oriental rug. Plain painted walls with pictures/paintings. High ceiling. Panelled doors or Japanese-style sliding screens?*

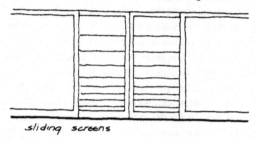

sliding screens

Ideas For Cloakrooms

➤ As an alternative to using the front porch to store outdoor apparel a cloakroom can be used. This will allow the inevitable clutter of coats, shoes, umbrellas and so forth to be somewhat concealed from casual observance. A cloakroom is, strictly speaking, not an essential space to have, as its function can easily be duplicated by a front or back porch.

➤ In terms of furniture and equipment, a cloakroom should be fitted out similarly to a front porch, with clothes hanging space, drawers, shelves and so on. Additional storage space for travelling luggage might also be incorporated.

➤ Most of all, one requires that a cloakroom be functional and easy to use. Natural light is not essential though it is desirable. This could come from the east or west. Proper ventilation will be essential to this space where damp or wet clothing will oftentimes be left.

➤ The proper location for a cloakroom is off either the back or front porch. If this is done, access can easily be gained to it without passing through any of the interior spaces of the house.

➤ The finishes in a cloakroom should be easily cleanable and hard wearing.

Sample Cloakroom Analysis

Activities: *Changing into/out of indoor/outdoor clothes and shoes. Standing/sitting to do this? Is mirror required for personal grooming?*
Furniture & Equipment: *Hanging space for clothes. Storage for shoes/slippers – no outdoor shoes allowed in house beyond this point! Umbrellas/wet weather gear – these may be brought home wet! Summer/winter clothing temporary storage. Mirror for personal grooming. Bench/seat for changing shoes.*
Abstract: *Pleasant. Well ventilated. Reasonably spacious – not cramped. Convenient to use and keep tidy.*
Location: *Off hallway, near to front door and living areas. Can the front porch and the cloakroom be in the same space? This would mean outdoor shoes could be left in front porch and hallway floor can be more easily kept clean.*
Surfaces: *Tiled/easily cleanable floor.*

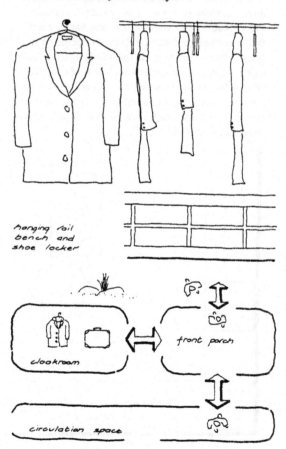

hanging rail bench and shoe locker

Ideas for Cloakrooms

Ideas For Kitchen/Dining Areas

➤ In many ways a kitchen is the heart of a house. It is an active informal space that will be in regular use throughout the day. Careful thought needs to be given to exactly the kind of kitchen that you want. This is a very personal choice and will be influenced by your style of cooking, eating and living.

The primary activity in any kitchen will be the preparation of food. This will happen with such regularity that unless the space is carefully thought out, using the kitchen will be difficult and inefficient. Apart from the cooking itself, the kitchen will serve as a meeting place for the family, friends and so on. The washing-up will also be carried out there as well as aimless chat, daydreaming and probably meal taking. A kitchen incorporates more activities than any other single space in the home and because of this needs careful thought.

➤ The equipment that a kitchen might have is almost limitless – fridges, freezers, microwaves, blenders, toasters, ovens, grinders, coffee makers, sinks, double sinks, dishwashers and halogen hobs. Whatever equipment you eventually decide on it will need sufficient space made for it to be fitted in and easily used. An almost essential item of equipment in a kitchen is an extraction fan. Steam, grease and cooking smells should be immediately expelled from this area. A good quality unit with a cleanable filter should be installed.

Kitchen furniture usually includes a table and chairs, worktops and, occasionally, a dresser. Equipment such as fridges, hobs, sinks and dishwashers can be accommodated in or beneath worktops, allowing a continuous easily-cleanable surface to be made. It is usual to place such worktops against walls, though freestanding 'island' units can be very successful. Such an island unit could contain a worktop and a cooking hob and would allow whoever was cooking to face into the room rather than face the wall. One side of the unit could also be used as a breakfast counter. An island unit can also allow the fridge, sink and the cooking surface to be placed quite near to each other which is very useful.

It is usual to provide storage space under worktops, though this is often inaccessible and difficult to clean. An alternative is to have open shelves under your worktops. Cupboards over worktops also suffer from problems of access and cleanability.

The storage of pots and pans is a difficult problem. These items are awkward to handle and store and it is not always desirable to have them on open display. Deep drawers can solve this problem and, if the items themselves allow it, some form of hanging arrangement could be utilised. A reasonably high ceiling would be needed to do this successfully. Storage space for pots and pans should be close to the washing-up area.

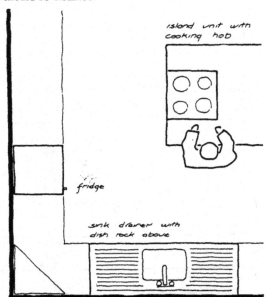

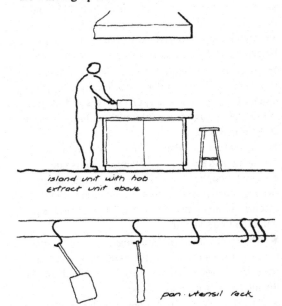

Ideas For Kitchen/Dining Areas

Crockery storage is best arranged in racks. If such racks are located above the sink/drainer they can be used to store the crockery immediately after washing them. A reasonable length of drainer surface is needed to do this.

➤ A southern aspect is very pleasant for kitchen/dining Areas as this will bring sunlight to the area during the day. Evening sun in a kitchen is also pleasant. The space should be friendly, welcoming and reasonably spacious. A view of the outside is very important and possibly a view of the path/driveway might be considered. Most of all a kitchen should not be at all difficult to cook, clean or wash-up in.

➤ A kitchen is best located in a central part of the house. A close connection to the front door is desirable as well as a proximity to the major living area. A direct connection can even be made between these spaces allowing them to be opened up to each other. A toilet and washbasin should be located nearby. The back porch should open into the kitchen.

➤ Cleanable surfaces are most essential in any kitchen area. As far as possible work surfaces should be made continuous to allow them to be easily cleaned. Built-in hobs and a separate oven offer a far better alternative to a built-in cooker which will interrupt the run of the worktop. The walls behind worktops should preferably be tiled, though tiling is not recommended for the worktops themselves.

Sinks should be carefully selected to ensure they can be easily cleaned when installed. The floor finish should be hardwearing and easily cleanable. Wood, tiles or linoleum could be selected.

Sample Kitchen/Dining Area Analysis

Activities: Cooking breakfast, lunch and dinner. Washing up. Baking. Preserving. Chatting with family and friends. Meal planning. Snacking. Eating.

Furniture & Equipment: Worktops/presses with natural wood finish. Storage for utensils, crockery etc. Sink and drainer – stainless steel or stoneware? Garbage – how best to do this? Should garbage be sorted for recycling? Cooking hob & oven – gas or electric? Extraction hood. Storage of cleaning implements – should this be in the utility room? Large dining table with six chairs. Dresser. Dishwasher?

Abstract: Sunny. Should have a good view to the outside. Friendly and relaxing. Warm. Convenient to use and easy to clean! Pleasant – whoever is cooking or washing up should not feel isolated!

Location: Close to front door. Beside utility room which will have back door in it. Separated from living area by two steps – up or down?

Surfaces: Smooth walls, painted finish. Tiles above worktops? Timber floor. Smooth painted finish to ceiling. Plaster cornice?

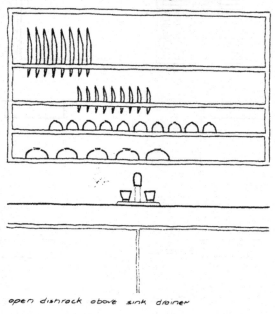

open dishrack above sink drainer

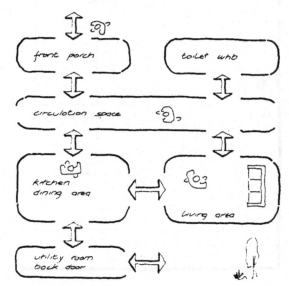

Ideas for Kitchen/Dining Area

37

Ideas For Living Areas

➤ Your living room is the room you should feel most at home in within the house. Here you will unwind, watch television and videos, talk, laugh, entertain your friends and do a multitude of other things.

➤ It is worth thinking carefully about the furniture and equipment that you wish to surround yourself with in this room. If your preference is for an especially large sofa and armchairs, you will have to give over plenty of space to accommodate them. If you wish to have an extra large video screen or to use a projector, you will also need to take account of the size these items are and the the amount of space they require when in use. All items such as televisions, stereos and video players need consideration in this regard.

➤ Your living room should be comfortable, relaxed and properly suited to your preferences and needs, whatever these are. In many ways the living room is the epicentre of territory and as such can be invested with calm, dignity and self expression. A south facing room will receive good natural light and a west facing window is very pleasant in the evening.

➤ A close connection between a kitchen/dining area is very desirable. The use of double doors or a slid-

ing screen to achieve this can be worthwhile. It is generally not a good idea to leave these spaces open to each other permanently. There are simply too many problems with this. Doors or screens however will give you the opportunity of temporarily opening the spaces to each other. Similarly, if a large hallway is to be incorporated into the design, doors or a sliding screen can be used to link the hallway and the living area occasionally. If large openings are required between spaces, sliding screens offer a more economical solution in terms of space use than double doors which have to swing through a large area to be left open. A toilet/washbasin area should be located near to the living area, as should the front porch.

➤ The various finishes that you select for your living area floor, walls and ceiling will all be subject to personal taste and style, in keeping with the furniture you choose. Plain wall finishes will allow you to highlight fabrics, floor rugs and so on, as well as allowing you to change your colour scheme fairly easily. A flat ceiling finished with a decorative plaster cornice can lend considerable style to an otherwise plain room. Living area ceilings should be kept fairly high.

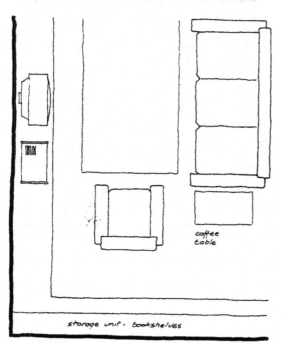

coffee
table

storage unit. bookshelves

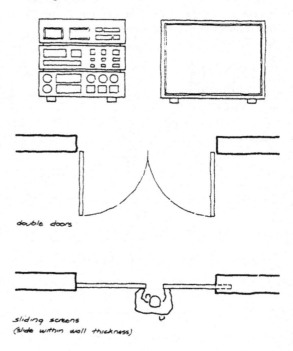

double doors

sliding screens
(slide within wall thickness)

Ideas For Living Areas

38

Sample Living Area Analysis

Activities: Relaxing. Reading. Watching TV/video. Listening to music. Entertaining visitors.

Furniture & Equipment: Easy chairs. Couch. Coffee tables. TV/video – built in unit? Music centre. Bookshelves/storage drawers. Open fire?

Abstract: Pleasant and welcoming. Comfortable. Sunny in evening especially. Relaxing! Warm. Expandable in future years?

Location: Beside kitchen/dining area – capable of being closed off from it? Connected to sunspace or outside terrace?

Surfaces: Plain painted walls with perhaps timber panelling on lower part of wall. Walls to have paintings, pictures or tapestries on them. These will be changed around regularly. Timber floor with loose rugs. High ceiling, plain white, with decorative plaster cornice.

Ideas For Study/Office Spaces

➤ A study/office can be used to operate a home based business in a professional manner. If no business is to be conducted there, such a space can offer a private location to write letters, pursue a hobby or for children to study in.

➤ A desk, chairs, shelves and perhaps a filing cabinet will well equip a study/office. A pinboard would also be useful. A built-in storage/worktop unit will cope with much of the normal storage needs of such a space.

➤ Privacy is desirable in a study/office, as is peace and quiet. The space should be reasonably formal but relaxing. South or west light would be pleasant.

➤ If the space is being used to run a business, it should be located close to the front porch and hallway. A toilet/washbasin area should also be nearby. A close proximity to the kitchen might also be desirable.

➤ The finishes in the study/office for the walls, floor and ceiling can vary according to taste and the style you wish to project.

Sample Study/Office Analysis

Activities: Writing. Telephoning. Faxing. Meeting visitors. Operating computer. Photocopying.

Furniture & Equipment: Desk. Chairs. Fax/photocopier table. Stationary storage. Bookshelves. Safe?

Abstract: Convenient. Pleasant. View outside. Warm. Private. Sunny if possible in afternoon.

Location: Close to front door/waiting area. Close to toilet/whb. Reasonably near kitchen.

Surfaces: Plain walls. Wood floor. Plain ceiling.

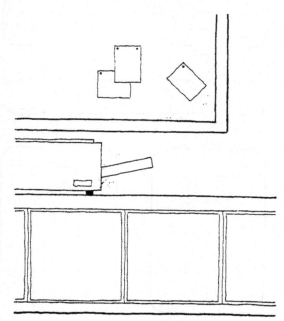
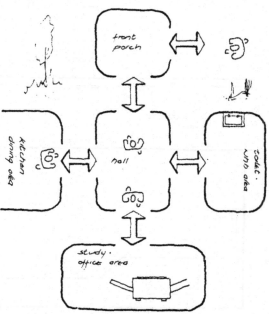

Ideas for Study/Office Spaces

Ideas For Toilet/Washbasin Space

➤ The function of this space is obvious. It will cope with the day and early nighttime needs of the family and visitors to the home, as well as providing a back-up service to the main bathroom when it is in demand.

➤ A toilet, washbasin and some storage space for towels, soap, toilet paper and cleaning items is all that is required in terms of furniture and equipment. A good towel rail should be installed and several hooks or pegs for hanging up clothing. A waste bin should be installed also.

➤ Good ventilation is essential for toilet areas and this is oftentimes best achieved mechanically. A reasonable amount of space should be incorporated into this area, allowing for the comfortable and easy use of the facilities.

➤ A close proximity to all living areas is desirable for this space.

➤ Easily cleanable surfaces are essential in this area. To this end it might be wise to enclose the toilet cistern, the washbasin and the storage unit within a built-in unit, thereby eliminating the difficult-to-clean spaces that can otherwise occur. Wall tiles might be used as a splashback behind the sink. A timber or tiled floor will be serviceable in this area.

Sample Toilet/Washbasin Space Analysis

Activities: Use of toilet. Handwashing. Shaving? Personal grooming.
Furniture & Equipment: Toilet and washbasin – matching units. Mirror with shelf. Towel rail.
Abstract: Pleasant and roomy. Convenient. Well ventilated.
Location: Close to living areas, kitchen, office and hallway.
Surfaces: Walls – tiled for easy cleaning? Wood floor or tiles? Cork tiles on wood floor? Plain ceiling.

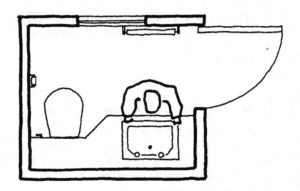

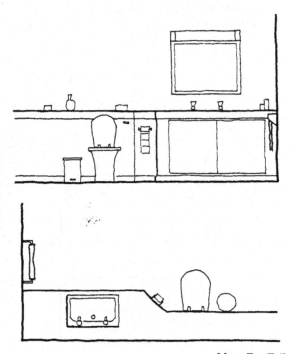

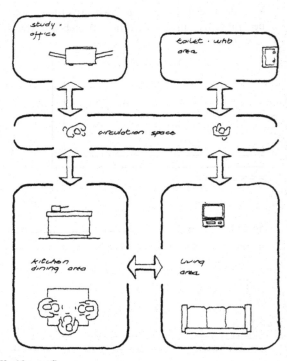

Ideas For Toilet/Washbasin Space

Ideas For Utility Rooms

➤ A utility room can be a most useful space in any home. The washing machine, a large sink for hand washing, soiled clothes storage, an ironing board, wine making facilities and a wide range of activities can be contained in this space.

➤ Equipment will depend on the use to which you will put the room, though, without doubt, a utility room is by far the best place in which to do the family laundry. A deep 'belfast' sink will be found useful for items requiring hand washing and will be a boon to wine makers. Worktop area, shelves and drawers will also be needed.

➤ Practicality is the keyword for utility rooms. East or west light will be fine and good ventilation will be essential. Sufficient space for all the activities you plan will also be important.

➤ The utility room should be close to, or open off, the kitchen. It should also be close to the back door to allow wet clothes to be easily taken out to dry. This proximity to the back door will allow the utility room to double as the place where outdoor clothing, shoes and so on are kept. If you do this, the space will need good organisation to work well.

➤ Cleanable and hardwearing are the qualities you want in the finishes for the walls, floor and worktops in this space. Tiling will serve well for this.

Sample Utility Room Analysis

Activities: Clothes washing – by machine and by hand. Pressing/ironing? Canned/dry goods storage.
Furniture & Equipment: Washing machine. Worktop. Deep sink. Shelving/storage.
Abstract: Convenient. Pleasant. Dry.
Location: Off kitchen. Close to back door for taking out wet washing. Utility room can act as draught lobby for kitchen? Should daily family coming and going be through utility room? If so, should it be the cloakroom instead of the front porch?
Surfaces: Tiled floor? Plain ceiling.

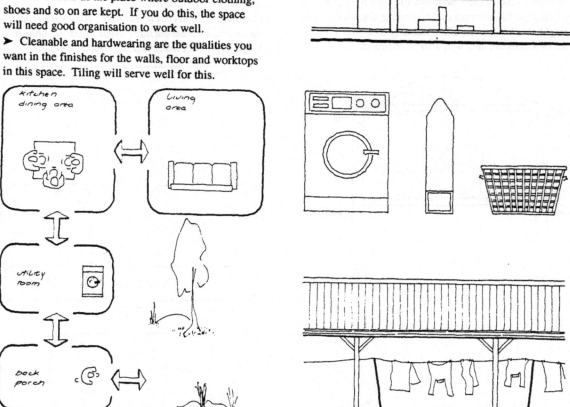

Ideas for Utility Rooms

41

Ideas For Workshops

➤ Anything from sculpture to dance to dismantling a car engine can happen in a workshop/studio space. Teaching, workshops, a home business or many other activities could be accommodated in this type of area.

➤ Furniture and equipment will depend on your needs. Basic tables and chairs and reasonable worktop/storage might be needed. If you plan on doing any heavy lifting a lifting device might need to be incorporated into the structure. Trestle tables that fold flat are very handy if you need to sometimes clear a large space. A sink will certainly be useful.

➤ Above all, a workshop/studio should be roomy enough for the activities that will be carried on there. Good light might also be important – from the south or west. A high ceiling will oftentimes be required.

➤ The location of this space will depend very much on individual need. Activities generating a lot of noise should be kept well away from living or sleeping areas. If visitors or students are likely to be brought to the workshop/studio, the door to it should be close to the front porch. A separate entrance might also be considered. Closeness to a toilet/washbasin area will also be required.

➤ The finishes in a workshop/studio will depend on the activities to be carried on there. If you wish to use it say, for dance, a good wood floor will be needed. For painting, a plain wood floor would be excellent. Wall finishes can be similarly chosen according to need. Inevitably, an area like this is disproportionately large in relation to the other spaces in the home and inexpensive materials have to be used to keep costs down.

Sample Workshop Analysis

Activities: *Woodwork. Artspace – painting. Teaching?*
Furniture & Equipment: *Worktops/storage. Sink? Shelving.*
Abstract: *Pleasant. Sunny. Warm. Spacious. View outside.*
Location: *Connected to hallway? Also with separate entrance from outside? Near toilet/washbasin.*
Surfaces: *Plain walls/ceiling. Wood floor.*

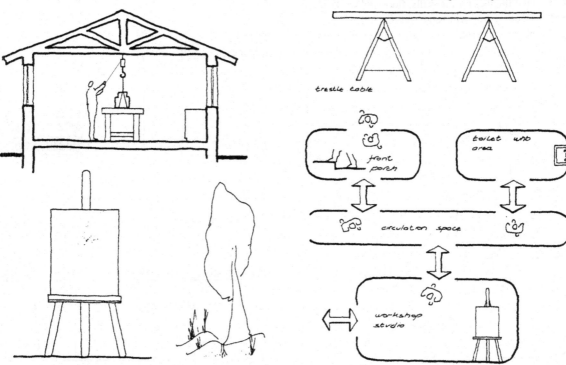

trestle table

toilet and area

front porch

circulation space

workshop studio

Ideas For Workshops

42

Ideas For Garages

➤ Strictly speaking, a garage is meant to house a car. In reality garages are used for a host of other things, such as the storage of goods and bicycles. Oftentimes they are converted into extra rooms. A proper garage should allow a vehicle to be easily stored under cover and allow work to be carried out on the vehicle while it is there. Ideally, a ramp or pit should be incorporated to allow work on the underside of the car to be carried out. This can be a relatively expensive space to make properly, so you should carefully think out the actual use a garage is likely to get. Incorporating such a space into a house is also a difficult exercise. A simple rain shelter will often suffice to protect a vehicle from the worst of the weather and would allow some work to be carried out under reasonable cover. If you opt for an enclosed garage make it generous enough in size to take a car, leaving enough room to walk all around it. If you will be storing bicycles in this space leave enough room for getting them in and out without scraping the side of the car.

➤ A good workbench is essential in a garage, as will be a sink, shelving and general storage. Other equipment will depend on individual need.

➤ While a garage might be intended to house the car, it might also get a reasonable amount of use for odd jobs, vehicle servicing and so on. From this point of view the space should be naturally lit. East, west or even north facing windows will be adequate.

➤ You may wish to be able to get directly from the garage into the main house and if this is so, some form of connection with the back porch could be made. While it is handy to be able to carry goods from the car directly into the house, it is nonetheless difficult to incorporate such a specialised space into a building that houses people. If a separate garage is made, some form of covered connection could be made to the back porch to give protection from the rain. Alternatively, a simple 'lean-to' arrangement outside the back porch would allow the car to be stored under cover and give convenience to the house occupants. Such a lean-to could also be used as a covered drying area convenient to the utility room. Whichever type of vehicle storage space you choose, a driveway will have to lead to it from the public roadway. The door of a garage will have to be quite large to accommodate a car passing through it. Good ventilation is essential in any enclosed garage.

➤ The floor of a garage should probably be concrete because of the weight involved. Walls and ceiling finishes should be serviceable.

Sample Garage Analysis

Activities: Parking/servicing car. Unloading/loading car.

Furniture & Equipment: Workbench/storage. Shelving. Pit?

Abstract: Comfortable size. Pleasant. Warm? What is best for the car?

Location: Connected to hallway or utility room? Connected to outside – double door for car and smaller door for people? Convenient to entrance gate/point.

Surfaces: Plain walls/ceiling. Strong hardwearing floor.

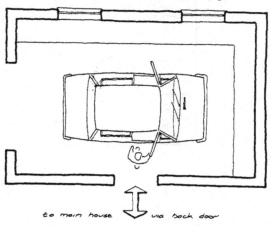

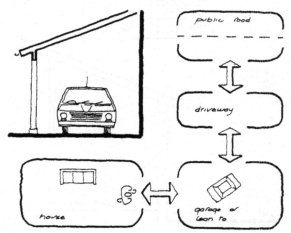

Ideas for Garages

43

Ideas For Sunspaces

➤ The function of a sunspace or solarium is to gather and store solar heat and feed this heat to the major spaces of the building. Such a space can also function to accommodate everyday activities. For example, a sunspace attached to the main living area of a building will not only collect solar heat, store it and distribute to the living space but it will also act as an extension of that space. Similarly, a sunspace attached to a kitchen/dining area or bedroom would act the same way. A sunspace might also be dedicated to a single task, such as an entry porch, hot-tub room or plant production area. Several sunspaces could be incorporated into a building.

➤ In terms of furniture and equipment, to function properly in the collection and storage of solar heat, the sunspace will need to be made from materials properly suited to this task. Large amounts of glazing are required to trap the solar energy and materials that can readily absorb heat while remaining relatively cool themselves are required for the heat storage. Effectively these materials – stone, brick and wood – will be used to make walls and floors but built-in furniture could also be constructed from these materials to contribute to the heatstorage capacity of the space. Sunspaces also need effective shutters for use over the windows at night. Timber shutters work excellently well in this regard.

➤ To be effective, a sunspace must face as near due south as possible. This will make the space bright and sunny, ideal for many household activities.

➤ The function to which a sunspace will be put will determine its location within the overall building plan. A proper orientation, however, is essential. If the sunspace is to be used as an extension of another space, sliding doors or screens will work to make this connection as easy and economical as possible.

➤ The surfaces of any sunspace must be chosen in regard to the solar energy collection, storage and distribution function of the space. Glass for the windows and materials such as wood, brick and stone for the floor and walls will be required. A dark surface will also be most effective in terms of absorbing solar heat.

Sample Sunspace Analysis 1

Activities: Front Porch. Arrival and departure.
Furniture & Equipment: Plants in clay tubs. Chairs. Small table. Mirror. Coat stand?
Abstract: Tall and dignified. Double height? Airy and bright.
Location: Close to all living areas and study/office. Close to driveway.
Surfaces: Timber floor or tiles? Brick or solid timber walls? Use black as dominant colour? Or terra-cotta? Water feature.

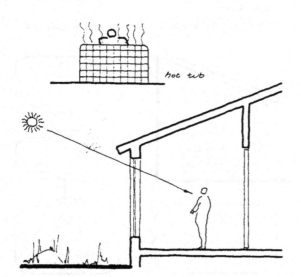

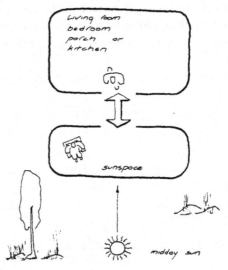

Ideas for Sunspaces

44

Sample Sunspace Analysis 2

Activities: Relaxing. Growing plants. Solar heat gathering/storage.
Furniture & Equipment: Table/chairs. Hot tub.
Abstract: Sunny all day. Sound of water inside?
Location: South facing. Adjacent to living/bedroom areas. Direct access to outside – especially in summer. What about privacy when using the hot tub?
Surfaces: Floor and walls to be heat absorbing. Double glazed windows.

Ideas For Bedrooms

➤ Bedrooms are the most intimate spaces in any dwelling and require careful thought and handling. In essence, a bedroom represents individual territory and any design needs to recognise this. While a bedroom might be considered to be a sleeping place only, many other activities not related to the bed at all can take place there. Reading, writing, watching TV/video, talking or listening to music are some of the activities that bedrooms can easily accommodate.

➤ Beds, bedside tables, clothes storage space, a dressing table, shelving and chairs can all be found in bedrooms. Music systems or TVs can either be permanently installed or brought in occasionally. A comfortable chair is a wonderful addition to any bedroom. The bed itself needs thought, especially if you are considering a large bed. If you want something extravagant like a four poster, the room will have to be big enough to take it. If study desks are being incorporated, enough room should be left for these.

➤ More than any other quality, bedrooms should be peaceful and relaxing. An easterly orientation will give a bedroom morning light. If you would prefer not to have this, a western aspect can be chosen. Pleasant textures and sensuous materials will all enhance the appeal of a bedroom.

➤ Because they are essentially private areas, bedrooms should be located away from the main living areas of the home. A close proximity to bathroom facilities is essential and indeed you might opt to have an en-suite bathroom arrangement. If children's bedrooms are likely to be noise producing, they should be organised so as not to disturb anyone.

➤ Pleasant, relaxing, intimate and warm are good descriptive terms for bedroom finishes.

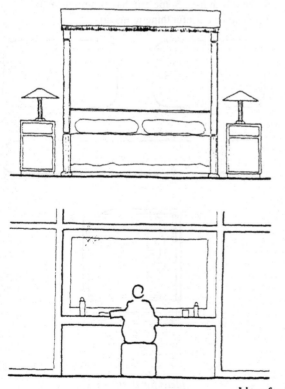

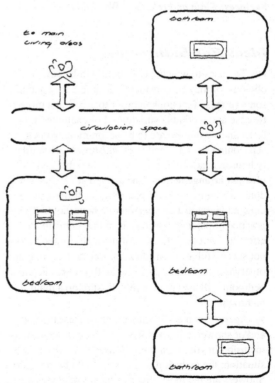

Ideas for Bedrooms

45

Sample Main Bedroom Analysis

Activities: Sleeping. Talking. Relaxing. Waking-up. Dressing/undressing.
Furniture & Equipment: Double bed. Bedside tables. Comfortable chair. Dressing table/stool. Clothes hanging space. Drawer/shelf space for clothes storage. Bookshelves? TV/video?
Abstract: Morning sun/south sun. Cosy. Relaxing. Warm. Sensuous.
Location: Near bathroom.
Surfaces: Plain walls. Plain ceiling with decorative plaster cornice. Wood floor.

Sample Bedroom Analysis

Activities: Sleeping. Talking. Relaxing. Studying. Waking-up. Dressing/undressing.
Furniture & Equipment: Bed/2 beds. Bedside table. Study desk(s)/chair(s). Clothes hanging space. Drawer/shelf space for clothes storage. Bookshelves. Music centre.
Abstract: Comfortable. Sunny in evening/morning. Warm. Relaxing. How many – 3 now, 1 later?
Location: Near bathroom.
Surfaces: Plain and relaxing! Wood floor.

Ideas For Bathrooms

➤ The uses to which a bathroom will be put are obvious. It may be considered desirable to separate some of these functions in order to arrive at a more flexible and workable situation. For example, if a toilet and washbasin are to be accommodated in a self-contained space and the bath/shower are similarly housed nearby, a more hygienic, flexible and pleasant arrangement will be arrived at. If this is not done, the entire range of bathroom facilities can be clogged up by just one person in a household. The practice of placing washbasins in bedrooms in an effort to overcome this sort of difficulty is generally not successful as it introduces a 'wet' activity into an otherwise 'dry' area. En-suite facilities attached to a bedroom will also relieve the pressure on a main bathroom.

➤ Apart from the WC, the washbasin and the bath and/or shower, a bidet is well worth consideration for inclusion in your bathroom. Certainly in an en-suite situation, the inclusion of a bidet should be standard. Showers are the most effective means of cleansing our bodies. Bath/shower combinations are not really successful. It is far better to create a purpose made shower cubicle rather than try to take your showers in the bath. Sliding or folding doors are very successful when used to enclose shower cubicles. Shower curtains simply do not work very well and should be avoided. A good shower tray is important – this is the part of the shower in which you stand. If there is the possibility of more than one person using the shower cubicle at any one time, the selected shower tray should be sufficiently big to allow this. Dual shower heads can also be installed. Thermostatically controlled units will allow a set water temperature to be maintained by mixing the hot and cold supplies. A shelf for shampoo bottles and soap should be fitted in the shower cubicle also. A timber 'duckboard' placed immediately outside the shower will be found useful for standing on immediately after showering. Baths should be selected on the basis of size, choosing a unit that is big enough for your needs. If you decide on a bath/shower arrangement, use a purpose made sliding door unit above the side of the bath to screen off the shower when it is in use. Some grip handles might also prove to be a useful thing to install.

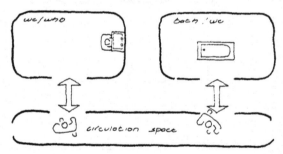

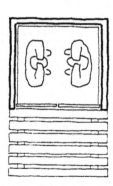

Ideas for Bathrooms

46

WCs should be selected for ease of cleaning. A unit that encloses the soil pipe exiting at the back and has a ceramic connection to the cistern rather than a pipe, will be found easiest to clean. A cistern can also be 'boxed-in'. Washbasins should either stand on a 'pedestal' or be housed in built-in units. A built-in unit will allow for easier cleaning. A shelf or cabinet, as well as a mirror, should be installed above the washbasin. Taps for both baths and washbasins should be of the mixer type, allowing a desired temperature of water to be run. The colour of WCs, washbasins, shower trays and baths should get careful consideration. It is important to think how a particular colour will look when it is in use. Oftentimes the standard white units will offer the most economical and 'cleanest' option.

A good extraction fan is vital in bathroom/shower room situations. This is especially true when large amounts of water vapour are being produced, for example, when someone is bathing or showering. Storage space for towels, soap, toilet paper and cleaning items is important to have. A built-in unit containing a washbasin will serve this purpose very well. A wastebasket will be needed also. Hooks, hangers and perhaps a chair will be required too.

➤ Making sufficient space in a bathroom/shower room is very important. Light can be brought in from the east or west, though with a toilet/washbasin arrangement a window is not essential. In such a case an extraction system will be needed and the operation of this should be linked to the light switch.

➤ Bathrooms/shower rooms should be located convenient to the bedroom areas.

➤ Hardwearing and easily cleanable surfaces are most important with bathroom facilities. Tiles are very successful in shower areas, above baths and washbasins and on floors. Timber is also very serviceable. As in all 'wet' areas, proper jointing of materials, especially in corners, is very important. This calls for careful workmanship when the finishing work is being done.

Sample Bathroom/Shower Room Analysis

Activities: Use of WC. Washing/shaving. Bathing/showering.
Furniture & Equipment: WC. WHB. Bidet. Towel rails – heated? Bath/shower or shower only? Hanging space for clothes. Towel storage space? Storage/shelves.
Abstract: Roomy! Comfortable. Sunny. Convenient. Warm. Well ventilated. Healthy!
Location: Near bedroom spaces.
Surfaces: Easily cleanable. Warm floor! Tiles? Wood?

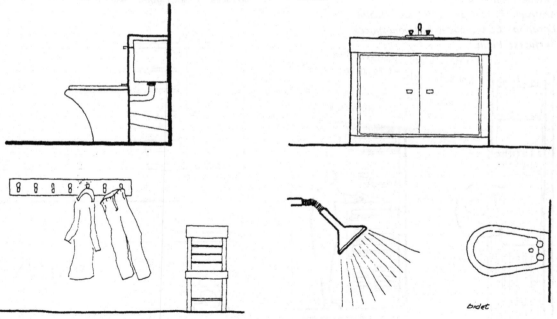

Ideas for Bathrooms

Ideas For Hot Presses*

➤ A hot press is normally used for the storage of fresh laundry. Heat is normally provided to this from the hot water cylinder. A small radiator could also be used for this purpose.

➤ Good shelving is essential in a hot press. Easy access to the shelves is also important and these should be located at a convenient height. If the hot water cylinder is to be properly insulated it will not give off much heat, so a small radiator can be located at the bottom of the hot press to pass warm air through it.

➤ Convenience in use is most important when thinking about a hot press.

➤ The press should be located in the most convenient place for the way in which the laundry cycle in the home will operate. A utility room can often be the handiest place for this or immediately adjacent to the bedroom areas. A hot press located in a circulation area will be very accessible.

➤ Slatted wood shelving will be found to be the most successful in use.

Sample Hot Press Analysis

Activities: Storage and retrieval of clothes/linen etc.
Furniture & Equipment: Heat source – hot water cylinder? Shelves.
Abstract: Easy to get at and use. Healthy!
Location: Convenient to bedroom spaces.
Surfaces: Plain.

*This is a very old-fashioned device to ensure that clothes and bed linen are fully dry before use.

A return to drying clothes on washing lines might see a return of this methodology!

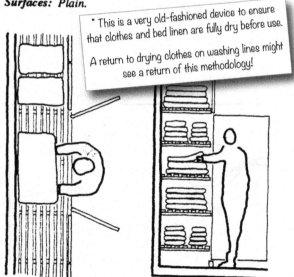

Ideas for Hot Presses

Ideas For Storage Space

➤ Proper, usable general storage space is essential in any dwelling. Such space can accommodate suitcases, vacuum cleaners, brooms, tools, family papers, mementoes – all the items in fact that you have no need for except occasionally.

➤ Shelving and drawers can be provided in whatever combination best suits your needs. High level storage will need a step ladder to reach, so space for a step ladder to be stored needs to be considered. A light in deep cupboards might be a useful inclusion.

➤ Accessibility is essential for storage spaces and the general circulation spaces of the home will be found to be the best place in which to locate them.

➤ Timber will prove itself to be by far the most usable material for storage units.

Sample Storage Space Analysis

Activities: Storage and retrieval of cleaning items, seasonal wear, family papers, boxes, mementoes etc.
Furniture & Equipment: Shelves. Drawers. Cupboards.
Abstract: Convenient to get at and to organise. Not hidden away.
Location: Convenient to all spaces! In the circulation spaces?
Surfaces: Plain. Wood smells good!

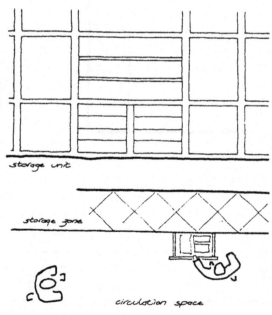

storage unit

storage zone

circulation space

Ideas for Storage Spaces

Ideas For Circulation Spaces

➤ The circulation spaces in any home will function to cater for the movement of people and goods between the various spaces within the building. They will also connect to the outside of the building.

➤ Circulation spaces should not be cluttered up with furniture but should be left clear. Open shelving can be introduced on one side of a circulation space as part of a storage unit containing drawers and other closed shelving.

➤ Above all, circulation spaces should be pleasant and, wherever possible, naturally lit. In many cases, some way of bringing in natural light overhead can be devised.

➤ By their nature, circulation spaces connect to all the individual spaces in a dwelling and also to the outside of the building.

➤ Many types of finishes can be selected for use in circulation spaces. Wood, floor tiles, plastered walls and ceiling will all prove serviceable in use.

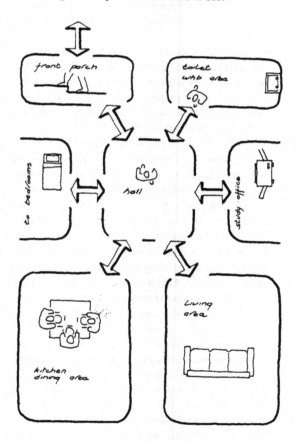

Ideas for Circulation Spaces

Sample Circulation Space Analysis

Activities: Moving from one space to another. Getting at storage spaces. Waiting.
Furniture & Equipment: Shelves, drawers and cupboards for storage. Chairs/tables. Pictures/paintings on walls? Stairs to upper floor?
Abstract: Roomy. Pleasant. Sunny if possible. View if possible. Warm. Well proportioned.
Location: Connecting spaces to each other and to the outside.
Surfaces: Wood floors. Plain walls and ceiling.

Ideas For Verandahs

➤ Verandahs allow for a pleasant extension of the indoor space of a building in periods of good weather. Playing primarily a leisure function, verandahs can also lend much to the outside appearance of a building.

➤ Tables, chairs, a barbecue, an open fireplace and a swing chair are all items you might consider putting out on your verandah. If such furniture is to be stored during wintertime, a storage space should be considered.

➤ Good orientation will be essential if a verandah space is to be fully enjoyed. A south or south/west aspect will be found to be the best. Enough space should be made to properly accommodate the activities you envisage carrying on there.

➤ A close connection to one of the major living areas, such as the kitchen/dining area will allow easy access to a verandah space and will prove convenient in use. A verandah outside one side of a living area will also be pleasant. It should be remembered that a verandah will tend to screen the spaces behind them.

➤ Wood or tiles are usable materials for the floor of a verandah. Timber supporting posts will prove to give the most pleasant finished appearance. The 'inside' of the verandah will be formed by the wall of the building and the finish will depend on the construction of this.

Sample Verandah Space Analysis

Activities: Relaxing. Star and moon gazing. Sunset watching. Possibly eating.

Furniture & Equipment: Hammock. Rocking chair. Swinging chair. Habachi.

Abstract: Pleasant to use. Sunny/shady. Can be enclosed in winter? Will it need fly screens in summer?

Location: Outside of Living and Kitchen/dining spaces.

Surfaces: Wood floor. Timber columns.

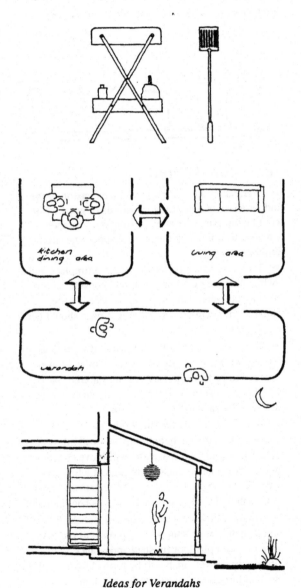

Ideas for Verandahs

Ideas For Outdoor Spaces

➤ The outdoor space surrounding a dwelling can accommodate a wide range of activities from recreation to entertainment or even food production. It is very important to focus on an image of how you intend to use the space around your building in order that the internal design can harmonise with it. It is all too easy to imagine the outdoor space as merely the space in which a building sits rather than as the space that will be seen when the occupants look out through the windows. In other words, do not merely consider how your building will look in relationship to the site but also consider how the site will appear while the occupants are inside the building looking out. Just what you intend to use the land surrounding your building for is vital to consider at an early stage. Children's play, sports, vegetable production, sunbathing and so on are all activities that are carried on outdoors. It is important to relate any such outdoor activities to the dwelling itself in order that a flexible and workable arrangement can be arrived at to harmonise the necessary links between the indoors and the outdoors.

➤ Seats, tables, chairs, slides, swings, sand-pits, hammocks, swimming pools, ponds, paths and tree houses can all be regarded as items of furniture and equipment for the purpose of studying outdoor space. Similarly, detached garages, workshops, playhouses, gazebos, greenhouses and so on can also be so regarded. The items you decide on will depend on exactly what you wish to do in the space surrounding your building. In any event, some form of driveway will be required linking the public roadway to the dwelling. A gate might also be considered necessary as might a cattle grid. Certainly a designated place for outdoor car parking will be necessary.

➤ Careful consideration should always be given to how the land surrounding a dwelling is to be developed. If a design that blends the house into a natural surrounding is required then one might wish to disturb the existing landscape very little. If a lawn is a requirement or a grass tennis court then invariably the existing contours will have to be altered and the existing vegetation disturbed. A natural garden can for all intents and purposes be self-sustaining and require no maintenance. A landscaped garden on the other hand can require constant attention. The growth of trees and shrubs on any site to the point where they contribute significantly to the landscape effects can take a considerable amount of time. Such planting can oftentimes be carried out before building work commences, though fencing and careful planning will be required to do this successfully.

➤ Outdoor space will normally surround a building and the internal circulation spaces will connect to this outdoor space via front and back porches. A gate will also connect the land to the outside world. Proper orientation, privacy and workable connections with the inside of the dwelling are all very critical.

➤ In regard to outdoor space, 'surfaces' might be considered as the vegetation, driveways, footpaths and so on. The outside appearance of the dwelling and any additional buildings or structures located within the outdoor space should also be considered in relationship to their natural surroundings.

Sample Outdoor Space Analysis

Activities: *Coming and going to/from house. Relaxing. Will be viewed from inside. Gardening? Games? Growing.*
Furniture & Equipment: *Garden shed for tools/implements. Greenhouse? Seat. Pond.*
Abstract: *Natural. Easy to keep. Beautiful.*
Location: *All around building.*
Surfaces: *Natural!*

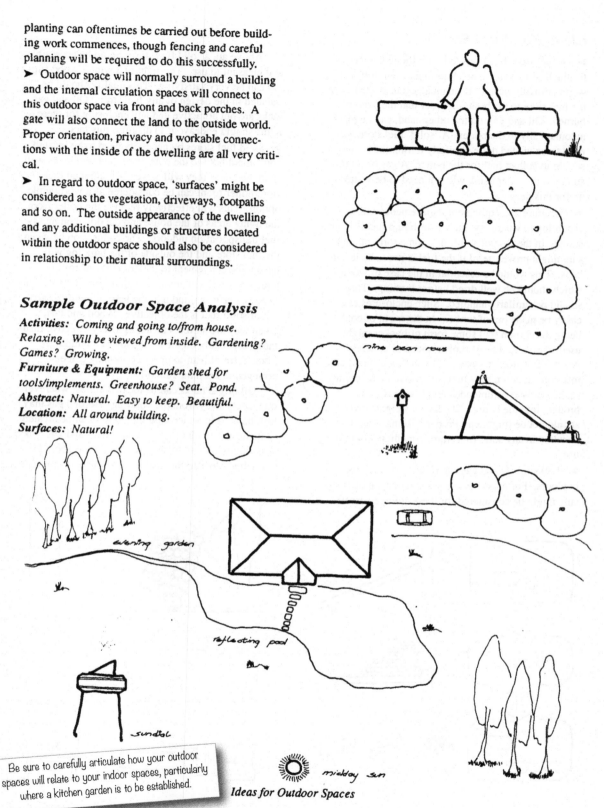

nine bean rows

evening garden

reflecting pool

sundial

midday sun

Be sure to carefully articulate how your outdoor spaces will relate to your indoor spaces, particularly where a kitchen garden is to be established.

Ideas for Outdoor Spaces

Ideas For Fuel Stores

➤ A fuel store functions to house the fuel necessary for the heating system in a building. Coal, turf and wood normally have to be manually transported from the fuel store to the boiler in order that they can be burned. Oil and gas, on the other hand, can be piped automatically to the boiler. A 'solid' fuel store will need to be visited quite regularly during the heating season to collect fuel for the boiler. A gas or oil fuel store, on the other hand, will not need to be visited at all for this purpose.

➤ Furniture and equipment requirements will vary according to whether solid, gas or liquid fuel is being stored. In the case of solid fuel, some form of enclosure might prove useful if the fuel is not to be left in bags. This would be essential in the case of wood, which should be well dried before burning. Turf should be similarly handled. Such enclosures can easily be made out of timber. In the event of coal being the chosen fuel some form of bunker might be used. This could be of timber, metal or concrete. Any type of storage system for solid fuel should take into consideration how fuel is to arrive at the premises, how it is to be unloaded and how it is to be brought into the house. The heavy weights involved should not be forgotten. Proper lighting should be installed in any solid fuel store to facilitate nighttime use.

➤ Tanks for oil and gas can usually be left exposed outdoors. For appearance's sake some type of enclosure might be considered for these storage vessels.

Above all, a solid fuel store should be accessible and pleasant to use. The sight of a winter wood supply can be very satisfying. This quality should be pursued in the design of any fuel store. Oil and gas tanks are not attractive and any enclosure for these items should endeavour to disguise this fact.

➤ Solid fuel stores by necessity need to be located convenient both to the outside of the building as well as to the boiler they will serve. A combined fuel store/boiler room can be considered as a worthwhile option. This will effectively remove the boiler from the living areas of the house and cut down on messy fuel transportation indoors. The connection between the fuel store and the outside of the building will need to be convenient to the driveway or road on which the fuel will arrive. At all points in the design exercise, bear in mind that the least amount of carrying of solid fuel is the objective. Wood and turf, when they are stored, can act as a very effective insulation especially on the north side of a building. Some form of lean-to or roof overhang can be arranged to keep the rain off.

Oil or gas tanks can be located almost wherever one wants away from the building. Bottled gas may also be used in which case the bottles can be located quite near the building. Delivery to oil and gas tanks is normally by road tanker, so these items should be located as close to the nearest roadway as is possible.

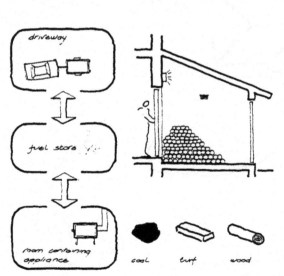

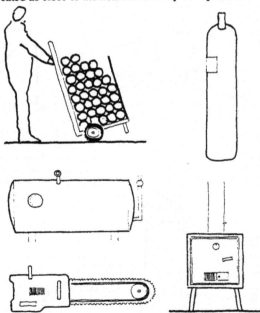

Ideas for Fuel Stores

Ideas For Boiler Rooms

➤ A boiler room will serve to house the boiler unit which will burn fuel to produce heat. Such boilers might burn oil, gas, coal, wood or turf. Oil boilers are normally independently housed. Gas boilers, being more efficient and less smelly, can be housed in a workshop space or a garage and do not strictly require separate accommodation. Solid fuel boilers and stoves are oftentimes located within the dwelling, though this practice is inefficient and dirt producing.

➤ Many types of boiler are available to burn oil, gas or solid fuel. No other furniture and equipment is likely to be required.

➤ Convenience is the major requirement for any boiler room. As there is no particular requirement for natural light in a boiler room, a northern aspect can be chosen.

➤ A central location for any boiler room will allow for an economical distribution of heat throughout the building which it serves. If a central location is desired, a boiler room located centrally below the main floor of the building will work effectively. Such an arrangement could well be combined with garage/fuel store/workshop accommodation. A boiler room can also be located on the north side of a building and used as an effective 'buffer', moderating heat losses. Such an arrangement can also allow easy access to the boiler room from the outside of the building.

➤ Due to the fact that controlled burning takes place in a boiler room, the surfaces enclosing such a space might need to be fireproofed. Several layers of plasterboard will be an effective fire barrier, as will concrete blockwork.

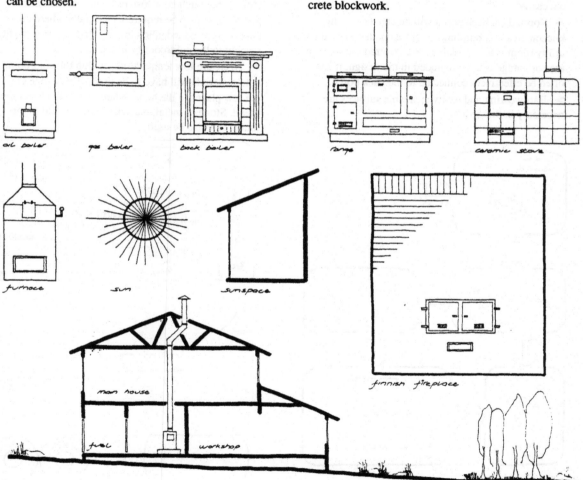

Ideas for Boiler Rooms

53

Ideas For Back Porches

➤ In preference to using the front porch as the main entry to your home, you might consider using the back porch to accommodate the daily comings and goings of the family. This would allow a more formal front porch to be planned and maintained. Alternatively, a back porch can merely function as a back door to your building.

➤ In terms of furniture and equipment, a back porch can be fitted out similarly to a front porch, fulfilling the function of coat, shoe and accessory storage. If a back door is all that is required, no furniture and equipment will be needed, though the creation of a proper draught lobby is essential.

➤ A back porch should be pleasant to use and naturally lit from the east or west. Enough space should be created to allow people and goods to move in and out easily.

➤ Normally, a back porch will be attached to the kitchen area of a building. A close connection with a utility room is also possible. If a covered car parking area or garage is to be included in the design, it can often be effectively connected to the back porch.

➤ Hardwearing and easily cleanable surfaces are necessary in this space.

Ideas For Coldrooms

➤ A coldroom incorporated into the design of a dwelling can provide valuable space for the storage of perishable goods. Milk, butter, eggs, vegetables, cheeses – items normally kept in a refrigerator – can be kept in a coldroom.

➤ Proper shelving is essential for this type of space – timber or even metal can be used for this. Some arrangement for hanging items might also be useful.

➤ As might seem obvious, a coldroom should be cold. A reasonable amount of space will also be needed for easy access. Good ventilation will also be required.

➤ A proper orientation is essential for a coldroom in order that the temperature can be kept to a minimum. A northwest aspect would be ideal. In terms of the other spaces in your design, the coldroom should be close to the kitchen. Close proximity to the back porch might also be required, especially where car parking is provided, allowing groceries to be brought straight to the coldroom from the car.

➤ To ensure low temperatures within the coldroom, cold materials will have to be used. This is one of the few places in the home where concrete blocks are ideal! Stone or metal, materials that are cold to the touch, can also be used.

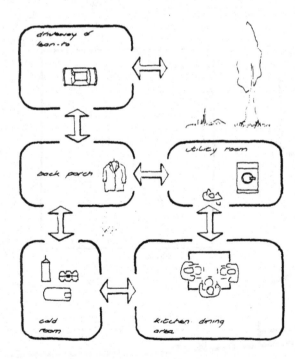

Ideas for Back Porches

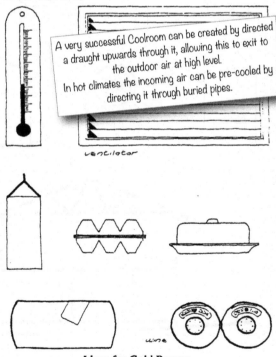

A very successful Coolroom can be created by directed a draught upwards through it, allowing this to exit to the outdoor air at high level.
In hot climates the incoming air can be pre-cooled by directing it through buried pipes.

Ideas for Cold Rooms

Looking At Spaces

The information that you set down about the spaces you want in your building will produce a wealth of very vital information about the kind of house you want to design and live in. It is from these blueprints that the design is made.

Any type of space can be considered in this way. While you may not feel confident to jot down straight away a description of a particular space, it will be found that looking at spaces in buildings will give you lots of ideas. Looking, at this stage, is very important. What something looks like on the outside can be deceptive. Imagine using things – not just looking at them! A house can be a hive of activity on a daily basis. Organising this activity so that it is easy to do can save a lot of time and effort day after day.

A house by no means has to be a series of inter-connected spaces. Apart from the need to provide an individual space for a toilet, a house can be a single space in which all the activities of the household take place. An infinite variety of other arrangements can also be arrived at, of course.

Looking At Activities

Particular activities, such as meal preparation, can be looked at closely in addition to the space analysis exercises *fig. 8*. These activities are activities that are likely to be repeated over and over within the building. By examining how these activities should best be carried out, the design can be made to conform to this. This will make it easy and straightforward to undertake regular household tasks.

For example, the activity of meal preparation will involve gathering ingredients, preparing them, it will involve using cooking utensils and cooking, washing up, disposing of packaging and waste and serving the meal. This activity might be repeated several times a day in your building. Finding the way that suits you best to cook meals and to wash-up will make life considerably easier on a regular basis.

Another good activity to analyse is washing. This will involve examining the clothes cycle in the home. Where do all the dirty clothes get left for washing? Who gathers them all up? Where will they be washed? Will they be washed by hand or machine, or both? How will the clothes be dried? Is a covered outdoor drying area a good idea – near the utility room/back door? Where will the clothes be

aired? Will some clothes need to be ironed? Where will this be done? How will the clean clothes get into the individual rooms?

Such an analysis will begin to produce a way of doing the washing that is simple, straightforward and efficient. It will also help you in deciding just where things and spaces in your house should be in relationship to each other.

Other activities that could be analysed are work and shopping. Looking at how food gets into your home and where it is stored there will make this regular activity much easier to face on a regular basis.

Buildings are made to serve the needs of the people that occupy them. It is looking at the particular needs you have and what you want to do in your building that will allow you to design a building to suit your needs.

activity analysis :
cooking :

gather ingredients
prepare ingredients
dispose of waste
cook
wash up pans / utensils
set table
serve meal
eat
clear table
wash dishes
store crockery / cutlery

If you are planning on growing food, include the fruit and veg harvesting and cleaning operations in your Activity Analysis.

Fig 8: Activities that are likely to be repeated over and over in your building should be clearly analysed.

5 Sheltermaker Design Programme
Analysing Regular Household Activities

Read *'Looking At Activities'* on page 55. This exercise is very important to the efficient functioning of a building. If such activities as cooking, dishwashing, food production and creativity are carefully looked at now, your design can be made to accommodate your preferred way of carrying out these tasks. If you are thinking of operating a business from your home it is important to look now at how this might be carried on successfully.

To assist in this exercise a *Sample Activity Analysis Sheet* has been drawn up. This describes the *Cooking/Eating Cycle* and *The Laundry Cycle* respectively. Print and read this. Now, create your own *Activity Analysis Sheet* or *Sheets* for the particular activities which you wish to carry on in your building. This is critical if any work or creative activity is to be carried on. Use the supplied *Activity Analysis Sheet* blank/s for this exercise.

Every home should be able to host work and creative activity easily. This is one of the keys to the adaptability of a design because it opens up a wide range of options. Remember, you are designing for an unseen future - in other words none of us knows what is going to happen ten or even five years down the road. The design you create should be able to adapt to any change either in the outside world or personal change. There is no doubt that creating your own house design will change you. This is part of the reason why no one can really do it for you. To facilitate such change you must be honest with yourself. This means searching within yourself and getting in touch with you own deep nature.

6 Sheltermaker Design Programme
Getting Organised

As soon as you begin filling out the *Space Analysis Sheets* and the *Activity Sheets* you will realise the need for good organisation to make the best use of your time. You will also need to get yourself properly equipped for the task in hand.

Read *'Getting Organised'* on page 58. This mentions 'working with others' or forming some kind of design team. It can be useful to work in groups, either family groups or groups formed around a common interest in sustainable shelter and living. Group energy can be a great motivator, though it is best that individual design solutions are developed rather than everyone trying to agree on a single solution. Generally speaking, caution needs to be exercised when working with others. Even the most harmonious design team will generate conflicts. It is critical to let these surface and to examine them closely, allowing differences to be seen in a positive light.

The first step in the direction of getting paperwork organised will be to obtain some supplies and equipment, as detailed on the *Equipment Worksheet*. There is no need to go out and buy everything at once. Simply obtain the items you need for the task in hand. At this stage these would be: *20 File Folders* some plain *A4 paper* and a *File Storage Box.*

Having obtained the file folders, dedicate one to each *Space* you intend to have in your design, writing on the front the name/number of the *Space*. Put the completed *Space Analysis Worksheets* into the relevant file along with any photographs and so on that specifically refer to that *Space*. While this might seem extravagant at this point, as work progresses these files will begin to fill up and might even begin to bulge! Keep the files in the box unless you have a dedicated workspace or desk with a file drawer. Keep everything close to where you intend working.

No building can be properly designed in a hurry, especially a home. The time spent in carefully evolving a design will only ever be a small fraction of the time you will spend within the completed building. Remember, being reasonably organised will allow you to get the best value out of your time. Also, it is best to spend a little time each day on the project rather than trying to cram a lot of work into a weekly session.

Read *'Time'* on page 62.

7 Sheltermaker Design Programme
Setting Out Your Budget

Economics is a critical aspect of your project - how much your site and building will cost and how it will be paid for. If you wish to build low-cost, you will inevitably have to become involved in the construction process yourself. Also, the choice of construction system, finishes and overall size will become very important. If you are borrowing in order to build, you will have to consider the attitudes of lending institutions towards property values and your own attitude towards work, resale values and property generally.

Read *'Money'* on page 60. You might also re-read page 22 of *The Introduction*. Money exerts a greater influence on building design and construction than any other single factor so it is critical that you get your thinking and your feeling straight on the matter. Basically, the more power you give to 'Money' in the design equation the more influence it will have. While this may seem like a truism, bear in mind that 'Money' is no respecter of persons or of life, so it can easily be the case that 'Money' rules the day to the detriment of Life considerations. In many ways this is the core of the struggle to achieve 'Sustainability'.

To get your *Budget* information underway print out and fill in the *Budget Worksheet*. You may wish to repeat the exercise several times. Set down your first estimate of how much you want to spend being completely honest in your estimates. It is critical that you reconcile your dreams with reality at this stage of the design process. Create a *Budget File* to keep this in.

Next: SDP8 - Assembling Furniture & Equipment Measurements, page 63

Getting Organised

Approaching the Brief by the careful analysis of activities and spaces will create much food for thought and much discussion between all those involved in the exercise. At this point the value of getting organised will become obvious. Clearly note on the top of each page which space the information refers to, as well as the particular aspect that is being considered *fig. 9*. Try keeping related pages clipped together and use a file folder for keeping information about each space separate *fig. 10*. Clearly note on the outside of each folder what it contains. What is going to happen from this point onwards is that more and more information is going to be gathered, as all aspects of the spaces are considered.

If the building you are designing is for more than just yourself, it is important to find a way to include

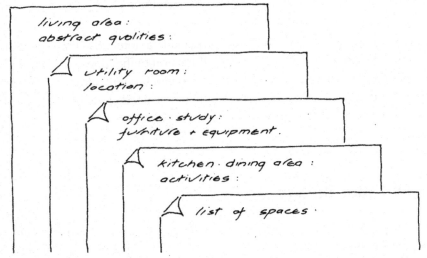

Fig. 9: The value of getting organised will become obvious very quickly. Clearly note on the top of each page which space the information refers to as well as the particular aspect of it that is being considered.

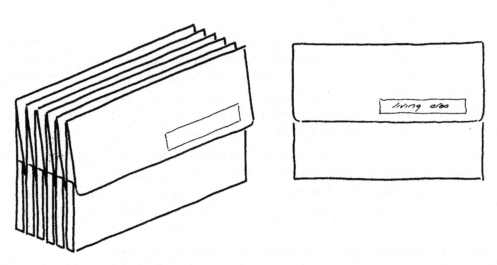

Fig. 10: Use file folders for keeping information about each space separate and clearly note on the outside of each file just what it contains.

everybody in the creative process. At the early stages of the design, there will be lots of ideas floating about as everyone fantasises about the kind of house they want. It is important to capture as many of these early ideas as possible. Someone will have to take overall responsibility for the work getting done. This is an organisational position, not one of power, so whoever is the best organiser should do the job.

The bulk of the work involved in designing a house can be done on a reasonably sized table *fig. 11*. Once the written information is stored in file folders these can be kept in a box and put away *fig. 12*. Meetings can also be held around the table. Organise your telephone so that you can sit and write down information while using it *fig. 13*. You may want to have all your information on the same size paper. If so, use A4 size plain, loose sheets.

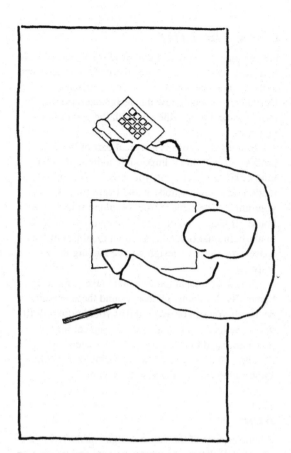

Fig. 13: Organise your telephone so that you can write down information while using it.

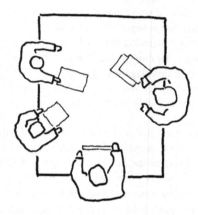

Fig. 11: The bulk of the work involved in designing a house can be done on a reasonably sized table.

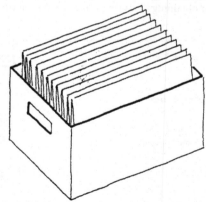

Fig. 12: File folders can be kept in a box and put away when not in use.

Information is only useful if it is information relevant to something you want to know or might want to know. As information becomes available to you, examine it before putting it away. If something is really of no interest or relevance to what you are doing, get rid of it. Useful information should be filed where you can gain easy access to it. It is important that, when you need to find out something from your files, you can find it out quickly.

This information will be coming from a variety of sources – from books, magazines, catalogues, newspapers and so on. Only take as much information as is relevant to your needs. Use photocopies to edit out of say, a book, a piece of information you need. Collect catalogues from shops and builders providers, use the phone and the post to search out ideas, products and prices. Talk to people about their houses and how they live in them. All this type of information gathering will allow you to make balanced choices and clear decisions.

Using The Brief

Formulating a clear Brief will produce as many questions as it will answers. Finding satisfactory answers to these questions involves making decisions. Decisions are what allow the design exercise to move forward to provide you with the sort of house you want.

Making decisions is a critical part of the design process. If you find it impossible to imagine what kind of kitchen you want, you must search out information on kitchens, study it and begin to make up your mind. The same is true for all the spaces in the house. If these kind of decisions are not made, particularly in relation to the Abstract Qualities of the spaces, the finished design will be lacking in these respects.

It is the personal touches that make a house a home. By designing a house around these personal decisions you can be assured that your house will fit you. The location of walls, floors and ceilings can all be arranged to suit your particular needs. It is deciding on these needs that will allow you to place these elements just where suits you best.

Money

All the aspects of the house design considered in the Brief relate directly to what you want and to what you can afford to pay to get it. The actual building of a home can be a very rapid process. After all the work of designing the house has been completed and the necessary permits or permissions have been obtained, the building can be made very quickly. At that point, all that might be needed to see the project realised might be money *fig. 14*.

Deciding on how much you have to spend is important right at the beginning of the project *fig. 15*. This amount should include the cost of a site. If you do not have all the money, how you are going to get it should immediately be brought under consideration. Borrowing money to build a house is now a very common practice. Such borrowing, or "mortgaging", carries with it certain restrictions that may not be compatible with the kind of house you want to make or how you want to make it. Broadly speaking, institutions which loan money for house construction consider such houses to be theirs and so apply restrictions to the design that have to do with protecting the investment. Such restrictions are based on considerations that have little to do with the comfort or happiness of the house occupants.

Designing your own home will not necessarily run counter to the lending institution's considerations but, it might. If so, you might have to search out an institution that is sensitive to your needs. Remember, borrowing money from a lending institution makes that money yours, not theirs. The important thing at this stage is to decide on a rough figure that is realistic for you. Decisions as to how to spend the money available can be made as the project unfolds.

If there are building grants available to you, it is important to find out the details attached to these. Again, it may be the case that the type of house you wish to create does not conform to the grant requirements. If this is the case you will have to decide whether to forego the grant rather than compromise your design. Alternatively, if you wish to benefit from the grant, you will need to be aware of the conditions for obtaining it, so that you can conform to these.

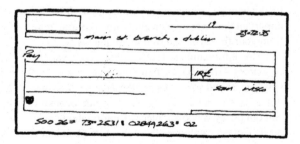

Fig. 14: After all the work of designing the house has been completed the building can be made very quickly. At that point all that might be needed to see the project realised is money.

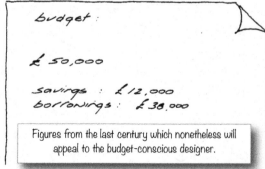

Fig. 15: Deciding on how much you have to spend is important right at the beginning of the project.

Once you have decided that you want to build to suit yourself, your way will be clear. The responsibility for the quality of the design and the construction will be in your hands and by virtue of this fact the building you design will, of course, be far superior to anything the lending institution might consider adequate. It is natural that the house designer wants to build carefully and well, and so protect the investment made. Deciding to get a mortgage is a very serious matter. Even if you reconcile yourself to the fact that the money that you have borrowed is yours, you are nonetheless committing yourself to repaying that money over a long period of time, a period in which your life will change, you will change and the life around you will change. What will not change are the monthly repayments due to the lending institution. The whole idea of mortgaging your future in order to pay for your house dates back to the growth of industrialised societies and their work ethic. Before that, people simply built the sort of homes they could afford, using their own hands and whatever materials were available to them.

Self-building can offer you a way of cutting costs as well as a way of you being directly involved in the construction of your home. Organisation is the key to successful building and time is required for this. If you already own a site and have even a modest amount of start up capital, self-building can allow you to remain outside of the conventional money market. You can design and build a small compact house that can expand as your need for space grows and finance this out of income. By building out of income, much of the pressure associated with mortgage repayments can be relieved.

If you are considering building a house yourself and have never tackled a major construction project before, it is important to gain experience of building. This can be done by taking a self-build course, or by building something in your existing back garden as a way of learning. Self-building is a very satisfying way of providing a home for you and your family. It requires reasonable capital resources, good organisation and, most of all, sufficient time to see everything through to completion. It really is not feasible to try to work and build at the same time. Also, there will be jobs such as wiring and plumbing that you may not be able to do for yourself. In such cases outside help will have to be brought in and invariably this will involve money changing hands.

The options open to self-builders expand considerably once a site has been obtained. Materials can be gathered, site preparations can be made, a caravan can be brought on site to act as an office or living accommodation and so on *fig. 16*. The construction of a small starter building can provide storage space for materials as well as acting as a kind of base camp, allowing work to proceed at a modest pace. If these types of self-building options are desirable, they should be included in the Brief *fig. 17*.

To bring a building project to the point where it is ready to be built is a time consuming job. It is this time, however, that will ensure your house is just how you want it to be when you move into it. Allow yourself plenty of time to feel it all through.

Fig. 16: The options open to self-builders expand considerably once a site has been obtained. Materials can be gathered, site preparations can be made, a caravan can be brought on site to act as an office or living accommodation.

Check out the EconoSpace on the next page!

Fig. 17: The construction of a small starter building can provide storage space for materials as well as acting as a base camp allowing work to proceed at a modest pace. If these types of self-building options are desirable they should be included in the Brief.

Time

To properly evaluate your needs and consider all the aspects of house design you need time *fig. 18.* If the design exercise is being carried out on a full time basis, then three months might be a reasonable time to allow. In practice, such a design will be done on a part-time ongoing basis. In this case, more like a year of time will be needed. Even this programme will require steady work to achieve.

The whole idea of designing your house is to enjoy it. It is a creative exercise that is fulfilling, and in truth, is an exercise that no one can really do for you. In comparison to the amount of time that will be spent in a building, the design time is negligible. Pressure to come up with a quick design solution is very difficult to deal with. A good design is a careful design. The care that goes into the design process will manifest itself clearly in the sort of house you make.

Using the Brief to honestly look at what it is you want in a house is a far cheaper and less traumatic process than trying to live in an ill considered design. It is a good idea to thrash out any differences of opinion within the design team as soon as they surface. It is inevitable that these will arise. If the differences seem insurmountable, try a different approach, like making two designs. No matter what happens, keep writing things down, keep looking into everything and asking questions, and remember that it is your money that you will be spending. Perhaps it will be borrowed money, but no matter, it is yours and it is you who can decide how it should be spent.

Summary

Write down a list of all the spaces you wish to have in your building.

Analyse each space individually under the following headings – Activities; Furniture & Equipment; Abstract Qualities; Location and Surfaces.

Analyse everyday Activities.

Organise the design team, a place to work and a filing system.

Decide on a budget for the project and consider money matters.

Give yourself time.

The EconoSpace is a simple building which can easily be made in the average backyard - or on-site as a 'starter' building. This is the ideal way to learn what are relatively simple skills. Check it out on page 286 or, online at: livingarchitecturecentre.com

Fig. 18: To properly evaluate your needs and to consider all the aspects of house design you need time.

8 Assembling Furniture & Equipment Measurementss

Apart from accommodating those who will use the building, the *Spaces* you create, [or modify in the case of an existing building], will also have to accommodate tables, chairs, storage units, books, electrical equipment and so on. It is important at this point to quantify the size that these items are likely to be.

Read the *Measurement* chapter. This hints at some of the Mysteries of Architecture alluded to in the *Introduction*. We normally do not think of *measurements* as being mysterious at all, but when you think about it, of course, they are. Even CEO's recognise this in their dedication to the bottom line! Essentially, measurements are about communication, the common language used by all those involved in the design and construction process.

Print the *Furniture & Equipment Worksheet*. As you will see this lists many common items in everyday use. You will notice that most items have three dimensions - length, width and height.

You are now going to 'size' items of *Furniture & Equipment* that you wish to install in the various *Spaces* of your design, entering this information onto the relevant *Space Analysis Sheets*. Items that do not appear on the *Worksheet* you will have to measure. To do this you will need a measuring tape and an A4 clipboard as listed on the *Equipment Worksheet*.

Begin with any one of your *Space Analysis Sheets*. Simply 'size' items listed under *Furniture & Equipment* by selecting dimensions from the *Worksheet* or measuring the particular item in question. Enter these dimensions into the *Furniture & Equipment* measurements portion of the *Analysis Sheet*. If there is not enough room use a blank sheet of paper attached to the *Analysis Sheet* with *'Item' 'Length' 'Width'* and *'Height'* columns.

Essentially, it will be the dimensions of items of *Furniture & Equipment* plus the activities associated with using these items that will dictate the size particular spaces will need to be.

Next: SDP9 - Drawing, page 69

Measurement

Many aspects of building design and construction are concerned with the sizes things are. For example, the height of the lofty ceiling you might want in your living room will have to be decided sooner or later, as will the sizes of all the furniture, rooms and circulation spaces. Similarly, all the doors and windows in your building will need sizes applied to them, as will the heights of the worktops and other items of built-in furniture *figs. 1 & 2*. In order to accurately communicate information about the sizes things are, measurements are used.

fig. 1: As the design exercise progresses the sizes of the various parts of your building will have to be decided, including the sizes of windows and doors.

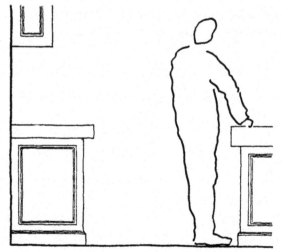

fig. 2: The sizes of the worktops and other built-in units will also have to be decided.

Human Scale

The dimensions or measurements of the human form have always influenced the sizes of buildings and their furnishings. The most obvious example of this influence is in the size of tables and chairs *fig. 3*. Beds are another good example *fig. 4*.

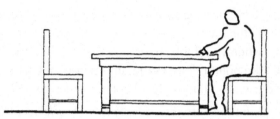

fig. 3: The dimensions of the human form have always influenced the size of buildings and their furnishings. The most obvious example of this influence is in the size of tables and chairs.

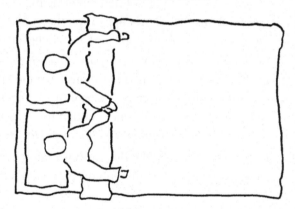

fig. 4: The size of a bed relates directly to the dimensions of the human form.

Room sizes are related to the activities carried on by people within them and stair gradients are set according to the ease with which people can negotiate them. Also, the heights and widths of doorways are determined by the space needed by people to pass easily through them. Windows are usually positioned to enable people to see out of them whether sitting or standing *fig. 5*.

The overall effect of taking the size of people into account in building design is to provide buildings with a human scale *fig. 6*.

fig. 5: Windows are usually positioned to enable people to see out of them whether sitting or standing.

fig. 6: The overall effect of taking the size of people into account in building design is to provide buildings with a human scale.

Body Measurements

The human body is the original measuring device *fig. 7*. Simple measurements are afforded by using the hands, the feet and the eyes to judge distance *figs. 8 & 9*. The outstretched arm can be used to judge height and depth. Both long and short distances can be measured by using the body as a ruler.

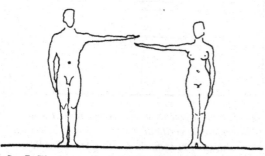

fig. 7: The human body is the original measuring device.

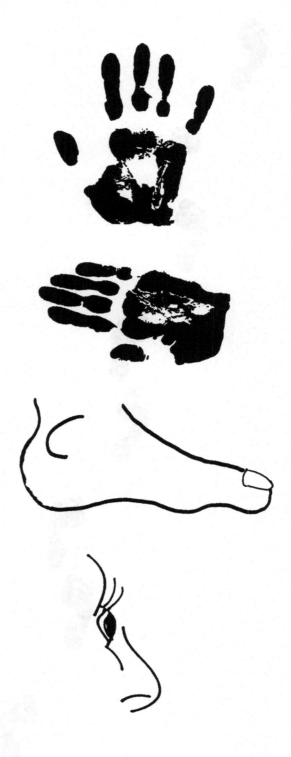

fig. 8: Simple measurements are afforded by using the hands, the feet and the eye to judge distance.

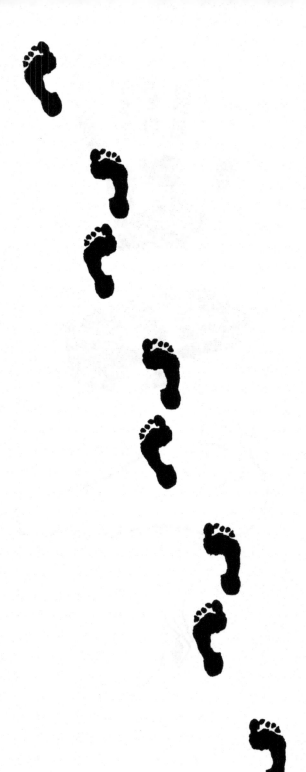

A ruler based on the human body is a highly individual one. It allows lengths, heights and other dimensions to be quantified in relationship to the body of the measurer. Such a loose system of sizing buildings has many advantages, especially in that it invests a human scale in any measurements determined in this way. This system does depend however on the close involvement of the measuring devices themselves, the rulers, in the actual process. Unfortunately, body measurements are impossible to communicate accurately because they are so personal. One way around this problem is to relate body dimensions to one of the Standard Measurement Systems.

Standard Measurement Systems

The simplest measurement system is that based on the human form. In a complex project such as the design of a building, such an individual system is unworkable. Instead, Standard Measurement Systems are used, replacing the human ruler. By doing this, accurate dimensional information can be communicated easily to all those involved in the building process.

Measurement Standards ensure that a quoted dimension is verifiable by reference to an agreed Standard, such as is marked onto a Standard Ruler. The Metric System and the Imperial System are two of the Standard Measurement Systems *fig. 10*. It is agreed by everybody who use these systems that their units, feet and metres, are a specific, exact length. Standards ensure accuracy and ease communications in the building process.

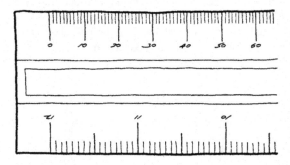

fig. 10: Measurement Standards ensure that a quoted dimension is verifiable by reference to an agreed Standard, such as is marked onto a Standard Ruler. The Metric System and the Imperial System are two of the Standard Measurement Systems.

fig. 9: The feet used as a measuring device.

66

fig. 11: Some Standard Measurement Systems retain links to their origins in the human form. The most obvious is the Imperial Foot.

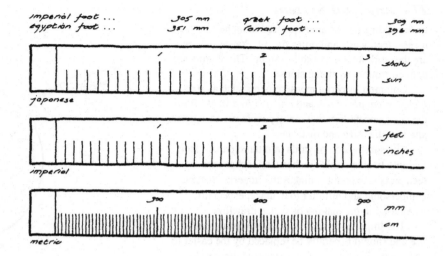

imperial foot ... 305 mm
egyptian foot ... 351 mm

greek foot ... 309 mm
roman foot ... 296 mm

japanese

imperial

metric

fig. 12: Japanese measure has its equivalent of the Imperial Foot in the shaku. The shaku is slightly shorter than the Imperial foot. The shaku is divided into ten parts called sun.

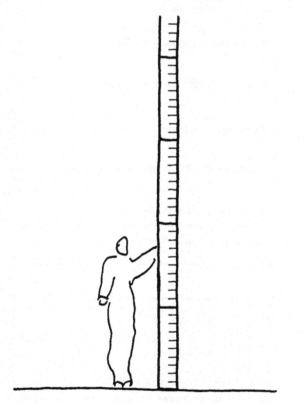

fig. 13: Where once the human form provided a living ruler, a marked standard has replaced it – the Standard Ruler.

Some Standard Measurement Systems retain links to their origins in the human form. The most obvious is the Imperial Foot *fig. 11*. Japanese measure has its equivalent in the *shaku*, another foot measurement. The *shaku* is slightly shorter than the Imperial foot. The *shaku* is divided into ten parts called *sun* in the Japanese measurement system *fig. 12*.

Adherence to any measurement system means a loss of the 'loose' dimensions provided by the hand, the foot or the raised arm. So, where once the human figure provided a living ruler, a marked standard has replaced it – the Standard Ruler *fig. 13*.

The Standard Ruler

Standard Measurement Systems consider all dimensions in relationship to the Standard Ruler, an object that otherwise has no connection to what is being measured or created. The accuracy that such a system guarantees and the ease of communication that it allows has ensured its supremacy in use. The loss that has occurred by the adoption of such systems has been that dimensions no longer refer directly to the human form. Where accuracy has been gained, the freedom of intuition and individuality has been lost and the eye has been discounted as a reliable measuring device.

The Imperial System

Imperial dimensions are expressed in inches, parts of inches, feet, yards and miles *fig. 14*. Yards and feet are the working units of this system. These units are derived from body dimensions.

Common Imperial measurements such as *six inches*, *a couple of feet* and *one hundred yards*, form the basic vocabulary that many people use to express and visualise size and distance.

The subdivision of yards into three parts – feet; feet into twelve parts – inches; and inches into sixteen parts – sixteenths, makes the Imperial System cumbersome and difficult to manage, especially when used in the making of scaled drawings.

The Imperial System is gradually going out of use and should generally be replaced by the easier to use Metric System. Familiar Imperial dimensions should be converted to their Metric equivalents as a way of adapting to the Metric system.

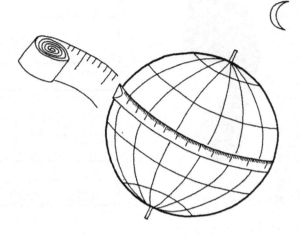

fig. 15: *The Metric System is a decimal system and is based on the measurement of the Earth itself and its subdivision into smaller units.*

---

1 Mile = 1760 yards

1 yard = 3 feet

1 foot = 12 inches

---

fig. 14: *Imperial dimensions are expressed in inches, parts of inches, feet, yards and miles.*

---

1 Kilometre = 1000m = 0.6214 miles

1 Metre = 1000mm = 1.093 yards

1 Centimetre = 10mm = $\frac{3}{8}$ inch

1 Millimetre = 0.0394 inches = $\frac{1}{32}$ inch approx.

---

fig. 16: *The units of the Metric System are, in descending order of magnitude: the kilometre, metre, centimetre and the millimetre.*

The Metric System

The Metric System is a decimal system and is based on the measurement of the Earth itself and its subdivision into smaller units *fig. 15*. These are in descending order of magnitude: the kilometre, metre, centimetre and the millimetre *fig. 16*.

A metre divided into a thousand parts makes millimetres, which are the basic working units of the Metric System and are roughly equivalent in size to the teeth of a comb *fig. 17*. This small unit of measurement allows dimensions to be expressed very exactly. Millimetres are always written as a number followed by the letters 'mm'. There are 25mm to the inch, 305mm to the foot and 914mm to the yard. Measuring and expressing all dimensions in millimetres allows for a very simple and accurate use of the Metric System.

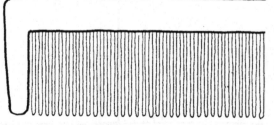

fig. 17: *A metre divided into a thousand parts makes millimetres. These are the basic working units of the Metric System and are roughly equivalent in size to the teeth of a comb.*

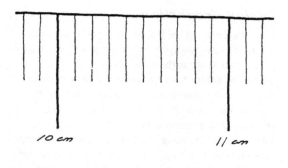

fig. 18: A Metric dimension that is commonly quoted is the centimetre. A centimetre is made up of 10mm and is usually expressed as 1cm.

		Exact		Loose
1 inch	=	25.4mm	=	25mm
6 inches	=	152.4mm	=	152mm
1 foot	=	304.8mm	=	305mm
1 yard	=	914.4mm	=	914mm
6 feet	=	1828.8mm	=	1829mm
100 yds	=	91.44m	=	91.5m
1 mile	=	1609.344m	=	1610m

fig. 19: The secret of getting used to the Metric System is to convert familiar Imperial Dimensions to Metric.

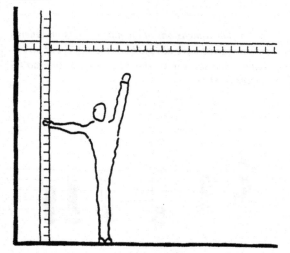

fig. 20: It is useful to mark out onto a wall vertical and horizontal measurements for reference.

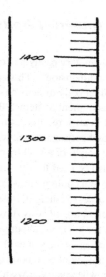

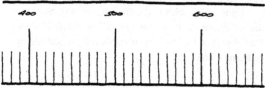

fig. 21: Copy dimensions from a Standard Ruler onto a tally roll and fix this to the wall.

A Metric dimension that is commonly quoted is the centimetre. A centimetre is made up of 10mm and is usually expressed as 1cm *fig. 18*. Centimetres tend to confuse the Metric System and their use should be avoided. If you come across a dimension that is expressed in centimetres, convert it into millimetres by multiplying it by 10. So, 50cm becomes 500mm and 3cm becomes 30mm.

With practice the Metric System can be mastered by anyone. The secret is to begin by converting familiar dimensions into millimetres. So, six inches becomes 150mm; an inch becomes 25mm and a yard, 914mm *fig. 19*.

It is useful to mark out onto a wall vertical and horizontal measurements for reference *fig. 20*. This can be done by copying dimensions from a standard ruler onto a tally roll and sticking this onto the wall surface *fig. 21*. It also helps to overlay these Standard Measurements with your own body dimensions. Eye heights, raised arm height and reach, if overlaid in this way, will immediately invest the Metric dimensions with a human scale. If these are displayed where they are seen every day these significant dimensions will become familiar very quickly.

Metric and Imperial Body Dimensions

Body dimensions can very easily be converted to Imperial or Metric dimensions. This can be done by measuring individual body dimensions using one of the Standard Measurement Systems. Body dimensions can be used in all sorts of situations – for "walking" a site and getting a rough idea of its size or for judging the height of a wall by raising your arm. They can also be used for estimating the size of items of furniture and equipment listed in your brief.

Hand, feet, stride, eye-height, raised arm height and sitting eye height are all body dimensions that you can discover for yourself, about yourself. If these are measured against a standard ruler and then listed, you will know your own body dimensions and you can use these whenever you wish *fig. 22*.

Familiarity with body dimensions will allow design decisions to be easily made in relation to the true object of building construction – the sheltering of human life.

Body Measurement	Length (mm)
Hand length	_____
Hand width	_____
Foot length	_____
Foot width	_____
Length of stride	_____
Standing eye height	_____
Sitting eye height (ave.)	_____
Raised arm height	_____
Length of reach	_____
Width of spread arms	_____
Head height	_____
Chin height	_____
Shoulder height	_____
Sitting head height (ave.)	_____

fig. 22: Hand, feet, stride, eye-height, raised arm height and sitting eye height are all body dimensions that you can discover for yourself, about yourself.

Divine Proportion

The dimensions of the human body and their measurements have always been the subject of investigation and study throughout the ages *fig. 23*. Interrelationships have been discovered between these common dimensions, which key the human form into a system of proportion which exists throughout nature and in music. This proportion, known as the Divine or Golden Proportion is considered pleasing to the eye. In music, these proportions, intervals or rhythms, are considered pleasing to the ear *fig. 24*. Divine proportion is interesting in relation to buildings because it connects the number world, the human form and the natural world together.

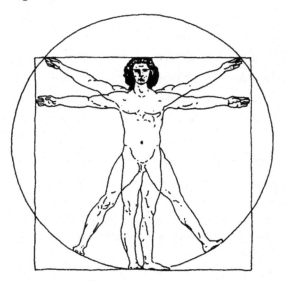

fig. 23: The dimensions of the human body and their measurements have always been the subject of investigation and study throughout the ages. Leonardo's Universal Man.

fig. 24: In music, certain intervals or harmonies are considered especially pleasing to the ear.

Proportion is the consideration of the size of something in relationship to something larger or smaller than it. Some proportions are considered more pleasing than others. The Divine Proportion is considered the most pleasing of all. In terms of the human form, the body can be divided into sections that are in numerical and visual harmony with one another. Subdivisions of these measurements also accord with Divine Proportion *fig. 25*.

In geometry, the generating form of Divine Proportion is the circle *fig. 26*. From the starting point of the centre of a circle, Divine Proportions can be created on a diminishing or on an expanding scale. Divine Proportion has the ability to reproduce itself and also to reduce itself, always returning to its original starting point – the centre of a circle. The geometry of Divine Proportion can also be used to form a spiral. In antiquity, Divine Proportion was seen as an expression of Divine Unity and the principles of Divine Proportion have been applied to building design throughout history, the most famous of these being the Parthenon of Athens *fig. 27*. The ancient theatre at Epidaurus, as well as most classical buildings, were similarly laid out using these proportions or harmonies.

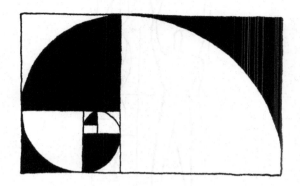

fig. 26: In geometry, the generating form of Divine Proportion is a point and a circle. These proportions are expressed mathematically by the ratio 1:1.618.

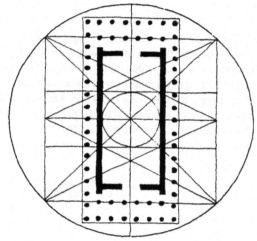

fig. 27: In antiquity, Divine Proportion was seen as an expression of Divine Unity and the principles of Divine Proportion have been applied to building design throughout history. The most famous of these is the Parthenon of Athens.

In building design, consideration of the size of the human form fulfills a twofold function. Firstly, it allows buildings to be made which have a human scale and secondly, it allows buildings to be created in harmony with the natural world in which they exist. In antiquity, the application of the principles of Divine Proportion was the work of priests. The knowledge of the proper application of these principles has, for all intents and purposes, now been lost. Attempts have been made to key into the mysteries of Sacred Numerology in modern times *fig. 28*.

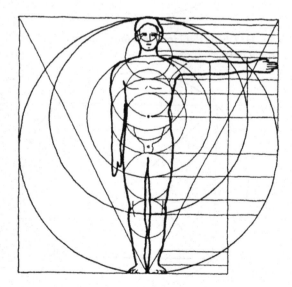

fig. 25: The human form can be divided into sections that are in numerical and visual harmony with one another, according to Divine Proportions.

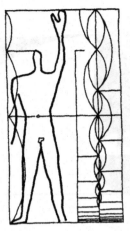

fig. 28: *Attempts have been made to key into the mysteries of Sacred Numerology in modern times. Le Corbusier's Modular Man.*

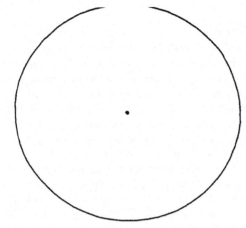

fig. 30: *Select a point and inscribe a circle around it.*

The creation of the Golden Section proportions is based on the selection of a point and the inscription of a circle around this *fig. 29.* Such a procedure can be carried out on site without elaborate equipment using a wooden stake and a line. On paper, the proportions can be arrived at by drawing a circle and the use of simple geometry *figs. 30-36.*

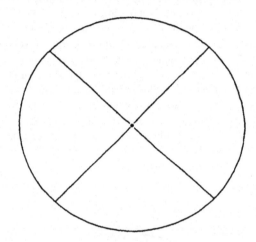

fig. 31: *Divide this circle into four quadrants or four equal parts.*

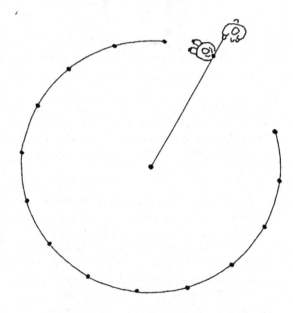

fig. 29: *The creation of the Golden Section proportions is based on the selection of a point and the inscription of a circle around this.*

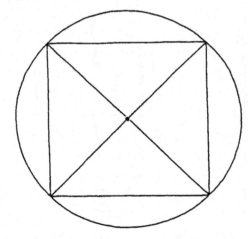

fig. 32: *Construct a square within the circle by joining the lines of the quadrants together.*

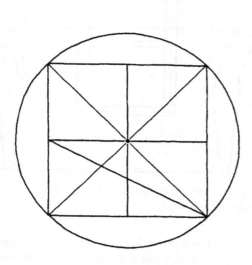

fig. 33: Divide the square into four equal parts and construct a diagonal from the mid point of one side of the square to the opposite corner.

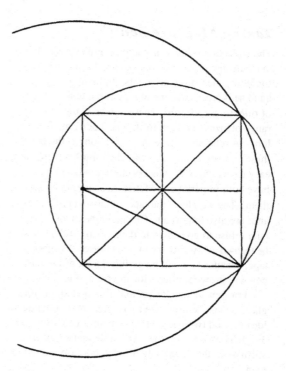

fig. 34: Using the diagonal as radius, and the mid point of the square as centre, construct an arc.

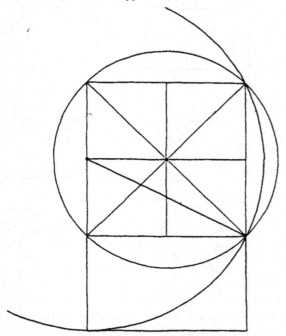

fig. 35: Extend the sides of the original square to intersect the arc and form a rectangle.

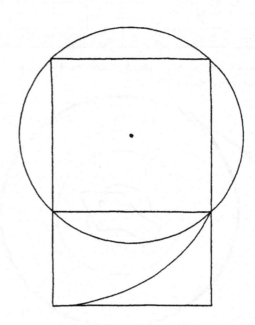

fig. 36: The proportions of this rectangle are in Divine Proportion to the original square.

Taking Measurements

The collection of measurements begins very early on in the design process. You will need a standard ruler for taking these measurements. In many ways the hand held retractable metal tape is the handiest type of ruler to use for this. These can be bought in a range of sizes from 2m (6'-6") to 5 or even 10m long. A retractable tape that is 3m long is the best of these. Choose a tape that has clear markings that are easy to read *fig. 37*. Most of these kinds of tapes have both Imperial and Metric measure marked onto them. The weight of the tape and its overall appearance are also important. Cheaper tapes sooner or later refuse to go back into their casing and have to be thrown away. So, try to get a reasonably good tape, because you will be giving it a lot of use and you will grow familiar with and fond of it.

For dimensions longer than 3m, a cloth or fibreglass tape is the best type to use *fig. 38*. Cloth tapes ideally need two people to use them successfully *fig. 39*. In contrast, with the retractable metal tape, the stiffness of the metal will allow you to use it on your own.

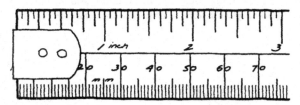

fig. 37: Choose a tape that has clear markings and that is easy to read.

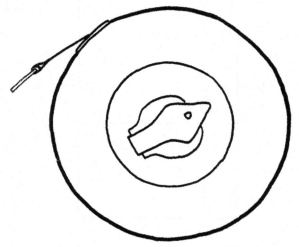

fig. 38: For dimensions longer than 3m, a cloth or fibreglass tape is the best type to use.

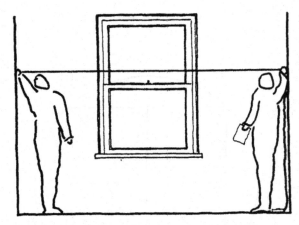

fig. 39: Cloth tapes ideally need two people to use them successfully.

The first things that you can begin measuring are those items of furniture and equipment listed in your Brief. Beds, chairs, tables, desks, worktops, fridges, cookers, stoves, baths, toilets, washhand basins, dressers – the list is endless *fig. 40*. These are the items that will be permanently in your home, besides yourself and your family.

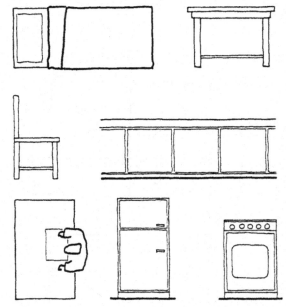

fig. 40: The first things that you can begin measuring are those items of furniture and equipment listed in your Brief. Beds, chairs, tables, desks, worktops, fridges, cookers, stoves, baths, toilets, washbasins, dressers – the list is endless.

The room sizes that you finally decide on will relate directly to the area needed to contain items of furniture and equipment and the area needed to do all the things you want to do in your house – eat, sleep, use the bathroom, relax, work, meditate, dream and so on. The thing to begin with is the sizes of the furniture and equipment and then to tackle the area you need for yourself. By designing your house in this way, by taking into account the sizes things are, a design can be evolved that will properly fit you and your belongings.

By considering what goes into a house and what activities are likely to take place inside it, a design can be evolved that will accommodate these best. A design evolved in this way will of course suit many people besides yourself, as all your measurements and dimensions will ultimately relate back to the human form. There are upward and downward variations in the sizes of people, but these variations, considered in the light of a building, are insignificant. In other words, designing exclusively for yourself and your family, would not exclude some other family from living happily in your house were you to sell it. Rather, the sensitivity to people displayed in the design would make it immediately attractive to a prospective buyer. People constantly adapt to the buildings they use. Adapting to a building that takes account of people is infinitely easier that adapting to one that ignores people altogether.

Measurements are a very exact language and it is this language that is most used in communicating about buildings. Measurements allow things to be planned out very exactly and related to each other. It is by planning exactly that a successful design will be evolved. If it is remembered that all measurements relate back to people and the natural world,

then the clinical nature of numbers and measurements can be tolerated.

By collecting measurements of the things that will be in your house and the activities associated with using them, all these diverse elements can be expressed in a common language – numbers. Numbers are a device that is useful to help you to get organised. So, where you may have listed in your Brief that you want a sink, a washing machine and worktop space in the utility room, you can do very little about relating these to each other with words alone. By putting measurements onto these items, however, they can all be referred to in terms of their size, and so they can be related accurately to one another *fig. 41*.

Many of the items listed in your Brief that will require measurement might already be in your possession, so you can measure them quite easily. Other items can be sized from catalogues or measured where you find them. It is a good idea to always carry a tape, so that you can do this. If you've left your tape behind, use body dimensions and translate them into standard measurements when you get home.

The amount of actual furniture you want to put in your home should be thought about very carefully at this stage. Furniture is a notorious user of space, leaving empty corners and odd bits of unusable floorspace all over the place. Much furniture is used for storage purposes only. Replacing this furniture with planned-in storage units will avoid this type of disruption and will make every square foot of your floorspace usable. In general, beds, tables and chairs are the only essential items of loose furniture you should need in your home.

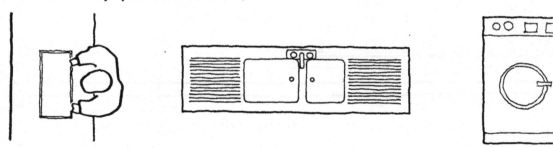

fig. 41: By putting measurements onto diverse items such as sinks, worktops and washing machines, they can all be referred to in terms of their size, and so they can be related accurately to one another. This is the function of measurement – everything can be expressed in the common language of numbers.

Recording Measurements

It is best to record all dimensions with a clear reference as to what they are of. Use the Furniture & Equipment lists to keep these records *fig. 42*. These sheets should be stored in the relevant file where they can easily be found whenever they are needed.

Summary

Get familiar with the Imperial and particularly with the Metric System.

Get familiar with body dimensions, particularly your own.

Begin taking measurements of items of Furniture & Equipment.

Record these dimensions on the Furniture & Equipment lists.

fig. 42: Record all dimensions with a clear reference as to what they are. Use the Furniture & Equipment lists to keep these records.

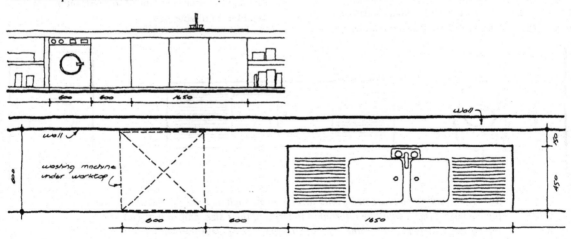

9 Sheltermaker Design Programme
Drawing

Recording information on paper is an essential part of the design and building process. Such information is usually recorded by drawing lines on paper. Many people say that they 'cannot draw'. This is OK. There is only one line you ever need to learn!

The prevalence of computer drawing programmes should not be a temptation to those wishing to shy away from the task of drawing. Drawing by hand is a certain way to activate our innate sheltermaking instincts. The benefits of such engagement can easily by lost if a computer is used.

First, you will need to obtain the following items from the *Equipment Worksheet* - pencils, a metal pencil sharpener, a plastic erase and some plain A4 paper.

Read pages 79-81 of *Drawing*, up as far as the section entitled '*Making Drawings*'. The key concept here is that drawings allow for effective communication within the design and construction process. In other words drawing is a language that you need to learn to read and write. This is not as daunting as it might seem.

Print out the *Drawing Worksheet*. Read through this, then begin practicing the drawing of '75 lines' using your clipboard, a pencil and plain A4 paper. It is essential to give yourself time with these drawing exercises and allow yourself plenty of practice. This will build your confidence and make the drawing of lines as familiar as writing your name.

Follow through the entire *Worksheet* until you are completely fed up but have achieved a level of competence that you are happy with. Remember that the key to freehand drawing is to turn the paper around so that your hand is always in the most comfortable drawing position and is always drawing the same line!

10 Sheltermaker Design Programme
Making Drawings

When you have mastered the drawing of lines as described in the *Drawing Worksheet* one can begin to make simple drawings of items of furniture and equipment listed on your *Space Analysis Sheets*.

First, read pages from page 81 '*Making Drawings*' to page 83, '*Scaled Drawings*'. The key piece of information here is the fact that drawings are 2-dimensional, allowing only one aspect of an object to be represented on paper at any one time. Because items of furniture and equipment are 3-dimensional - as are buildings themselves! - it requires at least two drawings to represent a 3-dimensional object on paper.

Using some of the furniture and equipment dimensions previously recorded on your *Space Analysis Sheets*, make some simple drawings of these items using the illustrations on page 82 as a guide. This will familiarise you with the need to make at least two drawings of 3-dimensional objects in order to represent them effectively on paper. Store these drawings along with the relevant *Space Analysis Sheet*.

11 Sheltermaker Design Programme
Making Scaled Drawings

The making of scaled drawings is the next step in the drawing process. First read from *'Making Scaled Drawings'* on page 85 to the end of page 87. The key piece of information here is the fact that scaled drawings are in exact proportion to the object they represent. Normal proportions used are 1:20, 1:50 or 1:100. This means that the drawings of objects made to these scales are exactly 20, 50 or 100 times smaller than the objects themselves.

To make scaled drawings you will need to obtain a Scale Ruler and some A4 Graph Paper as detailed on your *Equipment Worksheet*. Before you buy your Scale Ruler read the information on page 84.

Next, follow the exercise detailed on pages 85-87, taking your time. After that, try drawing to scale some of the items of furniture and equipment listed on your *Space Analysis Sheets*. Keep at this until you are familiar with the procedure. Resist the temptation to get on to the next level of the design work by skipping these exercises!

Next: SDP12 - Creating Furniture & Equipment Models, page 88

Furniture and equipment models installed in a Space Mock-Up

Drawings and Models

Drawings are simple pictures. They communicate much more directly than words and they allow you to visualise an item without it being there in front of you. Drawings are also invaluable when you are communicating your ideas to others *fig. 1*.

When you are collecting measurements, if the item you are measuring is drawn and dimensions of it are written against the drawing, you will not end up with a jumble of words and numbers that might be hard to interpret at some later date. These kind of drawings can be done very easily and they make the job of collecting measurements very straightforward.

fig. 1: Drawings are simple pictures. They communicate much more directly than words and they allow you visualise something without it being there in front of you. Drawings are invaluable when you are communicating your ideas to others.

Pencils and Pens

Drawings can be done either in pencil or in pen. Pencil has the advantage that it can be erased easily. Pencils are made from wood with a core of crystalline carbon called graphite or lead *fig. 2*. Graphite is made in a variety of softnesses and hardnesses ranging from a very hard lead, a 9H, to a very soft lead – a 6B. A hard lead – like the 9H, leaves very little graphite on the paper and so produces a very sharp, faint line. A 6B on the other hand is very soft and leaves lots of graphite on the paper making a fuzzy, dark line. Middle of the range leads like the H and the HB give the best results for general use. The secret of using pencils is to keep them sharp.

A sharp point makes an even line. When a pencil has been pared too much it gets very short and unbalanced, making it difficult to use *fig. 3*. When this happens a pencil needs to be thrown away.

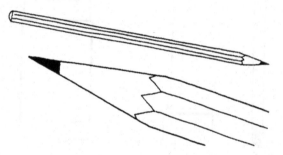

fig. 2: Pencils are made from wood with a core of crystalline carbon called graphite or lead. The secret of using pencils is to keep them sharp.

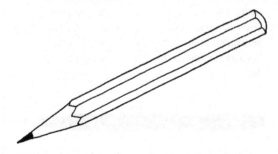

fig. 3: When a pencil has been pared too much it gets very short and unbalanced, making it difficult to use. When this happens a pencil should be thrown away.

One way of avoiding sharpening pencils and throwing stubs away is to use a clutch pencil. A clutch pencil is a permanent barrel with a lead inside it *fig. 4*. This lead can be sharpened without affecting the length of the barrel. Soft or hard leads can be used and these can easily be interchanged. Choose your clutch pencil for its feel, balance and its colour. You will also need a rotary pencil sharpener for keeping a point on the lead.

Pencil lines can easily be removed from paper by using an eraser. This is a very useful quality of pencil lines, allowing them to be easily changed. A plastic eraser is the best type to get. Choose one with a cover, as this will keep the eraser from getting too grubby *fig. 5*.

Occasionally rub the eraser on a piece of clean paper to produce a fresh, clean surface. Always use your free hand to hold the paper flat and stop it from creasing when you are using the eraser. Do not associate the use of an eraser with making mistakes, but rather with making changes.

After pencils, felt tip markers are the best instrument to draw with *fig. 6*. Pick a marker with a fairly fine line. Once you draw a line incorrectly with one of these pens you cannot remove it, so it is a good idea to sketch out the lines of a drawing first in pencil and then go over them with a pen.

Practising Drawing

Begin your drawing practise on a table or desk. Make sure that you have reasonable light and sufficient space to turn the page around as you work on it.

All drawings are made of lines. The easiest kind of lines to draw are freehand lines. They are also the quickest. You need no equipment, other than a pencil or a pen, to draw a freehand line onto paper. All you need is practise. Start with a sheet of plain paper and draw a series of freehand lines onto it. Plain A4 size paper is ideal for this. Make any sort of shapes you want *fig. 7*. It may help to outline some overall shape and then to fill this in using only straight lines. Try keeping your lines short and roughly parallel to each other. Turn the paper around as you draw so that your hand is always in the most comfortable position for drawing lines. The way you draw a line is as individual as your voice or your handwriting, so don't try to copy the way someone else draws, find your own way.

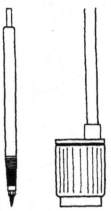

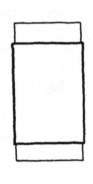

Use the Drawing Worksheet for your drawing practice. This can be downloaded from livingarchitecturecentre.com along with the other Worksheets

fig. 4: A clutch pencil is a permanent barrel with a lead inside it. You will need a rotary pencil sharpener for keeping a point on the lead.

fig. 5: Pencil lines can easily be removed from paper by using an eraser. A plastic eraser with a cover is the best type to get.

fig. 6: After pencils, felt tip markers are the best instrument to draw with. Pick a marker with a fairly fine line.

fig. 7: All drawings are made of lines. The easiest kind of lines to draw are freehand lines. Draw a series of freehand lines onto a sheet of plain paper, making any kind of shapes you want.

The drawings you do of Furniture & Equipment will usually be drawn where you find these things and will more often than not need to be done standing up, so you will also need to practise drawing while standing up. You will want something to lean on when you draw like this. A piece of stiff cardboard or hardboard is ideal. This only needs to be the same size as the paper you are using. Use a bulldog clip to hold your paper onto the board. Turn the clipboard around when you are working so that your drawing hand is always comfortable.

If you are on your own when you go to measure and draw a piece of Furniture or Equipment, you will have to hold the clipboard, the pencil and the tape measure and use these to draw, measure and write. You will also need to keep your eraser handy *fig. 8*. All this can be done easily enough with a little practise. Straight away you will see why the size and weight of the tape you buy is important.

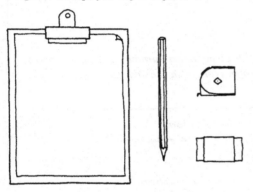

fig. 8: If you are on your own when you go to measure and draw something, you will have to hold the clipboard, the pencil and the tape measure while using these to draw, measure and write. This can be done easily enough with a little practise.

The drawings you will be making and the measurements on them will all be destined for inclusion in your Brief. Put a clear heading on each page you use to tell you what the drawing shows and which space in the building it is relevant to. Keep each page in its proper file where it can easily be found. This level of organisation is not difficult to achieve and it will allow you to store and retrieve information quickly and easily. If you cannot find a piece of vital information easily, you might as well not have it.

Making Drawings

The first thing you will find when you go to measure and draw some item from your Furniture & Equipment list will be that it has three major dimensions – Length, Width and Height *fig. 9*. A drawing will only allow you to show any two of these dimensions at a time – the Length & Height, the Length & Width or the Width & Height. To show all the dimensions of a three-dimensional object on paper, at least two drawings have to be made of it.

For example, you know the size of the single beds that you want to put into the bedrooms. They are 1900mm Long, 900mm Wide and 500mm High. You can make a drawing showing the Length & Width of the bed and write the dimensions in the appropriate places on the drawing *fig. 10*. A drawing showing the Length & Width of something is called a Plan.

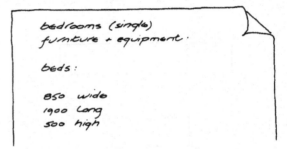

fig. 9: The first thing you will find when you go to measure and draw some item from your Furniture & Equipment list will be that it has three major dimensions – Length, Width and Height.

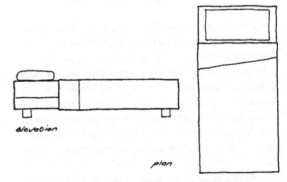

fig. 10: To show all the dimensions of a three-dimensional object on paper, at least two drawings have to be made of it. A drawing showing the Length & Width of something is called a Plan. A drawing showing a side view of something is called an Elevation.

To show the Height of the bed another drawing is needed. If you make a drawing of the side of the bed, this will show the Length & Height of it. Again, write the dimensions in the appropriate places on the drawing. A drawing showing a side view of something is called an Elevation.

Elevations can be drawn for all four sides of the bed. These will vary according to whatever side is being looked at *fig. 11*.

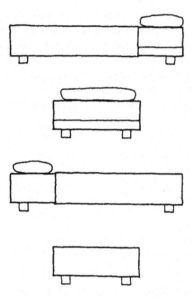

fig. 11: Elevations can be drawn for all four sides of an object. These will vary according to whatever side of the object is being looked at.

All the measurements of Furniture & Equipment listed in the Brief can be recorded in Plans and Elevations very easily. In addition, notes can be written onto these drawings, with additional information on material, colour, texture, feel, smell, age, quality and so on *figs. 12-14*. A combination of drawings, words and measurements allows a wealth of information to be communicated easily and accurately, both to yourself and, more importantly, to others.

At this stage of the design exercise you are only making drawings of three-dimensional objects that will be put into your finished building. The building itself is also a three-dimensional object however, and so can be represented by a plan and elevations also. For this reason, it is important to become accustomed to making these types of drawings.

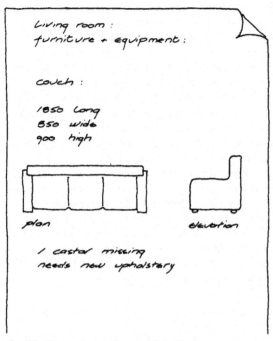

fig. 12: Living Room Furniture & Equipment measurements for couch and chairs.

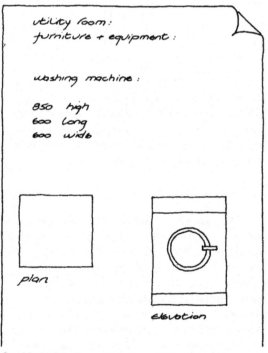

fig. 13: Utility Room Furniture & Equipment measurements for washing machine.

82

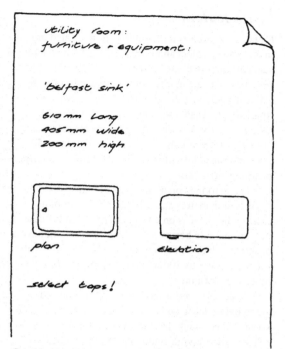

fig. 14: Utility Room Furniture & Equipment measurements for 'belfast' sink.

Scaled Drawings

The simple plans and elevations that you make while gathering measurements are usually made roughly proportional to what is being drawn. This is sufficient to show you or someone else what an object you measure looked like and what the accurate dimensions of it are.

As the project unfolds however, and you begin using this information, the measurements and drawings will become more and more important. It is useful, therefore, to make the drawings as precise as the measurements are. This will ensure accuracy, ease communications and, all in all, make the work manageable.

The process of drawing accurately is known as drawing to scale. What drawing to scale means is that the drawings made of an object are an exact number of times smaller than the object itself. The Imperial Measurement system lends itself to being divided into halves, quarters, sixteenths and thirty-second parts *fig. 15*. This means that drawings that are exactly one half, one quarter, one sixteenth the size of the original can be drawn using the Imperial System.

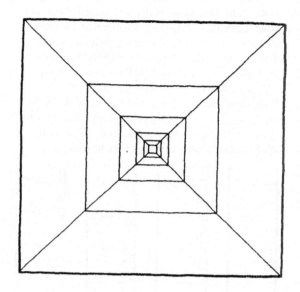

fig. 15: The Imperial Measurement system lends itself to being divided into halves, quarters, sixteenths and thirty-second parts. This means that drawings can be made smaller than the original in accordance with these proportions.

The Metric System, because it is decimal based, can be divided easily by numbers like two, five and ten itself *fig. 16*. This makes the Metric System more versatile for use to make scaled drawings.

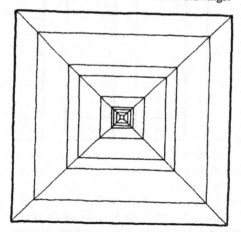

fig. 16: The Metric System, because it is decimal based, can be divided easily by numbers like two, five and ten itself. This makes the system quite versatile for the making of scaled drawings.

'One is to twenty' is a simple metric drawing scale. What this means is that a drawing done to this scale is exactly twenty times smaller than the object it represents. This scale is usually written – 1:20. Scales of this nature are usually referred to in words as 'One is to twenty; one is to fifty' and so on. A 1:20 scale is ideal for drawing Furniture & Equipment *fig. 17*. 'One is to fifty' is another drawing scale. A 1:50 drawing is fifty times smaller than the original object it represents. The 1:50 scale is used to draw house plans and room layouts.

Scale Rulers

Metric Scale Rulers are used to prepare scaled drawings. A scale ruler can be imagined as being a long standard ruler that has been compressed, so that it becomes an exact number of times smaller than the original ruler. A 1:20 scale ruler is exactly twenty times smaller than a standard ruler. A 1:50 scale ruler is exactly fifty times smaller. Scale rulers are normally 300mm long, which means that the 1:50 scale measures up to 15m while the 1:20 scale only measures up to 6m.

The markings on a scale rule are normally expressed in metres and millimetres – m & mm – exactly the same as on a standard ruler. In the case of the scale rule however, each millimetre will have a different value. For example, at 1:20 scale one millimetre represents 20mm, while on the 1:100 scale it represents 100mm.

Scale rulers are usually made of plastic and come in two basic types – oval and triangular *fig. 18*. Of these, the triangular variety is probably the easier to use. Choose your scale rule carefully. Make sure the markings on it are clear and legible. A triangular scale rule has six sides and at least one scale marked onto each of these sides. Sometimes there are two scales marked onto each side. This can make the scale rule difficult to read. The scales that you will be using most are 1:20, 1:50 and 1:100. Care should be taken that the edge of the ruler does not get chipped or broken.

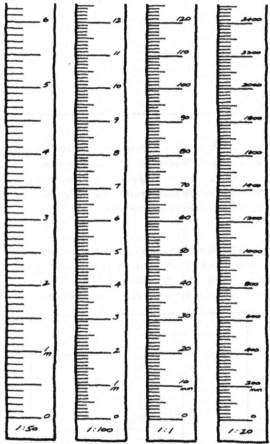

fig. 17: 'One is to twenty' is a simple metric drawing scale. What this means is that a drawing done to this scale is exactly twenty times smaller than the object it represents. This scale is usually written '1:20' and is an ideal scale for drawing items of Furniture & Equipment. 'One is to fifty' is another drawing scale. The 1:50 scale is used to draw house plans and room layouts. The 1:100 scale is used for drawings of large buildings. A 1:1 scale is represented by the Standard Ruler.

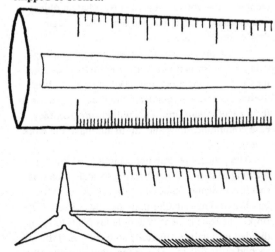

fig. 18: Scale rulers are usually made of plastic and come in two basic types – oval and triangular. Of these, the triangular variety is probably the easier to use.

84

The choice between flat and six sided scale rules is a personal one. Sometimes with the six sided variety it can be difficult to find the scale you want, as there are so many sides to choose from. Some of these types of rulers are colour coded to make this job easier. Flat type scale rules are made not quite flat, but more elliptical in cross section. This protects the edge from damage. It means, however, that the ruler has to be held down to measure a line or a distance between two points. In comparison, the six sided ruler can sit flat on the paper and is easier to use because of this.

Making Scaled Drawings

The best paper to use when preparing scaled drawings of Furniture and Equipment is A4 metric graph paper. This kind of paper has printed onto it a grid of feint lines one millimetre apart, with stronger lines at 5 and 10mm centres. This grid, matching as it does the divisions on the standard and on the scale rulers, is invaluable when you want to make scaled drawings *fig. 19*.

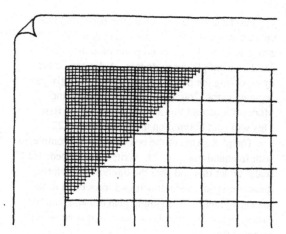

fig. 19: The best paper to use when preparing scaled drawings of Furniture and Equipment is A4 metric graph paper. This grid, matching as it does the divisions on standard and on scale rulers, is invaluable when you want to make scaled drawings.

To illustrate this we will use the drawing and measurements of a single bed that is 1900mm Long, 900mm in Width and 500mm in Height to make a 1:20 scale drawing. First examine the side of the scale ruler with the 1:20 scale on it. The major divisions on this will be numbered 200mm, 400mm, 600mm, 800mm and so on, all the way up to 6000mm *fig. 20*.

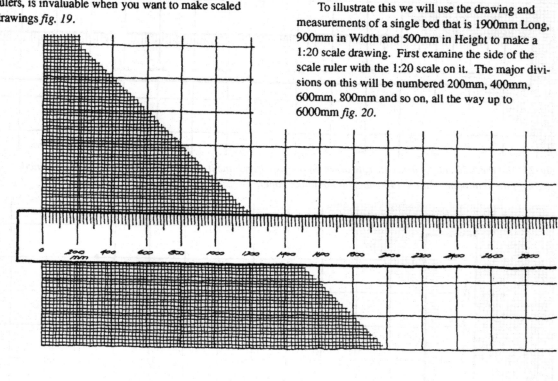

fig. 20: Compare the divisions on the 1:20 side of the scale rule with the markings on the graph paper.

Put the scale rule down on the paper and line it up with the grid lines. Using a pencil, mark off the zero point and the 1900mm point onto the paper *fig. 21*. Use a simple dot to do this. A dot can be made by revolving the pencil. A dot will always give an accurate mark. Join these with a freehand line. Mark off a second line at right angles to the first. This will read 800mm on the scale rule *fig. 22*.

The plan shape of the bed can now be completed with freehand lines *fig. 23*. Write 'Plan of bed: 1:20 scale' under this and note the dimensions. Noting dimensions on scaled drawings allows them to be read at a glance. This simple plan drawing can be further enhanced to make it clear what is being represented *fig. 24*.

Any one of the four sides of the bed can be drawn to illustrate the third dimension of height – either of the sides, the foot or the head of the bed. Whichever side or sides are chosen to be drawn, the procedure is the same as with the plan.

Choose one of the dimensions. Measure out the correct distance on the graph paper with the scale rule *fig. 25*. Mark the limits of the line using the point of a pencil. Draw a second line at right angles to the first of appropriate length. Complete the other two sides. This rectangular shape can have further lines added to it to indicate the height of the legs off the floor and the thickness of the mattress and base. The legs may also be drawn in.

The advantage of having scaled drawings is that they are exact and they can be measured by anyone with a scale ruler. For this reason, all scale drawings should carry an indication of the scale they have been drawn to. While scale drawings can be measured with a scale rule, in practise, to have written dimensions on a drawing saves a lot of trouble in finding out the size of something.

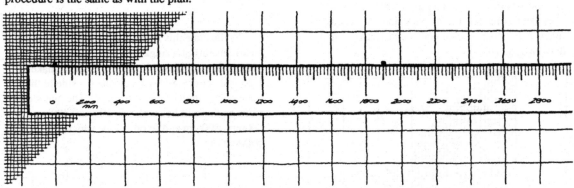

fig. 21: Put the 1:20 side of the scale rule down on the paper and line it up with the grid lines. Using a pencil, mark off the zero point and the 1900mm point onto the paper.

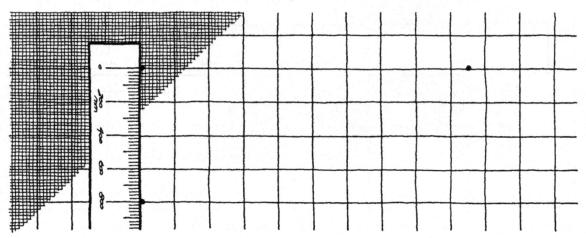

fig. 22: Mark off a second line at right angles to the first. This will read 800mm on the scale rule.

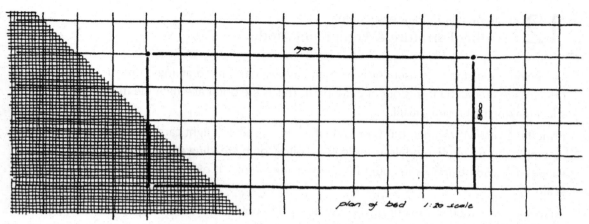

fig. 23: The plan shape of the bed can now be completed with freehand lines. Write 'Plan of bed: 1:20 scale' under this and note the dimensions. Noting dimensions on scaled drawings allows them to be read at a glance.

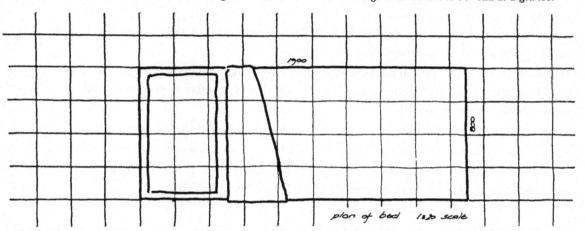

fig. 24: Simple plans can easily be enhanced to make it clear visually just what is represented in the drawing.

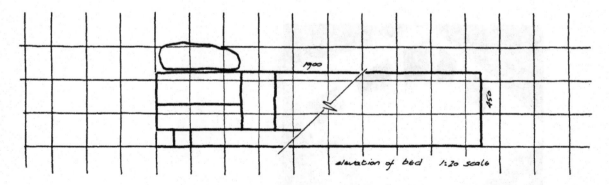

fig. 25: Any one of the four sides of the bed can be drawn to illustrate the third dimension of height – either of the sides, the foot or the head of the bed. This rectangular shape can have further lines added to it to indicate the height of the legs off the floor and the thickness of the mattress and base. The legs may also be drawn in.

Once you understand the usefulness (and limitations) of scaled drawings you can use such drawings to create 3D forms out of cardboard. This is the point at which the magic of spacemaking first reveals itself.

Print the *Model Worksheet*. It is best to do this onto a sheet of light card. Cut out, fold and assemble these sample models as indicated. Follow on by reading pages 89-95. Creating 3D shapes that will be *Spaces* in your building is a version of this exercise carried out on a larger scale.

To create some models of your own you will need to obtain some more equipment as listed on the *Equipment Worksheet* - Stanley knife and blades; 450mm steel ruler; Large 45° set square; protractor; sellotape and dispenser; masking/drafting tape; 1mm white card and a cutting mat. If you wish, light card can be used to make the models, though getting used to working with the 1mm white card will assist in later, and larger, modelmaking exercises. A box to keep everything in would be useful also.

Follow the exercise set out on pages 89-95, making sure that you do not cut yourself! Take your time and do not seek perfection in the first instance. Get a feel of your tools and materials and progress steadily.

When you are satisfied with your competence make some models of your own using measurements from your *Space Analysis Sheets*. Plenty of time is required to become familiar with drawing and modelmaking. This is all time that is very well spent and will pay you back one hundred fold when you progress deeper into the design exercise.

Next: SDP13 Creating Space Mock-Ups, page 101

Space-Mock-Up

Models

Once plans and elevations are drawn for three-dimensional objects, the flatness of drawings will become very apparent. This flat quality is caused by the two-dimensional nature of drawing, which means that only two dimensions of a three-dimensional object can be shown on any one drawing. To show all three dimensions, at least two drawings have to be made. By looking at two drawings of, say, a washing machine – a plan and an elevation – the washing machine can be imagined as a three-dimensional object *fig. 26*. This is not difficult to do. In designing a building however, where many three-dimensional objects are involved, the task of imagining a lot of three-dimensional objects together can be very difficult. A bedroom, for example, will contain beds, bedside tables, clothes storage space, chairs and other items that are three-dimensional in nature. While all these can be drawn to scale and imagined individually, how they all go together in the space of the room is very difficult to imagine.

To overcome these limitations, models can be made of three-dimensional objects. This makes if far easier to imagine what something will look like in reality. It also provides a very easy way of arranging three-dimensional objects in relationship to each other.

Models are made from scaled drawings. This ensures that all the models you make will relate to each other correctly in terms of size. Just as a 1:20 scale drawing is twenty times smaller than the object it represents, so too is a 1:20 scale model twenty times smaller than the object it represents.

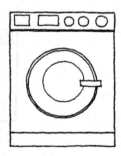

fig. 26: To show all three dimensions of a three-dimensional object, at least two drawings have to be made. By looking at two drawings of, say, a washing machine – a plan and an elevation – the washing machine can be imagined as a three-dimensional object.

Making Scale Models

The amount of equipment and material needed to make accurate scale models is very modest. 1mm thick white cardboard is excellent as a modelling material, though for small models thin cardboard from food packaging can also be used. The advantage of stiff white cardboard is that it is strong enough to support itself. White cardboard also takes paint very well. Being able to paint a model is a useful advantage to have. Cardboard can be bought in 20 x 30in or 30 x 40in sheet sizes *fig. 27*.

A sharp knife will be needed for cutting the cardboard. A heavy lino knife is good for this. A knife with a retractable blade is very handy. If your knife is not of the retractable type, tape the blade when the knife is being put away. Inevitably, fingers get cut when making models. Keeping some first-aid supplies in your modelling kit can minimise the trauma if the worst happens. The knife should be used with a steel edged ruler when cutting is being done. This ruler should be at least eighteen inches long *fig. 28*.

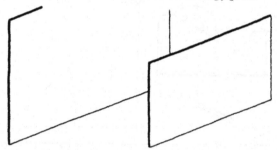

fig. 27: 1mm thick white cardboard is excellent as a modelling material. Cardboard can be bought in 20 x 30in or 30 x 40in sheet sizes.

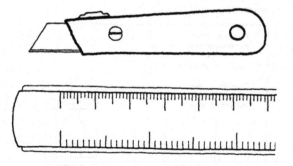

fig. 28: A sharp knife will be needed for cutting the cardboard. The cutting knife should be used with a steel edged ruler when cutting is being done. This ruler should be at least eighteen inches long.

A light scalpel is also useful for modelling work *fig. 29*. This will be suitable for cutting light card and trimming. Scissors can be used to cut card, though a knife will always make a cleaner, more accurate line.

When cardboard is being cut, a protective sheet of card or linoleum should be placed under it to protect the table surface.

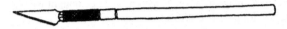

fig. 29: A light scalpel is also useful for modelling work.

Other equipment you will need is sellotape – preferably in a dispenser. You will also need a scale rule and a pencil, as well as a reasonably sized set square *fig. 30*.

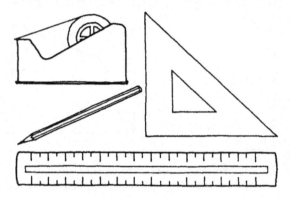

fig. 30: Other equipment you will need is sellotape – preferably in a dispenser, a scale rule, a pencil and a reasonably sized set square.

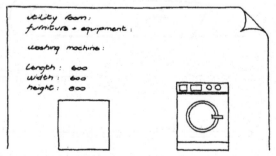

fig. 31: Simple drawings and measurements of a three- dimensional object are all that is needed to make a scale model.

Models of regular shaped objects should be made to begin with. First obtain the dimensional information of such an object. This kind of information will be recorded in your Brief or you can simply measure something handy. Simple drawings are all that is needed – a plan and an elevation *fig. 31*

A washing machine is a simple regular shape. Take your sheet of card, your scale ruler, your knife, your cutting board and ruler, your simple drawings, your pencil and your set square. You are going to mark onto the card a series of lines that will tell you where to cut when the time comes. The position of these lines is decided by the dimensions of the object you are making the model of. The washing machine is 600mm wide, 600mm deep and 800mm high.

Begin by imagining the washing machine squashed flat by some heavy weight so that the sides of it are spread out around the top of the machine *fig. 32* This is the picture that is going to be drawn onto the card. After cutting, the squashed machine is going to be reassembled.

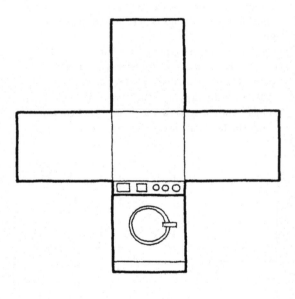

fig. 32: To make a simple model of the washing machine, begin by imagining it squashed flat by some heavy weight so that the sides of it are spread out around the top of the machine.

Start work in one corner of the card. Measure in from one edge the height of the machine on the scale rule. Mark the 800mm point by making a dot with the top of the pencil. A dot is more accurate than a line. Make several marks a couple of inches apart *fig. 33*. Draw a line through these *fig. 34*. The set square is ideal for doing this. In fact, if the cardboard sheet you are using has good clean edges that the set square can be lined up against, all you need to make is a single mark on the cardboard and line the set square up against this to draw your line.

Measure from this 1st line the width of the machine, 600mm with the scale rule, again making several marks. Draw a line through these again, using the set square *fig. 35*.

Measure from this 2nd line, a 3rd line that is again 800mm, the height of the machine. Make several marks. Draw a line through these *fig. 36*.

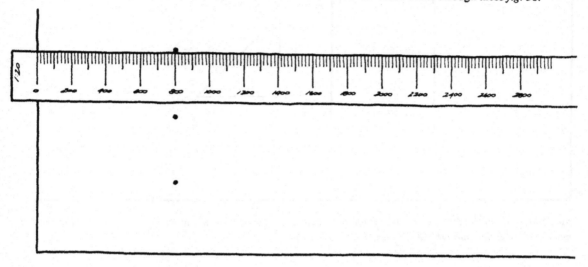

fig. 33: Start work in one corner of the card. Measure in from one edge the height of the machine on the scale rule. Mark the 800mm point by making a dot with the top of the pencil. Make several marks a couple of inches apart.

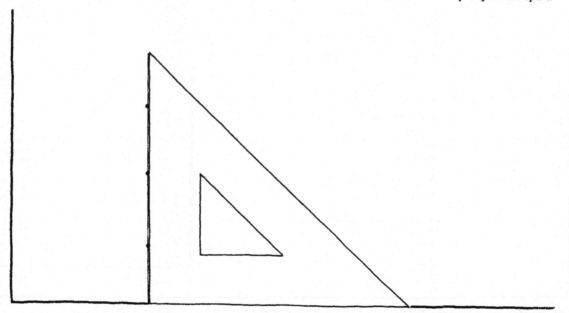

fig. 34: Draw a line through the pencil marks, using the set square aligned with the side of the sheet of card.

91

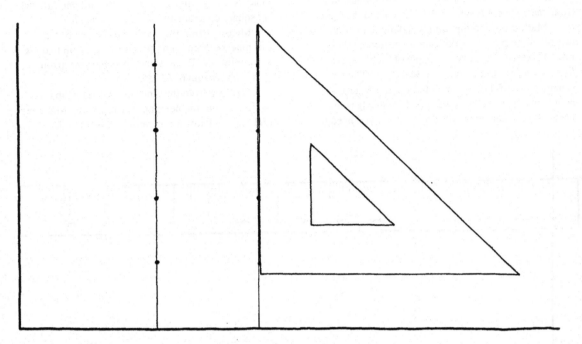

fig. 35 Measure in from the 1st line the width of the machine – 600mm – with the scale rule, again making several marks. Draw a line through these again, using the set square.

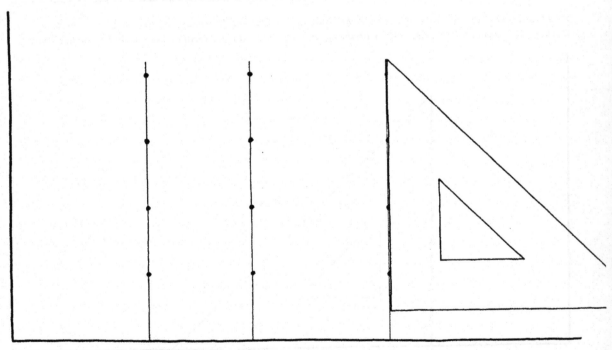

fig. 36: Measure in from the 2nd line, a 3rd line that is again 800mm, the height of the machine. Make several marks. Draw a line through these.

Turn the cardboard around and mark out three more lines, measuring in from the adjoining side. These measurements will be in order, the height of the machine, the depth of the machine and again the height of the machine. It is possible to use a 'running dimension' when doing this *fig. 37*. This will allow the three lines to be marked in at the same time. Running dimensions are dimensions which have been added together, in this case 800 + 600 = 1400 and 1400 + 800 = 2200. The 800, 1400 and 2200mm points are marked out onto the card using the scale ruler. Lines are then drawn through these points *fig. 38*.

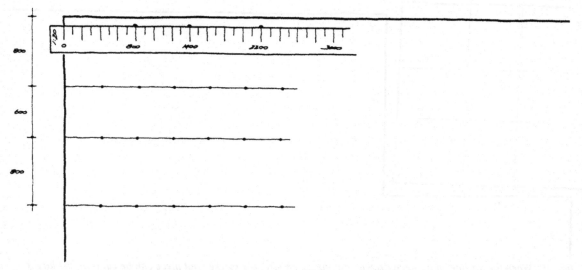

fig. 37: Turn the cardboard around and mark out three more lines, measuring in from the adjoining side. These measurements will be in order, the height of the machine, the depth of the machine and again the height of the machine. It is possible to use a 'running dimension' when doing this. This will allow the three lines to be marked in at the same time. Running dimensions are dimensions which have been added together, in this case 800 + 600 = 1400 and 1400 + 800 = 2200. The 800, 1400 and 2200mm points are marked out onto the card, at the same time, using the scale ruler.

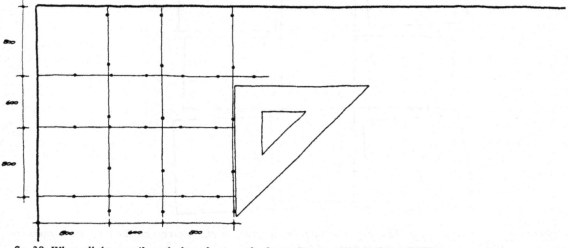

fig. 38: When all the pencil marks have been made, 3 new lines are drawn through them.

When the six lines have been drawn onto the cardboard the marked out piece can be cut from the larger sheet *fig. 39*. The excess pieces can then be trimmed off *fig. 40*. The excess will be the pieces of cardboard at the corners. All this trimming should be done with the knife and the steel edged ruler. Trimmings should be saved for further use.

fig. 39: When the six lines have been drawn onto the cardboard, the marked out piece can be cut from the larger sheet.

fig. 40: When the marked out piece has been removed from the larger sheet, the excess cardboard at the corners can then be trimmed off. The trimmings should be saved for further use.

94

After trimming, you will have a cross shaped piece of card with four lines marked on it *fig. 41*. If you want to draw anything onto the model, now is the time, while the cardboard is still flat.

The four lines at the centre of the piece of card are the fold lines. Lightly score along these lines using a scalpel and a steel edged ruler. This will allow the card to be folded easily into shape. Fold down the sides of the model and stick the edges where they meet with pieces of sellotape *fig. 42*. A dispenser will make this job easy, as you will be holding the folded model and will only have one hand free.

If you have not drawn anything onto the model to show what it is, you can number the model and keep a record of it on an A4 page *fig. 43*. By leaving models blank any one model can be used to represent several different things. For example, a model of a kitchen worktop unit can be used to represent a workbench or a dressing table. The A4 page recording the dimensions of models can be kept in a file marked *'Models'*.

The idea behind modelmaking is to introduce the third dimension into the design exercise. Modelmaking also allows one to get a sense of what size the various items of furniture and equipment are in relationship to each other. The exercise will also allow you to begin creating spaces to accommodate these objects.

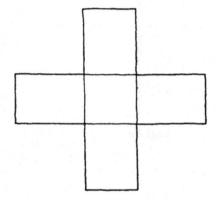

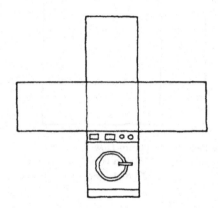

fig. 41: After trimming you will have a cross shaped piece of card with four lines marked on it. If you want to draw anything onto the model, now is the time, while the cardboard is still flat.

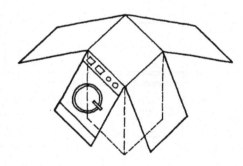

fig. 42: After scoring with the scalpel and ruler, fold down the sides of the model and stick the edges where they meet with pieces of sellotape.

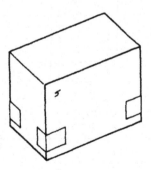

fig. 43: Models can be numbered. By doing this, any one model can be used to represent several different things. For example, a model of a kitchen worktop unit can be used to represent a workbench or a dressing table.

Models can be made for the bulk of items of Furniture and Equipment you have recorded in your Brief. Objects that are not quite regular in shape can be made up in several pieces. If models of worktops, tables, chairs, beds, wardrobes, the car, the TV and so on are made at 1:20 scale, they will serve as the furnishings for the next stage of the design process, which is to mock-up the individual spaces which will make up the building. You might even attempt to make a model of yourself and your family to lend more authenticity to the exercise!

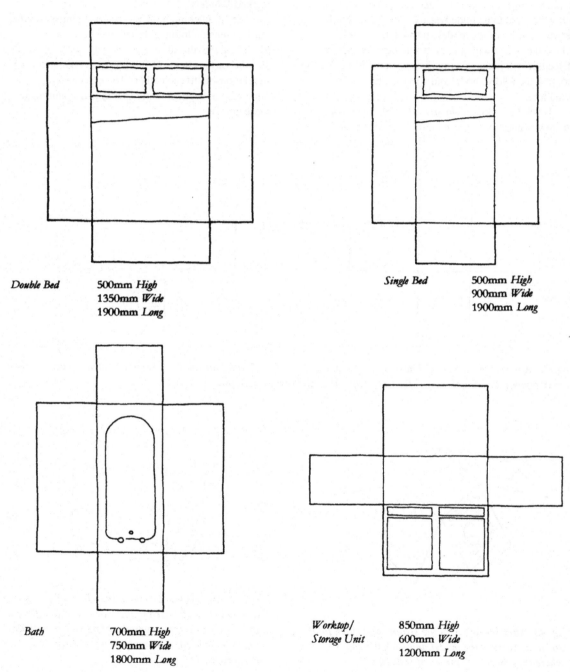

Double Bed   500mm *High*
1350mm *Wide*
1900mm *Long*

Single Bed   500mm *High*
900mm *Wide*
1900mm *Long*

Bath   700mm *High*
750mm *Wide*
1800mm *Long*

Worktop/   850mm *High*
Storage Unit   600mm *Wide*
1200mm *Long*

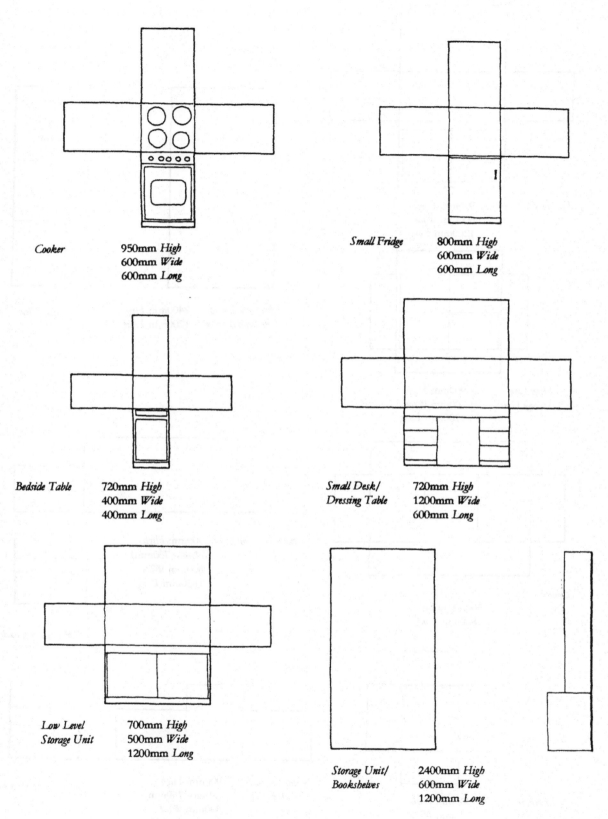

Cooker   950mm *High*
                       600mm *Wide*
                       600mm *Long*

Small Fridge   800mm *High*
                       600mm *Wide*
                       600mm *Long*

Bedside Table   720mm *High*
                       400mm *Wide*
                       400mm *Long*

Small Desk/   720mm *High*
Dressing Table   1200mm *Wide*
                       600mm *Long*

Low Level   700mm *High*
Storage Unit   500mm *Wide*
                       1200mm *Long*

Storage Unit/   2400mm *High*
Bookshelves   600mm *Wide*
                       1200mm *Long*

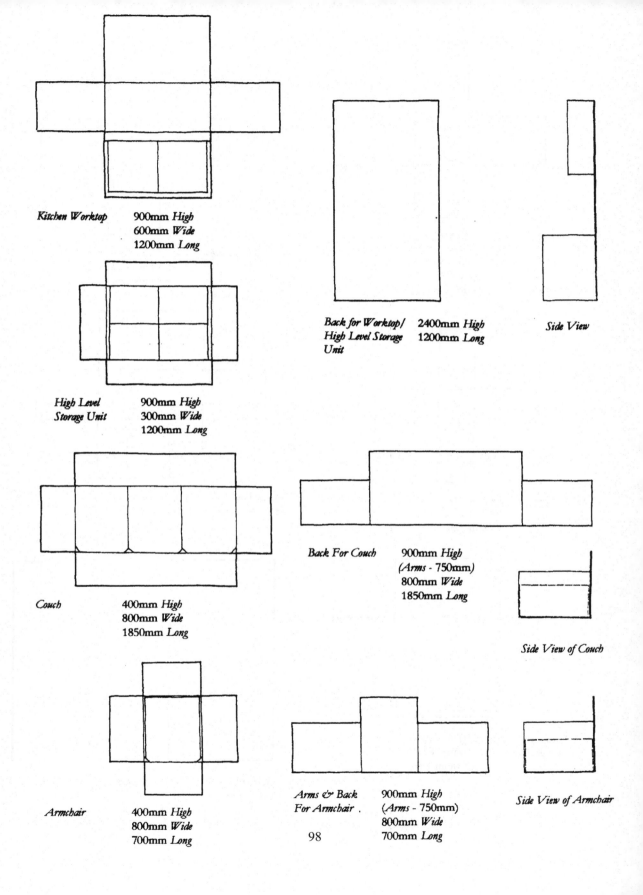

Kitchen Worktop   900mm *High*
600mm *Wide*
1200mm *Long*

Back for Worktop/   2400mm *High*
High Level Storage   1200mm *Long*
Unit

Side View

High Level   900mm *High*
Storage Unit   300mm *Wide*
1200mm *Long*

Couch   400mm *High*
800mm *Wide*
1850mm *Long*

Back For Couch   900mm *High*
(*Arms - 750mm*)
800mm *Wide*
1850mm *Long*

Side View of Couch

Armchair   400mm *High*
800mm *Wide*
700mm *Long*

Arms & Back   900mm *High*
For Armchair   (*Arms - 750mm*)
800mm *Wide*
700mm *Long*

Side View of Armchair

98

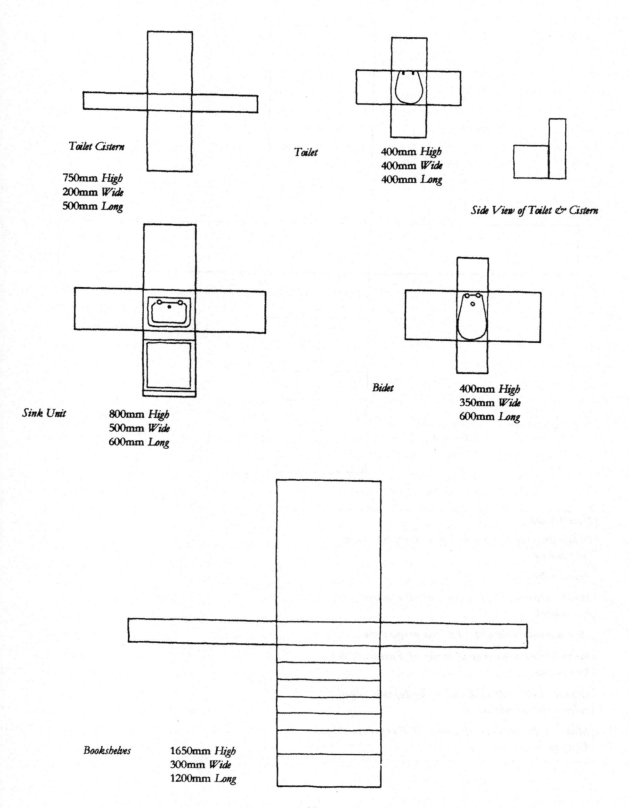

Toilet Cistern

750mm *High*
200mm *Wide*
500mm *Long*

Toilet

400mm *High*
400mm *Wide*
400mm *Long*

Side View of Toilet & Cistern

Sink Unit

800mm *High*
500mm *Wide*
600mm *Long*

Bidet

400mm *High*
350mm *Wide*
600mm *Long*

Bookshelves

1650mm *High*
300mm *Wide*
1200mm *Long*

Large Storage
Unit
2400mm *High*
600mm *Wide*
1200mm *Long*

Summary

Obtain drawing equipment – pencil, eraser, sharpener and pen.

Practise drawing.

Make drawings of items of Furniture & Equipment.

Obtain a scale rule and A4 metric graph paper.

Make scaled drawings of items of Furniture & Equipment.

Obtain white cardboard, cutting knife, steel edged ruler, sellotape and set square.

Make scale models of items of Furniture & Equipment.

13 Sheltermaker Design Programme
Creating Space Mock-Ups

When the knack of converting 2D information into 3D models has been mastered, the creation of architectural space can begin. *Space Mock-Ups* can be imagined as enlarged furniture and equipment models.

First read from page 103-113. From this it will be clear the numerous functions which the creation of *Space Mock-Ups* allows for - the planning, orientation and proportioning of individual *Spaces*; the estimation of overall floor area; the likely construction methodology for your building, and, the role of solar energy in the design process.

The critical aspect of mocking-up space is to grasp the fact that space is in fact invisible and what we actually see are the boundaries of space formed by the floor, walls and ceiling. Positioning these physical elements - floor, walls and ceiling - in relationship to each other is how architectural space is formed. Access to *Spaces* is achieved by creating opening in walls which is also how *Spaces* are naturally lit. A further aspect of creating *Space Mock-Ups* is that they allow the proportions of floor, walls and ceiling to be seen in relationship to each other, in other words, in 3-dimensions. These proportions can then be illustrated by drawing a plan and a cross section of the *Space* - the requisite 2 drawings required to represent a 3-dimensional object on paper.

Realistically, most people do not have the time to create *Space Mock-Ups* for all the *Spaces* in their *Brief*. Also, if the total floor area, calculated after all the *Space Mock-Ups* have been made, should exceed what one can afford, it's literally back to the drawing board! To speed up the process of estimating the likely floor area of your building - an essential requirement at this stage of the design process - a *Floor Area Worksheet* has been developed. This allows for the rapid calculation of likely floor area. Should this prove to be greater than the budget will allow one to build then the design can be scaled back before it proceeds any further. Use of the *Floor Area Worksheet* is explained on page 125.

The ultimate in Space Mock-Ups! A model which you can get your head inside. See page 291 for more on the HeadSpace.

While common sense will encourage one to reconcile floor area & budget now, as quickly as possible, the use of *Space Mock-Ups* for refining the 3D qualities of spaces should be remembered. It is therefore a good idea, once the various *Spaces* have become fixed as to their size, that they be mocked up. The latest stage at which one can do this is prior to embarking on item **SDP42 - Developing A Layout**. When this work has been completed the relevant figures should be entered onto the appropriate *Space Analysis Sheet*.

For those modifying or extending existing buildings the creation of a complete model of the existing structures will be required. How to do this is explained on page 136.

It should also be borne in mind that the exercises covered in items **1 - 13** of the **Sheltermaker Design Programme** are ongoing throughout the design process. Effectively this work continues in parallel with investigation and decision making relating to Structure, H&V, Materials, Construction, etc. So, you should not be overly concerned with mastering all drawing and modelmaking techniques before moving on.

Next: SDP14 - Estimating Total Floor Area, page 125

Space Mock-Ups allow one to see inside a space

Space
Mock-ups

When the furniture and equipment models have been made they are used to develop space mock-ups. Space mock-ups are made to the same scale as furniture and equipment models and they are also made out of 1mm thick white card. Space mock-ups allow the individual spaces in your Brief to be laid out and estimated in size. This is done by installing the appropriate furniture in the mock-up and by arranging walls and a ceiling around these to produce a pleasing space.

A piece of card is used as the base for the mock-ups. This represents the floor of the space. Besides the floor and the appropriate furniture for the space, some props are needed to act as walls and ceiling while the layout of the space is being done. These can be made very easily out of card also. It is by no means essential that the spaces you begin laying out and mocking-up should contain right angles. For the purpose of getting used to mock-ups though, the regularity of the shape dictated by the right angle is useful.

The exercise of making space mock-ups has several functions. It immediately makes apparent the three-dimensional nature of space. It also performs another important function in that it allows the size of the building to be estimated. The floor area you wish to cover can then be related to the budget figure to see if the project is financially viable. The amount of space you want and the amount of money you have to spend must be made compatible at this stage. If you want a lot of space, but you do not have a lot of money to spend, you will have to choose your materials carefully and perhaps even do some of the building work yourself. All these considerations need to be taken into account before the project moves much further.

At this point the design is still fairly loose. From now on, however, the building will begin to take on a more definite shape. If your Brief is clear and your space requirements are clear, the design can progress to its natural conclusion. If your design, however, is more extravagant than you can possibly afford you should recognise this now. If you go on, at some later point in the design process, you will probably have to retreat to this point in order to start again!

There is a large range of building types that can be made – for example, one can create a large amount of space relatively inexpensively, using low-cost materials and doing a large amount of self-building. Or, expensive methods and materials can be used to make a small, expensive, hand crafted building. Either way, it is important at this stage, to fix in a general sense, the overall size your building is going to be, how much it is going to cost to construct and how the work is likely to be carried out. This is done on a space by space, basis with additional floor area added on for general circulation, for fuel stores and for heating equipment.

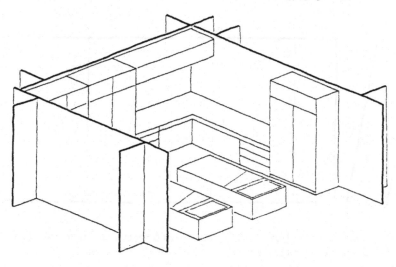

Making Space Mock-Ups

Your Brief will contain a file with the list of the spaces you want to have in your home. To start off, choose a simple space to mock-up – a bedroom for example. Keep everything simple. Make straight-forward shapes that are pleasing to the eye. The three-dimensional quality of the space will be readily visible in the mock-up. It is this quality that is invisible on paper. The only way it can be seen is either by building or by mocking it up. The location of windows and doors need not worry you at this stage.

Mark out a series of dots onto the long side of a sheet of card using a 1:20 scale ruler. The markings should be 2500mm in from the edge as measured with 1:20 scale ruler *fig. 1*. Cut the strip from the sheet. Mark off from one end of this a series of eight lines 600mm apart as measured on the 1:20 scale *fig*

. 2. Cut these off the strip. Cut the remaining strip into four pieces. Two of these should be at least 4000mm long and the other two 5000mm long at 1:20 scale *fig. 3*. If you do not have enough length in the strip you cut, cut another strip.

Using some glue *fig. 4*, fix two of the small strips to the back of each of the larger pieces you have cut. What you are doing is making freestanding walls that will temporarily enclose the rooms that you are laying out *fig. 5*. The support ribs need to be kept in from the ends of the wall pieces and they should be placed so as to allow the "wall" to stand upright. If a second strip of card is glued underneath these ribs, the freestanding walls will be further sta-bilised.

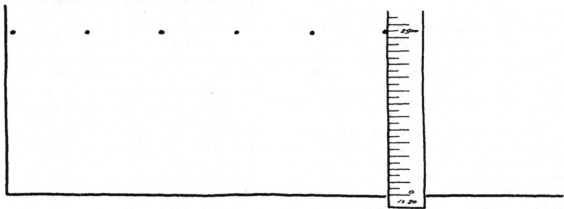

fig. 1: Mark out a series of dots onto the long side of a sheet of card using a 1:20 scale ruler. The markings should be 2500mm in from the edge. Cut the marked strip off the larger sheet.

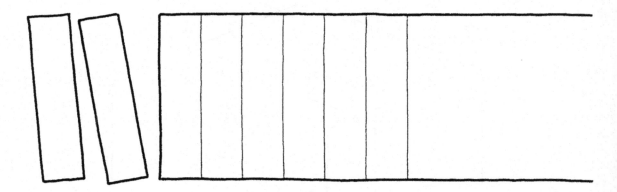

fig. 2: Mark off from one end of the strip a series of eight lines 600mm apart as measured on the 1:20 scale ruler. Cut these off the strip using the knife and the steel edged ruler.

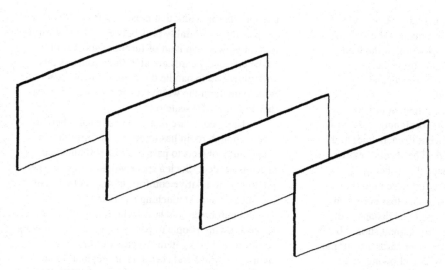

fig. 3: Cut the remaining strip into four pieces. Two of these should be at least 4000mm long and the two 5000mm long at 1:20 scale.

fig. 4: Use glue to fix two of the small strips to each of the larger pieces you have cut.

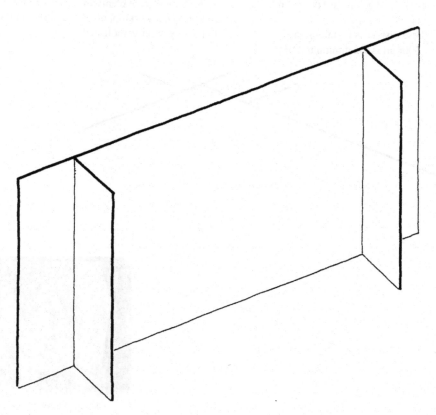

fig. 5: What you are doing is making freestanding walls that will temporarily enclose the rooms that you are laying out. The support ribs need to be kept in from the ends of the wall pieces and they should be placed so as to allow the "wall" to stand upright.

When the freestanding walls have been made and are dry, the mock-up can be made. The size of any space is controlled by the position of the walls and the ceiling. On the mock-up, these can be adjusted relative to each other, allowing an infinite variety of spaces to be created.

Collect the furniture and equipment models appropriate to the room you are designing. Erect two of the freestanding walls adjacent to each other at the corner of a sheet of card *fig. 6*. The sheet of card represents the floor of the space that is being designed. When arranging the furniture onto the model, it will be necessary to ensure that everything is well laid out. To properly judge the distances the various items of furniture and equipment should be apart, spacer cards are used. Spacer cards are simple strips of card of a particular width, allowing you to judge the distance items should be apart – the width needed for a person to pass between, say, the back of a chair and a wall, or between two beds. A spacer card representing the swing of a standard door can also be made *fig. 7*.

You can check these distances by taking measurements yourself. 500mm is the minimum effective circulation width that must be left in order that people can comfortably pass between items of furniture, or between an item of furniture and a wall. Make the spacer cards about 250mm long, as this will allow you to handle them quite easily. Also write onto them the width they represent. Measure this with the 1:20 scale rule.

Where people are likely to pass each other, or where enough room has to be left for furniture or other bulky objects to pass by, 750-800mm clear space is needed. Such a space would allow two people to pass in relative comfort, though not without touching or almost touching each other.

900mm is the standard width for circulation space allowing people to pass with ease and allowing furniture and bulky items to pass through easily. Stairs, doorways and corridors are regularly made this width. Within a room, a clear path of 900mm will allow easy unencumbered movement between objects or items of furniture. A clear width of 1200mm will give plenty of room both for someone to use, say, a worktop, or sit at a desk and for anyone to pass by them unmolested.

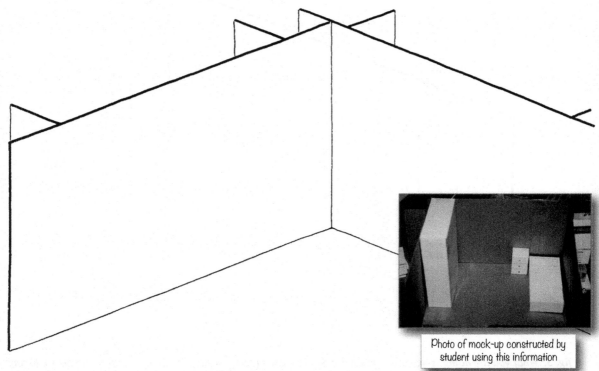

Photo of mock-up constructed by student using this information

fig. 6: Erect two of the freestanding walls adjacent to each other at the corner of a sheet of card. The sheet of card represents the floor of the space that is being designed.

fig. 7: Spacer cards are simple strips of card of a particular width allowing you to judge the distance items should be apart – the width needed for a person to pass between, say, the back of a chair and a wall or between two beds.

A standard width of 600mm should be used for all storage units. Well placed storage units can considerably reduce the amount of loose furniture that you will need in your home. A 600mm deep storage zone in, say, a bedroom, can incorporate hanging space, drawer space, a dressing table, a study table and bookshelves *fig. 8*. This type of unit can liberate the floor space of the room and leave it uncluttered. When you are installing storage zones into your lay-outs, think in terms of the zone extending the entire length of one wall. If you have several model storage units on hand in various lengths, you can install enough in any particular space to make any size unit you want. These should be installed against walls. The object of the current exercise is to become familiar with the creation of space and to estimate the overall amount of space that you need to build. So, take your time and have fun.

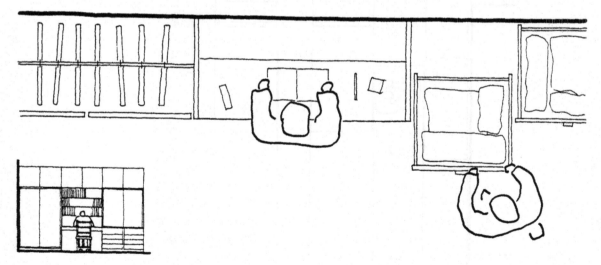

fig. 8: Well placed storage units can considerably reduce the amount of loose furniture that you will need in your home. A 600mm deep storage zone in say, a bedroom, can incorporate hanging space, drawer space, a dressing table, a study table and bookshelves.

The location of windows and doors can be given some general consideration at this stage. The final location and size of these, however, can only be decided in relationship to orientation, heating and to the relative position of the other spaces in the house. As you work, it will become clear that there are natural places for doors and windows in the spaces that you are laying out. These will be noted on the layout for use at a later stage, when the final positions of these elements can be fixed. It is important to remember that the design is still in its infancy and that the design is slowly built up as a series of layers, all of which are in harmony with your design objectives.

It is not difficult to make enough space to neatly fit you and your things in, but a room laid out like this will be a little like a caravan, an aeroplane or a cheap hotel room – there would be barely enough space, certainly not enough space to feel expansive or to throw a party in. The decision as to the size particular rooms are made must depend, not just on making enough space for you and your things, but on creating a sense of space appropriate to how you want to feel when you are in that space.

What is important now is that the spaces are made big enough for what you want to put in them and for the sense of space you wish to invest them with. Begin by erecting two of the freestanding walls at the edge of a sheet or large piece of card and then installing the model furniture and equipment in the corner made by these walls figs. 9 & 10. Use the spacer cards to properly distance these items from each other. When all relevant items have been arranged on the mock-up, locate the remaining two freestanding walls so as to create a complete enclosure fig. 11.

It will be found that square or rectangular spaces are the easiest kind of spaces to develop initially. With a little practice, more complex shapes, such as 'L' shapes, octagons or other geometric forms, can be mocked-up also by using various sized freestanding walls.

When a layout has been decided on, the mock-up ceiling height should be given some consideration. This can be done quite simply with a piece of card laid over the top of the freestanding walls. Only three of these walls should be left standing when this is being done fig. 12. This will allow a clear view inside the space, giving an effect similar to a stage set.

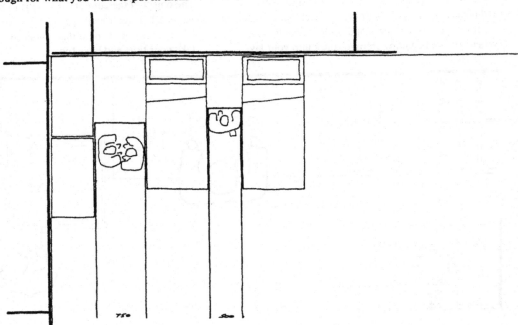

fig. 9: Begin by erecting two of the freestanding walls at the edge of a sheet or large piece of card and then installing the model furniture and equipment in the space made by these walls. Use the spacer cards to properly distance these items from each other.

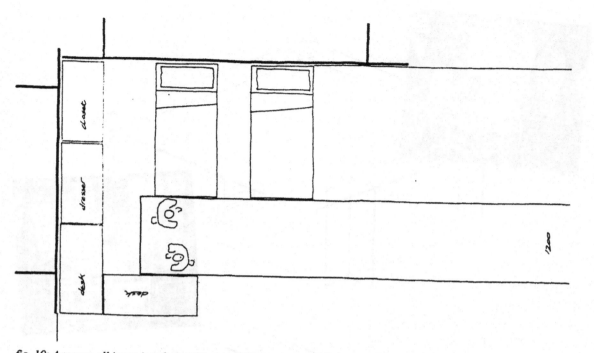

fig. 10: Arrange all items in relationship to each other bearing in mind the kind of use the room will be put to.

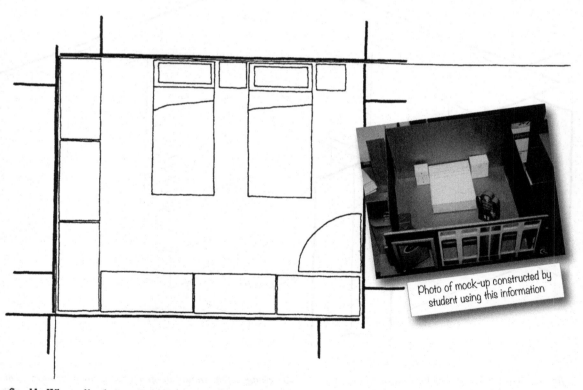

Photo of mock-up constructed by student using this information

fig. 11: When all relevant items have been arranged on the mock-up, locate the remaining two freestanding walls so as to create a complete enclosure.

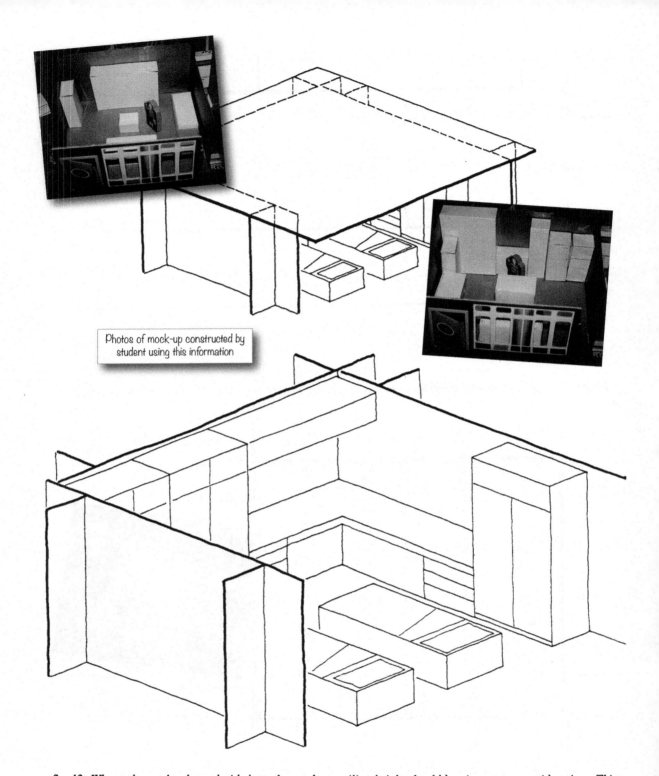

Photos of mock-up constructed by
student using this information

fig. 12: When a layout has been decided on, the mock-up ceiling height should be given some consideration. This can be done quite simply with a piece of card laid over the top of the freestanding walls. Only three of these walls should be left standing when this is being done.

The freestanding walls that have been made are 2500mm high. This is an appropriate height for small rooms, such as bedrooms, bathrooms, utility rooms and so on. Higher ceiling heights can be mocked up by making higher freestanding walls *fig. 13*. Freestanding walls can be made any height or length you want by cutting appropriately sized strips of card and putting ribs behind these. It helps to write on the back of the walls what actual height they are. This will save you measuring them to find the particular one you want. The minimum height that walls can be made is 2400mm. The walls and the

furniture are your props and you can use these to create any kind of space you want.

When the ceiling is placed onto the mock-up, it is important to look closely at the space being created. Getting down and looking closely at the mock-up is vital. The effect of doing this will be quite startling – you will actually see the space that you have created in miniature. This is the very practice of architecture and an essential forerunner to building full size spaces with real walls, floors and ceilings.

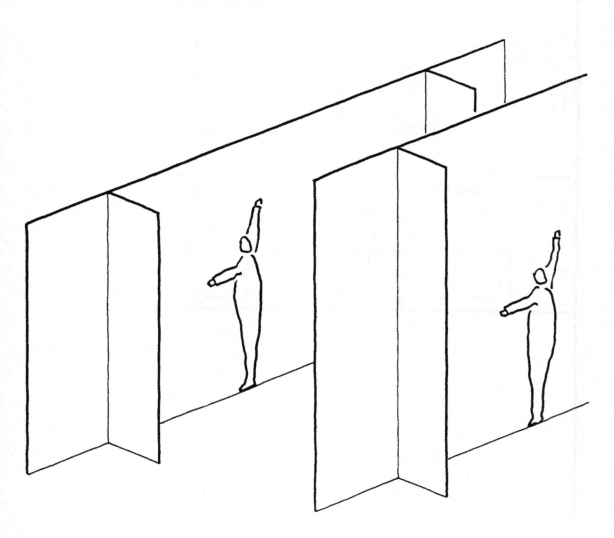

fig. 13: Higher ceiling heights can be mocked up by making higher freestanding walls. These can be made any height or length you want by cutting appropriately sized strips of card and putting ribs behind these

111

When a layout has been decided on, carefully remove the ceiling and mark with a pencil the position of the two walls standing on the sheet of card. Carefully remove each item of furniture outlining its shape on the card base and noting what it is *fig. 14*. Possible door and window positions should also be noted.

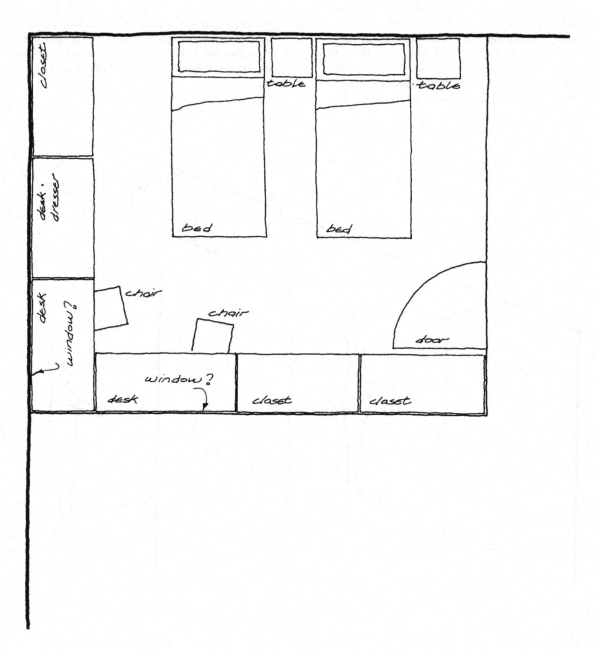

fig. 14: When a layout has been decided on, carefully remove the ceiling and mark with a pencil the position of the two walls standing on the sheet of card. Carefully remove each item of furniture outlining its shape on the card base and noting what it is. Possible door and window positions should also be noted.

Next, cut the room layout off the larger sheet of card. This will leave you with a "space plan card" that will show you the approximate size of the space, its furniture, its height and the possible location of windows and doors. Turn the card over onto its blank side. Measure with the 1:20 scale ruler the overall size of the space and note this on the back of the card *fig. 15*. Also, calculate the floor area of the space by multiplying the length by the breadth. This will be in square metres.

To obtain a figure for the floor area of a particular space in square feet, multiply the square metre figure by 11. This will give an approximate conversion that is sufficiently accurate. Also, note the estimated ceiling height and the title of the space on the back side of the space plan card. Depending on the size of the space you have made, the space plan card should fit in your file folder for that particular space.

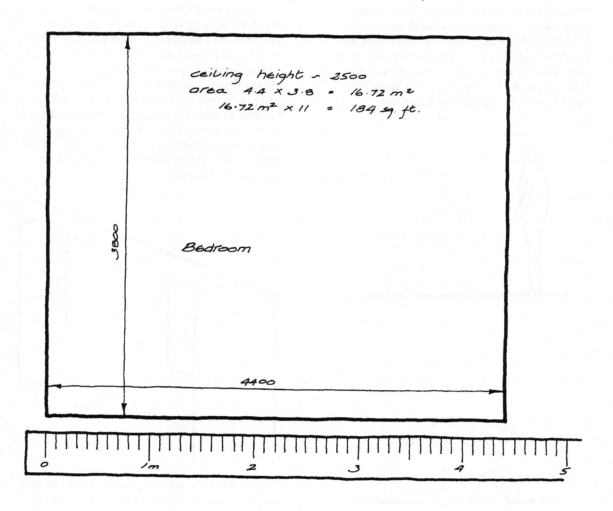

fig. 15: Turn the card over onto its blank side. Measure with the 1:20 scale ruler the overall size of the space and note this on the back of the card. Also, calculate the floor area of the space by multiplying the length by the breath. This will be in square metres.

113

Creating Space

Once the first mock-up has been made, it will become clear what the whole process of architecture is all about. It is about creating space. Providing enough space for furniture and equipment is one thing, but investing rooms with a sense of space is a process that has very few rules.

When looking at a mock-up, you have to remember that you are twenty times bigger than it is *fig. 16*. You have to scale yourself down in size. If you tower over the mock-up, you simply will not be able to sense the space it encloses. You must get down and peer inside it, turn it round, move walls, adjust the ceiling height and so on. Remember, the exercise of adjusting walls, ceilings and furniture in miniature is far easier, cheaper and less traumatic than trying to do the same thing when the building is being made or has already been completed.

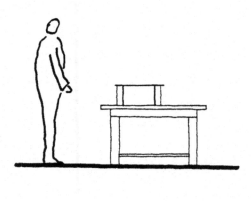

fig. 16: When looking at a mock-up you have to remember that you are twenty times bigger than it is. If you tower over the mock-up you simply will not be able to sense the space it encloses

Proportions

The key to creating pleasant spaces lies in creating pleasing proportions in three dimensions. That is, the length, breadth and height of a space should be in harmony. The best way of ensuring this is by creating the space in miniature and by adjusting its proportions until a pleasing space has been arrived at. The flexibility of the mock-ups allows this to be done very easily. The mock-up should be well lit when this is being done – a table lamp can be used for this or a strong torch.

When the mocked-up space is finally built full-size, it will be lit by windows. It is important to remember this – that some of the freestanding walls should, in fact, have windows cut out of them. It is a good idea to make up two freestanding walls with window openings cut in them *fig. 17*. These can be used as substitutes on the mock-up after the layout has been decided. Even though the window openings will not suit for every layout you come up with, their use will nonetheless give you a good idea of the kind of light a space is likely to get with windows placed in particular walls.

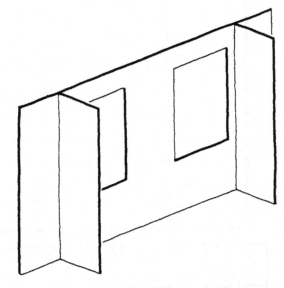

fig. 17: When the mocked-up space is finally built full-size it will be lit by windows. It is important to remember this – that some of the freestanding walls should, in fact, have windows cut out of them. It is a good idea to make up two freestanding walls with window openings cut in them. These can be used as substitutes on the mock-up after the layout has been decided.

You will need to put a ceiling on the mock-up to examine the light qualities of the space properly. This will effectively seal up the space, allowing you to see only through the windows. A 50 x 50mm hole cut in another freestanding wall will allow you to see inside the mock-up when it is being lit *fig. 18.* Use a strong torch or an angle-poise lamp to do this. If you use a lamp you can do this exercise alone, but with the torch you will need someone to hold it while you examine the space. Shine the light from various angles, remembering that the sun describes more or less a semi-circle every day and that it is high in the sky in summer and low in winter *fig. 19.*

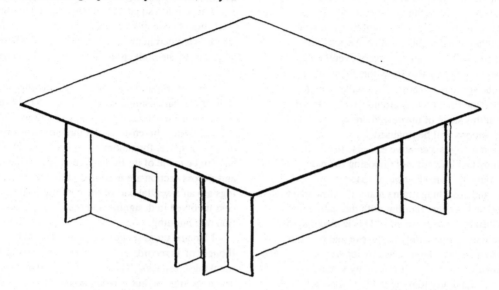

fig. 18: A 50 x 50mm hole cut in one freestanding wall will allow you to see inside the mock-up when it is being lit.

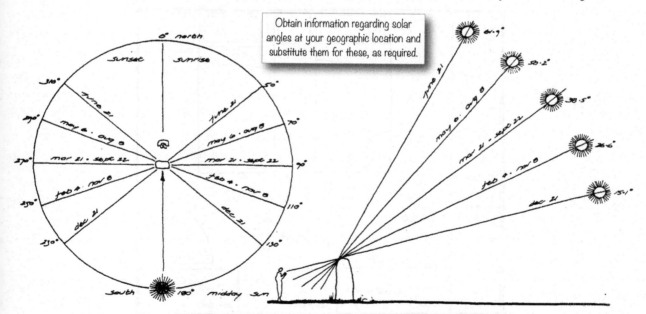

Obtain information regarding solar angles at your geographic location and substitute them for these, as required.

fig. 19: The sun describes an approximate semi-circle across the sky every day. The sun is high in the sky in summer and low in winter.

If there is a particular direction of the sun/torch that produces a quality of light within the space that is unique, this should be noted on the space plan card. Do this by drawing an arrow and giving this a direction. For example, if you want to reproduce that quality of light at midday every day in the full-size space, the direction would be South – this is where the sun will be in the sky at that time every day. If it is a quality of evening light that you wish to capture, then the direction will be West, as this is where the sun will be in the sky every evening *fig. 20*. It is a good idea to also show the direction of North on the space plan cards. This will come in useful when the final layouts are under way. It will not be until this stage of the design process that the window positions will be finalised.

Space-making is a creative exercise that you should enjoy tackling without imposing too many rules on yourself. The creation of space is an intriguing and absorbing drama that will allow you to conjure up and become familiar with the spaces that your finished home will contain. This is made possible by the remarkable ability of the eye and brain to allow us to imagine a large space by looking at a scaled down version of it. It is only by scaling yourself down and intently looking at the mock-ups that the full impact of this will be evident.

While space-making is essentially a creative exercise, there are some guidelines as to how pleasing spaces can be successfully arrived at – avoid creating long narrow spaces, these are unpleasant – you can mock this up very easily and see the effect that these kind of spaces create. If you create a large space, make sure you give it a high ceiling, otherwise it will appear too squat. Small spaces, on the other hand should have low ceilings. All these conditions can be examined in mock-ups or identified where they exist in the built environment around you *fig. 21*.

It is important to remember that drawings cannot show three-dimensional space. They can only show two dimensions of an object at any one time. To show the three dimensions of a three-dimensional object – a space, for example – at least two drawings have to be made of it. In the case of spaces, a plan and a cross section are used to do this. Such drawings are an essential part of the communication process involved in designing and realising the construction of a building.

Plan and cross section drawings should be thought of as records of the dimensions arrived at by mocking-up spaces. These records are then used when the final layout is being done.

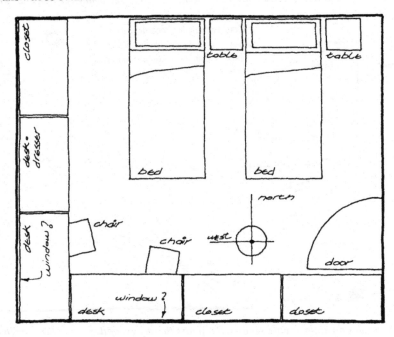

fig. 20: Note the preferred orientation on the space plan cards. It is a good idea to also show the direction of North.

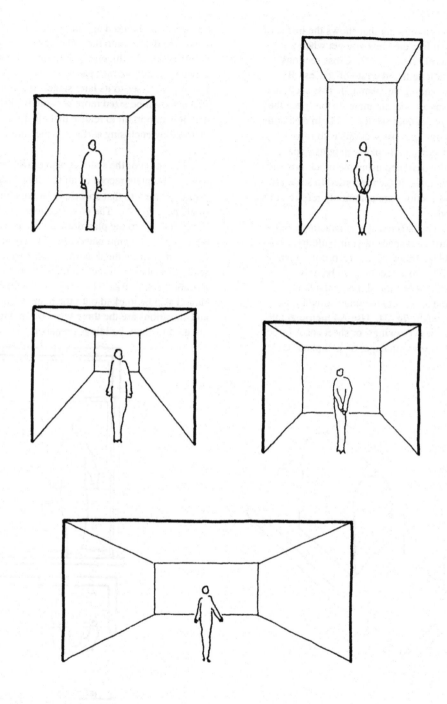

fig. 21: Avoid creating long narrow spaces, these are unpleasant. If you create a large space, make sure you give it a high ceiling, otherwise it will appear too squat. Small spaces, on the other hand should have relatively low ceilings.

117

Cross Sections

A cross section is a drawing that shows the inside of something, much like the view you get when you slice open a loaf of bread *fig. 22*. Cross sections show the height, length and width of spaces. By simultaneously reading the plan and cross sectional drawings of a space, you can imagine the space they represent, but you cannot see it *fig. 23*. In designing space, the function of cross sections is to record essential dimensions, particularly heights. Space should always be designed using the mock-ups and the essential dimensions then recorded to scale cross sections. Cross sections are commonly referred to as simply "sections."

When you have arrived at a satisfactory proportion for any particular space in your building, cross sections should be drawn of it to record its essential dimensions. Two cross sections can be drawn for any one space – one section showing the length and the height of the space and the other showing the width and the height *fig. 24*. Use A4 metric graph paper to make these drawings, or sheets of A4 tracing paper laid over graph paper on a clipboard. A 1:50 scale can be used and this will allow both sections to be drawn onto the same page. A nominal wall/floor/ceiling thickness of 150mm should be shown surrounding the spaces you draw. As the design progresses to its later stages, this nominal thickness will be sized more accurately. For the present, it is important to realise that all spaces are enclosed by enclosing surfaces which are of a certain width.

If the plan of the space is also drawn onto the A4 sheet, a complete record of all the dimensional information relating to that space can be contained on a single page *fig. 25*. The cross sections can be positioned relative to the plan drawing, so as to assist in their being read simultaneously. Clearly note on the page which space the drawings refer to, the relevant scale, and label each section individually as Section AA and Section BB. The line of each cross section should also be marked onto the plan. Plans, sections and elevations are the three types of drawings that are used to show buildings on paper.

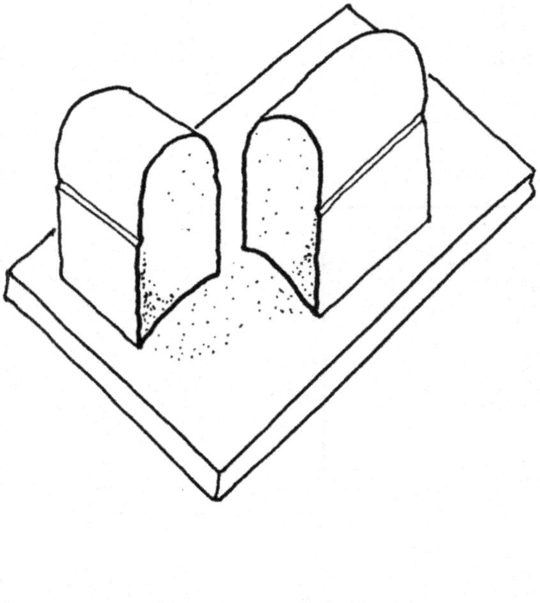

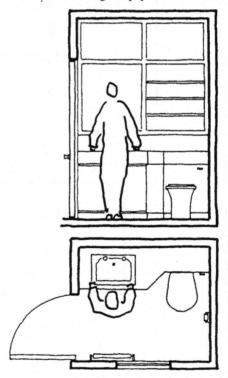

fig. 22: A cross section is a drawing that shows the inside of something, much like the view you get when you slice open a loaf of bread.

fig. 23: By simultaneously reading the plan and cross sectional drawings of a space you can imagine the space they represent but you cannot see it.

118

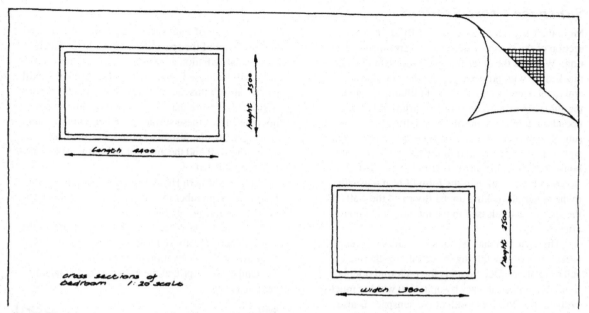

fig. 24: Two cross sections can be drawn for any one space – one section showing the length and the height of the space and the other showing the width and the height.

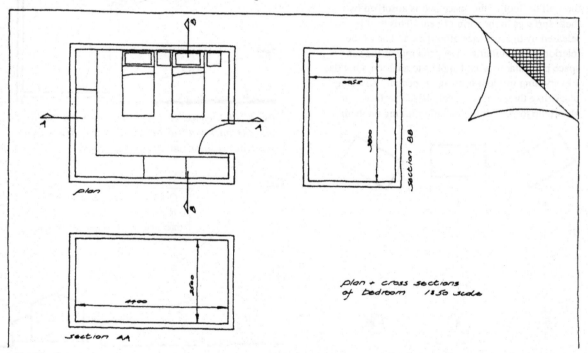

fig. 25: If the plan of the space is also drawn onto the A4 sheet, a complete record of all the dimensional information relating to that space can be contained on a single page. The cross sections can be positioned relative to the plan drawing so as to assist in their being read simultaneously. Clearly note on the page which space the drawings refer to, the relevant scale, and label each section individually as Section AA and Section BB. The line of each cross section should also be marked onto the plan.

Sunspace Cross Sections

More than any other space in your Brief, the cross section of the sunspace needs very careful consideration. Whereas the other spaces in your Brief can be mocked-up with proper regard to their proportions and to the kind of light that might illuminate them, the sunspace proportions must be primarily decided upon by reference to the angle and direction of the sun. The reason for this is because the sunspace, as well as performing as part of the habitable area of the house, functions to gather solar radiation. This is stored in the sunspace in the form of heat – usually in the materials making up the floor and the walls of the space – and released to the interior of the house after dark.

The direction that the sunspace faces is critical to its efficient functioning in regard to gathering solar radiation. Due South is the preferred orientation though this can vary by up to 30^0 without much problem *fig. 26*. The width of the sunspace is also critical. What actually happens in a sunspace is that sunlight, trapped behind South facing glazing, strikes the wall or floor of the space and is absorbed by these surfaces in the form of heat. This heat is released by the sunspace after dark and heats the interior of the building. The principle of the sunspace is similar to what happens to a car on a hot day – everything inside it heats up, especially anything black, like the steering wheel. Black surfaces can absorb up to 90% of the radiation falling on them.

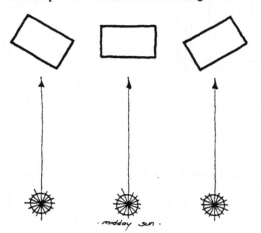

fig. 26: The direction that the sunspace faces is critical to its efficient functioning in regard to gathering solar radiation. Due South is the preferred orientation though this can vary by up to 30^0 without much problem.

In the case of a sunspace, you want the floor and the back wall of the space to be struck by as much direct solar radiation as possible *fig. 27*. These surfaces will be made from materials like brick that will readily absorb this radiation and store it in the form of heat. To ensure that as much direct radiation as possible strikes these surfaces, the height of the sunspace glazing, the distance behind it of the heat absorbing wall and the angle of the sun must be carefully coordinated.

In the Northern Hemisphere the heating season lasts from September to late April. During that period, the sun reaches its lowest elevation of the year, on Midwinters Day, December 21st. On that day the sun is a mere 15^0 above the horizon at noon. This contrasts with an elevation of around 40^0 in September and April, at the extremes of the heating season *fig. 28*.

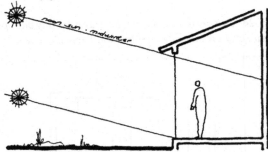

fig. 27: In the case of a sunspace you want the floor and the back wall of the space to be struck by as much direct solar radiation as possible.

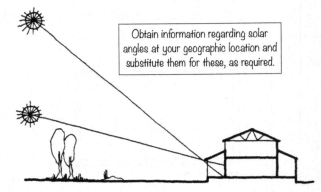

Obtain information regarding solar angles at your geographic location and substitute them for these, as required.

fig. 28: The sun reaches its lowest elevation of the year on December 21st. On that day the sun is a mere 15^0 above the horizon at noon. This contrasts with an elevation of around 40^0 in September and April, at the extremes of the heating season.

If the height of the south glazing and the width of the sunspace are made to be the same dimension – for example, 2500mm – then the floor and back wall of the space will be directly illuminated throughout the heating season *fig. 29*. The addition of a shallow reflecting pond in front of the south glazing will assist in directing sunlight into the sunspace, especially during the deepest part of winter. A sunspace can be used as part of the general living accommodation throughout the year. It is usual to situate further living accommodation behind the back wall of the sunspace to benefit from the gradual release of its heat.

If the south glazing is made to be quite high, for example 4000mm, and the width of the sunspace is made to be a similar dimension, it is possible to incorporate a second floor within a simple cross sec-tion *fig. 30*. The upper floor in such a situation would also benefit from the heat gathered into the back wall.

When the sunspace mock-ups are being made, careful regard should be paid to its height and width to ensure that the area will function efficiently in regards to the collection of solar energy. It is worth making a special freestanding south wall to examine the light characteristics of the space you evolve *fig. 31*. A torch with a strong narrow beam can be used to simulate the sun path in relationship to the mock-up.

The layout of the sunspace should be evolved using the appropriate furniture and equipment models and the information recorded on a space plan card in the usual way *fig. 32*.

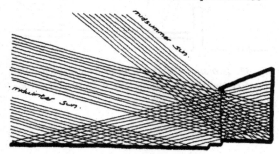

fig. 29: *If the height of the south glazing and the width of the sunspace are made to be the same dimension then the floor and back wall of the space will be directly illuminated throughout the heating season. The addition of a shallow reflecting pond in front of the south glazing will assist in directing sunlight into the sunspace, especially during the deepest part of winter.*

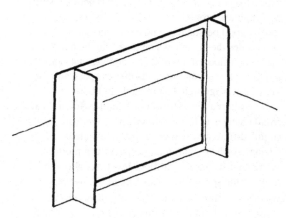

fig. 31: *It is worth making a special freestanding south wall to examine the light characteristics of the space you evolve.*

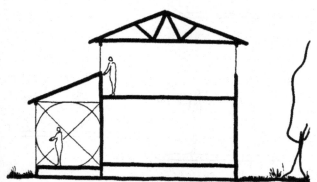

fig. 30: *If the south glazing is made to be quite high it is possible to incorporate a second floor within a simple cross section.*

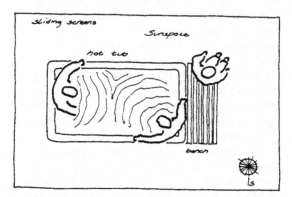

fig. 32: *The layout of the sunspace should be evolved using the appropriate furniture and equipment models and the information recorded on a space plan card in the usual way.*

Levels

A question that may have arisen in your mind at this point is levels. Should your house have two floors, one floor, changes in level and so on? Building on two floors is a generally cheaper way to build than creating the same amount of floor space on a single level, because the outside surface area of the building is kept to a minimum. The amount of wall area, roof and possibly circulation space will tend to increase if all the accommodation is on one floor only. Such a building might also be more difficult to heat.

Two storey houses tend to be stratified, however – the upstairs and the downstairs are very strongly separated *fig. 33*. A lot of human energy can also be expended going up and down stairs. There are solutions to these problems – balconies, two storey rooms, good personal organisation and so on. Oftentimes the best views on a site can be had from the second floor of a building – and yet that floor might well be given over to bedroom space and the view largely ignored during daylight hours.

An alternative to full floor height differences are small changes in level. These can range from "half-flight" differences in level to just a few steps. Changes of level within large spaces can produce interesting separations at floor level, yet allow the unity of the space to be undisturbed *fig. 34*. If you wish to incorporate such changes in level in your design, you should show this on the cross sectional drawings.

When the space mocks-ups are being made, it will be found that varying ceiling heights will be wanted over different size spaces. This will be especially true of living areas and such spaces as bedrooms and bathrooms. It is possible to incorporate such variations into the design by adjusting the floor levels *fig. 35*. At this point of the design exercise, the question of fixing floor levels and harmonising ceiling heights need not overly concern you. It is sufficient for these aspects of the final design to be in your head as options that can be firmly decided on at a later stage.

Attic rooms can oftentimes be incorporated above ground floor accommodation by constructing the roof in such a way as to leave a clear head height of 2400mm throughout two-thirds of the room. The remaining one-third of the ceiling can slope downwards allowing storage space to be incorporated along the sides of the space *fig. 36*.

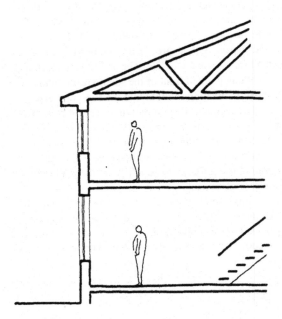

fig. 33: Two storey houses tend to be stratified – the upstairs and the downstairs are very strongly separated.

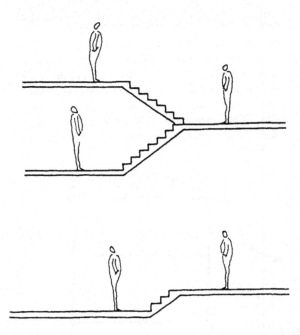

fig. 34: An alternative to full floor height differences are small changes in level. These can range from a "half-flight" differences in level to just a few steps.

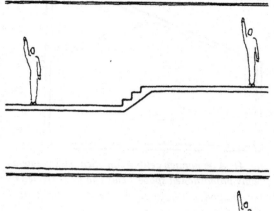

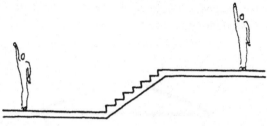

fig. 35: It is possible to incorporate variations in ceiling heights into a design by adjusting the floor levels.

Sloping Ceilings

If you wish to have other than a flat ceiling over a particular space, you can arrange this quite easily on the mock-up. If you want a ceiling to slope only one way you simply make 'sloped' freestanding walls, allowing the effect of a sloping ceiling to be mocked-up *fig. 37*. When the ceiling is placed over these it will be sloped. If the slope is so great that the ceiling slips off, use a piece of sellotape to fix it onto the mock-up.

Ceilings that slope two ways can be made by making freestanding wall to the required length and profile *fig. 38*. A piece of cardboard, folded to create the effect of a pitched ceiling, is then placed over these walls. You make the ceiling piece by marking the ridge line of the ceiling onto the piece of card, the size of which is gauged from the mock-up. Lightly score the card with a scalpel along the ridge line. Do not cut very deep. Fold the card along the score line *fig. 39*. Place this over the mock-up, using sellotape to hold it in position if necessary.

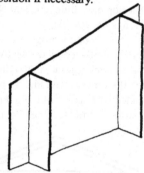

fig. 37: If you wish to have a ceiling that slopes one way you simply make 'sloped' freestanding walls allowing the effect of a sloping ceiling to be mocked-up.

fig. 36: Attic rooms can oftentimes be incorporated above ground floor accommodation by constructing the roof in such a way as to leave a clear head height of 2400mm throughout one half of the room. The remaining half of the ceiling can slope downwards to a height of 1500mm allowing storage space to be incorporated along the sides of the space.

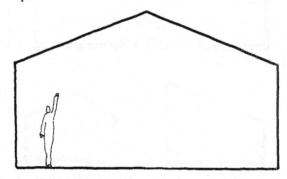

fig. 38: Ceilings that slope two ways can be made by making freestanding wall to the required length and profile.

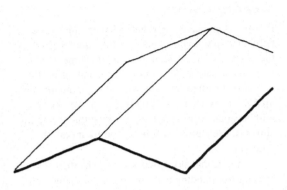

fig. 39: A pitched ceiling can be made by marking the ridge line of the ceiling onto a piece of card. Lightly score the line with a scalpel. Do not cut very deep. Fold the card along the score line and fix to the model with sellotape.

When the cross sections are being drawn for a space with a sloping ceiling, this will clearly show on the drawings *fig. 40*. A monopitch ceiling can oftentimes create an oddly proportioned space *fig. 41*. This can be corrected by the addition of a 'false slope' to balance the natural pitch of the roof.

Ground floor rooms with high or pitched ceilings can be blended with spaces of more regular cross section to create economical building profiles *fig. 42*.

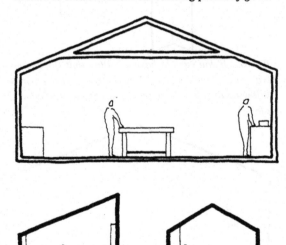

fig. 40: When the cross sections are being drawn for a space with a sloping ceiling, this will clearly show on the drawings.

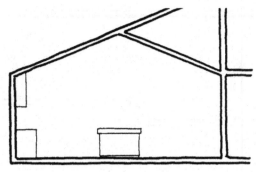

fig. 41: A monopitch ceiling can oftentimes create an oddly proportioned space. This can be corrected by the addition of a 'false slope' to balance the natural pitch of the roof.

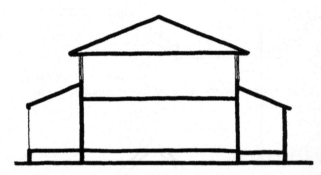

fig. 42: Ground floor rooms with high or pitched ceilings can be blended with spaces of more regular cross section to create economical building profiles.

Other Design Considerations

There is much more to the process of design than making mock-ups and drawing plans and cross sections. How the various spaces are to be interconnected has to be decided, how the building is to be made to stand up has to be figured out, what materials the building is to be made from has to be considered, a heating system has to be designed, the window locations have to be finalised, the plumbing and electrical services have to be incorporated, drains have to be taken into account – the list is not endless but it certainly is exhausting! *fig. 43*. All these things will influence the final design of the building. These considerations are secondary, however, to the creation of space. For this reason, it is the individual spaces that are created first in the house design and all other items are decided in relation to these and the sense of space that is desired.

Sheltermaker Design Programme
Estimating Total Floor Area

'Other Design Considerations' on page 124 gives an overview of where things now stand at this stage of the design process. Critical to the successful conclusion of this is the estimation of likely cost. Cost depends on many factors, one of which is floor area. If the total floor area is calculated, say in square metres or square feet, and that floor area figure is divided into the estimated construction cost figure, a cost per square metre or per square foot will be arrived at. This is a handy yardstick for assessing the financial viability of the project. It is critical to carry out this exercise out before proceeding too far with a design that may prove uneconomic to build.

So, read pages 132-134, bearing in mind that the illustrated figures date back to the early 90's - though they may be equally relevant now! Next, print the *Floor Area Worksheets*. You will also need your *List of Spaces* and your *Budget Worksheet* close at hand.

For every *Space* listed on your *List of Spaces Worksheet* choose a *Sample Area* figure (Small, Medium or Large) and enter this onto the *Floor Area Worksheet*. To estimate the floor area of *Spaces* not listed, select a similar *Space* from the *Worksheet*, or measure an existing *Space* that is the size you want and use that figure. Total the figures for all the *Spaces* and add 20% to cover circulation space. This total is the estimated size of your building in square metres.

For those modifying or extending existing buildings, create 2 *Worksheets* - one listing the new *Spaces* and the other listing the existing ones. When calculating the total floor area of the existing it is not necessary to add 20% to cover circulation space. To ascertain the size of these *Spaces* it will be necessary to carry out a survey. How to do this is explained on page 136.

Extract the estimate of construction costs from the *Budget Worksheet*. Divide your floor area total into this 'construction cost' figure. This will give you a construction cost per square metre or per square foot. This is an easy way of relating floor area to construction costs - very handy if you need to scale the project down. 'Cost per square metre' covers the construction of the building including all the services, finishes and so on. How the actual money will be spent to create the building will be the subject of further investigation as the design exercise proceeds.

For those modifying or extending existing buildings you will have to divide your estimated construction costs figure between the costs of modifications and the cost of the extension.

Your 'cost per square metre' figure needs to be compared with building costs in the area in which you wish to build. These costs will vary for various types of construction. There will also be a variation between the cost of self-building and the cost of employing a building contractor. What is critical now is to arrive at a realistic estimate of cost for the amount of floor space you wish to create based on a self-build or on a full contractual service. These can be seen as two extremes. While self-building may potentially look cheaper you have to be able to give the project time and consequently to pay yourself, even if this is a very small amount. At this early stage what one can do is to obtain some estimates locally and settle on a cost per square metre that is affordable for you. Those modifying or extending existing buildings will also need to obtain a guide price for modification work, though this is notoriously hard to gauge given the varying conditions that can be encountered.

As explained in the Manual, this is a reality check! If your budget is simply too small to pay for all the *Spaces* you wish to create then you have to scale back <u>now</u>! If you cannot do that phasing the construction might be an option. The one thing to be wary of is planning to borrow enough to do all that you want.

Once an overall cost per square metre has been set, or, in the case of those modifying or extending existing buildings, a cost for each type of work involved, it will be clear what segment of the market you are in. All design considerations from this point forward have to take this into account. In other words if you are working at the lower end of the spectrum you will not be entertaining thoughts of expensive heating and cooling technology, high cost materials or specialised contractors.

Next: SDP15 - Surveying, page 136

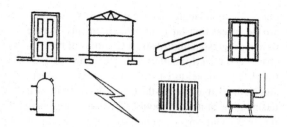

fig. 43: There is much more to the process of design than making mock-ups and drawing plans and cross sections. The list is not endless but it certainly is exhausting!

If all the spaces in the house are imagined as three-dimensional shapes – boxes! – the job of putting the spaces together correctly can be considered as a three-dimensional exercise. Each box can only be put beside certain other boxes. Some boxes are to be put on top of others. Certain boxes have to be slightly higher or lower than other boxes, and so on fig. 44. The final arrangement of all boxes is determined by the information contained in the Brief and relates to things such as location, orientation and so on. This final arrangement will in fact be the 'design' of the building, arrived at, as it is, by taking into account all aspects of the building.

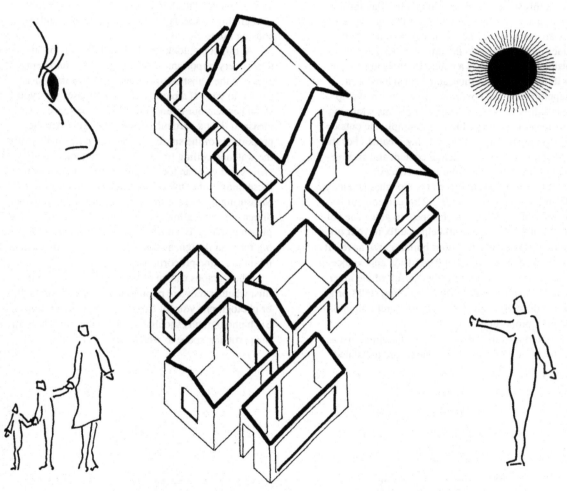

fig. 44: If all the spaces in the house are imagined as three dimensional shapes – boxes! – the job of putting the spaces together correctly can be considered as a three dimensional exercise. Each box can only be put beside certain other boxes. Some boxes are to be put on top of others. Certain boxes have to be slightly higher or lower than other boxes, and so on.

Even at this stage the Brief will contain a lot of information on how these boxes will be put together – the location of spaces relative to each other have been noted under *"Location"* and the *"Abstract"* qualities recorded for each space will give a broad indication of the orientation each space should have. The firming up of the layout however is a matter to be decided only after all the other major considerations have been taken into account. The crucial stage that has been reached now is to firmly decide on the type and scale of the building you are designing, how much it is likely to cost to build it and how the building work is likely to be carried out.

At this stage, it can be said that the way the various "space boxes" actually look on the outside when they are stacked together is an aspect of design that comes much later on in the project. Designing the outside of a building is a matter of choosing a style for it. In many ways this can be considered as a wrapping job – the boxes, or spaces, that make up the building are simply wrapped up! This wrapping can take any form you like – it is simply the outside of the internal spaces that are being created. For the moment, however, the internal content and arrangement of the building is your main concern.

It is worthwhile at this stage, though, to create a file entitled *'Design & Style'*. This can contain photographs of buildings which appeal to you. The collection of such images will help you fix in your mind the final appearance that your building will have. It should be remembered that the outside appearance of your home will in large part be a result of the inner harmony that is created. Many building styles originate in decorative effects and in the careful manipulation of proportions.

In terms of the interior of your building, just as the items of Furniture & Equipment are translated into a common language – measurements – so too are the spaces translated into measurements. As the design progresses, the Abstract Qualities of the spaces and the information on Surfaces are also translated into measurements. It is this use of measurements that allows all the different elements of the design to be united. It should always be remembered that underlying any given measurement is an object, a thing or a space. If the number is the only thing that is considered, a wealth of important data will be ignored. These omissions or oversights are caused by looking only at numbers, not at what they represent. Such omissions will produce a numerically biased design. This bias can be seen in many modern buildings, especially offices, apartments and housing estates.

At this stage, looking closely at existing buildings is very important. Looking at spaces and being aware of their abstract qualities will be of immense benefit to you. If a particular space pleases you, you should endeavour to understand why the space is so pleasant. Is it a particular quality of light? Are the proportions of the space gracious? Is it the quality of the wall and ceiling finishes? You can look at real spaces and you can look at photographs to discover these things. It is by looking that you will see. Measuring up a space that pleases you and noting the dimensions will allow you to record the size of a pleasing space. Even if that particular space is too big for your design, a scaled down version of it will retain the same proportions.

Photographs can be of invaluable assistance in this, whether they are photographs you take yourself, or photographs you cut from magazines and so on. Such photographs should be kept in the file folder for the particular space to which they refer.

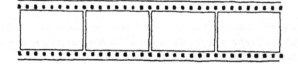

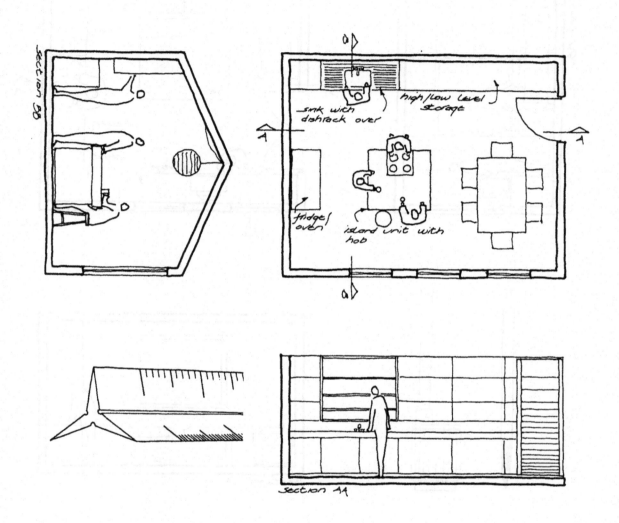

section BB

a

A ◀   ▶ A

sink with
dishrack over

high/low level
storage

fridge/
oven

island unit with
hob

a

section AA

Sketch plan and cross sections of kitchen/ dining area.

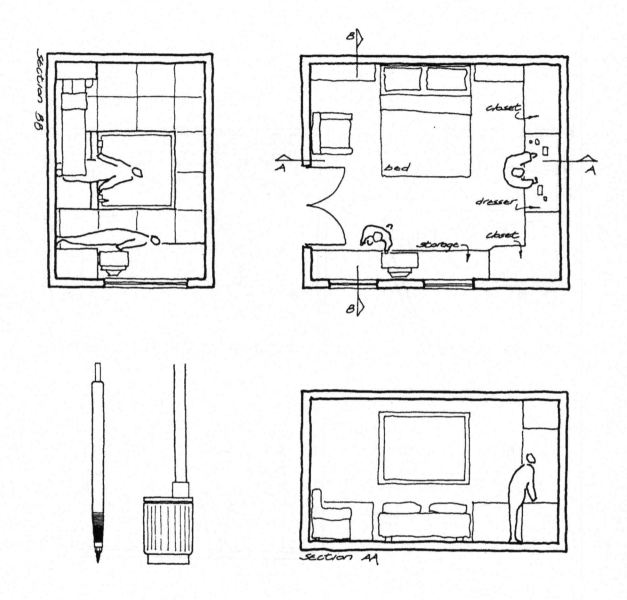

Sketch plan and cross sections of bedroom area.

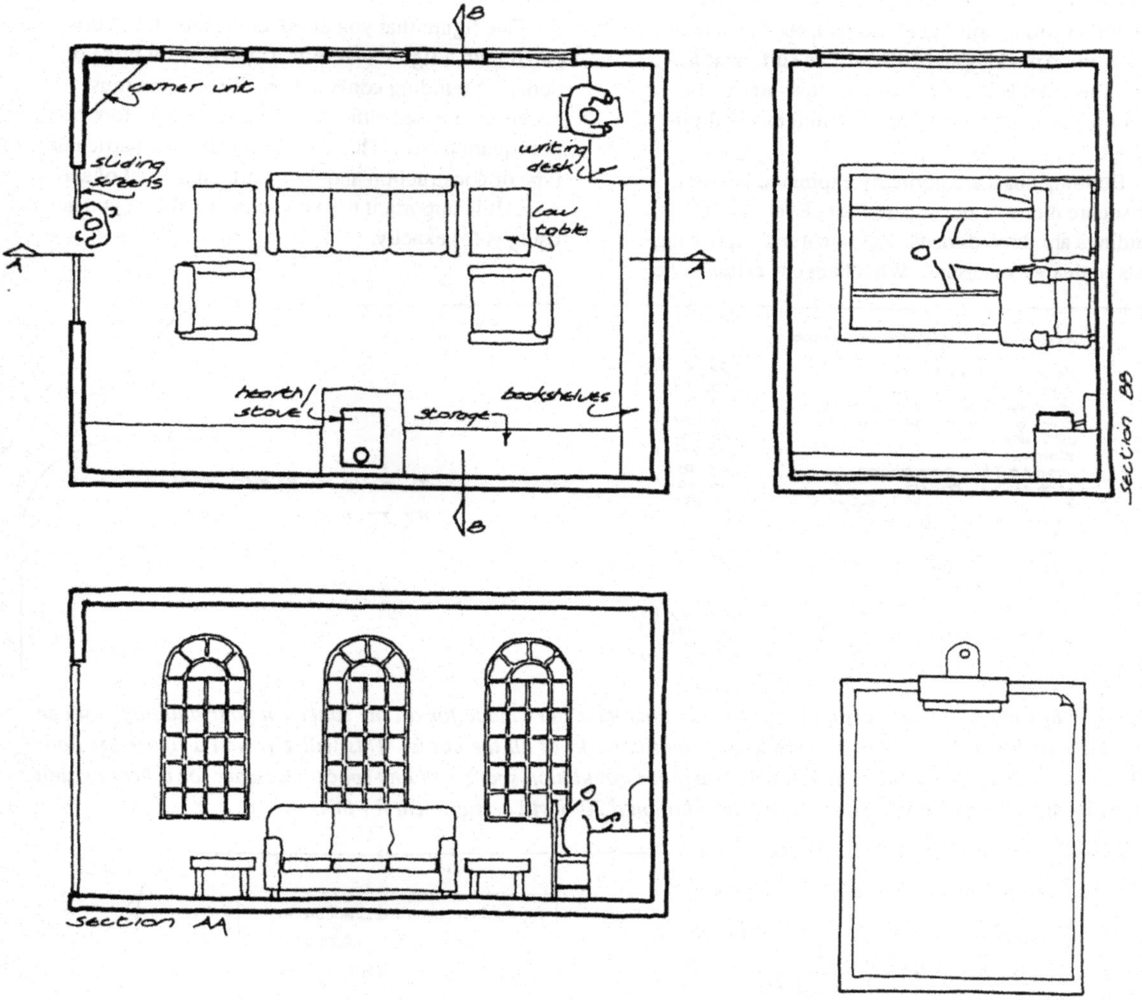
B
corner unit
sliding screens
writing desk
low table
A
A
hearth/stove
storage
bookshelves
B
section BB
section AA

Sketch plan and cross sections of living area.

Estimating Overall Floor Area

When mock-ups, layouts and space plan cards have been made for all the spaces in your building, you can total the individual floor areas that are written on the backs of all the cards. This will give you a figure for floor area to which must be added a certain percentage for circulation space and any space necessary for a heating unit to be installed, for fuel storage and so on. An additional 20% will be sufficient for this. This is added to the total you have arrived at for all the spaces you have laid out and mocked-up *fig. 45*.

Building costs are normally expressed in costs per square metre or per square foot. Even though buildings are three-dimensional in nature, expressing costs in this way is usual. What happens is this – the overall floor area of your proposed building is calculated and divided into your budget figure. This gives a budget construction cost per square foot or per square metre for that building *fig. 46*. This is a rough method of estimation which will act as a' guideline of cost.

The figure that you arrive at must then be compared with a figure that reflects the general price of domestic building construction. This figure must also be expressed either as a cost per square foot or per square metre. This cost will relate to a particular type of construction and for a particular level of service. It is important to know what the figure you are using is for exactly.

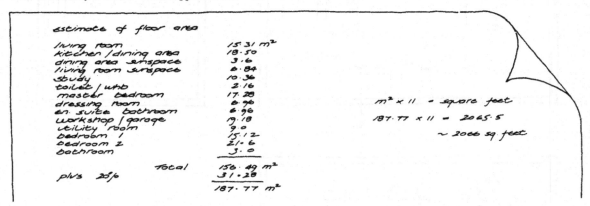

fig. 45: *When mock-ups, layouts and space plan cards have been made for all the spaces in your building you can total the individual floor areas that are written on the backs of all the cards. This will give you a figure for floor area to which must be added a certain percentage for circulation space and any space necessary for a heating unit to be installed, for fuel storage and so on. An additional 20% will be sufficient for this.*

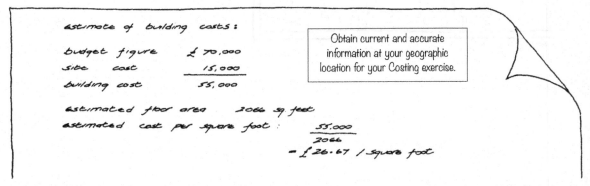

fig. 46: *Building costs are normally expressed in costs per square meter or per square foot. Even though buildings are three dimensional in nature, expressing costs in this way is usual. The overall floor area of your proposed building is calculated and divided into your budget figure. This gives a budget construction cost per square foot or per square metre for that building.*

You find out facts and figures by asking questions. Contractors, builders, real estate agents, timber frame suppliers, architects and surveyors will all have a figure that they can quote you for building work. The question you have to ask to learn these facts and figures is "What is the current cost of construction for a house?" You will rarely get a direct answer to this question. Alternatively you can ask "What is the price range for building a house?" This may elicit more response. You should be able to learn, within a fairly wide range, what buildings are being built for in a particular area or in the area you wish to build in. You must find out what the figures you have been quoted are for exactly – especially the type of materials and construction and the type of heating system that the price relates to. The more figures you are quoted the easier it will be to decide on an average figure.

This type of work is telephone work. Target your sources, formulate your questions and make your calls. Write down what you find out and start a new file for your Brief labelled "Cost". It is important that you let people know over the 'phone who you are, what you want and why you want it. You are playing detective to a large extent and you can be honest about this aspect of your enquiries – you are planning on building a house and you want to find out about costs. The project is at an early stage and you are making estimates and so on. People hesitate to give prices for things like building costs, because they vary so much. Ask for approximate figures that you are not going to hold anyone to. Some people will be more helpful than others and of course you will find some people do not want to help you at all!

Besides finding out the building cost figures, try to visit some newly built houses. Houses built for the speculative market are often put on show and you can visit these and find out a wealth of information from them. It does not matter if the showhouses you see are exactly opposite to the kind of house you want! You are not going to buy one, all you are doing is looking. You can find out the price of a show-house very easily. You might even be lucky enough to get a figure for the floor area also, allowing you to easily calculate a cost per square foot. The figure for floor area might be on some of the promotional literature. Failing this, you can actually measure out the floor area either with a tape or estimate it by stepping it out.

If you see a new house for sale that is £70,000 you can calculate the actual building cost fairly easi-

ly. The cost per square foot that you arrive at doing this is a working figure, not a rule or a standard or anything else. It will tell you what a particular sized house, constructed out of certain materials, is being sold for on the open market. This cost will include the speculator's profit. This makes the cost of the labour and materials difficult to quantify exactly.

To make a realistic comparison based on construction costs alone, a value has to be put on the site and this figure subtracted from the cost of the speculative house.. Let's say the site has cost the speculator £10,000 to buy and service, i.e. install public drains, bring in electricity and so on. The cost of building the house is then £60,000. If the floor area of the house is 2000 square feet, the building cost £30 per square foot to construct. This figure will be for a certain type of construction and certain materials.

The other way that one can discover building costs is to ask people who have built their own houses or have had their houses built for them. Again, it is important to realise that any building cost per square foot is for a particular type of construction, carried out in a particular way, in a particular place.

Relating the prices you unearth to your own budget figure is absolutely straightforward. You will immediately see whether your budget figure is realistic for the size and kind of house that you imagine making for yourself. Remember to take into account such items as hooking into the existing electrical, water and drainage services, Local Authority surcharges and so on. The site cost must not be forgotten about either! And remember the cost of furnishing the house needs to be considered *fig. 47*.

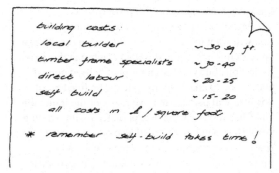

fig. 47: Relating known building prices to your own budget figure is absolutely straightforward. You will immediately see whether your budget figure is realistic for the size and kind of house that you imagine making for yourself.

This type of estimation is quite rough, though the exercise is vitally important. You will not alone realise that your building will cost money, but that it will have to be built either by you or by someone else. If your budget is unrealistic, you have a chance to rethink the project on paper before you go any further. Perhaps you can do with fewer rooms. Maybe you can shave a little off each space, thereby reducing your overall floor area. Or, you can plan to extend a basic house in three or four years when your finances will be better able to bear the financial strain. Alternatively, you can choose to carry out some of the work yourself, as a way of cutting costs.

In any event, this is a critical point in the design exercise. The relationship between the size and type of house you want must now be realistically related to your budget.

Your investigations of new houses, whether in the area in which you wish to build, or elsewhere, will reveal much. Conversation with self-builders, contractors and so on are also invaluable.

Freethinking

Once a realistic budget has been arrived at, the use of drawings has been appreciated and the first mock-ups have been made, the whole process of designing will be very much clearer. Like everything, practice will be needed to gain confidence and proficiency.

Your perception of what buildings and space are may change as you grasp the possibilities offered by this new knowledge. You may, in fact, wish to change many things in your Brief, to rethink certain spaces or even your whole approach.

An individual design is a very personal thing. You will want to get it all as right as you can, so that you can live happily in it. The keyword at this point is "responsibility." Designing your house yourself allows one to take responsibility. The freedom of this idea will perhaps remove many of the limitations and frustrations you have experienced with building designs up until now. It will also create a vast free space that you can roam in. This may be a little intimidating at first. It is essential to give yourself time. Time to look, time to think, time to change your mind. You cannot design a house in a rush. Well, you can, but it will have the rushed quality built into it and this will certainly be an unpleasant quality to live with.

It is time for taking stock. The project is underway and you know that you can do it. Give yourself the time and the space to think and feel the design all the way through. Go back carefully through the Brief and bring it up to date, changing the things that bother you.

Your files will now be growing. You will be accumulating photographs of buildings and spaces that please you. Your range of catalogues will be growing and you will have a strong sense of the things you are going to put into your house. You need to keep well organised. You should now have individual files for each space in your building, a cost file and so on.

Cost will, at this point, be a very critical factor in how the project progresses. It is vital that you begin investigations about the financing of the building. While you may gain assurance from a lending institution that a loan will be available to you, it is important to find out the conditions that may be attached to it.

Similarly, if you wish to take advantage of any grants that might be available to you, you should investigate the conditions attaching to these and the effect these are likely to have on your overall design.

Extensions To Existing Buildings

If you are designing an extension to an existing building, the procedure for mocking-up the spaces within the extension will be the same as for a new building. Similarly, the estimation of floor area and the cost calculation procedures will be the same.

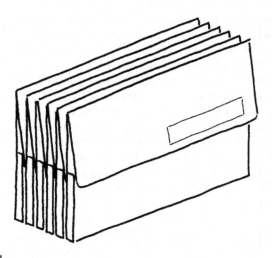

Sites

No mention of sites has been made so far, other than to mention their cost. In many ways a site can be a distraction when developing your ideas of the kind of house you want for yourself. Until you have become accustomed to making mock-ups and playing around with space, the implications of site should not be added to the design equation.

If you already own a site and you are preparing a design for it, the same approach is to be recommended. Many items have yet to be taken into consideration before the implications of the site are added to the design. What we are doing is designing the building from the inside out, allowing the design to grow outwards. Until this produces a firm design concept, the implications of the site should not be considered.

In the case of extensions to existing buildings, there will of course be an existing site, and, invariably, you will have some idea of where you wish your extension to be located relative to the existing structure. These factors can all be taken into account by surveying such a structure and by constructing a model of this structure. The procedure for this is described in the section entitled *'Surveying'*.

Summary

Make Mock-Ups of the Spaces included in your Brief.

Draw cross plans and cross sections of each space.

Estimate the overall floor area of your building extension.

Estimate your building costs.

Consider how your house will get built.

Review your Brief.

Organise your material and information.

15 Sheltermaker Design Programme
Surveying

If your project involves extending an existing building then you will need to survey that building in order to create an effective design. Techniques for this are described in the *Surveying* chapter. A method of making a scale model of a building is also described in this chapter. This is an essential exercise for those extending existing buildings as well as being a useful one for those becoming accustomed to techniques of measurement, drawing and modelmaking.

It is worth reading this part of the *Manual*, even if you think it has little direct relevance to your own project. You should, at this stage, be raising your awareness of buildings generally - looking at proportions, scale, natural lighting, materials, forms, layout and so on. The surveying information will allow you to do this more effectively and will inevitably lend assistance to progress on your own design path.

There is a wealth of further information in this part of the *Manual* focussed on other aspects of surveying buildings. 'Land Surveying' on page 153 will be of particular importance to those looking at potential building sites. This should be read in conjunction with the *Site Selection & Analysis* chapter on pages 197-210 in *Volume 2*.

Next: SDP16 - Understanding The Principles of Building Structures, page 174

More than any other subject, structure has the ability to strike fear into the heart

Surveying

Surveying is the investigation of land and buildings and the condition they are in. This is done by measurement and examination, and the information is recorded in drawings and words. This information can also be used to make scaled models of existing buildings.

Surveying activities can be divided into two broad categories – building surveying and land surveying.

A building survey covers all aspects of a building's construction, stability, condition and appearance, including its drainage, plumbing and electrical services. A further aspect of building surveying is the examination of the character of a building and of the quality of the spaces within it.

Land surveying involves measuring and examining land, levels, boundaries and vegetation.

Surveying existing buildings and closely examining the spaces within them will be good practice for those designing their own individual buildings. The production of plans, sections and elevations for an existing building, and the preparation of a scale model of that building, will also be of benefit to the designer. For those designing an extension to an existing building, the creation of a scale model of that building is essential.

Surveying Equipment

Very little is needed in the way of equipment for surveying. A reasonably long cloth/fibreglass wind-up tape is very useful, though not essential. This should be at least 10m long *fig. 1*.

A metal tape will also do the job, though over long distances these tend to bend. 5m is the longest metal tape you should try to use.

Survey notes are best recorded on plain, A4 size paper. Tracing paper of the same size is also useful. You will need a clipboard for leaning on, or a piece of plywood with a bulldog clip *fig. 2*. It is a good idea to use plenty of paper and to record different types of information on separate sheets. These should be clearly titled and numbered.

A fine felt tip marker is good for recording dimensions. A pencil might be preferred for drawing lines as errors can be easily erased. If pencil lines are initially used to outline a drawing, these lines can

then be gone over in felt tip pen to make them more legible.

You will also need someone to hold the end of the tape. A person who understands what you are doing will be best for this, so explain the process and make it a team effort. If one person calls out information and the other person writes it down, the survey notes will have a consistency to them. Remember that the information will be used to produce a report and drawings – make sure the information is clear and can be interpreted easily afterwards.

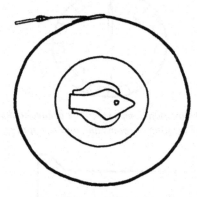

fig. 1: A reasonably long cloth/fibreglass wind-up tape is very useful for surveying. This should be at least 10m long.

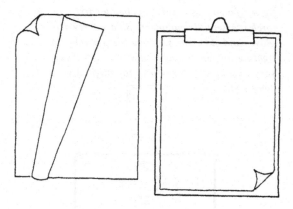

fig. 2: Survey notes are best recorded on plain, A4 size paper. Tracing paper of the same size is also useful. You will need a clipboard for leaning on, or a piece of plywood with a bulldog clip.

A direction compass will be needed to discover the orientation of rooms and outdoor spaces *fig. 3*.

If a condition survey is being carried out, a torch is essential equipment. So are screwdrivers, gloves and old clothes. If you are planning on investigating soil conditions, you will need a shovel at the very least for digging holes. You might also need some wellingtons *fig. 4*.

Photographs are invaluable for reference when surveys are being drawn up or reports are being prepared. When taking photographs, follow a logical sequence so that when you get your prints back you will know what you are looking at. The camera should have a flash attachment *fig. 5*.

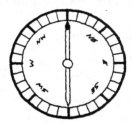

fig. 3: A direction compass will be needed to discover the orientation of rooms and outdoor spaces.

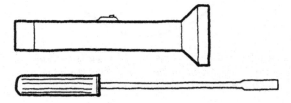

fig. 4: If a condition survey is being carried out, a torch is essential equipment. So are screwdrivers, gloves and old clothes. If you are planning on investigating soil conditions, you will need a shovel at the very least for digging holes. You might also need some wellingtons.

fig. 5: When taking photographs, follow a logical sequence so that when you get your prints back you will know what you are looking at. The camera should have a flash attachment.

Buildings with people or furniture in them are impossible to survey thoroughly. At the very least you need the building empty of people. Be prepared to shift things around, to lift carpets and poke into dark corners in your investigation.

For a building the size of a house you will need the best part of a day to carry out the survey work. This is all time well spent. If you acquire a building for your own use, you will spend a lot of time in it and you need to make sure beforehand that the building suits your needs. You must imagine the use to which you are going to put the spaces and look at it realistically. You must make it your own, get to know it and discover all the building's faults and merits. This is why it is important that the occupants, if any, are not present and why it is desirable to have the place empty of furniture and belongings.

If you are surveying a building that you already own or occupy for the purpose of designing an extension to it, you must be equally thorough in your investigations. It is very easy to assume that you are so familiar with the building that you do not need to measure it properly, or that you know exactly the condition it is in.

Building Surveying

Building surveying is carried out by taking measurements and notes, and the information gathered is converted into scaled drawings. The easiest way to become familiar with surveying buildings is to survey a building that you already know, from living or working in it.

Begin by sketching an outline of the entire area that is to be surveyed. If the building consists of more than one floor, begin by sketching out the ground floor area. The outline sketch should be made roughly proportional to what is to be surveyed and should fit comfortably on the page *fig. 6*.

fig. 6: Begin by sketching an outline of the entire area that is to be surveyed. If the building consists of more than one floor, begin by sketching out the ground floor area. The outline sketch should be made roughly proportional to what is to be surveyed and should fit comfortably on the page.

Select a room at one corner of the building and sketch the outline of the room onto the larger plan. The proportions of the space should be similar to those of the actual plan and all recesses, doors and windows should be shown *fig. 7*. When this has been done, move on to the next space and sketch out a plan of this, adjoining the first plan. Make sure to show the thickness of the wall between the two spaces. This is done by showing two parallel lines. Door openings will appear as gaps in these walls and the swing of the door is indicated by a quarter circle.

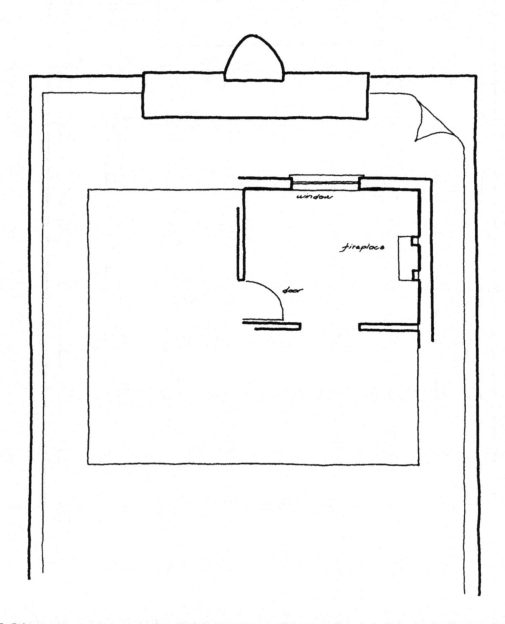

fig. 7: Select a room at one corner of the building and sketch the outline of the room onto the larger plan. The proportions of the space should be similar to those of the actual plan and all recesses, doors and windows should be shown.

Continue through all the spaces you wish to survey, sketching in the plans adjacent to each other *fig. 8*. If you make a mistake, simply erase this and draw fresh lines. If you run out of paper, try to continue on an adjoining sheet. External walls should be shown thicker than internal walls and, where windows occur in these outside walls, the window should be drawn in.

Sketching out a reasonable plan is a good start to making an accurate measured survey. Take your time with this, drawing in pencil which will allow you to correct any errors you might make. When the plan has been completed, the taking of measurements can begin.

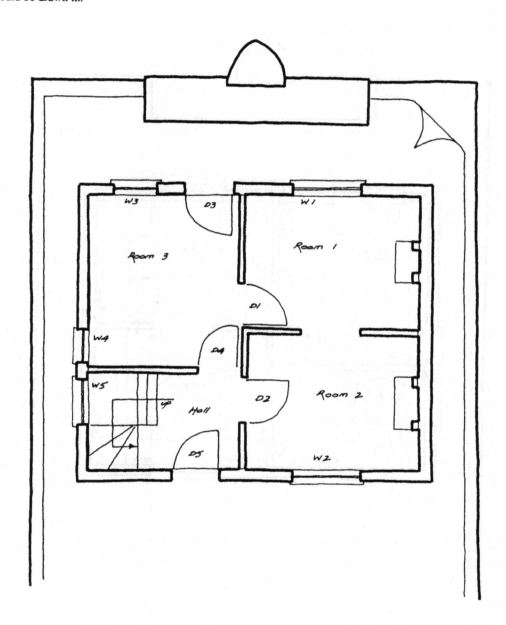

fig. 8: Continue through all the spaces you wish to survey, sketching in the plans adjacent to each other.

The easiest type of dimension to take is a 'running dimension'. A running dimension is taken in a straight line between two walls *fig. 9*. The points at which windows, doors or recesses occur on this line are read off from the measuring tape and written onto the survey sheet. Do this by first drawing a dimension line onto the survey sheet that reflects the line that the tape is being held on. Mark the dimension line where the measurement is being taken. These dimensions will be continuous, and will all relate back to the point where the tape is being held. A tape sufficiently long to stretch from wall to wall is needed to take running dimensions.

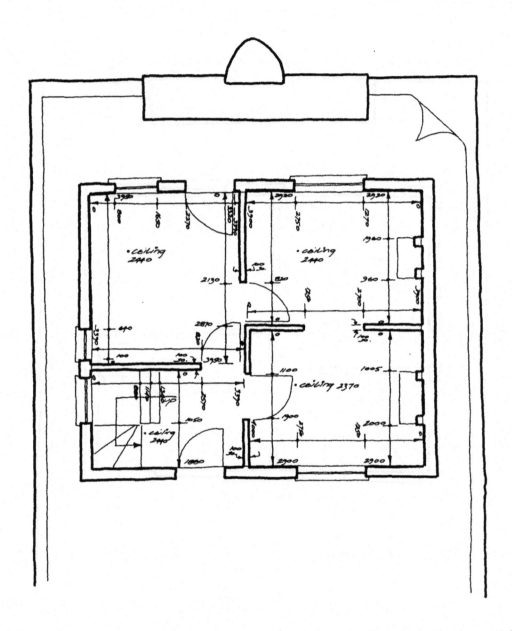

fig. 9: The easiest type of dimension to take is a 'running dimension'. A running dimension is taken in a straight line between two walls.

Another method of recording dimensions is to measure each item individually. Again a line is drawn on the plan to indicate where the measurement is being taken. Each dimension is then measured individually and the measurement written on the relevant part of the line *fig. 10*. If measuring in this way, an overall dimension should be taken on the same line. This should match the total of the individual measurements. Make sure that recesses such as are created by fireplaces are also measured.

Whichever method of recording dimensions is used, when the four sides of a room have been surveyed, diagonal measurements should be taken from corner to corner. These have the effect of acting as checks on the straight dimensions *fig. 11*. If an error has been made in reading off dimensions, when the survey is being drawn to scale, this error will manifest itself and can be corrected.

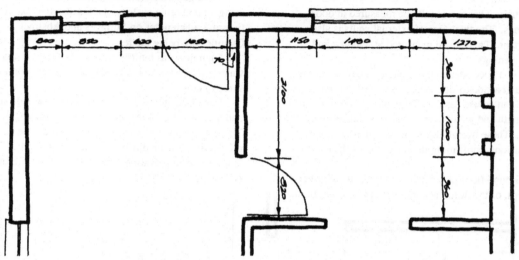

fig. 10: Another method of recording dimensions is to measure each item individually. Again a line is drawn on the plan to indicate where the measurement is being taken. Each dimension is then measured individually and the measurement written on the relevant part of the line.

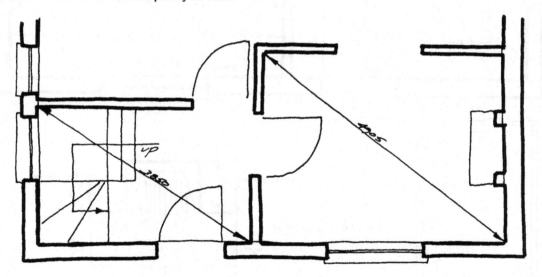

fig. 11: When the four sides of a room have been surveyed, diagonal measurements should be taken from corner to corner. These have the effect of acting as checks on the straight dimensions.

Information on heights must be included in the measured survey. The ceiling height should be noted, the sill and head height of the windows and the heights of the doors.

Where internal walls occur, it should be noted if they are solid or hollow. This can be discovered by knocking on them. A simple code, such as 'H' for hollow and 'So' for solid, is the easiest way to do this.

An indication of the thickness of walls is also important. This can usually be measured at door openings. The thickness of external walls is also important. This can be measured at window and door openings.

It is a good idea to try to get an internal front to back and a side to side measurement of the building. These can be used as check dimensions. Externally, the length and width of the house should be measured. These overall dimensions will act as check dimensions, confirming the thickness of the external walls.

Ground floor plans should indicate the number of steps, or the difference in level of the inside floor, level and the exterior ground level. This can be done at the outside doors.

It is not always possible to go back to a building that has been surveyed, so lots of dimensions and photographs are the order of the day.

Where there is a lot of detail in a small area, draw a plan of that area and measure it separately. Make sure you key this into the larger drawing fig. 12.

It is a good idea to indicate particular rooms by using a numbering system. This will prove extremely useful when notes on Surfaces and Abstract Qualities are being made.

Such items as built-in cupboards, sinks, baths, wash hand basins and WCs should be shown on the survey plans.

It is also a good idea to measure the outside sill and head heights of the ground floor windows. These will act as check dimensions and can be easily related to the same dimensions taken internally. This is useful when elevations and cross sections are likely to be made.

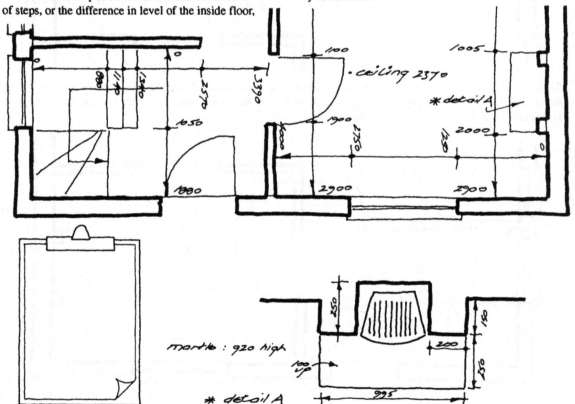

fig. 12: Where there is a lot of detail in a small area, draw a plan of that area and measure it separately. Make sure you key this into the larger drawing.

It is necessary for the drawing of cross sections to survey any attic space that exists. This is the worst part of surveying old buildings. Sometimes it is enough to simply measure the internal ridge height from inside the trapdoor. The width of the attic can be figured out from the survey plans where they show the width between the external walls *fig. 13*.

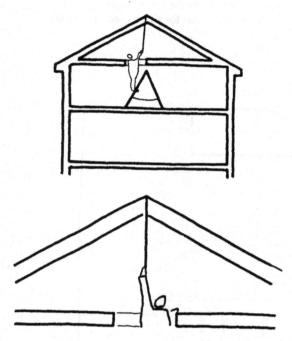

fig. 13: It is necessary for the drawing of cross sections to survey any attic space that exists. Sometimes it is enough to simply measure the internal ridge height from inside the trapdoor.

Surveying takes nothing more than practice to accomplish well. By surveying a building that you are considering buying, you will get to know it intimately. You will also end up with a set of drawings which will allow you to experiment with layouts or to consider where an extension might be located. If you are planning on making an extension to your existing dwelling, a measured survey will prove invaluable.

If two or more floors are being surveyed, a separate plan is made for each floor. In such cases the floor to floor heights should be measured and noted clearly. The easiest place to measure this is from the top of the stair landing down to the floor below *fig. 14*.

fig. 14: If two or more floors are being surveyed, a separate plan is made for each floor. In such cases the floor to floor heights should be measured and noted clearly. The easiest place to measure this is from the top of the stair landing down to the floor below.

Stairs appear on plans as a series of parallel lines *fig. 15*. A note should be made adjacent to this of the height of the step, called 'the riser', and the width of the step, called 'the going'. The number of risers should also be noted and the distance from the face of the first step to a wall or some other element that appears on the survey drawing. The width of the stairs should also be measured and the dimension noted.

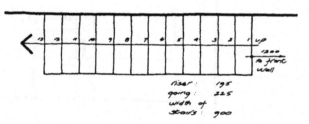

fig. 15: Stairs appear on plans as a series of parallel lines. A note should be made adjacent to this of the height of the step, called 'the riser', and the width of the step, called 'the going'. The number of risers should also be noted and the distance from the face of the first step to a wall or some other element that appears on the survey drawing. The width of the stairs should also be measured and the dimension noted.

Elevation Surveys

If elevations are being surveyed, the process is similar to that for plan surveys. A sketch elevation is drawn roughly proportional to the real thing *fig. 16*. The heights and widths of all windows and doors are then measured and the dimensions noted. The height of the roof eaves is also an important dimension. If the building is too high and the eaves cannot be reached from the ground, they can be measured from an upstairs window back down to the ground.

When the sketch elevation is drawn, pay particular attention to the roof. Note any chimneys or vent pipes coming through it. Note the position of gutters and downpipes.

When all this information is being transferred to scaled drawings, having a series of photographs for reference will make the job considerably easier.

Make elevations for all exposed sides of the house.

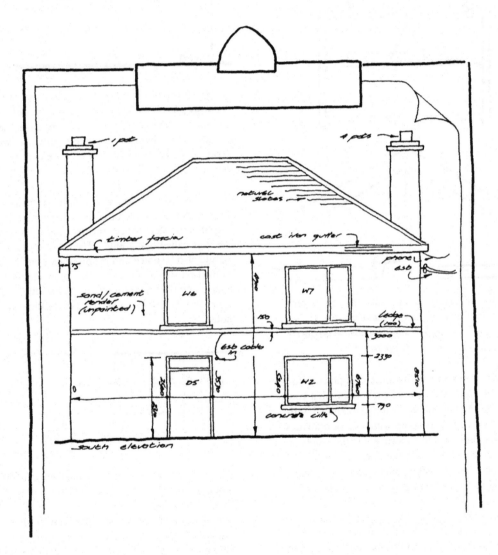

fig. 16: A sketch elevation is drawn roughly proportional to the real thing. The heights and widths of all windows and doors are then measured and the dimensions noted. The height of the roof eaves is also an important dimension.

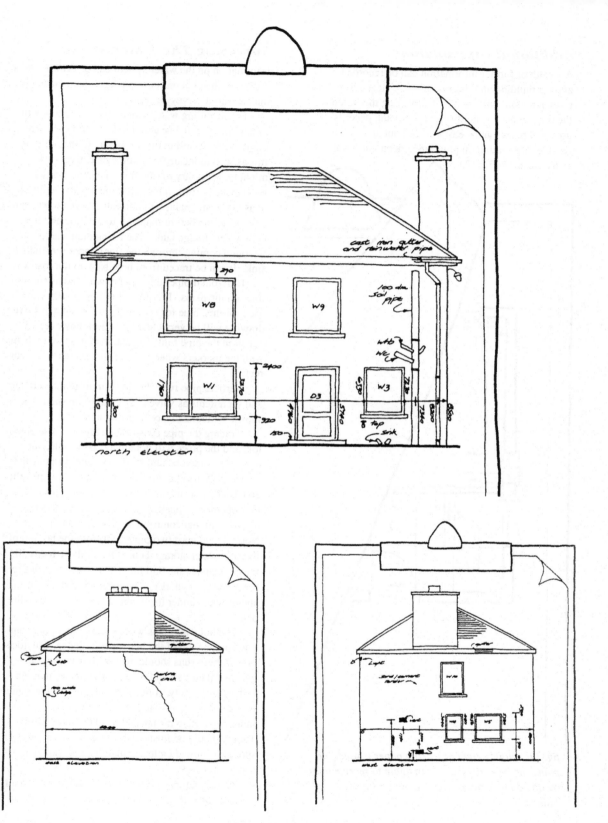

north elevation

cast iron gutter
and rainwater pipe

100 dia
soil pipe

W8

W9

W1

D3

W3

2400

920

150

8 tap
sink

north elevation

Additional Information

A wealth of further information can be recorded about a building and its condition. A clear system of room notation will assist in deciphering this when the time comes. If lightweight or tracing paper is used, the plans can be easily traced out again to receive information on plumbing, electrical installations and so on *fig. 17*.

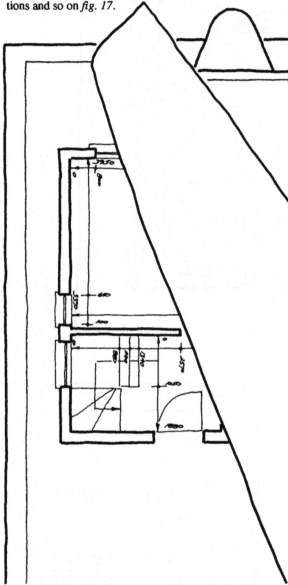

fig. 17: If lightweight or tracing paper is used, the plans can be easily traced out again to receive information on plumbing, electrical and drainage installations.

Surveying The Water System

Information on the water system can be drawn onto a tracing of the plan or plans that have been made for the measured survey *fig. 18*.

The incoming water supply to the building will usually be from the nearest road. A stop cock will normally exist to shut off the supply to the building. It is as well to locate this. Some detective work might be necessary to find this. The kitchen is a good place to start. This incoming supply, referred to as the rising main, will normally serve the kitchen cold water tap before rising up to the attic and the cold water storage tank. The rising main can often be found coming through the floor under the kitchen sink. It can be traced from here back to the roadway.

Horizontal pipe runs can be indicated as simple lines on the plans. If coloured felt tip markers are used for this, blue for cold and red for hot, the survey drawing will be very clear. It is best, however, to pencil in the pipe runs first and then to go over them with the markers when you are sure that they are correct.

Vertical pipe runs should be indicated by circles, and such items as valves, taps and so on should be shown symbolically, or by using notes.

Tracing the pipe runs is something of a detective job, and the pipes will not always be visible, but might be hidden behind skirtings, within floors and so on. The rising main usually rises up into the attic and discharges into a cold water storage tank. The tank should be checked, as well as the ballcock mechanism that controls the flow of water into it. Normally, at least two pipes exit from the bottom of the cold water storage tank. One of these feeds all the cold taps in the building. The other one runs to the hot water cylinder. The location of these pipes, and of the cylinder itself, should be drawn onto the plans.

The hot water taps will be fed from a pipe coming from the top of the hot water cylinder. The location of these runs should also be drawn onto the plans. All taps should be turned on to see that the water flows freely from them and to see if the water is clear. The taps should be left running for some time to ascertain the normal available pressure. Toilets should be flushed and, if there is a shower, it should be turned on to see that there is enough pressure in it *fig. 19*.

Notes on pipe condition, sizes and so on can all be made onto the survey drawings.

148

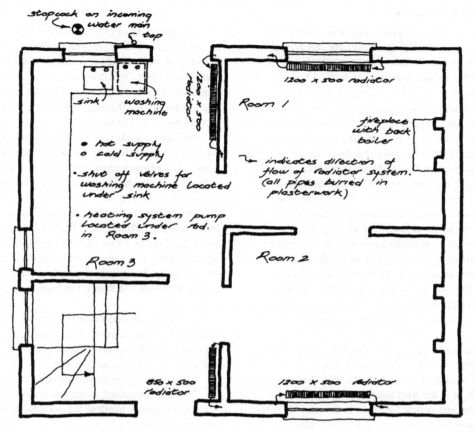

fig. 18: Information on the water system can be drawn onto tracings of the plans.

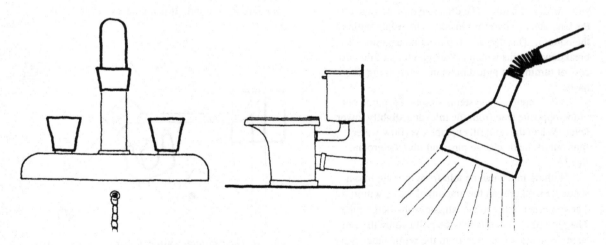

fig. 19: All taps should be turned on to see that the water flows freely from them and to see if the water is clear. The taps should be left running for some time to ascertain the normal available pressure. Toilets should be flushed, and if there is a shower, it should be turned on to see that there is enough pressure in it.

149

Surveying Drains

Surveying drains involves recording where and how used water leaves a building. Surveying and inspecting drains is no fun. In fact it's a horrible job, and because of this it often does not get done. There is no better way to confront the matter of waste than by examining a drainage system. Get properly equipped for the job – and properly dressed. Gloves will help and a heavy screwdriver or lever for prising up manhole covers. Wellingtons may also prove useful. The drainage system for any house comprises of a series of pipes that are connected to gullies, manholes and armstrong junctions *fig. 20*. Information on the size and location of these should be recorded onto a tracing of the ground floor plan *fig. 21*.

The covers on armstrong junctions and manholes should be lifted and the direction of the flow of water through them ascertained. This can be done by running taps, flushing toilets and so on. This information should be drawn onto a tracing of the ground floor plan, including notes on pipe condition, size and so on.

The drainage system should be followed to see where it leads to. This will be either to a public drain or to a septic tank. Follow the system to the septic tank, or to the road boundary where there is a public drain, and sketch the run onto the plan. If there is not enough room on the A4 sheet, make another plan.

Septic tanks are basically tanks that hold all the liquids and solids that go into your toilet and down your sinks and baths. The drainage pipe carries it to the tank and discharges it inside. The solids settle to the bottom. Through anaerobic action a natural breakdown begins which is the beginning of the process of turning the putrid mess into something less nasty.

Older septic tank systems simply discharge out of the opposite side from the inlet at a slightly lower level. When the tank fills up, the overflow water runs out of the discharge pipe and into the ground *fig. 22*.

Nothing much can be told from looking into a septic tank other than the amount of waste within it. The important thing to investigate is the outlet pipe. The ground around this may be polluted by the constant discharge of sewage from the septic tank. Very little breakdown occurs within the tank itself, it is when the 'sludge' goes into the ground that purification occurs.

For septic tanks to work properly, they need to be connected to proper percolation areas. Percolation areas consist of a series of perforated underground pipes that distribute the discharge from a septic tank over a wide area of ground. By doing this it is hoped that the natural ability of the earth to recycle the waste can be utilised.

Percolation areas take up a lot of space and their location has to conform to the local authority regulations. If an existing septic tank is to have a new percolation area attached to it, make sure that there is enough room to fit it in.

Regulations to do with drainage systems are quite stringent. Putting in a clean and efficient system should not be a case of Local Authority insistence. Rather, it is a matter for those using the system to satisfy themselves that their waste is being properly disposed of after it has been flushed out of sight.

The whole question of what goes into the septic tank is important. Unnatural substances, such as disinfectants and detergents, will upset the natural breakdown of organic matter within the system.

Septic tanks need to be desludged every year or so. The tank, therefore, should be reasonably accessible to a roadway to allow the desludging truck to service the tank.

It is usual for the rainwater system to be kept separate from the so called 'foul waste'. It is usual to run the rainwater to a soakaway, where it percolates back into the ground. It is not necessary to locate this.

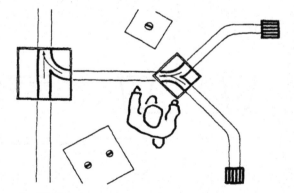

fig. 20: The drainage system for any house comprises of a series of pipes that are connected to gullies. manholes and armstrong junctions.

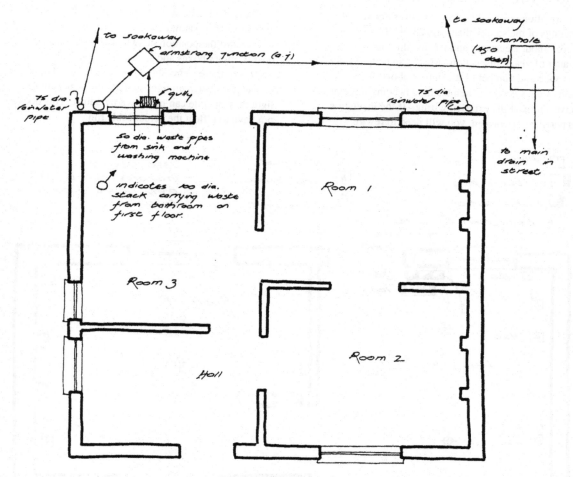

to sookaway

armstrong junction (a.j.)

to sookaway

manhole (450 deep)

75 dia rainwater pipe

gully

75 dia rainwater pipe

to main drain in street

50 dia. waste pipes from sink and washing machine

indicates 100 dia. stack carrying waste from bathroom on first floor.

Room 1

Room 3

Room 2

Hall

fig. 21: *Information on the size and location of pipes, gullies, manholes and armstrong junctions should be recorded onto a tracing of the ground floor plan.*

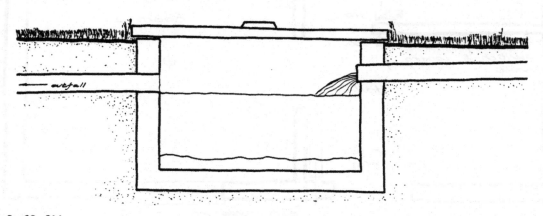

outfall

fig. 22: *Older septic tank systems simply discharge out of the opposite side from the inlet at a slightly lower level. When the tank fills up, the overflow water runs out of the discharge pipe and into the ground.*

Surveying The Electrical System

Information on the electrical system is drawn onto tracings of the survey plans *fig. 23*. Unless you know about electricity and wiring, this survey is a matter of visual inspection. Much can be told from the state and number of the outlets about the condition of the system. When the attic is being inspected, have a look at the exposed wiring. If the insulation is perished or cracked, you will need to rewire.

Check at the fuse board. If the panel is old looking then so is the system.

Record the position of switches, sockets, fuse boards, meter boxes and so on, using symbols. The heights of these items should be noted also. The connections between light switches and the actual light they operate can be shown by a line. This does not have to reflect the actual cable run.

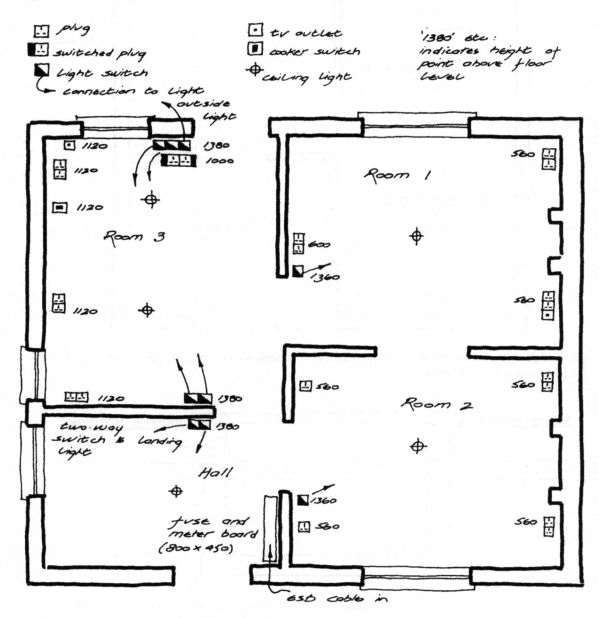

fig. 23: Information on the electrical system is drawn onto tracings of the survey plans.

Land Surveying

Land surveying involves measuring the ground that a new or proposed building sits on. In the case of an existing building, a land survey will cover all the ground from the walls of the house to the boundaries. Land surveying is concerned with areas and levels, and the information is recorded in plan form.

It is of great help to have an Ordnance Map of the property being surveyed. This will show the boundaries and the overall shape of the site *fig. 24*. Using a scale rule the lengths of the boundaries can be measured from the Ordnance Map and checked on site with a tape. A cloth tape at least 10m long will be needed for this.

Original Scale	Scale Required	% Enlargement
1:1000	1:500	200
1:1250	1:500	250
1:1250	1:1000	125
1:2500	1:500	500
1:2500	1:1000	250
1:2500	1:1250	200
1:5000	1:500	1000
1:5000	1:1000	500

fig. 25: The amount of enlargement needed to bring an Ordnance Map up to a desired scale will depend on the original scale of the map.

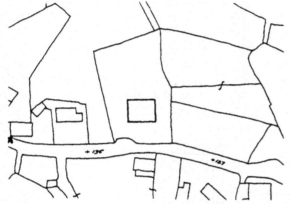

fig. 24: It is of great help to have an Ordnance Map of the property being surveyed. This will show the boundaries and the overall shape of the site.

Ordnance Maps cover large areas, and the site you are concerned with will appear quite small on the map. If enlargements are made of the portion of the map that contains the site, you end up with a more workable size of drawing for site measurements to be written onto. A half acre site will fit onto an A3 sheet at 1:500 scale. The amount of enlargement needed to bring an Ordnance Map up to this scale will depend on the original scale of the map *fig. 25*. Maps enlarged in this way cannot be relied upon to be as accurate as the originals they come from. Because of this, caution needs to be exercised in reading distances off enlarged maps. Original maps, on the other hand, are extremely accurate, despite the fact of their size. Site dimensions can oftentimes be found on the Title Deeds to a particular piece of land.

As with the internal building survey, check dimensions should be taken, in the form of diagonals when site dimensions are being taken *fig. 26*. When only a 10m tape is available, it is a good idea to have a few wooden skewers handy to push into the ground when you run out of tape. These will mark the end of the tape run and will make the job of totalling up the measured distances fairly easy to do.

When the boundaries are being measured, it is a good idea to record the type and size of walls, fences, trees etc. that occur along them. Quite a lot can be told from the trees, shrubs and plants that are growing on a property. If the trees are stunted and leaning over, for example, the wind has made them that way. Such evidence will tell you much about the local climate affecting the site.

Surveying is information gathering and it is as well to be thorough and to record as much information as clearly as possible. Surveying will also serve to familiarise one with a particular piece of land, to examine it intimately and consequently to get to know it very well.

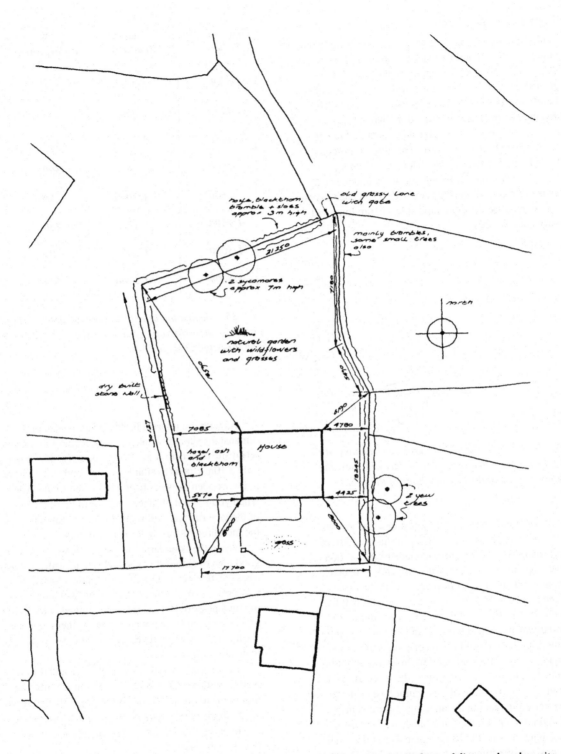

fig. 26: As with the internal building survey, check dimensions should be taken, in the form of diagonals, when site dimensions are being taken.

Surveying Levels

One of the most important aspects of surveying is levels. Ground levels are critical in many building situations. If the site for a new building is not flat, or almost flat, a survey must be carried out. If a house is to be built on, say, a south facing slope, then the angle of the slope will have to be discovered before an appropriate design can be made *fig. 27*. Levels are also important where drains have to be laid.

The normal way of ascertaining ground levels is with a surveyors level. This piece of equipment is basically a telescope that sits on a tripod. The telescope can be made to sit exactly level on this tripod. By viewing a graduated 'staff' through the telescope, the level of the ground in various places on the site can be figured out *fig. 28*. An imaginary grid is usually used for this and readings are taken at the various points on the grid and noted. The difference in the reading from one grid point to another represents the difference in level that exists in the ground. This information can be used to draw a contour map and site cross sections *fig. 29*.

Using a surveyor's level and a staff is a job for an experienced surveyor. If the site is particularly hilly or there is likely to be difficulty connecting into existing drains, the expense of having a survey carried out will be worthwhile.

fig. 27: Ground levels are critical in many building situations. If the site for a new building is not flat, or almost flat, a survey must be carried out.

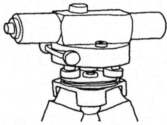

fig. 28: The normal way of ascertaining ground levels is with a surveyor's level. This piece of equipment is basically a telescope that sits on a tripod. The telescope can be made to sit exactly level on this tripod. By viewing a graduated 'staff' through the telescope, the level of the ground in various places on the site can be figured out.

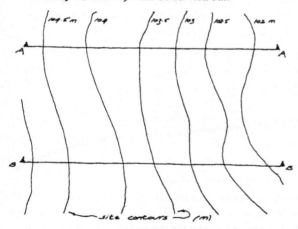

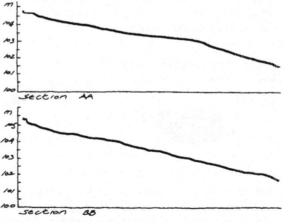

fig. 29: The information gathered from a level survey can be used to draw a contour map and site cross sections.

155

If an Ordnance sheet is examined, it will be found that levels are shown along roadways and, occasionally, a Bench Mark will be indicated against the face of a building *fig. 30*. These levels all relate to a fixed point – usually the sea level somewhere in the country. This point is known as the Ordnance Datum. It is normal for a professional surveyor to relate the levels he surveys on a site to the Ordnance Datum, for the sake of clarity and consistency. If this cannot be done, a convenient fixed point will be chosen on the site and a Temporary Bench Mark made. The top of a gatepost or some other permanent fixed object is normally used for this. This Temporary Bench Mark should be clearly indicated, both on the drawings and on the site, so that it can easily be located *fig. 31*.

If a level of 100m is given to the Temporary Bench Mark, all the other levels on the site can be related to this. This allows further surveying and design work to match into what has already been done. For example, the finished floor levels of a new design can be set to relate to this fixed point.

A simple alternative to a professional survey can be carried out without the use of a surveyor's level. This involves using a line and a spirit level. As with the normal survey, two people will be needed to carry it out. If a strong line is stretched between two points above the ground and the line is made level, the distance from the line to the ground can be measured and the slope of the ground ascertained *fig. 32*. If an appropriate grid is first marked out over the area to be levelled, the job will be made much easier.

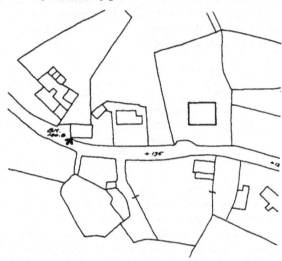

fig. 30: If an Ordnance sheet is examined it will be found that levels are shown along roadways and, occasionally, a Bench Mark will be indicated against the face of a building.

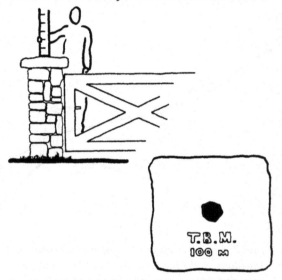

fig. 31: A Temporary Bench Mark should be clearly indicated, both on the drawings and on the site, so that it can easily be located.

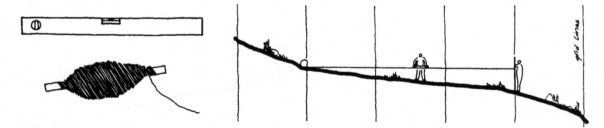

fig. 32: A simple alternative to a professional survey can be carried out without the use of a surveyor's level. This involves using a line and a spirit level. If a strong line is stretched between two points above the ground and the line is made level, the distance from the line to the ground can be measured and the slope of the ground ascertained.

Soil Survey

It may be necessary to discover the nature of the soil on a site, for a number of reasons. For example, when a septic tank or percolation area is being installed, you will need to find out the ability of the soil to absorb moisture. If building work is to be carried out, it has to be determined if foundations can be dug easily and there is no rock in the way.

Digging a deep hole will tell a lot about the soil and will allow simple tests to be carried out *fig. 33*.

Sun Survey

Every room in a building that is being surveyed should be checked to see if it gets direct sun into it or not. A compass can be used to check this *fig. 34*. Rooms that do not get any sun have a dreary quality that is hard to do anything about.

Also, check the outdoor spaces to see if they are sunny and during what part of the day the sun shines on them, winter and summer. Check whether the building is overshadowed by other buildings or trees.

This information can be drawn onto tracings of the survey plans.

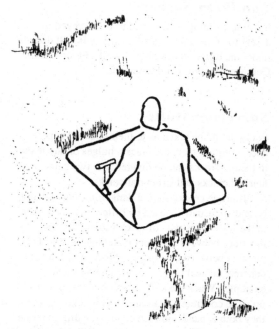

fig. 33: Digging a deep hole will tell a lot about the soil on a site and will allow simple tests to be carried out.

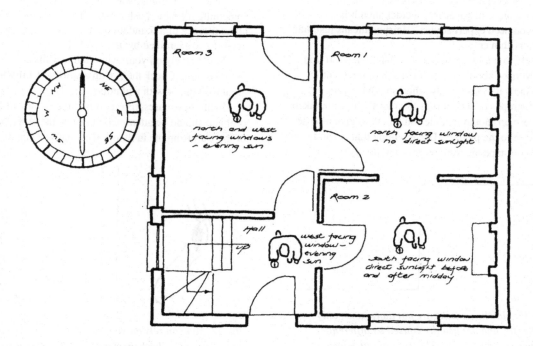

fig. 34: A compass can be used to check the amount of sun that any space is likely to get during the day.

Condition Surveys

Existing buildings often need to be surveyed to assess their condition. Such a survey is best done under the different headings – Walls, Floors, Roof, Ceilings, Windows and Doors etc.

Surveying Walls

Walls should be noted as to their outward appearance, noting if there are cracks, bulges or any leaning in them. Cracks can be divided into two categories, hairline cracks and structural cracks.

Hairline cracks are not dangerous, only unsightly, and are usually caused by differential movement in the wall. This type of crack usually occurs at junctions between different materials *fig. 35*. The junction between the concrete blocks in a wall and a concrete or steel lintel over a window is a good example. When the sun shines on the wall it heats up. The concrete blocks and the lintel heat up, but they both expand and then contract at different rates, tending to pull at each other ever so slightly. When the junction is covered up by plaster or render, the covering material will be touching both materials and will itself be pulled, and will thereby crack.

Cracks can lead to damp penetration. If you can shove a piece of paper into a crack then it is too big and you need expert advice. Hairline means just that – a very thin crack.

Photographs again are very handy here. If you are worried about a crack, take a photograph of it and show it to somebody who can advise you. Photographs of such things as cracks which are taken in close up should include some item to give a sense of scale to the picture. Use anything that is handy, like your tape measure or your torch *fig. 36*.

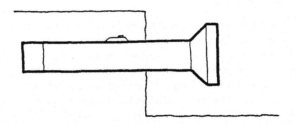

fig. 36: Photographs of such things as cracks which are taken in close up should include some item to give a sense of scale to the picture. Use anything that is handy, like your tape measure or your torch.

Structural cracks are a different matter altogether. These oftentimes run vertically down a wall but sometimes horizontally too. These type of faults are indicative of a failure in the structure. Whether a particular crack is dangerous or not is dependent on many things – what caused the crack in the first place, if it is getting progressively worse or not, and so on. All structural cracks should be looked at by an expert, either a structural engineer or a reliable builder. Again, photographs of the offending item are useful for this.

Leaning and bulging are usually caused by something trying to push a wall out or the failure or non existence of a foundation. This type of problem needs to be examined by an expert also.

You can rely on your eye to tell if walls are plumb or not. Check them with a spirit level if you are uncertain, or with a plumbob *fig. 37*.

In all these cases, trying to find the cause of the problem should be attempted. Look at the other side of the wall from the fault and see what you can discover.

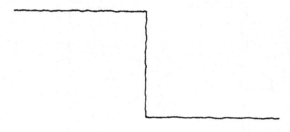

fig. 35: Hairline cracks are not dangerous, only unsightly, and are usually caused by differential movement in the wall. This type of crack usually occurs at junctions between different materials.

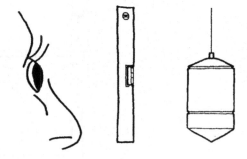

fig. 37: You can rely on your eye to tell if walls are plumb or not. Check them with a spirit level if you are uncertain, or with a plumbob.

Dampness is also a thing to look out for when surveying walls. Feeling the internal surface of a wall will give a reasonable indication if there is dampness present. This will likely be low down on the wall and will be caused by ground based moisture being drawn up by capillary action. Old buildings are particularly prone to this problem. If dampness in a wall is severe, some deterioration will be evident on the internal plasterwork. The plaster will be discoloured and flaky on the surface. Loose wallpaper is a sure giveaway. Polystyrene insulation is an indication that there is a dampness problem with the wall and an attempt has been made to rectify it. If a wall has been 'dry-lined', that is, the internal surfaces of the external walls have had timber studding and plasterboard put against them, the condition of the solid wall should be checked. You can tell a studded out external wall by the hollow sound it makes when you knock on it. Dry lining is not always carried out as an answer to dampness, but it is better to check. Finding a place to check may be a problem without causing some damage to the dry lining.

Water penetration may also cause dampness in outside walls. This can be caused by rainwater seeping through cracks or by seepage through the wall. Such dampness will occur in patches on the internal surface. Window and door openings in external walls are vulnerable to damp penetration and should be thoroughly checked.

The type and condition of internal and external wall finishes should also be noted clearly *fig. 38.*

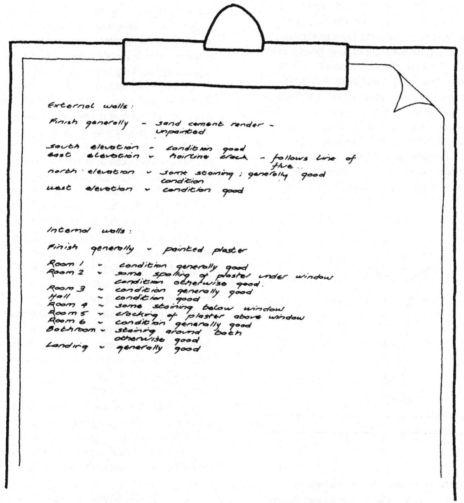

fig. 38: The type and condition of internal and external wall finishes should be noted clearly.

Surveying Floors

Ground floors are the most vulnerable floors in a building. In older buildings, especially houses, these may be of timber construction. The condition of such a floor can be visually assessed for signs of decay. You may have to lift carpets or other floor covering to do this.

A useful check as to the 'soundness' of timber floors can be carried out by standing in the centre of the floor and jumping up and down on it *fig. 39*. If the floor is 'sound', it will reverberate like a drum. If it is unsound, it will be dull and non-resonant. This will be the case if the floor has been affected by rot. Ground floors are more vulnerable to decay than upper floors because they are closer to the ground. If there is rising damp in the walls, it may affect the floor where it touches the wall. Check the outside of the building to see if there are vents in it *fig. 40*. These allow air to pass under the floor to ventilate the timber. If they are not there or have been partially covered up, there may be a problem of rot in the floor. Again, if you suspect that a problem exists, pursue your investigations until you are satisfied you have discovered all you can, then seek expert advice – an expert is a person who can answer your questions satisfactorily. Concrete floors need to be checked for dampness and cracking.

Upper floors are normally made of timber. Check these for soundness by jumping on them.

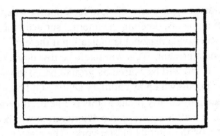

fig. 40: In a building with a timber ground floor check the outside of the building to see if there are vents in it. These allow air to pass under the floor to ventilate the timber.

Surveying Roofs

Roofs should be inspected inside and out. The outside inspection should note if the ridge is straight and the type and condition of the roof covering *fig. 41*. If there is sagging anyplace in the roof it indicates a problem. The cause of such sagging should be discovered by checking inside the roof.

Chimneys should be noted as to their condition also. This inspection can be carried out from the ground on all sides of the building. Here, again, a photographic record is invaluable.

The internal inspection of the roof is a messy business. Access can usually be had via a trapdoor. A lot of attics can be gotten into without a step ladder. It is never as easy to get out however! Be careful doing this. You are on unfamiliar territory and you may be alone. Bring something safe to stand on.

Be careful to walk only on top of the ceiling joists. Rafters need to be checked all along their length, though the most vulnerable point is at the junction of the rafter and the outside wall. This is the most difficult place to get at. A torch should be used to make this inspection. If any woodworm holes or severe discoloration of the wood is discovered, a problem exists. Fungus or obvious decay in the rafters are problems too. Check all over the attic, especially where the chimney goes through it. Check the roofing felt for tears or evidence of damp penetration. This is a detective job and care should be taken with it. Draughts from under the eaves should never be regarded as a problem. This is necessary to keep the roof timbers ventilated. If the attic is insulated the insulation should not hamper this air flow.

Ceiling joists should be inspected as to their condition also.

fig. 39: A useful check as to the 'soundness' of timber floors can be carried out by standing in the centre of the floor and jumping up and down on it.

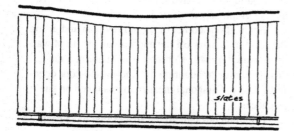

fig. 41: The outside inspection of any roof should note if the ridge is straight and the type and condition of the roof covering.

Surveying Ceilings

Ceilings should be visually inspected for signs of sagging, cracking or staining. Cracks at the junctions of ceilings and walls are normal and are not a problem. They are caused by differential movement.

Surveying Windows And Doors

Windows, especially timber windows, need to be checked to see what condition they are in. The soundness of the wood can checked by knocking on it. If it sounds dull, try pushing a small screwdriver into the frame. If the wood is rotten, the tip of the screwdriver will penetrate it quite easily. Paint is also a good indicator of condition. If the paint is flaked, chances are water has gotten into the wood and possibly set up decay.

Metal windows need to be checked for rust and their ability to open and close easily. The ability of all types of windows to open and close easily should be checked.

Modern uPVC windows should be checked for signs of discoloration. The welded corner joints should not have any gaps or holes in them. If there is water penetration, the steel core may have started to rust.

If there is a tendency to condensation, the internal frames and the sills of the windows will show signs of it. Any accumulated mould and dirt on the frames and sills means that there is a tendency to condensation.

All internal doors should be thoroughly checked for soundness and general condition. Try opening and closing them and see if the locks work.

Surveying Fireplaces

Fireplaces should be examined to assess their condition. Check the firebreasts for signs of cracking or staining. Evidence of either of these conditions is an indication that there has been a major chimney fire and that the chimney requires major repair work.

A lighted paper or papers set in a fireplace will also give a good idea if the draught is good on the fire.

The flues of woodburning stoves and ranges are more difficult to inspect. Again, excessive staining or any cracking of walls enclosing the flues are cause for concern.

Abstract Surveying

One aspect of surveying existing buildings that is rarely carried out is the examination of intangibles. These might be collectively described as the feelings within a building. If you are considering buying a building for your own use, it is important to become aware of the residual feelings within it that you will be buying as well.

There is no methodology for this investigation, other than to say that one should take your time doing it. Look into all the dark corners, under the stairs and in all cupboards and kitchen units. Buildings respond well to care. If a building has not been cared for, or cared about, it will appear neglected.

It is as well to carry out this aspect of the survey work without taking measurements or notes. You need to rely on your senses.

Try walking down the road from the building and approaching it as would a visitor. What impression does it give? Does it need a paint job? Do you like the appearance of the building or do you want to change it?

By looking at a building thoroughly in this way, you can honestly decide if it suits your needs or not.

Drawing Up A Plan Survey

When a survey has been completed, the dimensional information can be used to create scaled drawings. These are especially useful if an extension is to be made to an existing building. For those interested in creating an individual house design, the creation of scaled drawings of an existing building will be an invaluable exercise.

The equipment needed for this is as outlined in the Section entitled *Drawings and Models*. Scaled drawings should be made directly onto Metric graph paper or onto an A4 sheet of tracing paper with a graph paper underlay. An A4 size sheet will accommodate a plan size of up to 10 x 14m, drawn at 1:50 scale. This will suffice for most domestic buildings.

If the building you have surveyed is larger than this, use A3 graph paper.

Begin at one corner of the survey plan and, using the scale rule, mark off the appropriate length of wall as measured *fig. 42*. Complete one space at a time, paying particular attention to window and door openings. Use the diagonal measurements taken on site as checks.

Continue through all the spaces that have been surveyed. It is very important that wall thicknesses are shown correctly *fig. 43*. The benefit of taking lots of dimensions will be realised as the plan develops.

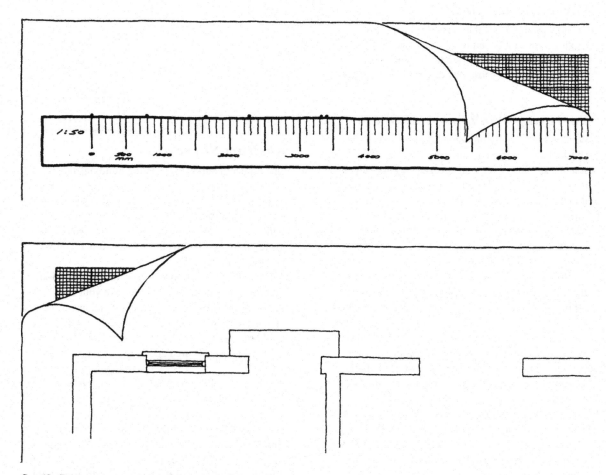

fig. 42: Begin at one corner of the survey plan and, using the scale rule, mark off the appropriate length of wall as measured. Complete one space at a time, paying particular attention to window and door openings. Use the diagonal measurements taken on site as checks.

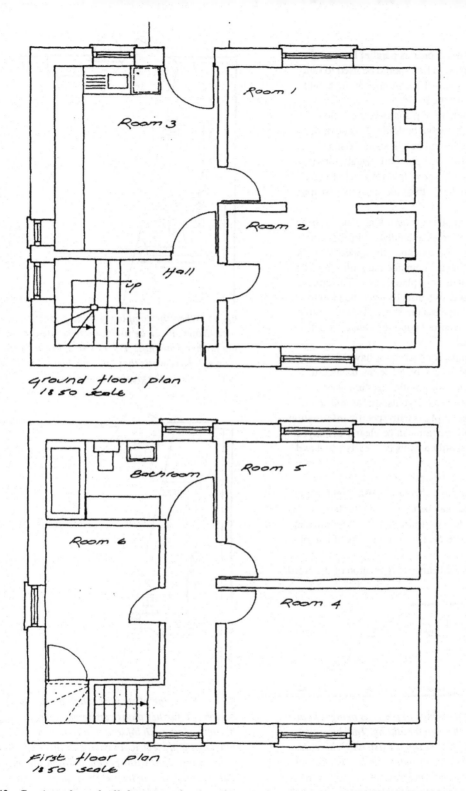

Room 1

Room 3

Room 2

Hall

up

Ground floor plan
18 50 scale

Bathroom

Room 5

Room 6

Room 4

First floor plan
18 50 scale

fig. 43: Continue through all the spaces that have been surveyed. It is very important that wall thicknesses are shown correctly.

Steps and stairs appear as parallel lines on the drawings. An arrowed line should be used to indicate which direction is 'Up'. A note of the height of the riser should also be made.

It is usual to think of plans as being a kind of horizontal slice through a building, 1m above the floor *fig. 44*. Where full height stairs exist, and where this is shown on a plan, it is usual to 'fade out' the stairs as they rise above this 1m level. In effect, this allows the underneath of the stairs to also appear on the plan.

When the complete ground floor plan has been drawn, it can be used as a template for producing further drawings. For example, the upper floor plan will have walls that are coincidental with some of the walls on the ground floor plan *fig. 45*. The upper floor plan can be drawn directly over the ground floor plan by using a tracing sheet. This can either be a sheet of greaseproof paper or a sheet of conventional tracing paper.

When the plans for each floor have been completed, further plans can be made, by tracing, to accommodate such information as dimensions, plumbing and electrical layouts, drains and so on *fig. 46*. By creating plans with specific information on them, this information can be clearly displayed. Such drawings should always be clearly titled and numbered.

Site plans will be drawn either to 1:100 or 1:200 scale. Again, a sheet of Metric graph paper and tracing paper can be used to create the drawing. Information on levels, drains and landscaping can be included on site plans or on tracings of site plans *fig. 47*.

All plans should carry an indication of the North point.

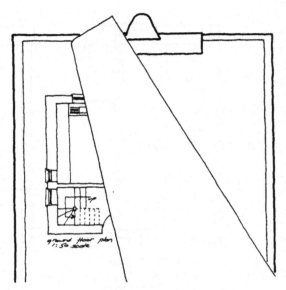

fig. 45: *When the complete ground floor plan has been drawn, it can be used as a template for producing further drawings. For example, the upper floor plan will have walls that are coincidental with some of the walls on the ground floor plan.*

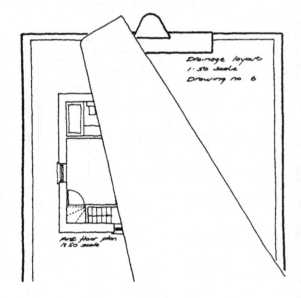

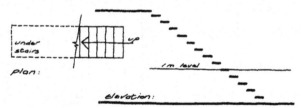

fig. 44: *It is usual to think of plans as being a kind of horizontal slice through a building, 1m above the floor. Where full height stairs exist, and where this is shown on a plan, it is usual to 'fade out' the stairs as they rise above this 1m level. In effect, this allows the underneath of the stairs to also appear on the plan.*

fig. 46: *When the plans for each floor have been completed, further plans can be made, by tracing, to accommodate such information as dimensions, plumbing and electrical layouts, drains and so on. By creating plans with specific information on them, this information can be clearly displayed. Such drawings should always be clearly titled and numbered.*

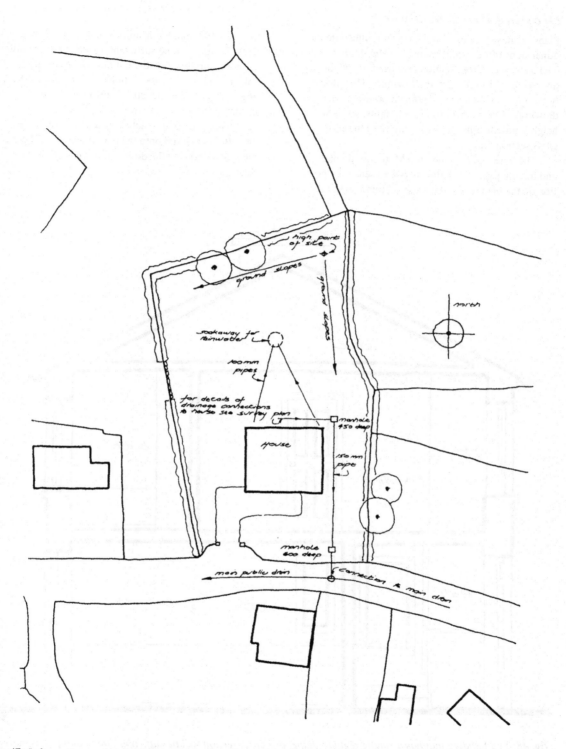

fig. 47: Information on levels, drains and landscaping can be included on site plans or on tracings of site plans. All plans should carry an indication of the North point.

Drawing Cross Sections

Plans are never enough on their own to illustrate the dimensions of Length, Breadth and Height that enclose space. Cross sections are used to add the dimension of Height to plan drawings. The information on these Heights will be noted on the survey drawings. Ceiling heights, door heights, window heights, attic heights and so on are used to create cross section drawings.

These are again made onto Metric graph paper and tracing paper. The first step is to select the position on the plan where the cross section is best taken.

In a building that has a simple regular shape, one cross section will be sufficient *fig. 48.* If the building is more complex, however, it may be necessary to take two or more cross sections. Cross section drawings also allow an elevation view of walls to be made.

The position at which cross sections are taken are always marked onto the plan drawings. These lines also indicate the direction of view of the cross section.

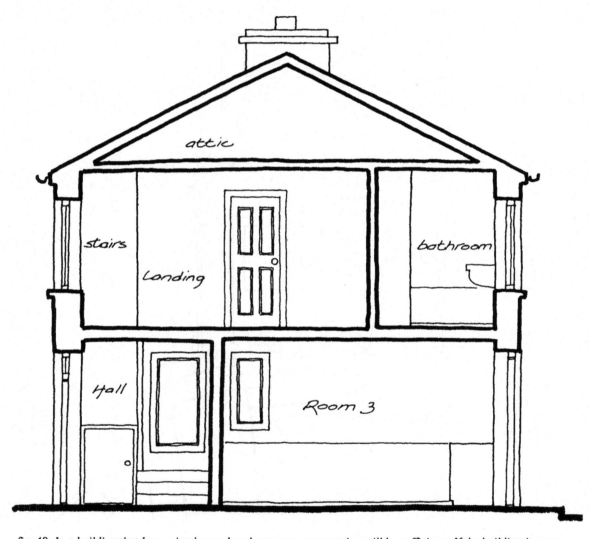

fig. 48: In a building that has a simple regular shape, one cross section will be sufficient. If the building is more complex, however, it may be necessary to take two or more cross sections. Cross section drawings also allow an elevation view of walls to be made.

166

Drawing Elevations

Elevation drawings are made onto Metric graph and tracing paper also. The dimensional information from the survey drawings is used to create these. Notes on materials, finishes, rainwater pipes and so on can all be included on elevation drawings *fig. 49.*

It is usual to designate elevation drawings by naming them North, South, East and West.

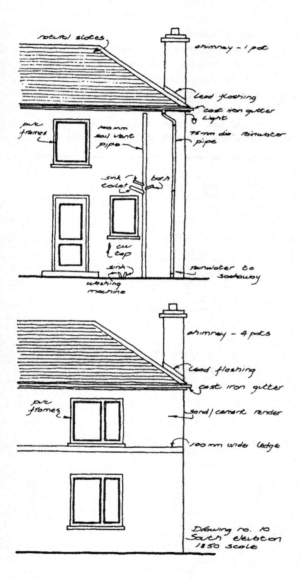

fig. 49: Notes on dimensions, materials, finishes, rainwater pipes and so on can all be included on elevation drawings.

Reproducing Drawings

The easiest way to make copies of plans, sections and elevations is to photocopy them. Photocopies of up to A3 size can be obtained on most machines *fig. 50.*

It should be remembered that copies of drawings using photocopiers are not always accurate. Because of this, one needs to be careful when measuring a photocopied scale drawing. To overcome this problem it is a good idea to have some measurements on every original drawing or, alternatively, notated vertical and horizontal scales that can be checked for accuracy.

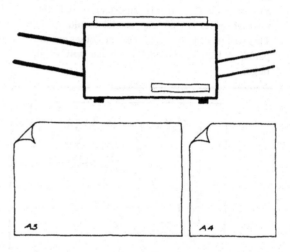

fig. 50: The easiest way to make copies of plans, sections and elevations is to photocopy them. Photocopies of up to A3 size can be obtained on most machines.

Percentage enlargement =

$$\frac{\text{Dimension required}}{\text{Original dimension}} \times 100$$

Percentage reduction =

$$\frac{\text{Original dimension}}{\text{Dimension required}} \times 100$$

Calculation of photocopier enlargement and reduction ratios.

Making A Scale Model

Even the most information laden drawings will not convey the three-dimensional quality of space. To gain a sense of the space enclosed by the walls and floors of a building, or to see the shape and form of a building, a model has to be made of it. This can be done quite simply. The equipment and materials required for this are outlined in the Section entitled *Drawings and Models*.

Scaled plans, sections and elevations of the building will also be needed. If these are to 1:50 scale, the internal spaces will be quite small and difficult to see. The overall model, however, will be of a manageable size. If it is important to study the internal spaces, a 1:20 scale model should be made. This will require that 1:20 scale drawings are prepared. A 1:20 scale model of a house will be quite large.

Begin by making copies of the plans and all the elevations of the building. Paste the ground floor plan onto a sheet of reasonably thick card – say 2mm. Trim this to the outside face of the wall *fig. 51*. Stick this onto a large sheet of card. The large sheet of card will represent the ground surrounding the building, so locate the plan as appropriate on this.

If the ground floor of the building has changes of level – for example a portion that is two or three steps different from the rest – the plan card should be cut where this change of level occurs *fig. 52*. Then, the two cards should be stuck down independently with the higher floor level being made higher by appropriately sized packing pieces.

Measure off the length of one of the internal walls on the plan – it helps to have a second copy of the plan for this, especially as the model making gets

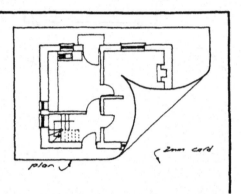
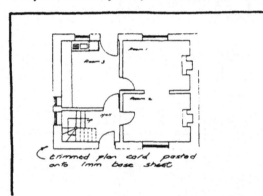

fig. 51: Begin the model by pasting a copy of the ground floor plan onto a sheet of reasonably thick card – say 2mm. Trim this to the outside face of the wall. Stick this onto a large sheet of 1mm thick card.

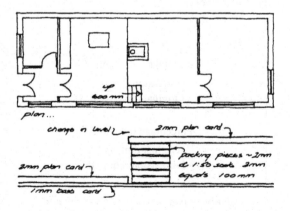
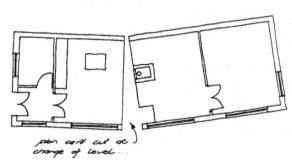

fig. 52: If the ground floor of the building has changes of level – for example a portion that is two or three steps different from the rest – the plan card should be cut where this change of level occurs. Then, the two cards should be stuck down independently with the higher floor level being made higher by appropriately sized packing pieces.

further developed. Check the height of the wall on the survey notes and cut the 'wall' out, making any openings in it that exist *fig. 53*. Place the wall onto the appropriate place on the pasted down plan. It can be held down using glue or sellotape *fig. 54*. Sellotape will give one the option of taking a model apart again quite easily.

Work your way through all the internal walls, placing them onto the plan and sticking them down. Walls that adjoin can be fixed together to make a rigid structure. Stairs can be shown as a strip of cardboard rising at an angle *fig. 55*.

If the building contains a second storey, paste the upper floor plan onto 2mm thick card and trim to

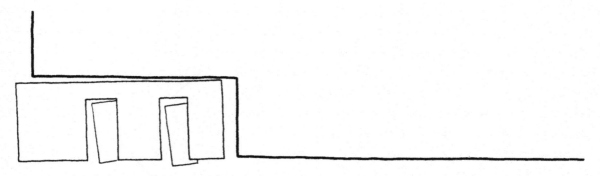

fig. 53: Measure the length of one wall, check the height of it and cut the 'wall' out, making any openings in it that exist.

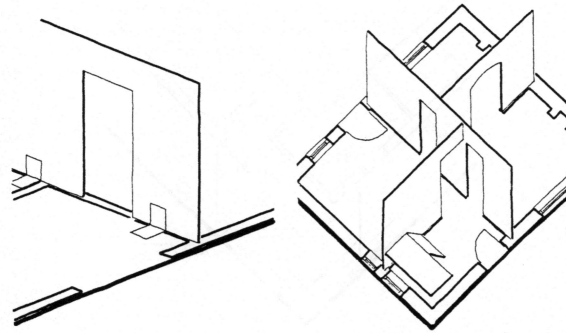

fig. 54: Place the wall onto the appropriate place on the pasted down plan. It can be held down using glue or sellotape.

fig. 55: Work your way through all the internal walls, placing them onto the plan and sticking them down. Walls that adjoin can be fixed together to make a rigid structure. Stairs can be shown as a strip of cardboard rising at an angle.

within 2mm of the outside face of the wall to allow for the external wall thickness. Cut out the opening for the stairs and place this over the ground floor walls, fixing it with glue or sellotape. Before this is done, it is a good idea to use it as a template to cut out another similar sized piece of card that will act as a ceiling for the upstairs rooms *fig. 56*. Proceed with the upstairs internal walls as was done for the ground floor. When this has been done, put the ceiling over these.

The external walls can now be made by pasting the elevations onto 2mm card and trimming these

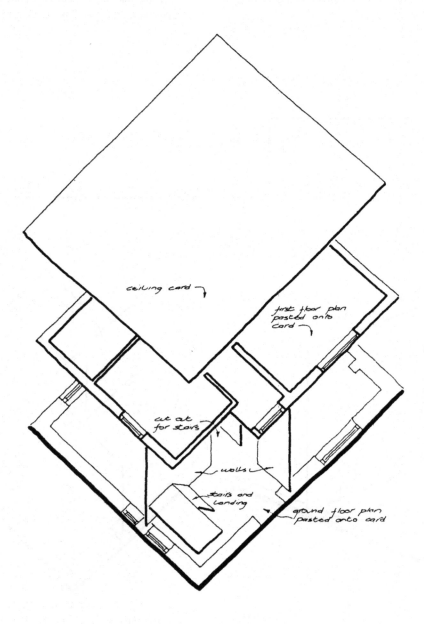

fig. 56: If the building contains a second storey, paste the upper floor plan onto 2mm thick card and trim to within 2mm of the outside face of the wall to allow for the external wall thickness. Cut out the opening for the stairs and place this over the ground floor walls, fixing it with glue or sellotape.

fig. 57. Windows and doors can be cut out of these. The walls can then be placed into position and glued or held in place with sellotape. All that remains to be made then is the roof.

The roof can be made by scoring a piece of card and folding it along the score line *fig. 58*. Ribs can be cut to fit inside this to make it hold its shape. The size of the roof can be calculated from the survey notes. If the roof overhangs the external walls, a piece of card can be cut to sit on top of the walls and the roof glued to this.

If the roof has a 'hip', a piece or pieces will have to be cut to complete the roof shape. The sizes of these will have to be worked out by trial and error. Chimneys or dormer windows, where they occur, can simply be stuck on to the roof *fig. 59*.

The model will then be complete. Paint can be used to colour the external walls and the roof, if so wished.

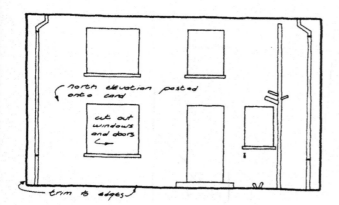

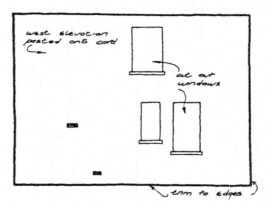

fig. 57: The external walls can now be made by pasting the elevations onto 2mm card and trimming these. Windows and doors can be cut out of these.

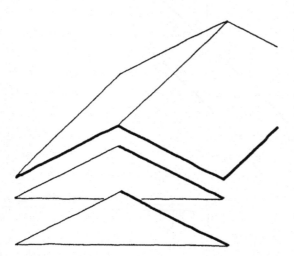

fig. 58: The roof can be made by scoring a piece of card and folding it along the score line. Ribs can be cut to fit inside this to make it hold its shape.

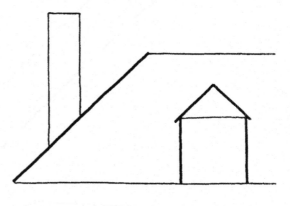

fig. 59: If the roof has a 'hip', a piece or pieces will have to be cut to complete the roof shape. The sizes of these will have to be worked out by trial and error. Chimneys or dormer windows, where they occur, can simply be stuck on to the roof.

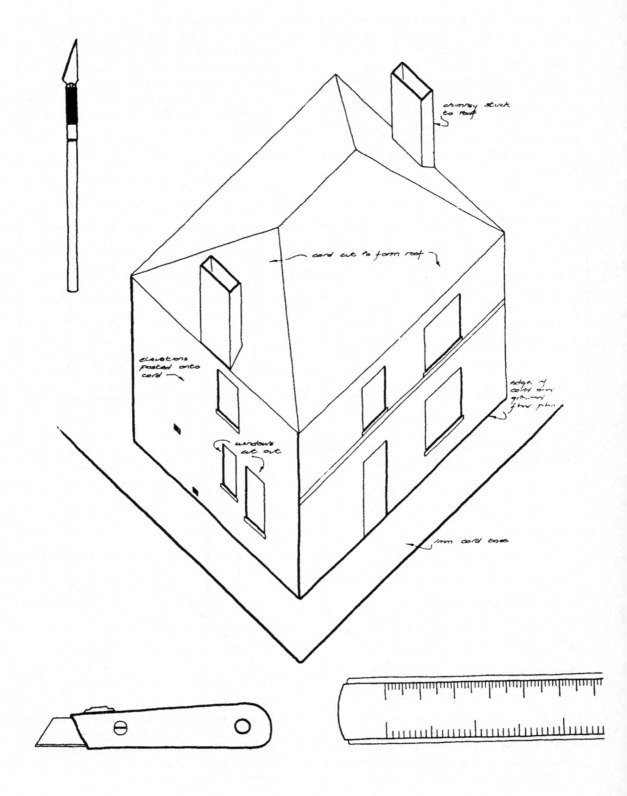

chimney stuck
to roof

cord cut to form roof

elevations
pasted onto
card

edge of
card over
ground
floor plan

windows
cut out

1mm card base

172

Summary

Organise surveying equipment.

Carry out a survey of an existing building.

Survey the site.

Carry out a condition survey.

Make scaled drawings.

Make a scale model.

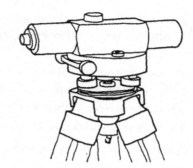

Part of timber frame

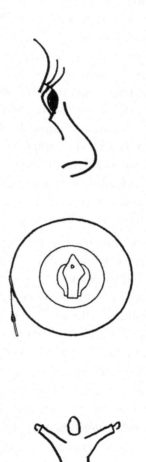

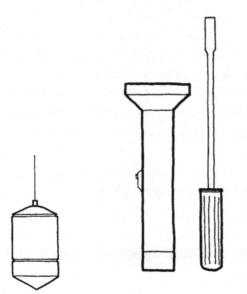

173

16 Understanding The Principles of Building Structures

More than any other subject *Structure* has the ability to strike fear into the heart. The reason for this is easy enough to grasp - if a building structure is not properly made then it might fall down! The consequences of this are obvious. However, bear in mind what my *Structures* professor was fond of saying: *'Nothing falls down until it absolutely has to!'*

The influence of fear on the design of building structures normally results in those structures being made excessively heavy and strong! Compare, for example, the structure of an aeroplane with that of a house. The aeroplane is made of extremely light materials of small section size fixed together so as to achieve maximum strength with minimum weight. In the case of a house - where weight is not as critical as it is with the aeroplane - heavy materials with a large section size are used to create strength and 'solidity'. This results in the making of extremely heavy buildings that are far stronger than is necessary to prevent them falling down. The reason for this is psychological more than it is physical. In other words we feel more secure in a massive building than we do in a flimsy one - even though we can happily consign ourselves to sit in the aeroplane which hurtles down the runway at almost two hundred miles an hour and then, at the end of the journey, lands on a rubber tyre filled with air! It is important, as you look at the issue of building structure, to bear in mind how it impacts us psychologically. Normally this results in buildings being made far more solid and massive than they need be.

The primary influencing factor in the design of structures is gravity. This is a mysterious force which pulls everything inward towards the centre of the earth. Structures also need to cope with the effects of wind. In a house design, the structural elements which will channel gravitational and wind energy will usually be the walls, floor and roof. This 'ties' structural considerations to the position of the walls, ceilings and floors. While this is not always ideal, it is economical as these elements are performing a dual function - enclosing *Space* as well as keeping the building standing upright. Where flexibility of internal layout or future extendibility are important design considerations it is best to separate the role of structure from that of enclosing space. In practice what this usually means is the use of a frame structure to carry the building loads, creating the option of opening up or entirely removed walls, without affecting the stability of the structure.

Read pages 175-184. The important thing to grasp in this is that gravitational and wind energies need clear paths to follow as they move through the building structure on their way to the ground.

Next: SDP17 - Distinguishing Between Types of Building Structure, page 185

Structure

The earth constantly exerts a force around itself called gravity. The effect of gravity causes objects to be pulled downwards towards the ground *fig. 1*. This effect is commonly referred to as 'weight'. The weight of an object is determined by its density and by the pull exerted on it by gravity.

The weight of a building can be quite considerable. This weight is made up of the combined weights of building materials, furnishings, occupants and so on, and is caused by the effect of gravity on these objects *fig. 2*. This gravitational pull, acting continuously, tries to drag the building and everything in it down into the earth.

Normally the weights that are of concern to building designers are called 'loads'. The majority of these are caused directly by gravity. If buildings are imagined as obstacles in a downward flow of gravitational energy, the principles of structure can be appreciated. This downward flow of energy, determined to make its way into the earth, sweeps through everything in its path. An object placed in its way must facilitate this flow by providing easy paths for it to follow *fig. 3*. This energy always wants to head in the same direction – directly down into the earth.

The preferred direction of gravitational flow can be observed by using a plumbob. This is made by tying a reasonable weight onto a string and suspending it freely above the ground *fig. 4*. Plumbbobs are used in construction to ensure that structures are standing up straight. They illustrate the ideal path to make for gravitational energy to flow through.

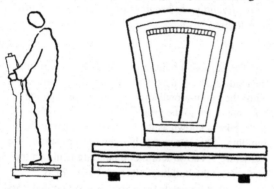

fig. 1: The effect of gravity causes objects to be pulled downwards towards the ground. This effect is commonly referred to as 'weight'.

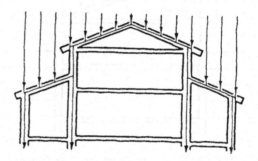

fig. 3: If buildings are imagined as obstacles in a downward flow of gravitational energy the principles of structure can be appreciated. Buildings must facilitate this flow of energy by providing easy paths for it to follow down into the ground.

fig. 2: The weight of a building can be quite considerable. This weight is made up of the combined weights of building materials, furnishings, occupants and so on, and is caused by the effect of gravity on these objects.

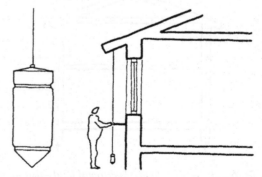

fig. 4: The preferred direction of gravitational flow can be observed by using a plumbob. Plumbbobs are used in construction to ensure that structures are standing up straight.

Vertical loads of this nature are not the only loads that a building has to contend with. Horizontal, or sideways loads also affect a building. Wind blowing against the side of a building, for example, will try to push the building sideways. Loads that are not quite horizontal do the same thing *fig. 5*. Like vertical loads, horizontal loads also wish to escape into the ground. Easy paths must also be provided for this to happen *fig. 6*.

Creating safe and easy paths for the vertical and horizontal flow of energy through a building to escape into the ground is the concern of structure. Energy or loads that cannot easily escape from a building's structure into the ground can literally break their way out and cause a building to become unstable or, worse still, to collapse *fig. 7*.

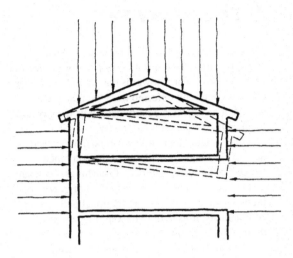

fig. 7: Energy or loads that cannot easily escape from a building's structure into the ground can and cause a building to become unstable or, worse still, to collapse.

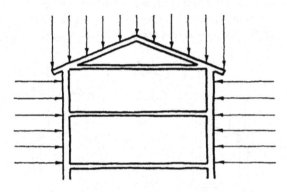

fig. 5: Vertical loads are not the only type of load that a building has to contend with. Horizontal, or sideways loads also affect a building.

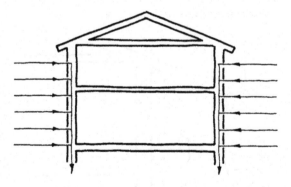

fig. 6: Like vertical loads, horizontal loads also wish to escape into the ground. Easy paths must also be provided for this to happen.

The parts of a building responsible for carrying the loads are known as the structure. These are the paths the gravitational energy follows through the building down to the ground. The form that these paths take is known as the structural system of the building. This is commonly referred to as simply the 'structure'. The structure of a building is in fact the skeleton of the building – its bare bones *fig. 8*.

A structure needs to be able to stand up under its own weight, as well as carry any other load that it might be burdened with. These loads are the weights of people, furniture, wind, and sometimes, of snow. What must happen to these loads is that they must be able to find their way easily through the structure into the earth *fig. 9*.

Some of these loads will be vertical and some will be horizontal or sideways loads. The building structure will be a series of paths for these to follow. These paths must all lead to the same place – down to the ground.

A structure needs to be stable as well as strong in order to be safe. Stability is achieved by creating balance within the structure and by providing clear paths for the flow of gravitational energy to find its way safely down into the earth. Strength is achieved by making the joints between the various parts of the structure as strong as possible, in other words, by connecting the skeleton together very well *fig. 10*.

fig. 8: The structure of a building is in fact the skeleton of the building – its bare bones.

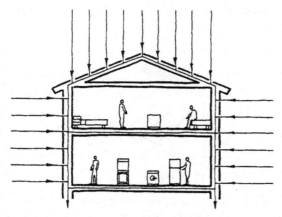

fig. 9: A structure needs to be able to stand up under its own weight as well as carry any other load that it might be burdened with.

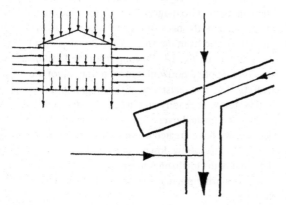

fig. 10: A structure needs to be stable as well as strong in order to be safe. Stability is achieved by providing clear paths for the flow of gravitational energy to find its way safely down into the earth. Strength is achieved by making the joints between the various parts of the structure as strong as possible.

The shape the structure of your building will take will be guided by the size and placement of your walls, floors and roof. These elements will dictate the location of the paths for the loads to flow safely through the building. In other words, the skeleton of the building – its bare bones or structure – will largely be made to conform to the shape made by the walls, floors and roof of the building. This shape is decided by the spaces that are being created within the building, in other words by the plan and by the cross sections fig. 11.

The size of the walls, floors and roof and how they are put together is decided by what these elements are to be made from – timber, steel or masonry – and by the loads that these elements will have to carry fig. 12.

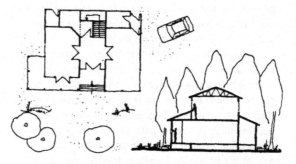

fig. 11: The skeleton of a building – its bare bones or structure – will largely be made to conform to the shape made by the walls, floors and roof of the building. This shape is decided by the plan and by the cross sections.

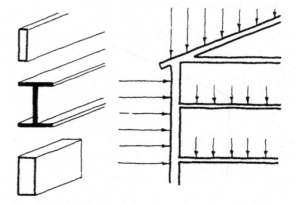

fig. 12: The size of the walls, floors and roof and how they are put together is decided by what these elements are to be made from – timber, steel or masonry – and by the loads that these elements will have to carry.

Structural Models

All building structures have to accommodate both the vertical and horizontal loads that might be imposed on them. These loads are channeled along paths that direct the loads through the structure down to the ground. These can be either vertical, horizontal or sloping paths.

    The nature of these paths can be observed fairly easily. Take a piece of 1mm card 150 x 100mm. Hold it upright on the table and press down on it from the top *fig. 13*. What you are doing is placing a vertical load on the piece of cardboard. As long as the card is held upright this load can follow a path vertically downwards to the ground, or in this case, downwards to the table. In reality this piece of card would be a wall in a building and the load you would be exerting with your finger would be the 'weight' of the wall plus the weight of anything resting on the wall. The weight of the roof, for example.

    Now, push the card to one side while still pressing down on it. You can only push it over a certain amount before it will slide on the table and fall over *fig. 14*. The reason for this is because the horizontal load you have imposed on the wall pushes it over, because there is no easy path for the energy to follow down to the ground. Because there is no readily available path for the energy to follow – in reality gravitational energy caused by the wind or some other sideways load – the energy in the horizontal load imposed by your finger leaps out of the structure and makes the wall fall over. Were this to happen in reality it would be akin to, say, a billboard being blown over in the wind *fig. 15*.

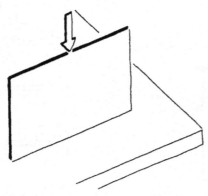

fig. 13: Take a piece of 1mm card 150 x 100mm. Hold it upright on the table and press down on it from the top.

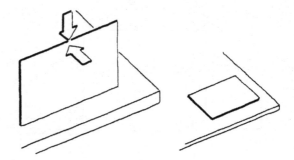

fig. 14: Push the card to one side while still pressing down on it. You can only push it over a certain amount before it will slide on the table and fall over.

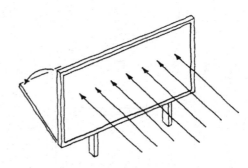

fig. 15: When a structure cannot properly channel a horizontal load, the effect is similar to a billboard being blown over in the wind.

    Now, cut a piece of cardboard 100 x 100mm and then cut this in two diagonally *fig. 16*. Glue the two diagonals onto the back of the larger piece. Keep them in a little from the end. When it is dry, stand the structure up *fig. 17*. Pushing from the front of the structure, apply a horizontal force to the top of the wall *fig. 18*. The resistance of the diagonal pieces will be felt very readily and in fact the structure cannot now be pushed over. The reason for this is because we have created a diagonal path for the horizontal load to follow downwards *fig. 19.* Creating diagonal paths to channel horizontal loads downwards is a principle that runs throughout building structure.

    If, instead of diagonals, we put square 100 x 100mm pieces on our model structure, the effect would be the same as with the diagonals insofar as directing the horizontal loads. In this case, the diagonal path would run within the square piece and the horizontal load will find its way naturally along it *fig. 20*.

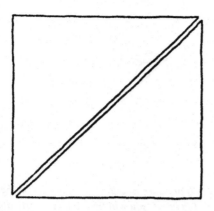

fig. 16: Cut a piece of cardboard 100 x 100mm and then cut this in two diagonally.

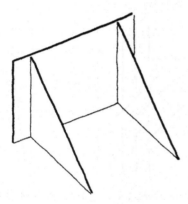

fig. 17: Glue the two diagonals onto the back of the larger piece. Keep them in a little from the end. When it is dry, stand the structure up.

fig. 18: Pushing from the front of the structure, apply a horizontal force to the top of it.

fig. 19: The structure cannot now be pushed over, because we have created a diagonal path for the horizontal load to follow downwards.

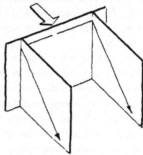

fig. 20: If we put square 100 x 100mm pieces on our model structure the diagonal path would run within this square piece and the horizontal load will find its way naturally along it.

If two 100 x 100mm square pieces are fixed close to the edges of two pieces of 150 x 100mm card, these four pieces would make a simple box fig. 21. Horizontal pressure can be applied to all the top edges of this box and the structure can direct these loads down through the 'walls'.

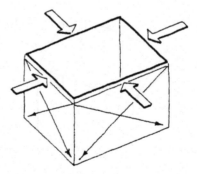

fig. 21: If two 100 x 100mm square pieces are fixed close to the edges of two pieces of 150x100mm card, these four pieces would make a simple box. Horizontal pressure can be applied to all the top edges of this box and the structure can direct these loads down through the 'walls'.

To complete this structure a simple roof can be made for it. Make this out of a piece of cardboard 150 x 150mm square. Draw a line dividing the piece in half and gently score along this line with a scalpel. Use a metal edged ruler to do this and only gently cut the card. Fold the card back along the score line and fix it onto the box. Use sellotape along the edges of the roof to do this *fig. 22*.

If pressure is applied downwards on the ridge of the roof, you will find that this vertical load is directed along the diagonal path made by the roof as far as the wall where the vertical load can begin to travel straight down *fig. 23*. Directing vertical loads onto diagonal paths in this way is a simple way of putting a roof over a structure.

The sellotape making the roof and wall junction allows the applied pressure or energy to change direction – if it were not there the roof would simply flatten out, as the rushing energy would not have a safe continuous path to follow. In reality the table would be the ground and the gravitational energy represented by your pressing finger would be the 'weight' of the roof.

This exercise illustrates the importance of strong junctions between the various parts of a structure, particularly where the structure changes direction. What this means is that where the path for gravitational energy changes direction, a strong joint must be made to allow the energy to easily change direction too. Otherwise this energy will leap out of the structure – break the joint – causing the structure to become unstable *fig. 24*.

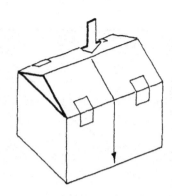

fig. 23: If pressure is applied downwards on the ridge of the roof, you will find that this vertical load is directed along the diagonal path made by the roof as far as the wall where the vertical load can begin to travel straight down. Directing vertical loads onto diagonal paths in this way is a simple way of putting a roof over a structure.

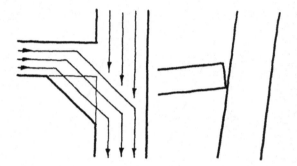

fig. 24: Where the path for gravitational energy changes direction, a strong joint must be made to allow the energy to easily change direction too. Otherwise this energy will leap out of the structure – break the joint – causing the structure to become unstable.

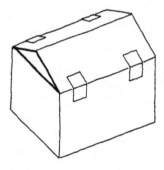

fig. 22: To complete the structure a simple roof can be made for it. Make this out of a piece of cardboard 150 x 150mm square. Use sellotape along the edges of the roof to fix it to the structure.

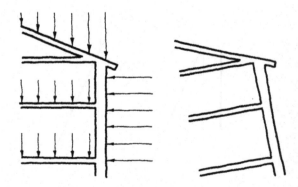

fig. 25: When gravitational energy passes through the structure of a building the vertical and horizontal loads tend to make the structure turn or bend.

Tension And Compression

When gravitational energy passes through the structure of a building, the vertical and horizontal loads tend to make the structure turn or bend *fig. 25*. This causes stress in the structure as it tries to resist this bending tendency. These stresses fall into two categories that are known as tension and compression. Tension is when the stresses in the structure are stretching the structure and compression is when the stresses are causing the structure to be compressed *fig. 26*.

You can see the separate effects of tension and compression by bending a piece of cardboard in two. On one side the surface of the cardboard has been pulled apart and on the other it has been crushed *fig. 27*. The tearing apart of the surface is caused by tension stresses and the crushing is caused by compression stresses. These two conditions exist side by side in structures. They are caused by the vertical and horizontal passing through the structure on their way to the ground. When the structure resists this flow of energy passing through it, stress occurs *fig. 28*. This resistance, in the case of a large structure such as a building, is offered by securely fixing the structure to the ground. If this were not done, the structure would simply turn over when a large horizontal load was applied to it.

Compressive loads press things down. Tension loads are loads that are trying to pull things apart or loads that are directly opposed to each other, like teams in a tug of war. Compressive and tensile loads, as these loads are called, are part of every structure and are caused when a structure resists the gravitational energy – weight or loads – passing through it on its way to the ground *fig. 29*. The resistance to these loads or weights, in the case of large structures such as buildings, is always provided by the ground the structure rests on.

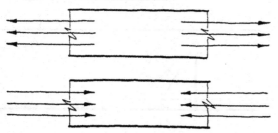

fig. 26: Tension stress occurs when the loads in the structure are stretching the structure and compression is when the stresses are causing the structure to be compressed.

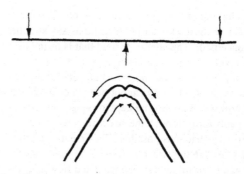

fig. 27: You can see the separate effects of tension and compression by bending a piece of cardboard in two. On one side the surface of the cardboard has been pulled apart and on the other it has been crushed.

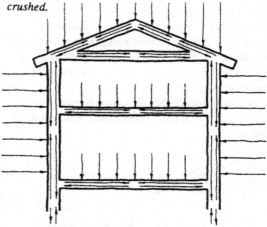

fig. 28: Tension and compression stresses exist side by side in structures. They are caused by the vertical and horizontal passing through the structure on their way to the ground. When the structure resists this flow of energy passing through it, stress occurs.

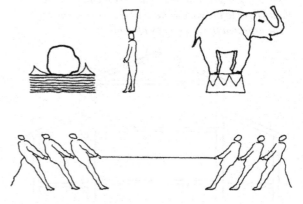

fig. 29: Compressive and tensile loads are part of every structure.

Gravitational energy in the form of weight and loads is a constant occurrence as far as any structure is concerned. The energy or load that is trying to get down to the ground is being pushed from behind by more energy – the energy is bumper to bumper you might say. Energy cannot be managed like traffic, however, but must be kept moving constantly, so the paths for it through the structure have to be made as efficient as possible. This means that the paths through the structure have to be made wide enough to accommodate the expected flow of energy along them, as well as ensuring that the changes in direction are made so as to guide the energy flow smoothly round the corners *fig. 30*. Changes in direction are the potential weak points in any structure. These are the places – normally the joints between the various parts of the structure – where the energy, if it cannot flow easily, may try to break out of the structure. Such an occurrence can be imagined like a series of speeding cars trying to negotiate a bend in the road – if the bend is too sharp and the track they are on too narrow, the cars may shoot off the road, being unable to safely make the turn *fig. 31*.

Triangulation

Triangulation is a way of providing convenient paths in structures to ensure that gravitational energy – vertical and horizontal loads – can easily pass through the structure on its way to the ground *fig. 32*. The tensile and compressive stresses that are set up when the structure resists the loads being applied to it can also be easily balanced by this configuration. This can be illustrated with a simple model.

The model can be made using 1mm card and sellotape. Cut a piece of card 100 x 150mm. Mark two lines onto the centre of this using a pencil and gently score along the lines with a scalpel *fig. 33*. Fold the card along the score lines so as to make a triangular structure. Secure the open edge of the structure with two pieces of tape. It will be found that considerable pressure can be applied to the apex of this structure without causing distortion. This is because the triangulated form provides convenient paths for the vertical loading to follow. The effect of the tensile stress set up in the structure by the applied load can be seen in the way the tape is stretched underneath the structure. When the load is removed the tape slackens off again.

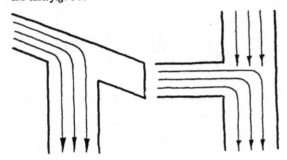

fig. 30: The gravitational paths through any structure have to be made wide enough to accommodate the expected flow of energy along them.

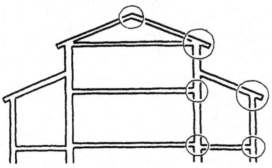

fig. 31: The joints are the potential weak points in any structure.

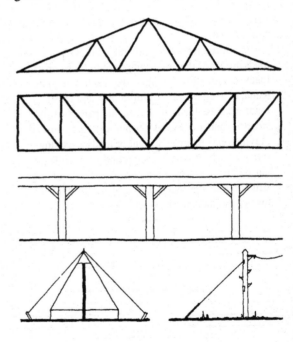

fig. 32: Triangulation is a way of providing convenient paths in structures to ensure that gravitational energy – vertical and horizontal loads – can easily pass through the structure on its way to the ground.

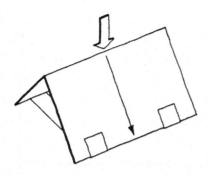

fig. 33: A simple model can be made to illustrate the principles of triangulation.

Horizontal loading can also be easily dealt with in this type of simple structure, because a diagonal path is provided within the structure for the horizontal load to follow downwards. Triangulated structures can be made immensely strong because of this facility to cater for both vertical and horizontal loads.

Another simple model can be made to illustrate this principle. You will need some thread and some light dowels to do this. Take two dowels and tie them together close to one end. Open them apart and stand them on the table. Any vertical load that is applied to these will result in the dowels spreading apart *fig. 34*. If you take a third dowel and tie it to the free ends of the first two dowels however, making a triangle, the shape will be found to be quite rigid and quite an amount of pressure can be exerted on it. If the thread holding the dowels together is not firmly tied it might be found that the thread will slip when the load is being applied. If sellotape is placed over the thread this slippage can be prevented. Such failure, however, illustrates the weak points in any structure – the joints.

If a second triangle is made, similar to the first, and both triangles are connected together with more dowels, a three-dimensional structure can be made *fig. 35*. When this structure is put sitting on the table and a horizontal load is applied from the end however, the structure can be pushed over quite easily. This weakness can be overcome by making diagonals from the ridge down to the opposite corners. These diagonal paths channel horizontal loads safely downwards by making additional triangulated shapes. What has been created is a strong, stable, three-dimensional structure that can withstand any horizontal or vertical loading that is applied to it.

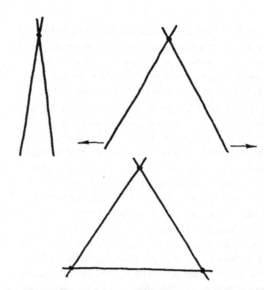

fig. 34: Take two dowels and tie them together close to one end. Any vertical load that is applied to these will result in the dowels spreading apart. If a triangle is made however, the shape will be found to be quite rigid and quite an amount of pressure can be exerted on it.

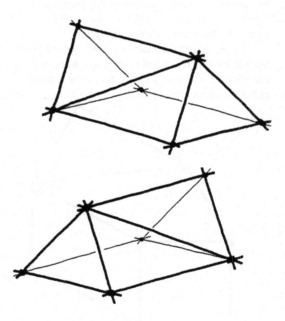

fig. 35: If a second triangle is made similar to the first and both triangles are connected together, a three-dimensional structure can be made. Strengthen this structure by using diagonals.

183

If this structure is imagined as being a simple roof, then walls can easily be made to go under it *fig. 36*. This can be done by using more dowels and thread. It is best to separately make two frames for the walls and to then attach them to the roof *fig. 37*. Make each wall frame from four dowels, putting two vertically, one horizontally across them close to one end and by putting the fourth dowel diagonally across these. Tie all the dowels with thread and put sellotape over the knots to stop the thread sliding. In a real life frame, the knots will in fact be bolts and nails and it is these places in the structure that will tend to be weak, just as your knots are.

Make the two frames and then attach them to the roof frame on opposite sides of the structure. You may need a hand to do this, because until all the pieces are firmly tied to each other the structure is not complete and, therefore, not stable. When the two frame walls have been attached to the roof, use more dowels to complete the two open sides of the structure *fig. 38*. This can then be stood upright on the table. The structure will be remarkably strong and will accept vertical and horizontal loads very easily. This is a model of a simple frame structure. Frame structures are in fact structures made up of clearly defined paths for loads to follow. Frames are very light structures and very strong.

Pieces of cardboard can very easily be cut to size and placed over the model to represent walls and roof *fig. 39*. In this way the model can be enclosed and made into a model building.

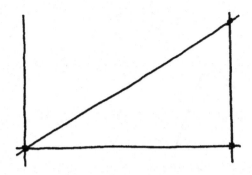

fig. 37: Make each wall frame from four dowels, putting two vertically, one horizontally across them close to one end and put the fourth stick diagonally across these. Tie all the dowels with thread and put sellotape over the joints.

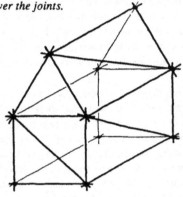

fig. 38: Attach the wall frames to the roof frame on opposite sides of the structure. When the two frame walls have been attached to the roof, use more dowels to complete the two open sides of the structure.

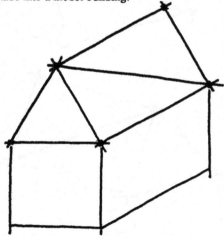

fig. 36: If the structure is imagined as being a simple roof, then walls can easily be made to go under it. This can be done by using more sticks and thread.

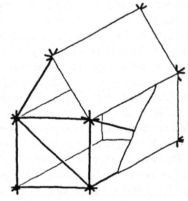

fig. 39: Pieces of cardboard can very easily be cut to size and placed over the model to represent walls and roof. In this way the structure can be enclosed and made into a model building.

Distinguishing Between Types Of Building Structures

Pages 186-194 set out details of the two main structural types. These can be described as 'solid' and 'frame' structures. A 'solid' structure would be one made with stone or blocks usually with a concrete floor while a 'frame' structure would be a skeleton made of timber with, possibly, a timber floor.

Essentially both types of structure provide paths to 'channel' gravitational and wind energy down to the ground. 'Solid' structures, once constructed, are difficult to modify because the entire construction acts as a path for the movement of energy. Frame structures, on the other hand, provide clearly defined paths for energy to follow. Such structural 'skeletons' are easy to work around, allowing changes to be made to a building without disturbing the paths which the flowing energy uses to find its way to the ground. Many buildings combine both types of structure - for example, a 'solid' building made of concrete blocks will normally have a timber 'frame' roof, or a timber frame structure might have a masonry outer covering.

While the choice between 'solid' and 'frame' structures is, in part, made on the basis of in-building flexibility there are other consideration involved the the choice of structural type. For example, insulation, self-building and cost all play a role. What is important at this stage of the design process is to grasp the principles of structural design; to acknowledge the influence of psychology on our choices and to commit oneself to the observation of *Structures* in the real world.

If you are renovating an existing building or planning an extension to one it is essential that a clear understanding of the structure of this is understood. How to gather such information can be found on pages 158-159, in the *Surveying* chapter.

Essentially, timber framed elements such as walls and floors are easy to remove or modify because usually they do not carry any of the building loads. Solid walls or floors, on the other hand, are more cumbersome to modify. Also these can oftentimes be carrying some of the building loads, in which case their alteration needs to be carefully managed.

Generally speaking, caution is the order of the day. Examine the building structure thoroughly and carefully. Seek the advice of someone experienced in such matters if you are unsure of some aspect of the structure. Also, bear in mind that modifying or removing a solid, load-bearing element of a structure can be a slow, cumbersome and expensive business.

Next: SDP18 - The Role of Foundations, page 195

Types of Structures

Structures can be divided into two major categories – loadbearing structures and frame structures.

Loadbearing structures are usually made of stone, brick or concrete blocks. These structures rely on size and weight, as well as on being supported at right angles for stability *fig. 40*. If such support is not provided, loadbearing walls can easily fall over in a strong wind or when they are subjected to a strong horizontal load. The reason such support is needed for loadbearing walls is because they are made from materials that perform poorly under tensile loading. What this means is that when an unsupported concrete block wall is subjected to a strong horizontal load, the wall might not be able to resist the tension stresses that this load creates. The reason for this is because loadbearing walls are usually made from small pieces of masonry stuck together with mortar. While the masonry and the mortar can perform well under compression loading they have no strength whatsoever when they are being pulled apart.

Loadbearing walls that are made from reinforced concrete are an exception to this general rule. This is because the steel within the concrete performs excellently under tension loading *fig. 41*. The combination of concrete, which works well under compression loading, and steel, which works well under tension loading, has made reinforced concrete a very common way of creating loadbearing structures.

Loadbearing structures are usually confined to walls that are roofed over with frame structures *fig. 42*.

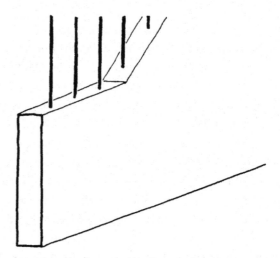

fig. 41: Loadbearing walls that are made from reinforced concrete contain steel bars which perform excellently under tension and compression loading.

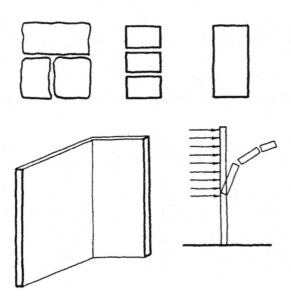

fig. 40: Load bearing structures are usually made of stone, brick or concrete blocks. These structures rely on size and weight, as well as on being supported at right angles for stability. When an unsupported concrete block wall is subjected to a strong horizontal load, the wall might not be able to resist the tension stresses that this load creates.

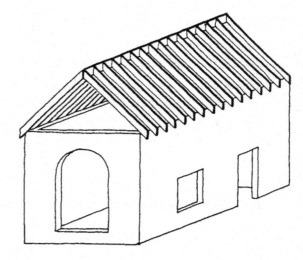

fig. 42: Loadbearing structures are usually confined to walls that are roofed over with frame structures.

186

Frame structures are by nature lightweight and rely on providing smooth, easy paths for horizontal and vertical loads to flow through and reach the ground *fig. 43*. Such paths are made up of beams attached together. A typical frame structure wall is made up of vertical beams with some form of diagonal bracing.

A typical framed roof structure is made up of beams called rafters. Such rafters provide the paths for the roof loading by forming diagonals that run over to the walls, where the loads can continue on a downward path. The reason this type of diagonal arrangement is used in roof structures is because it allows large areas to be covered over economically and simply. In a typical roof structure, the two diagonal rafters lean against each other and so balance each other, much like two people might lean their weight against each other. The tendency for such rafters to push out the top of the walls they are sitting on is counteracted by tying the bottoms of the rafters together. Frame structures are ideal for roofs because they are light and strong.

Beams

The beam is a principle element of frame structures. Depending on their location, such beams are called joists, rafters or purlins. The natural strength of beams can be observed by laying a ruler between two books. When the ruler is flat and it is pressed down in the middle it will bend or deflect very easily *fig. 44*. If the ruler is turned on its side however, and is again pressed down it will be much stiffer and will easily carry the applied load across to its supports. If the tendency of the beam to fall over sideways is counteracted by supporting it at right angles, a considerable load can be applied to the ruler without it breaking *fig. 45*. When several beams are used in this manner and are supported so that they cannot fall over, frame structures of considerable lightness and strength can be made *fig. 46*. Such a configuration of beams can be used to make floors, walls, roofs – in other words, entire building structures.

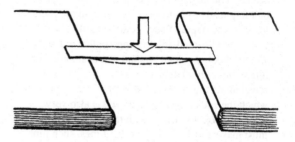

fig. 44: The beam is a principle element of frame structures. The natural strength of beams can be observed by laying a ruler between two books. When the ruler is flat and it is pressed down in the middle it will bend or deflect very easily.

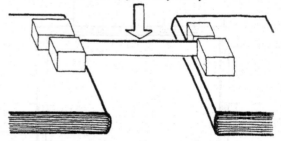

fig. 45: If the ruler is turned on its side and is pressed down it will be much stiffer and will easily carry the applied load across to its supports. If the tendency of the beam to fall over sideways is counteracted by supporting it at right angles, a considerable load can be applied to the ruler without it breaking.

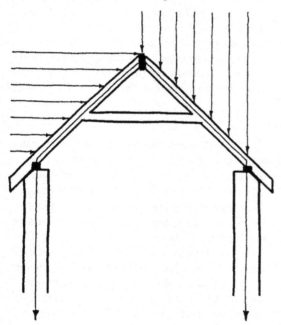

fig. 43: Frame structures rely on providing smooth, easy paths for horizontal and vertical loads to flow through and reach the ground. A typical framed roof structure is made up of beams called rafters. Such rafters provide the paths for the roof loading by forming diagonals that run over to the walls, where the loads can continue on a downward path.

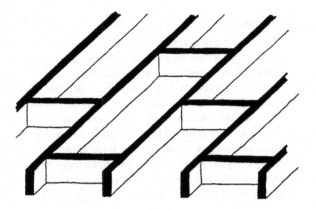

fig. 46: When several beams are used side by side and are supported so that they cannot fall over, frame structures of considerable lightness and strength can be made.

Frame structures utilise the natural strength of beams to make paths for vertical and horizontal building loads to follow on their way to the ground fig. 47. The depth of such beams is critical to their ability to withstand any loading applied to them fig. 48. In effect, any load applied to a beam must be turned through 90 degrees in order for the load to travel along the beam to its support. The manner in which the ends of beams are fixed is also very important fig. 49. Here again the building loads must make a difficult turn. Oftentimes, such junctions are widened by the addition of triangular brackets which have the effect of providing a more generous path for the building loads to flow through. Such junctions need to be securely fixed.

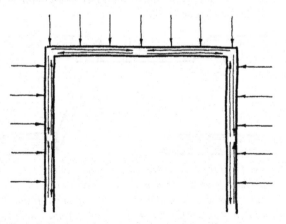

fig. 47: Frame structures utilise the natural strength of beams to make paths for vertical and horizontal building loads to follow on their way to the ground.

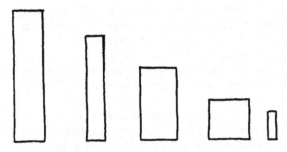

fig. 48: The depth of beams is critical to their ability to withstand any loading applied to them.

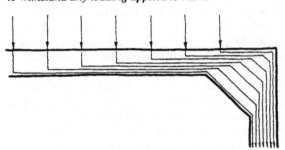

fig. 49: Any load applied to a beam must be turned through 90 degrees in order for the load to travel along the beam to its support. Oftentimes, such junctions are widened by the addition of triangular brackets which have the effect of providing a more generous path for the building loads to flow through.

The loads that beams must normally cope with are divided into two categories – Uniformly Distributed Loads and Point Loads. Uniformly Distributed Loads, or UDLs, are loads that are spread across the entire length of a beam, whereas Point Loads are concentrated at a single point or points on the beam fig. 50. In normal domestic building, Uniformly Distributed Loads occur with the greatest frequency. Such loading would be caused by furniture, people and so on and these weights would be distributed evenly across the beams by the floorboards. In the case where a partition for an upper floor was to be constructed across the beams – joists – making up the floor, a Point Load would occur fig. 51. Point Loads, because they concentrate the load at a particular point on the beam, can cause considerable stress at that point if the load is very great. Such stress can be relieved by the addition of a further beam under the Point Load. This additional beam would be subject to a UDL by the partition above it.

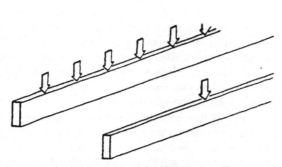

fig. 50: Uniformly Distributed Loads, or UDLs, are loads that are spread across the entire length of a beam, whereas Point Loads are concentrated at a single point or points on the beam.

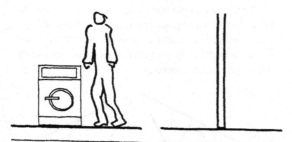

fig. 51: In normal domestic building, Uniformly Distributed Loads occur with the greatest frequency. Such loading would be caused by furniture, people and so on and these weights would be distributed evenly across the beams by the floorboards. In the case where a partition for an upper floor was to be constructed across the beams – joists – making up the floor, a Point Load would occur.

The ability of any beam to carry either Uniformly Distributed Loads or Point Loads without the beam deflecting unduly, depends on the strength of the beam as well as on its depth. The manner in which the ends of the beam are fixed is also important.

Timber beams are normally graded into various Strength Classes, and tables are published indicating the ability of beams of particular Strengths and depths to carry typical domestic loads fig. 52. For example, a Floor Joist of Strength Class A Sitka Spruce that is 150mm deep and 44mm wide will be able to span across a distance of 3280mm without support. Such a floor would require that all the beams were laid 300mm apart. If the joists were to be laid 400mm apart, they could only span 2980mm. The reason for the variation in the span of the joist at various distances apart has to do with the number of joists you end up with – the further apart the joists are, the fewer there will be. Consequently, each joist will have to carry more weight and this reduces its span capability.

While beams in frame structures are normally made of solid wood, they can also be constructed from small sections of timber securely fixed together fig. 53. Laminated beams are made from small sections of timber glued together. Box beams are made from sections of timber and plywood glued or nailed together. These can be very strong in relationship to their weight. Plywood web beams are similarly strong. These are also made from plywood and sections of solid wood.

Floor Joists									
Strength class									
	SC A			SC B			SC C		
	Spacing of joists								
	300	400	600	300	400	600	300	400	600
	permissable span of joists in mm								
Size of joist (mm)									
35 x 100	2021	1812	1481	2123	1923	1671	2212	2000	1743
35 x 115	2332	2074	1693	2435	2212	1924	2543	2303	2000
35 x 125	2543	2243	1832	2654	2402	2093	2761	2500	2183
44 x 100	2193	1985	1663	2291	2087	1813	2394	2162	1891
44 x 115	2521	2283	1894	2632	2393	2071	2742	2481	2162
44 x 125	2743	2481	2052	2871	2592	2251	2980	2712	2351
44 x 150	3824	2982	2434	3441	3123	2721	3582	3251	2832
63 x 150	3714	3773	2915	3894	3521	3074	4043	3642	3201
75 x 150	3945	3582	3112	4124	3742	3261	4295	3891	3404

fig. 52: Timber beams are normally graded into various Strength Classes, and tables are published indicating the ability of beams of particular Strengths and depths to carry typical domestic loads.

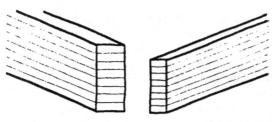

fig. 53: Laminated beams are made from small sections of timber glued together. Box and web beams are made from sections of timber and plywood glued or nailed together.

Frame Structures

Frame structures can accept vertical and horizontal loads with ease and direct these safely and efficiently to the ground. They do this by providing clear definite paths for weights and loads to follow. In the case of a building, the materials making up the walls, floors and roof are fixed to this frame, and the weight of these covering materials is transferred to the ground by the frame fig. 54.

An electricity pylon is a good example of a frame structure. Or the Eiffel Tower. You can imagine fixing walls to the outside of these and enclosing the space inside very simply. Such walls could be put up and taken down very easily, as they are merely a skin that is fixed to the bare bones of the structure. Frame structures can be erected very easily and quickly.

fig. 54: Frame structures can accept vertical and horizontal loads with ease and direct these safely and efficiently to the ground. The materials making up the walls, floors and roof are fixed to this frame, and the weight of these covering materials is transferred to the ground by the frame.

The wigwam, the A-frame, the triangulated truss, and so on are all structural forms that are based on the principles of triangulation fig. 55. Factories, pylons, hay barns, bridges, tents, scaffolding and platforms all use the principle of triangulation to make strong, lightweight structures.

An important consideration in the construction of frame structures is the materials from which they are made. Because frame structures cater for both vertical and horizontal loads, they are subjected to both compressive and tensile stresses. The materials making up frame structures must therefore be capable of withstanding the effects of these stresses. Compressive stresses cause materials to be pressed in on themselves, while tensile stresses cause materials to be stretched or pulled apart fig. 56. Materials which perform well under these stress conditions are wood and steel. These materials are often used in the making of frame structures.

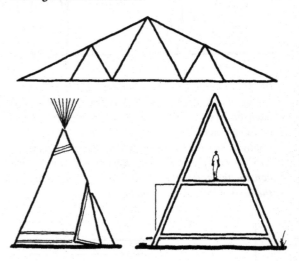

fig. 55: The wigwam, the A-frame and the triangulated truss are all structural forms that are based on the principles of triangulation.

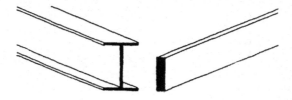

fig. 56: The materials making up frame structures must be capable of withstanding the effects of compressive and tensile stresses. Wood and steel perform well under these stress conditions.

Some parts of frame structures only ever have to perform under tensile stress *fig. 57*. In these situations, materials which act well only under tensile stress can be used. All types of ropes and cables fall into this category.

A simple model can be used to illustrate this. Take two dowels and tie them together near one end. Take a piece of cord of a length equal or slightly longer than the dowels. Tie either end of the cord to the ends of the dowels *fig. 58*. Use sellotape to secure all knots. When a vertical load is applied to this structure the cord will tighten indicating the tensile stress it is being subjected to. Such tension members, as such parts of structures are called, mean that frame structures can be made to be very lightweight. Guy wires for tents, aerials and masts all fall into the category of tension members *fig. 59*.

Frame structures are normally covered with a variety of different materials to make floors, roofs and walls. Wood, slates, tiles, brick and concrete blocks can be used for this. Frame structures have the advantage of being very light, strong and quick to erect. They in fact provide a multitude of paths for loads to flow through, in comparison to loadbearing structures which provide one continuous path. Balloon frames, platform frames, post and beam structures, Segal frames and common stud walling are all common types of frame structures.

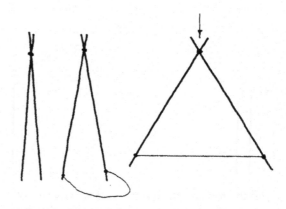

fig. 58: A simple structure can be made to illustrate the use of tension members.

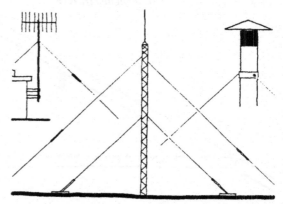

fig. 59: Guy wires for tents, aerials and masts all fall into the category of tension members.

Roof Structures

Frame roof structures utilise the principle of triangulation to span over wide distances *fig. 60*. Such structures can either be made up of individual beams or rafters, or they can be made up of triangulated trusses. Rafters normally need to be supported midway along their length to stop them from sagging unduly. Such a support is known as a purlin *fig. 61*. Rafters must also be prevented from spreading apart. Collar ties or ceiling joists are used to do this.

Triangulated roof trusses are made from light sections of timber that are firmly fixed together in a factory. They have the advantage of being very light and strong *fig. 62*.

Frame roof structures, when they are used to enclose loadbearing walls, are fixed to sections of timber that are known as wall plates *fig. 63*. Such wall plates are in turn firmly fixed to the walls they are resting on.

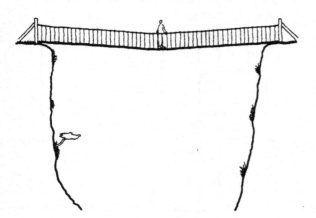

fig. 57: Some parts of frame structures only ever have to perform under tensile stress. In these situations, materials which act well only under tensile stress can be used. All types of ropes and cables fall into this category.

191

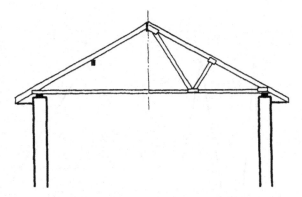

fig.60: Frame roof structures utilise the principle of triangulation to span over wide distances. They can either be made up of individual beams or rafters, or they can be made using triangulated trusses.

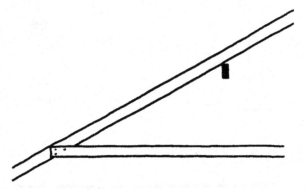

fig. 61: Rafters normally need to be supported midway along their length to stop them from sagging unduly. Such a support is known as a purlin. Rafters must also be prevented from spreading apart. Collar ties or ceiling joists are used to do this.

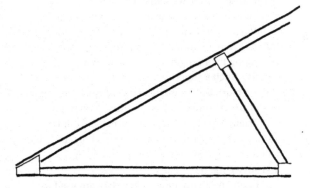

fig. 62: Triangulated roof trusses are made from light sections of timber that are firmly fixed together in a factory. They have the advantage of being very light and strong.

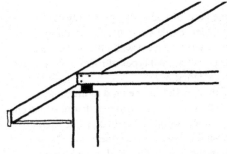

fig. 63: Frame roof structures, when they are used to enclose loadbearing walls, are fixed to sections of timber that are known as wall plates. Such wall plates are in turn firmly fixed to the walls they are resting on.

Loadbearing Structures

Both frame and loadbearing structures have to be capable of transferring vertical and horizontal loads safely to the ground. How these two structural types do this is quite different. Frame structures rely on the creation of clear paths and on triangulation to channel gravitational energy, and are made using materials such as wood and steel which perform well under both tensile and compressive stress. Loadbearing structures, on the other hand, are made using materials such as stone, brick and concrete block which act well under compressive stress but have no ability whatsoever to withstand tensile stress. If a material such as a concrete block is subjected to a load that stretches the block in any way, the block will simply break apart fig. 64.

It has been pointed out that all structures are loadbearing. This is true.

fig. 64: Loadbearing structures are made using materials such as stone, brick and concrete block. If a material such as a concrete block is subjected to a load that stretches the block in any way, the block will simply break apart.

To overcome this limitation, loadbearing structures rely on the creation of vertical loads that far outweigh the horizontal loads acting on the structure *fig. 65*. This is achieved quite easily, as the materials used to make loadbearing structures are in themselves very heavy. In creating such an imbalance between the vertical and horizontal loads that a structure must contend with, tensile stress in the structure is kept to an absolute minimum.

Vertical loads are made large in loadbearing structures by making them heavy. Stone, brick and concrete blocks are commonly used. These materials act well in compression, that is, under vertical loads. Under tensile loads, however, these materials have very little strength. To overcome this limitation, the horizontal loads acting on a loadbearing structure are channelled within the thickness of the wall which provides diagonal paths for the horizontal loads to follow down to the ground. Alternatively, piers, buttresses and supporting walls are used to channel these horizontal loads downwards *fig. 66*. The model described in *figs. 14-22* clearly illustrates the principles behind loadbearing structures.

As with the loadbearing wall, the loadbearing roof must be made out of heavy materials whose strength lies in their abilities to accept compression loading. The dome is a structural form that carries compression loads very successfully *fig. 67*. A completely loadbearing structure would be a structure with a dome or a conical roof sitting on vertical walls. Any such roof structure is difficult to make, because it is not completely strong until the last piece has been put in place – the keystone. To make such a loadbearing roof the structure has to be supported until the final piece is set in place.

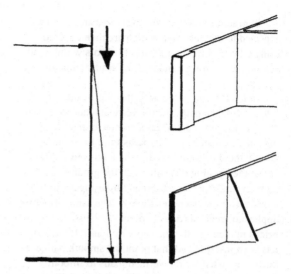

fig. 66: *Horizontal loads acting on a loadbearing structure are channelled within the thickness of the wall which provides diagonal paths for these loads to follow down to the ground. Alternatively, piers, buttresses and supporting walls are used to channel these horizontal loads downwards.*

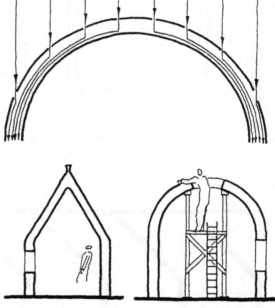

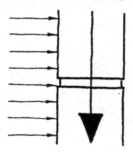

fig. 65: *Loadbearing structures rely on the creation of vertical loads that far outweigh the horizontal loads acting on the structure. This is achieved quite easily, as the materials used to make loadbearing structures are in themselves very heavy. Stone, brick and concrete blocks are commonly used.*

fig. 67: *The dome is a structural roof form that carries compression loads very successfully. A completely loadbearing structure would be a structure with a dome or a conical roof sitting on vertical walls. Any such roof structure is difficult to make, because it is not completely strong until the last piece has been put in place – the keystone.*

In practice. loadbearing structures are usually confined to making walls which are then covered using a frame structure. Similarly, floors within loadbearing structures are made using frame techniques *fig. 68*.

In loadbearing structures, the walls of the structure provide the paths for the vertical loads to follow down to the ground. When it comes to making openings in a loadbearing wall, paths have to be made around these openings so that the load coming from above the opening can still reach the ground. Such paths around openings are made by using an arch or a lintel over the openings *fig. 69*. The same principle applies to arches as does to domes – the stones or bricks in them need to be supported until the last one has been inserted. At that point the smooth path has been completed for the vertical loads to smoothly flow towards the ground *fig. 70*. Lintels, on the other hand, need to be solid and are simply set into place in one piece *fig. 71*.

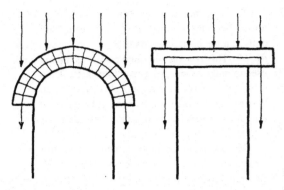

fig. 69: When it comes to making openings in a loadbearing wall, paths have to be made around these openings so that the load coming from above the opening can reach the ground. Such paths around openings are made by using an arch or a lintel.

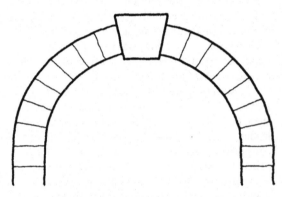

fig. 70: The same principle applies to arches as does to domes – the stones or bricks in them need to be supported until the last one has been inserted. At that point the smooth path has been completed for the vertical loads flow towards the ground.

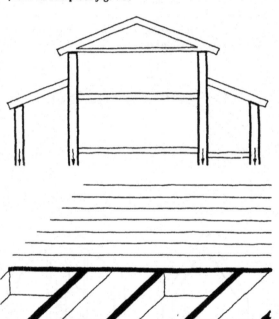

fig. 68: Loadbearing structures are usually confined to making walls which are then covered using a frame structure. Similarly, floors within load bearing structures are made using frame techniques. The walls of the structure provide the paths for the vertical loads to follow down to the ground.

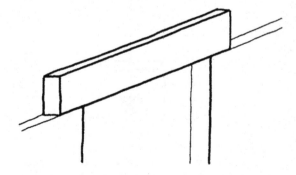

fig. 71: Lintels need to be solid and are set into place in one piece. They are usually made of wood, steel or reinforced concrete.

18 Sheltermaker Design Programme
The Role Of Foundations

All building structures sit on foundations which is the interface between the building and the earth. This is where the energy passing through the structure is 'transferred' to the ground to continue its journey.

How foundations manage to do this is described in *Structure*, pages 196-198. You should read this bearing in mind that the construction of foundations can eat up a huge proportion of one's budget if care is not taken to keep things as simply as possible. Essentially, 'solid' structures require quite massive foundations to prevent any movement whatsoever in the structure they support. This is done to prevent cracking, as the least movement will provoke this. Frame structures, on the other hand, where they are 'clad' with flexible, lightweight materials, can be supported on quite simple 'pad' foundations and can absorb a certain amount of movement without adverse consequences.

Apart from issues of stability, it should be borne in mind that the deconstruction of buildings is an important aspect of building sustainably. Solid structures usually require mechanical force to knock down and remove whereas frame structures can be disassembled, removed and even relocated with manpower alone.

Next: SDP19 - Taking On Board Compliance with the Building Regulations, page 199

Foundations are the interface between a building and the earth

More than any other subject, structure has the ability to strike fear into the heart.

Foundations

The structure of any building always sits on foundations, which transfer the building loads to the ground. The earth has a natural ability to carry any load placed upon it *fig. 72*. It does this by spreading the applied weight over a considerable area. This phenomenon can be easily demonstrated.

Take a bowl and fill it with two inches, 50mm, of sand or sugar. This will represent the ground. Take a pencil and push the blunt end of it into the sand *fig. 73*. The pushing that you are doing represents a building load and you can push the pencil quite easily all the way to the bottom of the bowl. Take the pencil out and smooth out the sand. Take a piece of 1mm cardboard 50 x 50mm and lay it across the surface of the sand. Place the blunt end of the pencil in the middle of the card and again press down *fig. 74*. This time you will only be able to push the pencil and the cardboard a little way down into the sand, no matter what load you exert on it.

The reason for this is because the cardboard spreads the load of the pencil across a large area of sand, allowing more paths to exist in the sand for the load to follow and escape. In a real life situation, the sand or sugar would be the earth. A loaded post or column placed directly on the ground would sink into the ground without the benefit of a foundation under it.

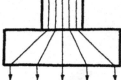

fig. 72: The structure of any building always sits on foundations which transfer the building loads to the ground. They do this by spreading the weight over a considerable area.

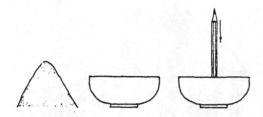

fig. 73: Take a bowl and fill it with two inches, 50mm, of sand or sugar. This will represent the ground. Take a pencil and push the blunt end of it into the sand.

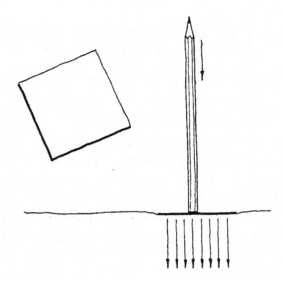

fig. 74: Take a piece of 1mm cardboard 50 x 50mm and lay it across the surface of the sand. Place the blunt end of the pencil in the middle of the card and again press down. The cardboard spreads the load of the pencil across a large area of sand, allowing more paths to exist for the load to follow. In a real life situation the sand or sugar would be the ground.

Stiletto heels or stilts concentrate the weight of a person onto a very small area *fig. 75*. If the surface that someone wearing stiletto heels or stilts walks on is soft, they will sink into it just like the pencil sank into the sand.

Nature has provided us with in-built foundations – our feet *fig. 76*. These spread our body weight over a reasonably large area, allowing us to walk on surfaces impossible to those wearing stiletto heels or stilts!

This is the fundamental principle of foundation design – spreading the load of a building over as wide an area of ground as possible. Almost all types of ground are capable of carrying the type of loads made by small buildings, provided that foundations are placed beneath them.

Loadbearing structures require continuous foundations underneath their walls *fig. 77*. Such foundations, normally made from concrete, are known as strip footings. Frame structures can either be supported on strip footings or they can be supported at selected points, where the frame itself is brought to the ground *fig. 78*. Such foundations are known as pad foundations.

fig. 75: *Stiletto heels or stilts concentrate the weight of a person onto a very small area. If the surface that someone wearing stiletto heels or stilts walks on is soft, they will sink into it.*

fig. 76: *Nature has provided us with in-built foundations – our feet.*

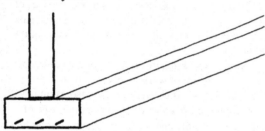

fig. 77: *Loadbearing structures require continuous foundations underneath their walls. Such foundations, normally made from concrete, are known as strip footings.*

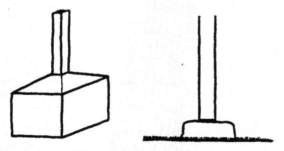

fig. 78: *Frame structures can either be supported on strip footings or they can be supported at selected points, where the frame itself is brought to the ground. Such foundations are known as pad foundations.*

The Bearing Stratum

The place in the ground that is considered able to carry the weight of a building is called the bearing stratum. This exists immediately under the first six inches of the ground, in other words beneath the topsoil *fig. 79*. Topsoil is very active and can easily be compressed so it is not considered stable enough for building on. Once the topsoil is cleared away, firm ground will be uncovered. This is the bearing stratum.

In practice, foundations are laid deeper than this to protect them from rain and frost. Normally a depth of 3 feet or 900mm is considered deep enough *fig. 80*. Burying foundations also has the advantage of spreading the loads of the building more effectively through the surrounding earth. Nowadays, foundations are usually made of concrete. Traditionally, stone was always used and even timber.

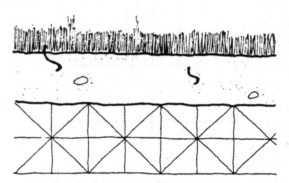

fig. 79: *The place in the ground that is considered able to carry the weight of a building is called the bearing stratum. This exists immediately under the first six inches of the ground, in other words beneath the topsoil.*

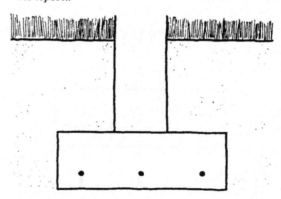

fig. 80: *In practice, foundations are laid to a depth of 3 feet or 900mm.*

The idea of balance is one that runs through the entire process of building design. Where this applies to the foundations, it can be interpreted as the balance created by the loads exerted by the building structure being resisted by the earth pushing back, or resisting *fig. 81*. If the ground does not have the ability to resist the load applied to it by the foundations, the foundations will sink. In practice, it is unusual for this to happen unless the ground the structure is resting on moves in some way. This might happen in a landslide, or it might happen due to earthquake movement. It also might happen if a structure rests on ground that is unsettled, for example ground that has been made up from rubble and fill *fig. 82*. This type of ground can begin to settle when the load of a building is placed on it. For this reason, fill of any kind should only be built on with extreme caution.

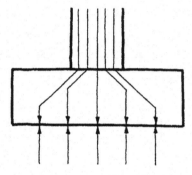

fig. 81: The idea of balance is one that runs through the entire process of building design. Where this applies to the foundations, it can be interpreted as the balance created by the loads exerted by the building structure being resisted by the earth pushing back, or resisting.

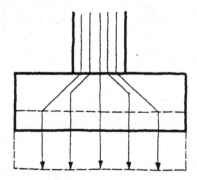

Building Regulations

In regard to structural design and construction, Building Regulations require that the combined loads affecting a building can be safely carried by the structure and can be transmitted safely to the ground without causing any deflection or movement of any part of the building.

While it may not be a requirement that structural calculations be submitted to illustrate a structure's likelihood to do this, such information might be requested by the authorities and so should be available for submission to them. Such information is, in any event, necessary for the proper design of any structure.

Clear guidelines are issued by the regulating authorities as to the design of loadbearing masonry structures. Compliance with such guidelines will meet the requirements of the regulations without specific calculations being necessary. Loadbearing structures falling outside the scope of the guidelines will, however, require calculations to be done for them.

In regard to timber frame structures, the sizes of the various components of these will have to be calculated in order to comply with the provisions of the regulations.

Strictly speaking, this is a job for a qualified person. The amount of work involved in completing such calculations is not very great. Also, computer programmes exist which can carry out this type of calculation rapidly and with ease. Such programmes are normally used by timber frame manufacturers.

fig. 82: If the ground does not have the ability to resist the load applied to it by the foundations, the foundations will sink.

Taking On Board Compliance With The Building Regulations

Regulations embody all of the fear issues which the topic of *Structure* manages to raise. An outline of these, as set out in pages 198 & 200 of the *Structure* chapter, will strike fear into the bravest soul. If you are working in a jurisdiction other than Ireland refer to your local *Regulations* which will address issues particular to the conditions pertaining in your area.

In reality these issues are 'down the road' from where your design presently stands. However you do need to take on board the fact that for your completed design to be constructed it will require a set of Working Drawings to be prepared for it. Such drawings concern themselves with the minutiae of the design including the issue of the *Structure* complying with the *Building Regulations*. Architects, Engineers and Building Technicians are all qualified to prepare such Working Drawings. Indeed any person with a basic knowledge of materials and construction can competently design a *Structure* to meet the *Regulations*.

The issue however is not one of qualification but rather one of liability. Where a mortgage is to be put in place to finance the construction of a building, the lender will require that the construction be Certified as to its compliance with the relevant *Building Regulations*. Such certification must be backed up with professional indemnity insurance so that, in the event of a problem arising, the lender has someone to sue. This makes building professionals very cautious in their approach particularly if they are not familiar with a particular structural system - for example, breathable timber framing, post and beam, hemp/lime, straw bale or cob, for example. In the case of a conventional timber frame, one way round this is to employ an engineer or a specialist Timber Framing Company to 'design' the frame and to meet the relevant *Regulations* as far as the *Structure* is concerned. For more innovative building systems one may need to seek out a professional familiar with the particular approach you wish to take. In the case of replanning or extending an existing building, compliance with *Building Regulations* will also be required.

Create a file entitled *'Regulations'* and use this to gather information on the issues involved - especially the strings attached to mortgage financing.

Next: SDP20 - Environment, page 203

It is important that advice on structural matters, if it proves to be necessary, be sought at an early stage of the design process. Normally this would be when a general decision in regard to structural type has been made and when a preliminary layout has been completed. If an early consultation is made, any changes deemed necessary can be incorporated into the design without undue difficulty.

While any qualified person might be deemed capable of making the necessary calculations for you it is important that a person be chosen that you can get along with fairly well. In this regard, it is important that you present yourself and your design information as clearly and as straightforwardly as possible. In the world of professional architecture, advice is regularly sought from engineering professionals in regard to the structural form of the buildings that are being designed. At all points in such consultations the architect leads the design team.

Companies that design and erect timber frames will undertake the compilation of structural calculations on behalf of their clients. If you intend to use the services of such a company, this will obviate the need for you to engage a structural engineer.

The requirements of the Building Regulations in regard to structural stability and strength means that the structure of a building must be designed in such a way that the loading it is subjected to in normal use will not cause it to move in any way. To meet this requirement, the wind and snow loading that the finished building is likely to be subjected to, the weight of the structure itself and the loading caused by the furniture, fittings and people must be quantified. The design of the structure is then based on these values.

Wind and snow loading figures are available from regulating authorities. The values indicated in *Code of Practice (CP) 3, Chapter V, Part 2, 1972* can also be used.

The load caused by the structure itself will depend on the materials used in the construction. The values given in *British Standard (BS) 6399 Parts 1 & 3* can be used in calculations. Loads resulting from the occupancy of the dwelling should accord with the values given in the same document. Codes of Practice and National Standards are reference documents that treat specific topics, such as building loading, in great detail. Euronorms relating to topics covered by National Codes and Standards may also be used for the purpose of making structural calculations, provided such Eurocodes are sub-

ject to the requirements of the National Application Document for these codes.

Generally, loadbearing structures should be designed in compliance with *Irish Standard (IS) 325, Part 1, 1986* or *BS 5628, Part 3, 1985*. Timber frame structures should comply with *SR 11, 1988, BS 5268, Part 2, 1991* and *IS 193, 1986*. In regard to the external cladding of frame structures, the provisions of *BS 8200, 1986* should be followed. Timber cladding should conform with the provisions of *BS 5268 Part 2, 1989*. Steel cladding with *5950, Part 1, 1985, BS 5950, Part 5 1987* and *BS 449, 1969*. Profiled sheet cladding should conform with *BS 5427, 1976*.

The above information is not intended to intimidate the reader but is included as a matter of record and for reference purposes. The translation of these codes into clear guidelines to assist the designer is covered in the chapter entitled *'Construction'* in Volume 2.

In regard to foundations, Building Regulations require that the building be designed and constructed in such a way that movements of the subsoil will not impair the stability of any part of the building. The provisions of *BS 8044, 1986* should be adhered to in this regard.

In effect, these requirements necessitate a proper and careful examination of the soil conditions on any proposed site and require that foundations be designed appropriate to these conditions. Made-up ground, subsoils with wide variations in subsoil types or weak soil at depths below normal foundation level all present difficulties in regard to meeting the regulations. Such conditions, of course, also present difficulties in practice.

The excavation of 1200mm deep test holes at several locations within the area that a proposed building is likely to occupy will provide a clear indication of the soil conditions existing on any particular site. Clearly, the proper examination of a proposed building site should be carried out in advance of purchase of such a site. If this is not possible, a proper examination of an existing site should be carried out at an early stage of the design exercise.

A further provision of the regulations in regard to foundations stipulates that the construction of a new building, or any extension to an existing one, should not in any way impair the stability of any part of an existing building. This provision largely relates to extensions to existing buildings and the care that is needed to avoid disturbing the existing foundations in any way.

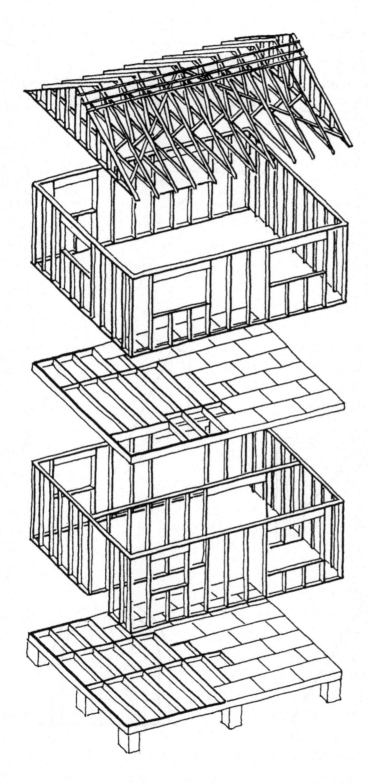

Typical timber frame structure using 4x2" (100x50mm) sections and plywood sheeting and flooring.

Summary

Make structural models and observe the effects of vertical and horizontal loading on these.

Consider engaging a professional engineer if structural calculations must be submitted with a planning application.

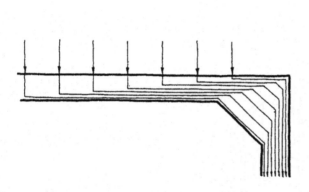

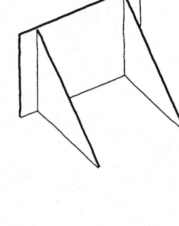

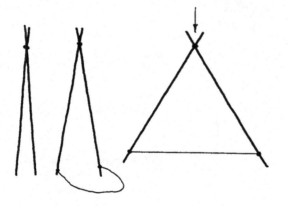

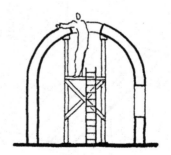

202

It is very important that the healthiness of a building's 'environment' is recognised at this point. This encompasses both the 'internal' environment as well as the 'external' environment within which the building is located.

Environmental considerations encompass both physical as well as psychological issues. What this means is that the building design that is being created must be seen as a 'living' thing, not merely as an assemblage of inanimate objects. Equally, the relationship of this living architecture to the 'outside world' must be considered as a dynamic living relationship.

Such an approach acknowledges that human life is marked by self-awareness and is composed of visible and invisible aspects. While the visible aspects of life are, by definition, visible to the eye, in order to detect its invisible aspects a different form of attunement is required. Such sensitivity must be consciously acknowledged otherwise one can remain blind to the effects of these invisible 'forces'. This is particularly true of electromagnetic radiation, earth energies, dirty electricity, odours, vibrations and so on.

Read 'Environment'. Then print the Environment Worksheet and outline your environmental preferences on this. Create an Environment File in which to store this and other relevant items.

If you are designing an extension to an existing building you need to assess the environmental quality of this, particularly where manufactured materials have been used in the construction. It is also important to assess a property for to the presence of invisible 'forces' such as detrimental earth energies, electromagnetic radiation, dirty electricity etc. as these can cause pollution of the local environment which might easily be overlooked in the desire to extend or renovate as a means of improving a place.

Next: SDP21 - Introduction To Heating & Ventilation, page 213

Masonry, or, ceramic stove

Environment

The physical world we inhabit is made from the interaction of four major elements – earth, air, fire and water *fig. 1*. These elements, of which we are composed and that compose all the natural world, exist in and around us in a harmony that is self-sustaining and beneficent to life.

fig. 1: The physical world we inhabit is made from the interaction of four major elements – earth, air, fire and water.

Our bodies are made of and sustained by a combination of earth, air, fire and water elements. Of these, water is the most abundant and air the most essential. Fire exists in our bodies in the form of heat, and sunlight has a considerable effect on our emotional well-being. The actual solid matter of our bodies derives from the earth itself and returns to the earth when we die.

The combination of major elements that comprises our bodies inexorably links us with nature and with the processes of nature. These processes are essentially cyclical. This means that they are natural, harmonious and balanced. In this way our natural world is constantly changing and reshaping itself – but always out of the same things – the four elements of earth, air, fire and water. Of these, fire is the only element that is constantly being added to the world *fig. 2*. The other three elements exist only in the amounts originally combined to make our world and are processed over and over again *fig. 3*. This natural recycling process allows life to exist and propagate on the planet.

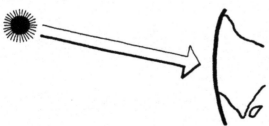

fig. 2: Fire is the only element that is constantly being added to the world.

fig. 3: The other three elements exist only in the amounts originally combined to make our world and are processed over and over again. This natural recycling process allows life to exist and propagate on the planet.

Besides these physical aspects of the world, as expressed in the existence of the four major elements of earth, air, fire and water, are the phenomena of radiation and magnetism *fig. 4*. These phenomena constantly impact the earth and all physical matter in the form of electromagnetic radiation. Detectable but invisible radiation travels in waves *fig. 5*. Light, radio waves, microwaves and gamma rays all exist in the electromagnetic spectrum. The electromagnetic spectrum is the range of electromagnetic radiations that are known *fig. 6*. The major source of natural radiation is the sun, but radiation from the moon and the planets can also affect the earth. Manmade radiations also exist.

 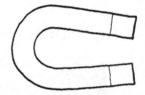

fig. 4: Besides the physical aspects of the world, as expressed in the existence of the earth, air, fire and water elements. There exist the phenomena of radiation and magnetism.

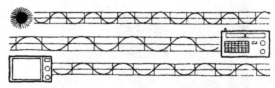

fig. 5: Detectable but invisible radiation travels in waves. Light, radio waves, microwaves and gamma rays all exist in the electromagnetic spectrum.

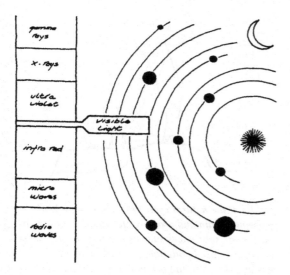

fig. 6: The electromagnetic spectrum is the range of electromagnetic radiations that are known. The major source of natural radiation is the sun, but radiation from the moon and the planets can also affect the earth. Manmade radiations also exist.

Some forms of electromagnetic radiation are essential for the life process, particularly light. Radiations such as ultra violet in large doses can be harmful. Large amounts of radiation are screened by the atmosphere before they reach the earth fig. 7. This is part of the harmony of the natural world.

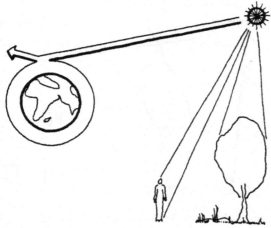

fig. 7: Some forms of electromagnetic radiation are essential for the life process, particularly light. Radiations such as ultra violet in large doses can be harmful. Large amounts of radiation are screened by the atmosphere before they reach the earth.

The Natural World

Environment is the word we use to describe the harmonies and cycles of the four elements, earth, air, fire and water, their combination with radiation and magnetism and the effect this has on our lives.

A good example of the natural harmony of our world is the way in which water is collected and deposited on the earth in a natural cycle fig. 8. Sun and wind cause water to evaporate from the sea, from lakes and rivers, from plants and from people. This evaporated moisture rises into the atmosphere to form clouds. The water is then transported in cloud form and deposited elsewhere as rain, snow or dew. Where this falls on the earth it becomes available to plants, animals and man and then finds its way into the groundwater system. From here it makes its way back into the sea, or rivers and lakes, and the cycle begins again.

This cycle is composed of a balance between the elements of earth, air, fire and water, as well as electromagnetic radiation and magnetism. Water is evaporated from the earth by fire – the heat of the sun. While fire and heat can be regarded as being a physical element, the heat of the sun reaches the earth through the vacuum of space by means of electromagnetic radiation. The evaporated moisture created by this heat is transported on the air and redeposited on the earth by means of gravity. After the water has been used by plants, man and animals, it returns to the earth which cleanses it as it makes its way into the groundwater system. The interdependence between these four elements is an example of natural balance and. as such, is characteristic of life.

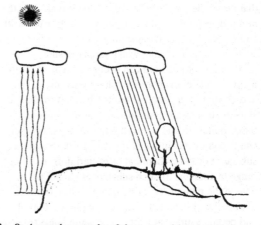

fig. 8: A good example of the natural harmony of our world is the way in which water is collected and deposited on the earth in a natural cycle.

Our physical bodies are made up of the four major elements. They are also subjected to the effects of radiation and magnetism. When we die, our bodies decompose and return to the earth again. Our bodies are also naturally attuned to the movements of the sun, the moon and the planets. The earth's gravity and magnetism affect us also *fig. 9.*

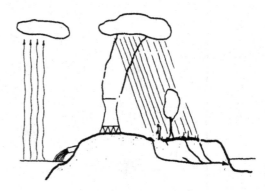

fig. 10: If the natural cycle of evaporation, cloud movement, rain and groundwater runoff is tainted by man-made substances such as are contained in smog or ground based pollution, the water moving through the cycle can become contaminated.

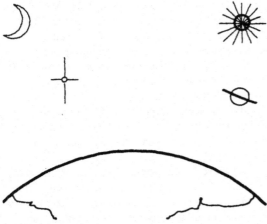

fig. 9: Our bodies are naturally attuned to the movements of the sun, the moon and the planets. The earth's gravity and magnetism affect us also.

Natural Balance And Harmony

Any disruption of the natural cycles of the environment can be threatening to life. For example, all life depends on water for survival. If the supply of water is stopped, life itself stops.

It is not these extreme circumstances, however, that prove the greatest threat to our survival. It is the minor disruptions to the natural cycles of birth, death and regeneration that reduce the quality of life that such things as a reliable water supply ensure.

Threats of this kind can occur very easily. If the natural cycle of evaporation, cloud movement, rain and groundwater runoff is tainted by man-made substances such as are contained in smog or ground based pollution, the water moving through the cycle can become contaminated *fig. 10.* These polluting substances can be chemical or bacterial, from a wide range of sources. If such substances cannot participate in the natural recycling process, they begin to disrupt the system and to affect the plants, animals and people using that water. The same holds true for all natural processes, not just those concerned with the water supply.

The effects of pollution on life are usually slow moving and not immediately devastating. Our bodies, for example, are well equipped to deal with any unpleasant input to our individual life systems. Any threat to our bodily well-being that is caused by pollution is normally efficiently dealt with by our immune systems. Such pollution can take many forms and can be chemical or electromagnetic. Man-made chemicals and radiations are particularly threatening *fig. 11.*

fig. 11: Any threat to our bodily well-being that is caused by pollution is normally efficiently dealt with by our immune systems. Such pollution can take many forms and can be chemical or electromagnetic. Man made chemicals and radiations are particularly threatening.

206

Bodily response to any perceived danger is controlled by the immune system. If the immune system is put under constant strain to keep the body healthy, it will be weakened considerably. Such strain can occur when regular small scale threats must be endured by the body. Such strain can impair the system's ability to cope with a major threat to the body. The immune system's response to sensory input is an automatic one that we are not always aware of. Strains on the system can easily go undetected. This is especially true when the environment is largely man-made and the body is surrounded by danger.

This makes it even more important that the home environment places as few strains on the body as possible. In this way the natural defence mechanisms can be relaxed and the immune system given a chance to renew itself *fig. 12*.

We perceive the environment through our senses of touch, smell, taste, sight and hearing *fig. 13*. These five senses deliver to our brains information on the state of our surroundings – the environment. This information enables our bodies to adjust to our surroundings and, consequently, to survive.

For example, if we smell gas when we are within a building, we immediately become alarmed, seek out the source, open doors to allow fresh air in, and generally do everything we can to ensure our survival. Another example of our sensory perception protecting us is using our feet – our sense of touch – to 'test the ground'. If we are walking on very soft ground or on something unstable we do this automatically *fig. 14*.

fig. 13: We perceive the environment through our senses of touch, smell, taste, sight and hearing. These five senses deliver to our brains information on the state of our surroundings – the environment. This information enables our bodies to adjust to our surroundings and, consequently, to survive.

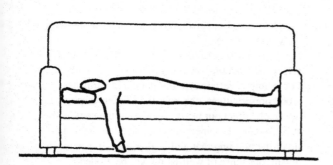

fig. 12: It is important that the home environment places as few strains on the body as possible.

Survival Instinct

One of the primary forces behind the desire to create buildings is the human urge to survive and flourish.

We interpret the physical world through our senses and rely on the information gathered in this way to ensure our survival. A shelter of any kind is inevitably part of the wider environment in which it exists. Because it is created in response to such a deep urge in us – the urge to survive which is assisted by our senses – any shelter that we create must satisfy the senses in order to best protect us in this quest for life.

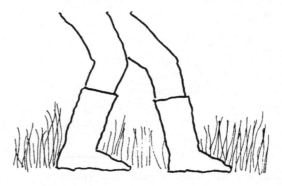

fig. 14: We use our feet – our sense of touch – to 'test the ground' if we are walking on very soft ground or on something unstable. We do this automatically.

207

The messages that our brain receives from our senses determine the response that our bodies have to make to adjust to the local environment. If we sense that our bodies are cold, we respond by heating them up – by putting on more clothes, by closing an open window or door, by lighting a fire and so on. The easier it is for our bodies to adjust to the local environment the better it is for our bodies – the less work they will have to do. Other forms of threat to our health are dealt with by our defence mechanisms – our immune systems.

The creation of any building involves the modification of the local environment and the creation of an internal man-made environment. This internal environment must also achieve a balance between the four life sustaining elements of earth, air, fire and water, just as the natural world does. The creation and regulation of this internal environment is a very important aspect of any building design. Such an environment should pose no threat whatsoever to its inhabitants. If this is done, the building will provide an environment in which the body can relax, renew itself and enjoy a sense of general well-being *fig. 15*.

The way in which a house is built, the materials that it is made from, the way that light enters it and the quality of the air within it all impact our senses, which in turn signal our brain as to the state of our surroundings – our environment. This triggers whatever bodily responses are necessary to ensure our survival. If no bodily threat whatsoever is offered us in our home environment, we can relax and so enjoy being alive. A further benefit will also be available to us in that we can recover from the rigours of the modern world which inevitably threaten our well-being.

fig. 15: The internal environment of a building should pose no threat whatsoever to its inhabitants. If this is done, the building will provide an environment in which the body can relax, renew itself and enjoy a sense of general well-being.

Using Common Sense

In practical terms, the selection of building materials and the way in which they are put together to form the internal environment of a building should be made in relation to how they are likely to affect us in use.

The abstract qualities enumerated in the Brief are the keys to telling us the type of internal environment we wish to make. For example, if we want a 'light and airy' kitchen then we want our sense of sight to be impacted in a certain way in that kitchen. When the light aspect of the internal environment is being considered, it must be designed to please that sense – our sense of sight. To achieve this we have to pay close attention to the windows in the kitchen, to the orientation of the room and possibly to the final colour scheme.

It is by impacting our senses with good news – something good to look at, something nice to touch, something nice to smell, something pleasant to hear and, to top it all off, something nice to taste, that allows our sensory mechanisms to relax and fill us with a sense of well-being. This is what relaxation is – we are at ease, we are in harmony with our surroundings and our surroundings are in harmony with the world at large.

To create this kind of environment, you need to select very carefully the materials that it is made of. For example, certain types of paint and varnishes, wood preservatives, chipboards and even carpets can adversely effect our health because of the chemicals they contain. If something is included in the makeup of the building that will trigger our defence mechanism, our sense of well-being will be eroded. Furthermore, the ability of our immune system to fight off a major attack can be lessened from being in a constant state of alert. Because our response to our environment is an automatic thing, it is almost impossible to switch our senses off – otherwise we would simply die.

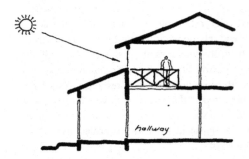

The Sixth Sense

While the input to the five major senses can usually be physically isolated, input to our sixth sense is abstract and non physical. Our response to this is through the organs of perception. Unlike our ears, our eyes, our tongues, our noses or our skin, the organs of sixth sense perception are not physically evident in our bodies. This type of perception is expressed in the way we feel about something.

Our preoccupation with the physical world and our senses that interpret it, oftentimes neglects this vital sixth sense. As with the physical senses, any disturbing input channelled through this sense will automatically trigger a defensive response to ensure our survival. The defensive responses triggered by this sense are very strong because the urge to survive, itself, is a sixth sense.

The operation of the sixth sense is witnessed in the way we feel about things. It is what is left over after the other five senses and their responses have been isolated and physically identified. It is very important to attune ourselves to this sixth sense and to allow our interpretation of it – our intuition – to properly hold its place alongside rational interpretation based on the other five.

Earth

The earth, and the nature of the earth, plays a major role in influencing building design. Inevitably, buildings stand on the earth and so must conform to the ability of the earth to support them. The exceptions to this would be tree-houses and houseboats.

Many building materials are derived from substances found in the earth – stone, sand, clay, gypsum and glass, to name but a few. Some of these materials retain strong 'earthy' qualities which are oftentimes exploited in building design.

Trees and plants also fall into the category of earth materials. Wood, of course, is the single most useful building material known to man. Trees can also provide oils, scents, food, medicine and fuel. Plants provide pigments and dyes, materials such as cotton and linen, as well as food.

Oil is an earth substance which is used to make many products used in modern building. Plastics, paints, adhesives, synthetic fabrics and many types of chemicals and synthetics are produced by the petrochemical industry. Oil is also used as a major fuel for heating purposes.

All types of metals are of earth origin. Metals are used to make nails, reinforcing bars, door and window latches, hinges, wires, stoves and so on for use in buildings.

Earth based materials, such as stone and clay, can be used to store heat, either from conventional heating systems or in passive solar heating systems.

Air

Air is particularly important in the built environment. Our bodies depend on air for breathing and for recycling exhaled air. Also, the water that we expel when breathing, as well as perspiration, are recycled by the air. Air also plays an important role in the drying process involved with many construction techniques – the drying of concrete for example. Air functions as a means of cooling our bodies, as well as all types of mechanical apparatus.

Air is composed mainly of nitrogen and oxygen that exist in a balance ideal for sustaining and creating life. Oftentimes this natural balance of air is disturbed by the presence of other gases which are produced by burning and by chemical reactions. Our bodies must process this air, in order to extract from it the oxygen that is essential to our survival.

While most bad air might be regarded as being 'outside' air, this of course is not always the case. Polluted air is everywhere, including within the buildings we live in. Oftentimes we can pollute the air within a house by unwittingly adding to it gases that are harmful to life. These gases can come from adhesives, synthetic fabrics, cleaning products and many modern materials that are artificially produced. While our bodies can breathe air that has been polluted with gases that are not particularly good for us, the strain that this puts on our defence systems is enormous. Many gases that are harmful are produced by burning. Dust, bacteria and fungi are also present in the air. Headaches, itchy or watering eyes, nose and throat infections, dizziness, nausea, colds, asthma, bronchitis and allergies are all symptoms of polluted indoor air.

To minimise the risk of creating a polluted internal air environment, one should choose very carefully all materials and products used in its construction and furnishing. A clean and efficient heating system is also critical to this. Buildings also need to be properly ventilated. Ventilation is the renewal or changing of the air within the building. Ventilation is necessary for the provision of fresh clean air to replace air that has been breathed and air that has been polluted with gases and so on.

Our sense of smell depends on the air. This sense is thousands of times more accurate than the sense of taste. As with our other senses, our sense of smell helps us to survive. By reacting to unpleasant smells, our bodies warn us that we are breathing something which is bad for us. If you ignore these warnings, your system may become overtaxed and this causes stress or even illness. Olfactory fatigue is a condition whereby your sense of smell adapts to a danger and ignores the warnings being given you. This can happen where you are exposed to polluted air on a regular basis. We would normally describe this as 'getting used to something'!

Because the internal environment you create within your home is under your control, it is possible to make this environment totally safe for you and your family. This is in marked contrast to the outside world, which you can do very little to control. If the air in your home is healthy, you and your family will be able to relax and allow your natural defences – your immune system – to recover from the stresses that it is regularly subjected to in the outside world.

Air can carry natural electrical charges. The natural electrical balance of air is five positively charged air molecules, or ions, to every four negatively charged ions. This natural balance is believed to give people a sense of well-being. Any change in this balance that produces an excess of positive ions creates feelings of tension, irritability and depression and can even account for physical disorders. Accidents rise at times when there is an excess of positive ions in the air. Such excesses occur before thunderstorms or in certain types of winds, such as the *Mistral* and the *Santana*. At these times the negative ions lose charge and the positive ions dominate. In the domestic environment, negative ions are depleted by the electrical fields from TVs and VDUs. The natural electrical balance of air can be restored artificially by the use of ionisers. An open fire will also function to create negative ions. 'Breaking water', such as is produced by a fountain or waterfall in the vicinity of the dwelling, will also serve to do this.

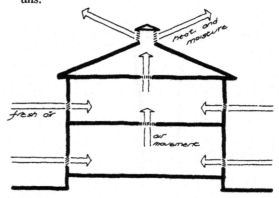

Fire

The most obvious application of fire in the creation of living environments is for heating purposes. Fire is also used in the production of many building materials, especially metals.

Fire, in the form of solar heat and energy, is responsible for the growth of plants and trees from which many building materials are derived. Similarly, the sun contributes to the production of edible plants. Fire is also essential to the cooking process.

The sun is the embodiment of the element 'fire'. Oil, coal, wood and turf, which produce heat when burned, are, in fact, releasing stored solar energy in the process.

The energy of the sun plays a vital role in nurturing our well-being. Without some exposure to the sun, human beings can develop a syndrome related to sunlight deprivation.

Water

Water is involved in almost all aspects of designing an internal environment and to the creation of buildings. Our bodies are largely composed of water and we exhale considerable amounts of water when we breathe. Water is also essential to the cooking process, as well as being a very important beverage. A source of pure drinking water is very desirable within any dwelling – this is not always possible due to the low level pollution in many piped in supplies. Filters can rectify this to some extent. Without water our bodies dehydrate and die. This is in marked contrast to food, which our bodies can do without for long periods of time. Water, of course, is essential to food production.

Some building processes require large amounts of water. The making of concrete for example. Up to 2500 gallons of water can be used in the building of a house using 'wet' construction techniques.

Water is normally used for cleansing purposes – for washing as well as for the removal of bodily wastes from the home. It is in these processes that much pollution can be caused, by the introduction of chemicals and foreign bodies into the natural water cycle.

Water also plays a part in heating systems, as it is capable of storing large quantities of heat that can be then easily moved from place to place in pipes.

Finally, water is an important constituent of air. The addition of water vapour to very dry air 'humidifies' that air, making for a more pleasant atmosphere. In planetary terms, the oceans play a major role in keeping the planet cool by absorbing heat from the sun.

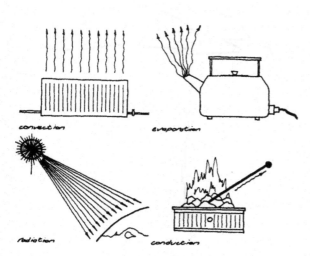

convection   evaporation

radiation   conduction

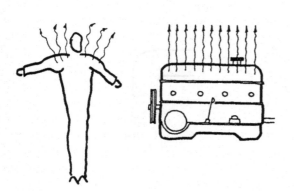

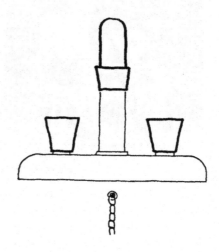

Radiation and Magnetism

Light is the most familiar type of electromagnetic radiation affecting our daily lives. Infra-red and ultra-violet radiations also regularly impact the earth. The earth's magnetic field operates at all times. Radio waves, microwaves, radioactivity as well as radiation from man-made electricity constantly surround us and the world we live in.

The human body operates on the basis of weak electrical signals within the nervous system. Any disturbance to this subtle control mechanism can have serious consequences for our health and well-being. Such disturbance can be caused by overexposure to large amounts of electromagnetic radiation. The effects of radioactivity on the human body are well known. The effects of exposure to high tension power lines are also well documented. Microwave ovens as well as microwaves used for communications systems can also be harmful to life.

It is believed that past cultures had a highly developed awareness of the natural electromagnetic 'grid' enmeshing the earth. This energy grid, fed from the sun, the moon and the planets as well as from earth sources, was delineated by 'ley lines', evidence of which remains detectable to this day.

Summary

Consider the world as a four-part harmony composed of the elements earth, air, fire and water.

Consider the existence of Radiation and Magnetism and their effects on the planet.

Consider the natural recycling process of our environment and how this contributes to order and balance on the earth.

Consider the importance of a healthy environment in nurturing our well-being and the effects of environmental imbalance on the body's immune system.

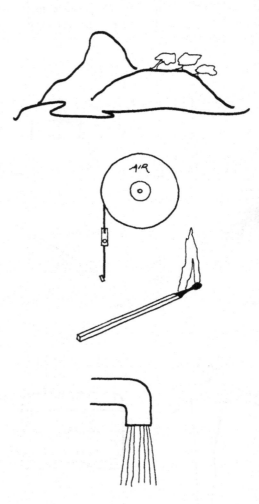

Exploring harmony

212

21 Sheltermaker Design Programme
Introduction To Heating & Ventilation

Heating and its companion, *Ventilation*, play a huge part in influencing the layout, orientation and siting of a building as well as influencing its structural type and the choice of materials required to construct it. *Heating & Ventilation* are also critical to the likely energy performance of a building. This will have meet minimum standards set by national energy regulation bodies - before it is constructed! Also, *H&V*, as it is commonly referred to, has a bearing on the creation of a healthy internal environment and affects the external environment also. The topic of *H&V* also includes the subject of *Cooling* and should properly be referred to as '*Heating, Cooling & Ventilation*'.

Approach the subject of *H&V* gently. The *Heating & Ventilation* chapter contains a wealth of information, facts and figures that can easily overwhelm. So, begin by absorbing it slowly using this *Design Programme* as your guide. More than any other aspect of building design, this topic will key one into the crucial aspects of sustainability - climate change; the burning of fossil fuels; solar energy; waste; pollution and so on.

Begin by reading pages 214 - 219. The critical facts are as follows:

a) Heat always tries to move towards cold.

b) Our bodies produce too much heat.

These two facts are the basis for creating a healthy and workable *H&V* system.

Item b) begs the question - '*What are we heating when we heat a building if the people within it are normally shedding heat in order to remain at a comfortable temperature?*'

It is worthwhile creating a *H&V* File at this stage and to begin the assembly of information on fuels, boilers, stoves etc.

If you are working on an existing building an assessment of its *H&V* systems and their performance will be necessary. Refer to the *Surveying* chapter for guidance on this. Boilers, heat pumps, solid fuel stoves, fuel tanks and fuel stores, pipe runs, flues, exhaust fans, etc. should all be inspected and tested and the details recorded in the *H&V* file. Assessing how fresh air gets into a building and stale air exits is also important. Estimating the insulation values of the external walls, the floor and the roof is necessary also - though oftentimes this can be difficult, particularly in respect of external walls and solid floors. The thickness of external walls however can serve as a useful guide to the amount of insulation they might contain. The external building fabric should also be carefully inspected for signs of condensation, dampness, etc. Internal relative humidity levels should be tested, particularly when cooking or bathing activities are taking place and at times of high occupancy.

Next: SDP22 The Role of Air & Water in Heating & Ventilation, page 220

Heating and Ventilation

Properly, this should read Heating, Cooling & Ventilation!

Heat is an abstract, but nonetheless physical, concept. We speak of things being 'hot' or 'cold' and we measure these physical states in 'degrees of temperature' called Centigrade. Temperatures are normally written as °C and sometimes simply as 'K'.

Heat always tries to move to somewhere colder than where it is. For example, air that has a temperature of 23°C will automatically try to go somewhere that is cooler than 23°C. You can experience heat movement if you put your hand on a block of ice. Heat will immediately leave your hand and go into the ice which will begin to melt from this transfer of heat. This transfer will occur so rapidly as to be painful after a short time. Similarly, if you stand on a cold floor in your bare feet you will experience severe heat loss.

Heat moves in a number of ways. These types of heat movement are called *convection, conduction, radiation* and *evaporation fig. 1.*

Convection heat movements rely on air in order to take place. In other words the heat moves in the air on its journey to somewhere colder – warm air always moves to where there is a lower temperature.

Conduction heat movements rely on a solid or liquid in order to take place – a poker placed in a hot fire will rapidly conduct the heat of the fire along the poker. Metals are generally good conductors of heat. Materials such as timber are not so good. Water is an especially good conductor of heat.

Evaporation heat movements rely on a combination of water and air in order to take place. This happens, for example, when so much heat has been applied to water that it boils. Boiling water is water that is shedding excess heat in the form of a gas – water vapour. This hot gas, a mixture of water and air, then moves to somewhere colder. Towards the kitchen window, for example, where the water vapour cools down – releasing its heat – and promptly turns back into water. This process of water vapour cooling and turning back into water is called *condensation.*

Radiation heat movements are more mysterious than any of the other ways in which heat moves. This is because no actual physical medium is needed to accomplish the heat transfer from a warm place to a cooler place. The best example of radiant heat movement is the way in which the sun radiates heat to the earth. This is achieved by waves of heat energy crossing through the vacuum of space from the hot sun to the cooler earth. When this radiation strikes something – for example the tar on the road – the radiation changes its wavelength and in the process releases its heat. This is the heat we feel on our skin when we expose ourselves to direct sunlight.

The sun is not the only source of radiant heat. Almost any material that can be warmed up – a metal poker, for example – will radiate out some of its heat to the cooler objects in the vicinity. An open fire will warm your hands because it is sending out heat radiation which releases its heat when it strikes your hand. Radiant heat waves travel in straight lines and radiate out in all directions from a warm surface to a cooler one.

While it can be accepted that heat always moves from a warm place to a cold one in these certain ways, it is a curious question to ask 'what really happens to the heat – where does it eventually go?' The answer to that is simply that it is absorbed into the ground, radiated off into space at night, or absorbed by the many cold regions that exist across the planet.

Heat is a form of energy and much of this energy has its origin in the sun. All fossil fuels were formed by the action of the sun on the earth. The heat energy in wood is also derived from the growing tree absorbing sunlight. Usually heat is released from fuels by burning.

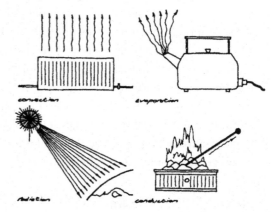

fig. 1: Heat moves in a number of ways – by convection, evaporation, radiation and conduction.

214

Body Heat

The amount of heating and ventilation that a building requires relates primarily to the needs of the human body and the way in which it functions. The human body, like a car engine, produces heat while it works *fig. 2*. This excess heat must be constantly expelled from the body to prevent overheating and to maintain an even body temperature.

Our bodies strive to maintain an even temperature at all times by shedding the excess heat that they produce. This shedding of excess heat must happen in an orderly way and at a reasonably steady rate for the body to feel comfortable.

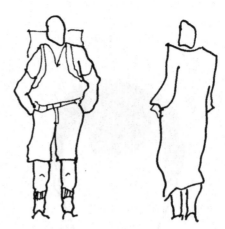

fig. 3: *Normally, clothing is used to control the rate of heat loss from the body's surface.*

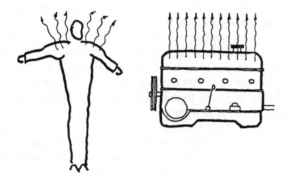

fig. 2: *The human body, like a car engine, produces heat while it works.*

Air plays a major role in removing excess heat from the body by convection. In other words, the excess heat is carried away on the air. Because of this fact, and because air is in other ways essential to life, the heating requirements of any building are always considered together with the fresh air requirements of the building. In other words Heating and Ventilation is regarded as a single question in building design and not as two separate subjects. This is normally referred to simply as '*H&V*'.

Normally, clothing is used to control the rate of heat loss from the body's surface *fig. 3*. Clothes do this by protecting the body from direct exposure, especially to cold air and cold surfaces. Even warm air passing over a body will carry away heat by convection. If the amount of heat carried away like this is too great, the body will loose heat too rapidly and will be made cold. By adjusting the amount and type of clothing we wear we can protect the body, maintain an even body temperature and so be 'comfortable'.

Clothes that work well in respect of controlling the flow of air to and from the body surface are usually natural fabrics like cotton, silk and wool. Such fabrics 'breathe', allowing air to pass through them, as well as holding within their fibres a certain amount of heat. Non-breathable fabrics such as nylon or plastic cause the body to overheat because they restrict the flow of air to the skin. Because the fibres of synthetic fabrics do not hold any heat within them, we regard them as being 'cold' to the touch.

Apart from carrying away excess heat, air also plays an important role in removing waste matter from the body. Skin particles, carbon dioxide, microbes and so on, are all carried away from the body by the action of air movements.

Heat is also radiated out from our bodies, especially from the top of the head *fig. 4*. Our hair controls the rate of heat loss from this part of our bodies. Hats and headscarves, when they are worn, work to minimise these radiant heat losses. Gloves work in a similar fashion for the hands.

Heat is also lost from the human body by evaporation. When we breathe we exhale warm moist air. This air is carrying water vapour and heat and on a cold morning we can see this moisture 'condensing' when it comes in contact with the cold air around it. Evaporation also occurs from the surface of the skin, especially in very hot conditions. Perspiration is moisture that has been expelled from the skin carrying excess heat with it. Such moisture is then evaporated away on the air.

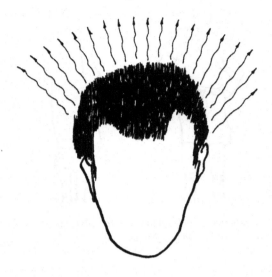

fig. 4: Our bodies radiate out heat, especially the top of our heads.

Conduction heat movements from the body occur when we come into direct contact with a surface that is much colder than the body – a slab of concrete, for example, or a stone floor *fig. 5*. These surfaces will draw away body heat, causing excessive heat losses, resulting in bodily discomfort. Normally we insulate ourselves from such losses by carefully choosing the surfaces that we come into contact with and by wearing shoes to protect our feet from coming into contact with cold materials.

When the H&V system for a building is being considered, it is important to remember that the people occupying the building will in fact be producing more heat than they need to stay warm, assuming that they wear a reasonable amount of clothing to protect themselves from excessive heat losses. These losses of excess body heat by convection, evaporation, radiation and conduction are the means by which we maintain an even temperature. Our body heat balance is primarily controlled by the radiant energy exchange with the immediate environment. In other words, we shed most of our excess body heat by radiating it out to cooler areas. This radiation occurs from all parts of the body, particularly those that are left exposed. Convection losses account for the second largest heat loss, and evaporation the third. Conduction heat losses account for the smallest proportion.

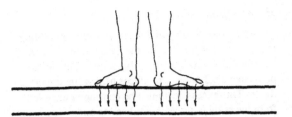

fig. 5: Conduction heat losses from the body occur when we come into direct contact with a surface that is much colder than the body – a slab of concrete, for example, or a stone floor.

H &V System Design

Why H&V systems are needed at all is because the temperature of a building and of the air within it, need to be controlled to bring them into balance with normal body temperature, thus preventing excessive heat loss from the occupants as well as providing them with fresh air. A H&V system does this by supplying fresh air and heat within the building as well as providing a means for expelling stale air *fig. 6*. The expulsion of stale air performs the function of removing moisture and microscopic particles from the interior of the building to the outside air, where they can be recycled naturally.

Like so many of the concepts behind building design, the notion of balance is critical when it comes to designing and choosing a H&V system. It is our bodies and the way in which we clothe them that provide us with the approach needed to design a balanced system.

In the case of needing to cool a building, the ideal is to use good ventilation to achieve this. The best method of all in regards to cooling is to keep a building from heating up in the first place - shading is the ideal way of achieving this.

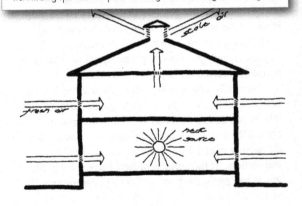

fig. 6: A H&V system supplies fresh air and heat to a building and provides a means for expelling stale air.

The notion of heat loss is one that is essential to understand in order to properly create a working heating and ventilation system. Heat losses in a building, as in our bodies, are caused by convection, evaporation, radiation and conduction. Convection and evaporation losses are losses due to air passing over a warm object and carrying heat away. Radiation losses are caused by an object radiating out heat if it is warmer than the surfaces surrounding it. Conduction losses are caused by heat being conducted through a solid material .

The majority of body heat losses occur by radiating out this heat to the colder surfaces within a building such as the walls, floors and ceilings *fig. 7*. If these surfaces are appreciably colder than the occupants, too much body heat will be radiated out, causing excessive heat loss, making the occupants feel cold. To moderate these heat losses the H&V system has to increase the temperature of these surfaces thereby bringing them more into balance with body temperatures. This results in a reduction in the radiant heat transfer from the occupants to the cold surfaces of the building and so contributes to maintaining bodily comfort. As an alternative to this, the H&V system can heat the internal air to such an extent that the occupants continue to feel warm, despite being surrounded by 'cold' surfaces.

Convection accounts for the next largest loss of body heat after radiation. These losses occur when air passes over the occupants of a building *fig. 8*. The temperature and speed of this internal air is very critical in maintaining a comfortable balance and moderating heat losses. If the air is too cold or it is moving too fast it will simply carry away too much heat, making the occupants cold. To moderate these losses the H&V system has to warm up cold incoming air and control the rate at which it moves through the building. This results in a reduction in the convective heat transfer from the occupants to the internal air that circulates through the building.

Because fresh air is essential to life, and because stale air carries out a kind of waste disposal function also, the introduction of fresh air into a building and the emission of stale air is essential to the creation of a balanced and healthy internal environment. Just as our bodies themselves breathe in fresh air and breathe out heat and moisture, so too does 'the body' of the building *fig. 9*.

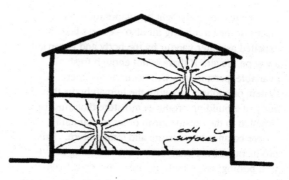

fig. 7: The majority of body heat losses occur by radiating out this heat to the colder surfaces within a building such as the walls, floors and ceilings.

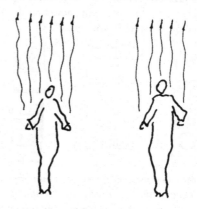

fig. 8: Convection body heat losses occur when air passes over a person.

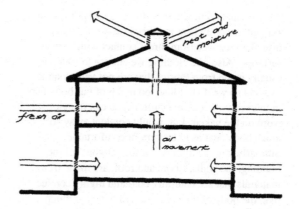

fig. 9: Just as our bodies themselves breathe in fresh air and breathe out heat and moisture, so too does 'the body' of the building.

The loss of body heat by evaporation occurs by means of the circulating air also – excess heat is expelled as water vapour by the body and is carried away on the air. If there is not enough fresh air available, perspiration will occur as an emergency system of cooling. As with the human body, the body of a building produces moisture that must be expelled to the outside air in order to maintain a proper balance of moisture and temperature. This production of moisture arises from cooking activities, boiling water, bathing and showering, from washing machines, from people and from drying and airing clothes *fig. 10*. Moisture production can also occur from the drying out process immediately after a building has been completed. As with the human body, if a building does not have enough fresh air to expel airborne moisture it will 'sweat'.

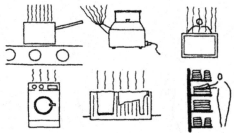

fig. 10: Moisture production within a building arises from cooking activities, boiling water, bathing, showering, from washing machines and from drying and airing clothes.

Conduction heat losses do not account for a large amount of bodily heat loss because we normally insulate ourselves from direct contact with very cold surfaces. Also, the clothing we choose to wear is usually made from fabrics that are not very conductive and so we do not lose too much of our body heat in this way. A concrete shirt, if you can imagine it worn on the naked skin, would conduct away so much body heat as to be very uncomfortable. Similarly with a building – if the 'clothes' of the building, the walls, floors and roof, are made from materials that are naturally cold and highly conductive, the body of the building will have too much heat drawn away from it for comfort. This is especially true of where the building fabric connects with the ground. Cold ground can draw a considerable amount of heat through the fabric of the building. This would be akin to standing barefoot on a stone floor *fig. 11*.

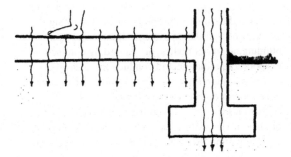

fig. 11: Cold ground can draw a considerable amount of heat through the fabric of the building.

The best model on which to base the design of a building H&V system is the human body *fig. 12*. A building should be imagined as a body with the walls being clothing and the roof the head. The building fabric will have openings for air circulation and will experience heat losses by means of conduction, radiation, evaporation and convection heat movements. These heat movements will create a balance of temperature, air and moisture that will be in harmony with the natural state of the human body. If a building is imagined in this way it will be realised that the selection of 'clothes' for the body of the building is very critical. If naturally warm clothing is used the body of the building will always be comfortable. If 'cold' materials are used – a concrete shirt – it is difficult to achieve this.

fig. 12: The best model on which to base the design of a building H&V system is the human body and the way in which it is clothed.

218

Where food is the fuel that generates heat in the human body, the body of a building requires specialised fuel to generate heat within itself. Oil, gas, wood, coal and turf are all fuels that can be used to generate heat within a building *fig. 13*. This is usually done by burning these fuels, thereby releasing the heat trapped within them. As with food, the heat content of fuel is measured in calories. The heat of the sun can also be utilised for heating purposes. This, of course, can be done without burning. Heat can also be released from wood by setting up a natural decay process in a pile of wood chips. The advantage of this lies in the fact that there is no burning involved and therefore no fire. A valuable mulch is also produced in the process. Heat can also be generated by the use of electricity, though the economics of this are not attractive.

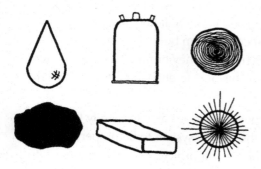

fig. 13: Oil, gas, wood, coal and turf are all fuels that can be used to generate heat within a building. The heat of the sun can also be utilised for this.

The generation of heat within a building must always be considered in relationship to the facts of heat movement and heat loss. Just as the human body loses heat to its surroundings, so too will the body of a building loose heat to its surroundings. These losses are inevitable and the best one can hope to do is to reduce these losses to an absolute minimum by careful design. It must also be remembered that the warm air movements that carry heat and moisture away from a building also carry out a kind of garbage collection service by carrying away noxious gases, skin particles, dust, microbes and so on, helping cleanse the interior of the building. This in fact means that the H&V system of the building very much controls the quality of the internal environment that is created.

Building Regulations require that buildings be designed and constructed so as to secure, as far as is reasonably practicable, the conservation of fuel and energy. The proper ventilation of buildings must also be achieved. Because the H&V system plays such a vital part in the proper functioning of the internal environment of any building, it is necessary at an early stage in the design process to decide in principle the type of system that is to be used. It is also necessary to estimate the capacity of the heating unit that will be required to provide the necessary heat.

All H&V systems influence both the internal planning of buildings as well as their orientation and siting. They also influence the selection of building materials, window design and location, as well as affecting the actual construction of the building. It is for these reasons that the H&V system must be given detailed consideration at an early stage in the design process and clear decisions must be made as to the type of system that is to be used in the finished building.

Proper consideration must also be given to the requirements of the Building Regulations in regard to H&V systems. A file entitled *'Heating & Ventilation'* should be created at this stage and information on all aspects of the subject gathered into this. The vital function of the H&V system in the creation of a healthy internal environment should be borne in mind and adequate time given over to the selection of a healthy, efficient and workable system.

Air

Fresh air is essential to life and to its continuance. It is vitally important that fresh air can get into a building and stale air can escape to the outside air where it can be recycled naturally. How fresh air gets inside a building and stale air gets out is critical in creating a healthy internal environment. Once inside a building, the temperature of the air, the way it moves and the amount of water vapour it holds create the internal living environment.

The question of fresh air getting into a building and stale air getting out is called *'ventilation'*. The purpose of ventilation is to provide fresh air for breathing, to dilute and remove from the interior cooking or body odours; to provide cooling in summer; to increase a low moisture content or to remove an excess of moisture. Stale air removes waste from the interior of a building, expelling it to the outside air where it can be recycled naturally.

The Role Of Air & Water In Heating & Ventilation

Air & water play critical roles in the design and operation of any *H&V* system, particularly in the creation of healthy buildings. Details of these roles are described in pages 219-229.

It is critical, when reading those pages, to understand that a building is a living environment and that the operation of the *H&V* system, to a large extent, is the heart or, hearth, of that environment. The human body and its living functions are the models to follow in the design and creation of an efficient and healthy system. An internal environment must be not only healthy, but *energising* to its occupants.

Some climates require that buildings are provided with protection from the sun and oftentimes require cooling! Ironically, passive solar designs in cool climaters oftentimes suffer from excess heat gains at either end of the heating season. The first principle is to avoid a building overheating in the first place. This can be achieved by the use of blinds, shutters, roof overhangs, verandahs, etc. Also, cool air can be channeled into a building through pipes that are buried in the ground or submerged in water. Such cool air can be 'drawn' through a building much the same as smoke is 'drawn' upwards by a chimney or flue. It is a good idea to refer to traditional solutions to heating/cooling problems by reference to parts of the world that have similar climates to your location.

As to the facts and figures regarding *Ventilation* in pages 219-229 - you can merely take them on board as the numerical expression of the need of the 'living' system to be properly supplied with air. In reality, at the detailed design stage of your project, you will refer back to these facts and figures and apply them to the specifics of your design. For now it is the principles of the *H&V* system design that concerns you, particularly the fact that the choice of materials will be affected by this system design as will the internal layout of the building and its orientation and siting.

Next: SDP23 - Heat Losses & Heat Gains; Thermal Mass & Insulation, page 231

Ventilation occurs in buildings via openings through which fresh air can enter and stale air can get out *fig. 14*. Generally, warm stale air will rise and leave a building at a high level and cooler fresh air will be drawn in at low level. The location of inlets and outlets, their relative sizes and the difference in temperature between the stale air and the fresh air will determine just how rapid the movement of air will be through the building. In older buildings, especially those with open fireplaces, the infiltration of fresh air occurs through loose fitting doors and windows, through cracks and so on. In modern, tightly sealed constructions, supplying fresh air to the interior of a building, is a more difficult task. Traditionally, windows have served the function of allowing fresh air into a building but the opening of a window will normally allow too much air into a building, creating draughts which will carry away too much heat. Fresh air inlets located on the sides of a building exposed to the wind will allow for a natural movement of air into a building. Outlets located at high level on the sheltered sides of the building will allow for stale air to make its way outside.

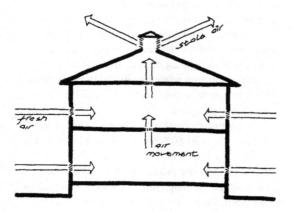

fig. 14: Ventilation occurs in buildings via openings through which fresh air can enter and stale air can get out.

In addition to providing specific ventilation openings, the construction of a building can be made to 'breathe'. If this is done, air moves through the fabric of the building much as air moves through our clothing. There are benefits in using this type of arrangement, not least of which is how the system parallels the way in which we clothe our bodies.

An adequate supply of fresh air for the occupants of any building is of critical importance. If this is not done there will simply not be enough oxygen to breathe, and what air there is within the building will become stale and noxious. Building Regulations require that buildings be provided with adequate means of supplying fresh air to their occupants and to any heating units within them.

Figures vary as to the amount of fresh air that is required in any particular situation. Anything from one to four air changes per hour might be required to maintain a proper supply of fresh air for breathing, within a building. That is, all the air within a room or building will need to be replaced anything from once to four times every hour. Because the air within a building is normally warm and so tries to escape to the colder outside, heat losses due to ventilation can account for a considerable proportion of the overall building heat losses.

Water & Air

Water has an amazing ability to hold heat. So has air. Our bodies expel quite a large amount of moisture and heat, both by exhalation and by evaporation from the skin. Air and water work very well together in carrying away this excess heat. Moisture expelled from the body is normally in the form of water vapour. Water vapour is water in the form of a gas. Such vapour contains heat. Exactly how much water vapour air can carry depends on the temperature of the air.

We normally describe air that contains a lot of water vapour as being humid. In a humid atmosphere our bodies perspire, because the air around us is saturated – in other words it is carrying as much water vapour as it can and it can carry no more. Faced with this state of affairs, our bodies must find another way of getting rid of the excess heat normally shed by evaporation. This is done by using water itself as a vehicle for shedding heat – our bodies perspire. Humid conditions are relieved by introducing fresh air, that is, air that can absorb some of the excess water vapour and carry it away. Inducing an artificial draft by means of a fan will also relieve such conditions. This will produce a flow of air which will carry heat and moisture away with it. As with our bodies, a building also produces water vapour and this must be expelled to the outside air, otherwise the building will begin to sweat or perspire.

Sources of water vapour production within a building are cooking, bathing and showering. Washing machines, fridges and human activity also produce moisture which must be absorbed and processed by the internal environment. It is very important to remember that it is heat that assists in the removal of moisture and other waste from a building. The price one pays for this is the loss of this heat to the cold outside air. If this heat loss is accepted as a vital part of the internal environment, it will not appear at all wasteful that precious heat is ventilated away. In any event, moisture production from cooking and washing should be kept to an absolute minimum and, where possible, be expelled directly to the outside air by means of an extract fan *fig. 15*.

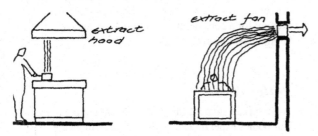

fig. 15: Moisture production from cooking and washing should be kept to an absolute minimum and, where possible, be expelled directly to the outside air by means of an extract fan.

Because they are such efficient heat carriers, water and air are usually employed together in heating systems. Central heating uses hot water to distribute heat via pipework, and air is used to carry such heat throughout a building by convection from radiators. Radiators are primarily convectors and not radiators as their name implies.

It is interesting that early central heating systems were developed for use in hothouses and not for domestic situations. In these early systems, humid conditions were required for tropical plant production. By putting large amounts of heat into the air in the presence of water, these early systems allowed for the creation of steamy internal conditions. Later developments imported such systems into houses – without the liberal use of water, of course. By heating the air, however, there was still a tendency to high levels of humidity. This tendency continues to be a feature of modern central heating systems. The measure of the amount of water vapour present in air is referred to as *relative humidity*.

Relative Humidity

An important factor in the creation of a balanced and healthy internal environment is relative humidity. Expressed as a percentage, relative humidity is a measure of the balance between air, water and heat. For example, air that has a relative humidity of 50% is holding half the water vapour it can hold at that particular temperature. If the temperature goes up, that air can hold more water vapour, if the temperature drops, it can hold less. When that air is holding as much water vapour as it can at a particular temperature it is said to be saturated – and it has a relative humidity of 100%. Relative humidity is sometimes referred to as vapour pressure. Hygrometers are used to measure relative humidity levels.

The degree of relative humidity of the internal air of a building is important in building design, because relative humidity is a factor in determining comfort levels, as well as being a factor in various medical problems. Relative humidity below 40% – excessively dry air – can lead to respiratory infections as well as inducing allergic and asthmatic symptoms. A relative humidity above 60% – excessive humidity – can lead to fungal growth, the proliferation of bacteria and viruses, the release of gas from products containing formaldehyde and it can cause asthmatic and allergic symptoms also. This makes the control of the internal relative humidity very critical in building design. Because relative humidity is directly related to air and to temperature it must be carefully considered when the H&V system is being designed.

The optimum comfort and health zone for relative humidity is 40-60% *fig. 16*. A high level of relative humidity can be moderated by carefully controlling moisture production within a building. A well designed building fabric – the materials used to make walls, floors and roof – can also make a significant contribution to moisture balance indoors. This moisture will be coming from occupants, cooking, washing machines, showers and so on. If materials are used which naturally absorb and release water vapour, an internal environment can be created that can achieve a natural balance of relative humidity, keeping it within the 40-60% zone. Such a building fabric, when the internal air is very dry, will contribute the necessary moisture needed to bring the relative humidity up to an acceptable level by releasing some of its moisture to the dry air. When the opposite condition exists and the relative humidity indoors is very high, the building fabric can absorb excess moisture, bringing the relative humidity down

222

to an acceptable level. Timber works excellently
well in this respect. Excess moisture in the air is
readily absorbed by timber and rereleased when drier
conditions prevail. Bricks, lime mortar and gypsum
plaster also have good characteristics in this respect.
Materials that function well in respect of absorbing
and releasing water vapour are called *'hygroscopic'*.
If such materials are not used in the interior of a
building, excessive ventilation will be needed or else
some form of mechanical dehumidification.
Increasing the ventilation within a building will lead
to increased heat losses.

When the relative humidity inside a building is
higher than the relative humidity outside, the warm
moist air will try to get out any way it can *fig. 17*.
This can happen by the water vapour passing through
walls, floors, roofs and so on. Such movement of
water vapour can cause severe condensation problems in buildings. Because it is by nature 'warm',
water vapour is drawn to cold surfaces where condensation can easily occur.

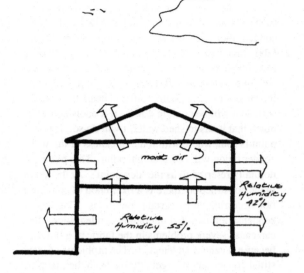

*fig. 17: When the relative humidity inside a building
is higher than the relative humidity outside, the
warm moist air will try to get out any way it can.*

Condensation

When a building is in use, the air within that building
will have moisture added to it by virtue of the building being occupied. This moisture or water vapour
will tend to move to a place where less moisture
exists in the air. Normally, this will be the exterior of
the building. To reach the outside air, water vapour
will pass through the building fabric – the walls,
floors and roof – where it can, if no other means of
escape is possible. When this happens, there will be
a risk of condensation occurring.

When the temperature of moist air drops, the
amount of water vapour it can carry drops too! In
other words, the air has to get rid of some of the
water vapour it contains. It does this by turning
some of its water vapour back into water. Water that
has been jettisoned by falling air temperatures is
called condensation.

Condensation happens when warm moist air
meets cold air. When this happens in our atmosphere
we call the condensation that results rain or dew.
Condensation also occurs on cold surfaces that cause
the vapour laden air to cool down suddenly. A
kitchen window or a cold wall surface is a good
example of this – vapour laden air hits the cold surface, the temperature of the air drops and it leaves
water on that surface. Condensation needs water
vapour and cold to actually happen.

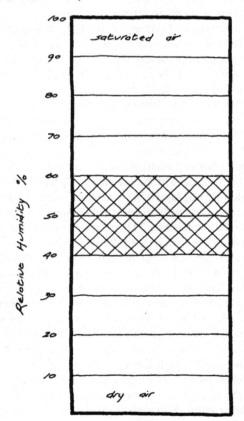

*fig. 16: The optimum comfort and health zone for
relative humidity is 40-60%.*

Usually, condensation happens on cold surfaces, such as windows and walls, and is called surface condensation. It can also occur within the building fabric that warm moist air is passing through. For example, vapour laden air passing through the thickness of a wall in its effort to get outside *fig. 18*. As the air passes through the wall and nears the outside surface it will be cooling down. If it cools down so much that it has to shed water it will do so. If this point is somewhere within the thickness of the wall, condensation will occur at that point. This point is normally referred to as the 'dewpoint'. At this point in the construction, there is a likelihood of condensation occurring under certain conditions. This type of condensation is called interstitial condensation. It can cause severe problems in the fabric of a building, because it can go undetected. The problems of interstitial condensation largely derive from the inappropriate location of insulating material and from inadequate ventilation provision. The inside of roofs can be prone to condensation, due to the fact that warm moist air rises naturally into the roof in its effort to escape outside.

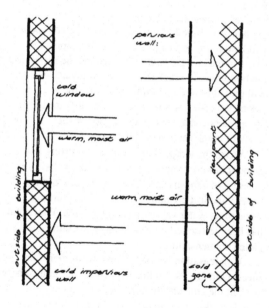

fig. 18: Usually, condensation occurs on cold surfaces, such as windows and walls, and is called surface condensation. It can also occur within the building fabric that warm moist air is passing through. This is called interstitial condensation.

All condensation can be avoided by having a plentiful supply of fresh air available and by being careful about the amount of water vapour that you put into the air in your building. Avoiding the creation of cold surfaces is also very important, as is the proper location of the insulating materials. Building Regulations require that adequate provision be made to prevent excessive condensation, particularly in roofs or in a roof void above an insulated ceiling. A roof void would in fact be any sort of attic space. This requirement of the regulations can be met by the proper location of the insulating materials used in the construction and by the provision of sufficient ventilation also.

Breathing Buildings

While the bulk of the air coming in and out of a building might do so through ventilators. air can be made to enter and leave through the walls, floor and roof of the building. This leads to the descriptive term *breathing buildings*. Breathable construction works in the same way as clothes do – the building fabric partially controls the flow of air to and from the interior or body of the building. It is important to think of the inside of a building as a living space. This expression, 'living space', frequently quoted, is a very accurate description of the interior of a building.

Clothes work by helping to control the rate of heat loss from our bodies by shielding our naked skin from radiating out its heat and by protecting us from direct contact with the outside air. Clothes create a slow moving layer of air next to our bodies, which carries away sufficient heat and moisture to allow us to feel comfortable. This escaping air leaves the surface of our bodies, especially at the neck. The expression 'hot under the collar' describes what happens if warm, moist air cannot escape from our bodies if our clothes cannot breathe or are too tight at the neck. Some air also passes through the fibres of the clothing. Natural fibres such as cotton and wool are ideal for clothing as they allow such 'breathing' to take place naturally. They regulate the passage of this warm, slightly moist air by trapping some of it within their fibres, thus allowing them to warm up. This is why wool, a natural fibre, is described as being warm. Man made fibres such as nylon do not breathe naturally and cause the body to heat up and to begin losing water – perspiration – as a way of shedding heat.

If the interior of a building is imagined as a living body and the building fabric – the materials from which the walls, floor and roof are made – is imagined as clothing for that body, the notion of breathable buildings will become clear *fig. 19*. In the same way that clothes act to moderate the flow of fresh air to and from the body and regulate the passage of stale air from the skin, so, too, the fabric of a building can act relative to the body of the building.

Depending on how wind will blow across your building, some walls will be allowing air to seep in through them and others will allow air to seep out *fig. 20*. In the case of external walls allowing air to seep in, such air will be gently warmed by the walls as it passes through them, as well as being naturally regulated or balanced for moisture. In the case of walls allowing air to seep out, the air will release heat and moisture to the material in the wall and then escape to the outside. When we refer to 'moisture', we mean the water vapour contained in the escaping air.

> A breathing building is not a means of providing the building occupants with air to breathe! Rather it is an approach to the design of the <u>fabric</u> of the building in order to eliminate the risk of condensation, to help regulate relative humidity levels, etc.

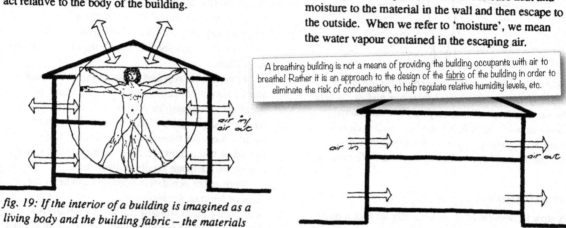

fig. 19: If the interior of a building is imagined as a living body and the building fabric – the materials from which the walls, floor and roof are made – is imagined as clothing for that body, the notion of breathable buildings will become clear.

fig. 20: Depending on how wind will blow across your building, some walls will be allowing air to seep in through them and others will allow air to seep out.

While our bodies produce too much heat, they of course do not produce enough heat to warm the body of the house. It is the heating unit itself that will function to do this, in conjunction with the ventilation system. The internal spaces of a building and the building fabric surrounding it are similar to the human body and its clothing. This fabric or clothing, if it is made from naturally warm and breathable materials, will result in a naturally regulated interior environment.

If breathable construction is desired, the choice of materials for the building fabric and the way in which they are assembled becomes very important. By creating a properly balanced construction, the air exiting from the building that is carrying away excess heat and moisture can release some of this heat and moisture to the walls, floors and roof of the building before reaching the outside air. This is exactly similar to the function carried out by our clothing. In other words, the fabric of the building can act like clothes, filtering and trapping the heat from warm air, thus keeping the body of the building at a comfortable temperature and in balance with the natural heating of the occupants.

This is what makes breathable materials such as timber, brick and lime invaluable in the creation of the fabric of any building. Air can slowly pass through them releasing its heat and its moisture as it goes. This function is very desirable. Just as wool or cotton traps warm air and moisture, adjusting itself to our natural body temperature, so, too, does timber act in the same way. Not alone is the moisture content of the air naturally regulated by this, but also the fabric of the building becomes warm. This drastically reduces the radiant heat losses from the occupants to the surfaces surrounding them. Radiant heat losses account for the major losses of heat we experience from our bodies. Where the surrounding surfaces are considerably colder than the body itself, the body will radiate too much heat to those surfaces *fig. 21*. What this means, as far as your building is concerned, is that if your walls, floor and ceilings are cold your body will radiate out too much heat to them, making you feel cold. With 'warm' construction, excessive radiant heat losses are eliminated.

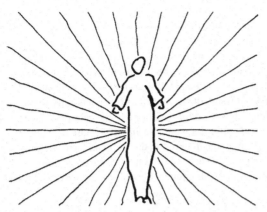

fig. 21: Radiant heat losses account for the major losses of heat we experience from our bodies. Where the surrounding building surfaces are considerably colder than the body itself, the body will radiate too much heat to those surfaces. With 'warm' construction, these excessive radiation losses are eliminated.

Ventilation

A slow movement of air is generally all that is needed to provide adequate ventilation within a building with non-breathable construction. The amount of air that will get into such a building will depend on the external wind speed, the size and location of the ventilation openings and on the internal and external temperatures. This air flow results from the effect of varying pressure drawing cold air in at low level and expelling warm stale air at high level *fig. 22*.

Building Regulations require that adequate means of permanent ventilation must be provided in buildings to supply their occupants with fresh air. These requirements, in effect, mean that fixed venti-

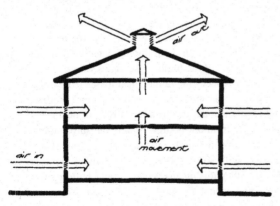

fig. 22: Air flow due to varying pressure draws in cold air at low level and expels it at high level.

lation openings of a particular size must be provided within certain spaces in a dwelling. Generally, these permanent openings must connect directly to the outside of the building. It is also a requirement of the regulations that a means of rapid ventilation be installed in all habitable rooms, kitchens, bathroom, shower and toilet areas. This provision ensures that airborne pollutants and moisture, when they occur, can be rapidly diluted with large quantities of fresh air. Habitable rooms are rooms used for living or sleeping purposes. A kitchen with a floor area of less than 6.5m² has specific requirements in regard to ventilation.

Even if it is proposed to use a system of breathable construction, permanent and rapid ventilation openings should also be provided. Utility rooms, workshops, garages etc. have no specific requirements set out for them in the regulations. Care should be taken, however, to ensure that such spaces receive an adequate supply of fresh air.

Permanent ventilation openings can be in the form of louvres, airbricks, grilles or permavents incorporated into window frames. Generally, these openings should have a smallest dimension of at least 8mm, so as to minimise resistance to the flow of air through them. Screens, fascias and baffles, however, can contain smaller openings than this. A flue or an open fireplace cannot be considered to be a permanent ventilation opening.

Openings for rapid ventilation can be in the form of openable windows, louvres or some form of adjustable ventilator. Some part of such openings must be at least 1750mm above floor level.

Building Regulation Ventilation Requirements for Habitable Rooms (including kitchens larger than 6.5m² in floor area):

Permanent Ventilation – Openings of total area at least 6500mm² in area. (65 x 100mm.)

In the case of a habitable room with an attached Sunspace, where it is not possible to ventilate directly to the outside, ventilation to the habitable room can be provided through the Sunspace. Such a Sunspace must itself be provided with a permanent ventilation opening of at least 6500mm² in area and an opening of similar size must be provided in the wall separating the two spaces.

Rapid Ventilation – Openings of at least 5% of the floor area of the space. Some part of this opening must be 1750mm above floor level. In the case of a habitable room with Sunspace attached, openings of at least 5% of the combined floor areas of the habitable room and the Sunspace must be provided in the wall between the spaces. Some part of this opening must be at least 1750mm above floor level. The Sunspace itself must also be provided with an opening or openings of similar size, connecting directly to the outside air.

Building Regulation Ventilation Requirements for Circulation Spaces:

Permanent Ventilation – Openings of total area at least 2% of floor area of hallway or corridor.

Alternatively, if the circulation space is wholly enclosed and is used for access only, continuous mechanical extract ventilation can be used. Such a system must be capable of providing the space with one air change per hour and be run continuously.

Rapid Ventilation – No requirement.

Building Regulation Ventilation Requirements for Bath & Shower Rooms:

Permanent Ventilation – No requirement.

Rapid Ventilation – Openable window or ventilator providing an opening of at least 5% of the floor area of the room. Some part of this opening must be at least 1750mm above floor level.

Alternatively, a system of mechanical extract ventilation can be used. This must be capable of extracting at a rate of 15 litres per second. This does not have to run permanently.

Building Regulation Ventilation Requirements for Toilet/Washbasin Areas:

Permanent Ventilation – No requirement.

Rapid Ventilation – Openable window or ventilator providing an opening of at least 5% of the floor area of the room.

Alternatively, a system of mechanical extract ventilation can be used. This must be capable of extracting at a rate of 3 air changes per hour. This does not have to be run continuously but should have a facility for a 15 minute overrun.

Building Regulation Ventilation Requirements for Kitchens less than 6.5m² in floor area:

Permanent Ventilation – Openings of at least 6500mm² in area.

Alternatively, a system of mechanical extract ventilation can be used if this is run continuously and is capable of providing the kitchen with one air change per hour.

Rapid Ventilation – Ventilation openings with a total area of at least 10% of the floor area of the kitchen. Some part of this opening must be at least 1750mm above floor level.

Alternatively, a system of mechanical extract ventilation can be used. This must be capable of extracting air at a rate of 60 litres per second. If this extract unit is incorporated into a cooker hood, an extraction rate of 30 litres per second is acceptable.

These requirements allow for the provision of a small kitchen area within a dwelling. They are specifically designed to allow internal kitchens to be incorporated into modern apartment buildings. In an individual dwelling, the use of an internal kitchen is questionable and the reliance on mechanical ventilation is hardly desirable. This applies, of course, to the other areas within the dwelling where mechanical ventilation might be considered for use.

Information on the requirements of the regulations in regard to ventilation should be entered into the appropriate 'Space' files at this stage of the design process.

Ventilation Openings

Apart from the specific requirements of the Building Regulations, ventilation calculations can be carried out which will allow the designer to estimate the amount of fresh air that is likely to enter and leave a building through ventilation openings. Such calculations will allow for the proper sizing and location of ventilation inlet and outlet openings to ensure that the required number of air changes per hour are met. Building Regulations generally do not set requirements for the number of air changes required in a building every hour. Such requirements may be specified by the individual designer however.

For winter ventilation, fresh air inlets should ideally be at high level. These should be well distributed so that the entering cold air will mix with the heated air in the building and thus reduce the risk of draughts. For summer ventilation and cooling, fresh air inlets should ideally be at low level. A compromise between high and low level inlets for summer and winter ventilation can be achieved by locating inlets anywhere from 700-1000mm above ground floor level *fig. 23*.

While openable windows will bring in air effectively, in practice only a gentle air flow is required to provide adequate ventilation, and opening a window will produce a more vigorous flow than is needed, though for rapid ventilation openable windows will be most effective. Adjustable ventilation grilles for background ventilation are likely to give the most satisfaction in practice. These should be designed to achieve the minimum openings required by the regulations, where they are located in rooms to which the regulations apply. Ventilation openings on the windward side of a building will allow fresh air to enter a building directly. Outlets should be located on the sheltered side.

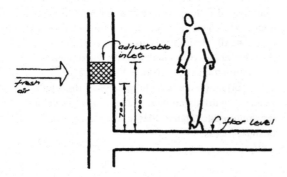

fig. 23: Fresh air inlets can be located from 700-1000mm above floor level.

Generally roofs will have stale air passing through them, except for the side of the roof facing the wind that has a gradient that is more than 30 degrees. A grille in a sheltered gable wall or an old fashioned ventilator atop the highest point of the roof will allow stale air to readily escape from a building. How the stale air reaches this point of exit to the outside air is a matter of leaving a clear path for the stale air to rise within the building fig. 24. Rooms not containing a fresh air inlet connected to the outside air should have either a gap under the door for fresh air to get in or a ventilation grille incorporated into the door itself. A grille for exhaust air should be located above all internal doors. In this way stale air can make its way out. The circulation space onto which such grilles open will also be the circulation space for the stale air! In a two storey building, the stairwell will provide the means for such stale air to make its way towards the roof. It will be necessary to provide a grille in the ceiling at the highest point of any interior to allow the stale air to make its way to the grille or ventilator connecting to the outside air.

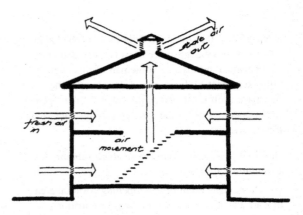

fig. 24. How stale air reaches the point of exit to the outside air is a matter of leaving a clear path for the stale air to rise within the building.

The amount of fresh air that you let into your building will be decided by the type of internal environment you wish for, the prevailing climate, the time of year and the Building Regulations. Figures such as two air changes per hour can be quoted for the amount of fresh air humans need, based on medical studies and so on. Fresh air requirements can be expressed in litres/second fig. 25.

Fresh air supply per person in litres per second

Air space per person m³	Recommended (Smoking)	Recommended (Non-smoking)	Minimum
3	22.4	17.0	11.3
6	14.2	10.7	7.1
9	10.4	7.7	5.2
12	8.0	6.0	4.0

fig. 25. Fresh air requirements expressed in litres/second.

The methods of calculating inlet and outlet sizes which follows, relates to inlets on the exposed sides of buildings and outlets located on their sheltered sides. While the values expressed in the calculations might be interpreted as being exact and therefore infallible, as with all natural processes variations and fluctuations will regularly occur. For example, as the wind speed varies, so also will the amount of fresh air entering the building vary.

To regulate the intake of air in such a situation a sophisticated control mechanism would be required. This would sense the wind speed and the temperature of the air and adjust the inlets accordingly. In reality, few people would opt for such a system, even though in theory this is what is required to maintain a fixed supply of fresh air. The calculations should therefore be seen as an indicator of the factors involved in properly ventilating a building, rather than an exact prediction of reality. These factors are – the amount of fresh air required per person per hour, the wind speed and the relative size and location of the ventilation openings.

It is sufficient to say that we all need fresh air, and that if you do not have it you will be putting up with a level of discomfort that is unnecessary, as well as setting up potentially unhealthy conditions. The worst of these would be condensation and oxygen starvation. In any event, the ventilation system needs to be adjustable beyond a minimum level to allow it to properly cope with a wide range of possible conditions. At the end of the day, there will be no instrument more accurate than your body, when it comes to sensing the perfect balance for your system.

The size of ventilation openings is calculated by reference to the amount of air required within the building, the relative size of inlets and outlets and the wind speed. In a situation where the size of inlets and outlets are to be made the same, the formula $V = 3150 \times A \times v$ can be used, where V is the volume of air required in cubic meters per hour, A is the area of the inlets/outlets in square meters and v is the wind speed in miles per hour. The figure for wind speed will depend on location, though a figure of 5 mph will prove adequate for most situations. The figure '3150' is a multiplier value based on the ratio of the outlet area divided by inlet area.

In a building with a volume of 500 cubic meters requiring two air changes per hour, openings that will allow 1000 cubic meters of air to enter and exit every hour in a 5 mph wind will require inlets/outlets of $1000 = 3150 \times A \times 5$. Therefore A = 0.0635 square meters. This is the equivalent of a single opening of 100mm long by 635mm wide, though in practice multiple smaller openings distributed along the windward side of the building will be used.

Where there is to be a difference in size between the inlets and the outlets, alternative multiplier values are used for calculation purposes *fig. 26*. For example, where the area of outlets is to be only half

If Total Area of Outlets ÷ Total Area of Inlets		
gives ratio of: 1	use	3150
2	use	4000
3	use	4250
4	use	4350
5	use	4400
3/4	use	2700
1/2	use	2000
1/4	use	1100

fig. 26. Wind pressure calculations: multiplier values for various outlet/inlet ratios.

the area of the inlets, an inlet area of 0.05m² or 100 x 500mm will be required.

When wind speeds vary, as they inevitably will, adjustments will be necessary in the ventilation opening sizes. For example, in a 10 mph wind, if the inlets are only half opened and the outlets are left fully open, the volume of air entering the building will be calculated by $4000 \times 0.0529 \times 10 = 2116$ cubic meters. This is far in excess of actual needs. In theory, by adjusting the inlets and the outlets according to the actual wind speed the proper amount of air can be be made to enter the building at all times. In practice, this will require a reasonably sophisticated control mechanism that will make these adjustments automatically. If this is not done, too much air will be coming in to the building, causing too much heat to be lost. This is one of the problems with such methods of ventilation. The tendency is to restrict the inflow of air to overcome this problem, though this can lead to problems of condensation and lack of oxygen. In any event, outlet sizes will normally be fixed and adjustments to the inlets size will be the adjustment that will normally be made.

Natural ventilation will also occur through permanent ventilation openings, when the air inside a building is warmer than the outside air. This is called 'stack pressure' ventilation. The 'draw' of a flue or chimney is an example of stack pressure. The rate of air flow induced by stack pressure will vary according to the difference in internal and external air temperatures, the difference in height between the inlets and the outlets and the size of the ventilation openings themselves. The rate of air flow when the outlet and inlet openings are equal can be calculated from the equation: $V = 540 \times A \times \sqrt{h \times t}$, where V is the air flow in cubic meters per hour, A is the area of the inlet in square meters, h is the height in meters between the inlet and the outlet and t is the temperature difference in °C between the inside and the out-

If Total Area of Outlets ÷ Total Area of Inlets			
gives ratio of:	1	use	540
	2	use	680
	3	use	720
	4	use	740
	5	use	745
	$^3/_4$	use	455
	$^1/_2$	use	340
	$^1/_4$	use	185

fig. 27. Stack pressure calculations: multiplier values for various outlet/inlet ratios.

side of the building. If the area of the outlets and the inlets vary, the value '540' is substituted by an alternative multiplier value *fig. 27*.

For example, in the case of the ventilation opening already calculated – 0.0635 square meters – if the outlet were to be the same size and the height difference were to be 4m between outlet and inlet, for an 18 °C difference in temperature the air flow would be:

$$V = 540 \times 0.0635 \times \sqrt{4 \times 18}$$

$$= 540 \times 0.0635 \times 8.482$$

$$= 290.85 \; cubic \; meters/hour$$

It is usual to calculate both the air flow due to wind pressure as well as the air flow due to stack pressure and to choose the larger estimate as being the one more likely to reflect the real situation.

To calculate the number of cubic meters of air in your building, multiply the floor area of each space by the height of the space, making sure that all your measurements are in meters. Include all the spaces in the building, not forgetting the circulation spaces. If some spaces have sloping ceilings, be sure to calculate the volume of these rooms properly. To make a preliminary calculation as you evolve your design, use the figures recorded in your Space files to estimate the expected building volume. The percentage area that you have allowed for circulation space in your design can be multiplied by 2.5m to give you a figure for its volume.

If you require two air changes per hour within a building of 500m³, you will need to supply 500 x 2 cm³ of air to that building every hour. Alternative figures can be arrived at based on individual requirements in terms of litres/second of fresh air. 1m³/hour is the equivalent of 1000L/hour.

Mechanisms can be used to recover some of the heat from stale air that is being vented out of the building. Heat Pumps and Heat Recovery Units can be utilised to do this. The salvaged heat can then be used to either heat incoming fresh air or to heat water. The incorporation of heat absorbing materials into the path that warm stale air takes on its way out of the building will also allow some heat to be recovered. The effect of this would be the warming of part of the internal fabric of the building and the consequent benefits of this.

Breathable construction is also an excellent way of bringing a certain amount of air into a building. Not only does the air come in slowly, but it also can be warmed and its moisture content adjusted to suit the prevailing conditions. This happens when cold, dry air passes through the building fabric and is warmed and humidified on its way through. Breathable internal walling and flooring, as well as room inlets and outlets, will allow the air once it is within the building to move.

Even if breathable construction is used, controllable inlets and outlets will also be required. The sizing of these should follow the regulations or the procedure set out above. Because breathing buildings operate at lower air temperatures than 'cold' buildings, their ventilation heat losses will consequently be less for comparable volumes of air.

If the fresh air coming into a building is simply too cold and is cooling the occupants too much, even though it is moving gently, the air will have to be heated. Similarly, if the surfaces enclosing the internal spaces are too cold and the occupants are radiating out too much heat to them, these surfaces also will have to be heated. It is for these purposes that a heating unit is needed – the warming of the internal air and surfaces. Heating the internal air and surfaces in a building can be done by using solar energy or by burning coal, gas or oil. Of these, solar energy is the cheapest and the cleanest. Of the others, gas or dry wood are preferable.

It is important to remember that warm air rises and tries to escape to somewhere colder. In terms of a building, this is invariably the outside of the building. The more the internal air of a building is heated, the more it tries to escape outside and so precious heat is lost. It is therefore better to only heat the internal air of a building very gently, to mimimise ventilation heat loss. This is also compatible with the primary function of ventilation – supplying the building's occupants with fresh air.

Pages 232-239 of the *Heating & Ventilation* chapter concern themselves with the 'mechanics' of any *H&V* system. Essentially, buildings loose heat through their 'fabric' - walls, windows, floors and roofs. Heat is also lost when warm air is vented away. Also, buildings gain heat from their occupants, from appliances, lights and from the sun. A *H&V* system makes up for the difference between these losses and gains by generating and distributing heat. Sometimes the *H&V* system also has to cool a building down.

In your reading of these pages you should, as before, concern yourself with the principles involved rather than trying to completely understand all of the figures and calculations. These can be referred back to when required. What is critical at this stage is understanding how buildings gain and loose heat and how best to create a building fabric that will perform best in the conditions that are likely to prevail when it is constructed. In many ways choosing a suitable building fabric is a little like choosing ones' clothing to suit the weather.

Common Heating Methods' on page 232 provides a good summary of the types of choices that now confront you - to heat the air within the building or to heat the building fabric itself. Consider this carefully and set down on the *H&V System Worksheet* your general preferences, bearing in mind that you can always change your mind at any point.

If you are working on extending or replanning an existing building you will have to be versatile and realistic in your approach. Some even relatively new housing stock is so deficient in respect of energy performance that it might be prohibitively expensive (as well being impractical) to upgrade it to a 'liveable' standard. In such cases it might be best to consider creating a highly efficient extension which might be isolated from a cold house, rather than try to upgrade existing poorly insulated external building fabric to an acceptable standard.

Next: SDP24 - Measurements & Calculations, page 240

Common Heating Methods

Broadly speaking, there are two ways in which a building can be heated. The first of these is where the building fabric – the walls, floor and possibly the ceilings – is warmed up, bringing it into balance with the temperature of the occupants and so eliminating excessive radiation losses. Radiant heating, as it is called, allows for a more natural internal environment to be created, as well as allowing for the inclusion of naturally warm, breathable materials in the building fabric. The gentle heating of the internal air is a natural consequence of radiant surface heating.

The second method of heating a building is to warm the internal air by means of radiators or some such device, leaving the building fabric cold. When the internal air is warmed in this way, problems of humidity and condensation can result. Due to the relatively high air temperatures involved, a high degree of heat loss can also occur.

Oil, coal, gas, wood and turf can all be used to create both radiant and convective heating systems. Solar energy can also be used, particularly for radiant systems. At this point in the design exercise some thought should be given to the type of system – radiant or convective – that you might wish to use. A preference in terms of fuel should also be expressed. This preference should take into account the realities of supply, handling and burning of fossil fuels, particularly in terms of the wider environment.

Building Heat Losses

A building will lose heat in the same way that the human body does – by convection, evaporation, radiation and conduction. A building, like a person, also needs to control the rate of these heat losses in order to maintain a comfortable state. This is achieved, in the case of a building, by regulating the amount of heat that is generated, by controlling fresh air intake, and by controlling the amount of heat that is lost by convection, evaporation, radiation and conduction *fig. 28*. The heat losses that occur in any building not alone carry away heat but also expel stale air and help to maintain a healthy internal environment. This is an important function of the H&V system.

Building heat losses by convection movement can account for a very large portion of overall heat loss, especially in a building that is heavily insulated and well sealed from draughts. These losses occur

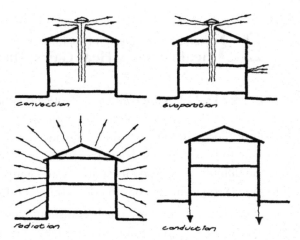

fig. 28: A building will lose heat in the same way that the human body does – by convection, evaporation, radiation and conduction.

when air that has been heated makes every effort to escape from the building to the outside air which is colder than the internal air. The movement of air within the building which this sets up means that fresh air is drawn in at a low level and that warm stale air is expelled, usually at, high level. Generally, air is drawn in on the windward side of a building and expelled on the sheltered side.

Once fresh air is within a building and it is heated, it rises. The speed at which this internal air moves and its temperature are very critical to the comfort level that is to be achieved *fig. 29*. For example, if the speed of the moving air is too fast, too much heat will be carried away from the occupants for comfort. If the speed is too slow, there will not be sufficient fresh air coming in for the occupants to breathe. Oftentimes fresh air gets into a building through gaps in window frames and under doors. This type of infiltration is difficult to control. In a building that is well sealed, fresh air has to be brought in through purpose made vents.

Building Regulations recommend minimum standards for inlet ventilator sizes. The reliance on opening windows to provide fresh air in buildings is too cumbersome and difficult to control, though Building Regulations stipulate that habitable rooms be fitted with an openable window. This is to ensure that such rooms can be rapidly ventilated if necessary. Breathable construction naturally regulates itself and can be supplemented by controllable vents.

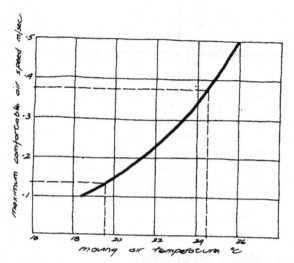

fig. 29. Comfortable air speed/temperature graph. Air speed of less than 0.1m/s is considered stuffy.

Buildings are also subject to convection heat losses, because of the movement of air outside them fig. 30. For example, a building constantly subjected to a steady cold wind blowing across it will lose a considerable amount of heat to the wind. This is similar to the effect of a fan on a car radiator, generating an artificial wind and carrying away excess heat with it. Similarly, a person standing naked in front of an electric fan will experience considerable heat loss by convection. Proper siting of a building in relationship to the prevailing wind is very important.

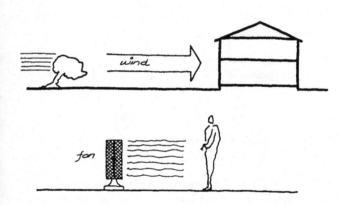

fig. 30: Buildings are also subject to convection heat losses because of the movement of air outside them.

Heat losses by evaporation from buildings take place via the flow of air through the building. Evaporation of moisture and heat will occur from people, cooking activities, washing and from the drying and airing of clothes fig. 31. This heat will be in the form of water vapour, a gaseous form of water, and it will travel on the air and rise through the building following the natural air flow upwards. In the case of breathable construction, some of this moist air will pass through the building fabric. Where large amounts of water vapour are being produced, for example when cooking and boiling is being done in the kitchen, a separate extraction system is required over the source of the water vapour – for example over the cooker – in order to remove the moisture from the building as quickly as possible. If this is not done and the water vapour cools down excessively, it will turn back into water, causing condensation. Proper ventilation and the creation of warm internal surfaces will act to eliminate the risk

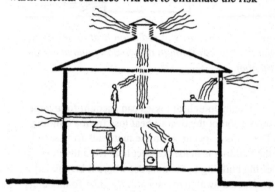

fig. 31: Heat losses by evaporation take place via the flow of air through the building. Evaporation of moisture and heat will occur from people, cooking activities, washing and from the drying and airing of clothes.

The majority of radiation losses from buildings occur through the windows and also from the roof fig. 32. In a night-time situation, where a warm space is exposed to the black sky through a window, this warm space will radiate out its heat to that cold sky. Similarly, roof glazing, particularly in conservatories, will radiate out any heat that is within the building to a black night sky. If the heat generated within the building is to seep out through the walls of the building, making them warm, these walls will then radiate out their heat to their colder surroundings. This will also be true of the roof of a building which will directly face the cold night sky and so will radiate out any heat it has to this. Radiation losses from buildings can be rigidly controlled by using curtains or insulated shutters over windows and by carefully constructing the roof and walls so that they do not radiate out heat. This is done by properly insulating the construction. Radiation from buildings does not carry out any other function of the internal environment, unlike convection and evaporation which use heat to dispose of moisture and other waste.

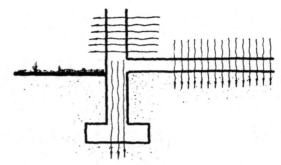

fig. 33: Conduction heat losses from a building occur when the materials from which the building is made conduct heat from the interior of the building to the outside, where it is radiated or conducted away into the earth.

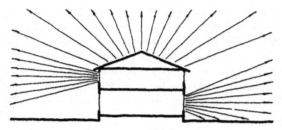

fig. 32: The majority of radiation heat losses from buildings occur through the windows and also from the roof.

Building Heat Gain

Lights, refrigerators, people, televisions, computers, motors and many domestic appliances give off heat when they are operated. Also, the sun can add considerably to the amount of heat within a building fig. 34. This heat gain can contribute significantly to the heating needs of a building.

Conduction heat losses can account for a large proportion of the overall heat loss from a building. These losses occur when the materials from which the building is made conduct heat from the interior of the building to the outside, where it is radiated or conducted away into the earth fig. 33. To moderate these losses, the materials from which the building is made and the way in which they are assembled need very careful consideration. As with radiation, conduction heat losses can be kept to an absolute minimum in any building, as they do not carry out any function in respect of the regulation of the internal environment. Convection and evaporation losses on the other hand are regulators of the internal environment and so must be accepted as being inevitable, though the amount of these losses can be moderated by careful design.

Building Regulations require that buildings be designed and constructed so as to secure, as far as is reasonably practicable, the conservation of fuel and energy. It is recommended that this be achieved by the proper design of the building fabric, to minimise heat losses, and by the proper control of the heating system output.

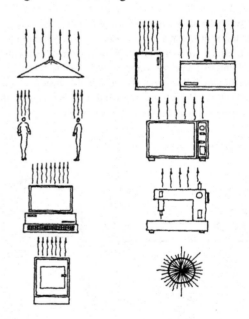

fig. 34: Lights, refrigerators, people, televisions, computers, motors and many domestic appliances give off heat when they are operated. Also, the sun can add considerably to the amount of heat within a building.

To 'capture' heat that is being produced within a building, materials have to be used which have an ability to store heat. If this is done, heat that otherwise would be ventilated away – lost through convection and evaporation – can be held within the fabric of the building, warming it up. If this happens, a proper balance between the internal surface temperatures and the occupants can be achieved. This will contribute to the provision of a proper level of comfort and a healthy internal environment. Capturing heat within the fabric of the building is an important principle in H&V design, particularly in relation to radiant heating systems. Materials that 'capture' heat and store it are referred to as the 'thermal mass' of the building.

Building Regulations encourage the maximisation of solar heat gains in new building design. A decision to utilise solar heat gains to contribute to the heating of a building will exert a strong influence on the internal planning and on the siting of the building.

Thermal Mass

The heat storage capacity of a building is called its Thermal Mass. Thermal mass is in fact materials within the fabric of the building which have an ability to 'warm up'. Materials with good thermal mass characteristics are dense, like certain types of stone, brick and water. Timber is also a good heat storage medium. Water is the most efficient heat store of all. Dry earth has good heat storage capabilities also fig. 35.

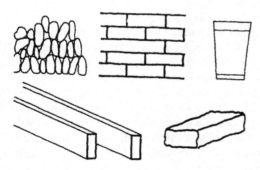

fig. 35: Materials with good thermal mass characteristics are dense, like certain types of stone, brick and water. Timber is also an excellent heat storage medium. Dry earth has good heat storage capabilities also.

To incorporate heat storage capacity into a building, thermal mass has to be introduced into its fabric. This, in practical terms, means selecting materials with good heat absorption and retention characteristics. This thermal mass will absorb heat, store it, and release it when the internal conditions demand it back – in other words when the heat source has been turned off. The electrically operated storage heater functions on this principle. Thermal mass allows for the creation of warm internal surfaces in a building, thereby minimising radiant heat losses from the occupants.

Brick introduced into the internal fabric of a building will retain the heat that would otherwise be carried too quickly away by convection and conduction. Dry turf, earth, stone and timber also function well in this capacity. While water has a remarkable capacity to hold large amounts of heat, it is difficult to contain such water within the fabric of a building. For thermal mass to properly do its work of storing heat it should be isolated from contact with any potentially cold area. Insulation should totally enclose the thermal mass to prevent any heat leaking out of it fig. 36. This loss would occur by heat being conducted or radiated away.

Thermal mass is different from insulation. Insulation slows the rate of heat loss because it is made from materials that are poor conductors of heat. Thermal mass actually warms up and holds heat within itself. When such thermal mass is then insulated the stored heat cannot escape, except back into the internal space of the building.

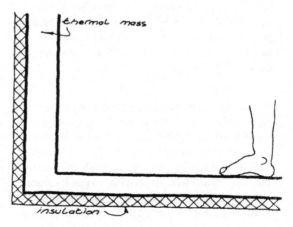

fig. 36. Thermal mass should be isolated from contact with any potentially cold area. Insulation should totally enclose the thermal mass to prevent heat leaking out of it.

While insulation cannot strictly be regarded as having a heat storage capacity, air, which comprises in many cases the main constituent of thermal insulation, is a very good heat storage medium. The difficulty with using air as a heat storage medium is that it wants to move as soon as it heats up!

How the thermal mass of a building is heated up is quite important. Ideally, this should be done by applying heat to the interior of the heatstore materials *fig. 37*. The commonest example of this would be underfloor heating where hot water pipes are embedded within a concrete slab thereby heating up the slab. Low temperature hot water is used for this purpose as the process is a slow and gradual one to which low temperatures are best suited. In such a situation, the concrete slab absorbs heat from the water circulating in the embedded pipes and the temperature of the concrete gradually rises, radiating out heat as well as setting up a gentle convection current, where heat is carried away from the floor by air passing over it.

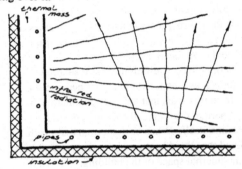

fig. 37: How the thermal mass of a building is heated up is quite important. Ideally, this should be done by applying heat to the interior of the heatstore materials. Normally, low temperature hot water is used for this purpose.

An ancient Roman system of heating – the *'hypocaust'* system – used warm air circulating under floors and within walls to gently heat these stone surfaces. Similarly, an old-fashioned fireplace, with its gentle, slow-burning fire, gradually heated the stone chimney breast above it, so that it radiated out its heat to the room *fig. 38*. In all these situations, gentle heat is applied to the heatstore materials from within, maximising the amount of heat absorbed and ensuring a gradual rise in the surface temperatures of these materials. This is a very critical aspect of incorporating thermal mass into a build-

ing – it must be realised that the process is gradual and involves low temperatures. These surfaces, because they are warm, do not 'demand' heat from the internal air or from the occupants of the building and so achieve a gentle balance within the internal environment. Because the heating of thermal mass from its 'cold' state is a gradual process, it is preferable that such materials are maintained in a relatively 'warm' state.

fig. 38: An old-fashioned fireplace, with its gentle, slow-burning fire, gradually heated the stone chimney breast above it, so that it radiated out its heat to the room. The heating up of thermal mass always involves low temperatures.

If heatstore materials are allowed to get 'cold', when heat is applied to them the temperature rise is gradual and so is the achievement of the desired temperature balance within the internal environment – in other words the building is slow to heat up. This situation is frequently referred to as the 'thermal response' of the building.

Just as a building with a large thermal mass is slow to heat up, so, too, it is slow to cool down again. This is in contrast to heating systems where the internal air is used to carry the heat produced by the heating unit. Because air can absorb a large amount of heat very readily and will immediately move once it has been heated, air is frequently used to distribute heat within buildings. This is done at relatively high temperatures by heating air with radiators, stoves or storage heaters. The 'thermal response' of such systems is very fast, as high temperatures are used, and the heat can be distributed rapidly by convection air currents. When such systems are switched off, cooling occurs very rapidly. Because convection heating systems rely on air to distribute heat, there is a necessary movement of warm air upwards within the building. Essentially, this air is trying to escape to the cold outside. This tendency is not only undesirable because of the heat losses involved, but also because the air movements thereby set up tend to carry heat away from the occupants, unless the temperature of the air is quite high. Any effort to 'trap' warm air within a building in an attempt to stem heat losses, will result in severe problems with maintaining a balanced and healthy internal environment. Problems of condensation can also occur. It is in this regard that the use of warm internal surfaces incorporating 'thermal mass' is far preferable to the use of convective heating systems, despite the quick response of these. Warm internal surfaces, because they allow for a natural balance between themselves, the occupants and the internal air, considerably reduce the radiation losses from the occupants that occur when the internal surfaces are left cold. In addition to this, the risk of condensation can be eliminated.

Thermal mass can be heated directly by the radiant heat available from the sun. This is done by arranging a glass enclosure for it *fig. 39*. The sun shines through the glass and strikes the thermal mass, releasing its heat. A wall, or a wall and floor, can be arranged in this way. As well as acting as a solar heat collector and heat store, such space can also be used as part of the built accommodation. Such a space is normally called a solarium or sunspace. A wall that functions to gather and store solar heat is called a Trombe Wall. Such a wall can be arranged as part of the space it is intended to heat. Dark surfaces, especially black, absorb the greatest amount of solar radiation. Because of this, the surfaces within a Solarium, Sunspace or Trombe Wall should be of a dark colour.

Another way of heating up the thermal mass of a building is by allowing warm air to pass over or through it *fig. 40*. Such warm air can come directly from a stove or a furnace, or it can come from a skirting radiator. Such radiators are connected to a water heater or boiler. When the radiator is filled with hot water, the air around the radiator warms up and carries heat into the wall by convection. Such heat, making its way through a heatstore wall, would be absorbed by it, though pipes arranged within the thermal mass are the preferred way of applying the heat. A bonus of having warm internal surfaces is that the risk of condensation is totally removed.

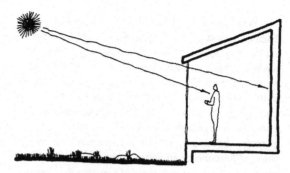

fig. 39: *Thermal mass can be heated directly by the radiant heat available from the sun. Such a space is normally called a Solarium or Sunspace.*

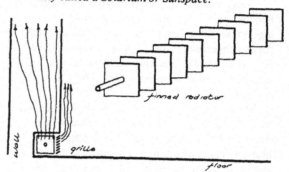

fig. 40: *Thermal mass can also be heated up by allowing warm air to pass over or through it.*

Heatstore Materials

The amount of heat that any given piece of material can hold depends on its density and on its Specific Heat. Specific Heat is a measurement of the amount of heat that is required to raise a Kilogram of a material by 1^0 C. Some materials, such as metals, have a low Specific Heat, which means that when a kilo of metal is heated up, very little heat is required to raise the temperature of the metal by 1^0 C. Water, on the other hand, has a very high Specific Heat and so a large amount of heat is required to raise the temperature of 1 kilo of water by 1^0 C. The boiling of a kettle will show this to be true – the kettle itself will heat up very quickly when the heat is applied to it, while the water within the kettle will heat up relatively slowly. If the weight of the water within the kettle and the weight of the kettle itself are comparable – let's say for argument that they both weigh 1 kilo – then it can be appreciated that the kettle will be hotter than the water after a couple of minutes on the fire. This is because the Specific Heat of water is high and that of metal is low.

While it might be imagined that the metal, because it heats up more quickly, would be the better material to use in the creation of warm internal surfaces, this is not the case. The reason for this is because the metal will in fact get too hot and so will cause convection air currents to be set up which will carry away the heat too quickly. A material which can absorb large quantities of heat without its temperature shooting up is what is required in the creation of heatstores and warm internal surfaces. If such materials are used, the surfaces that they create will become warm, not hot, and so contribute to a gentle balance in the internal environment.

Ideally, the average temperature of the internal building surfaces should be equal to, or preferably higher than, the air temperature within the building. An air temperature of 18^0 C and a surface temperature of 20^0 C are acceptable. With convection heating systems, an air temperature of $22-24^0$ C is normally used.

Water is a remarkably versatile heatstore material, but the difficulty of containing it in large quantities is very great. Usually, the use of water as a heatstore material is confined to piping it through a circuit containing radiators which set up convective air currents to carry away the heat.

Brick and baked clay are materials of relatively high Specific Heat so they have a large heatstorage capacity. Concrete blocks have only about one third of the heatstorage capacity of bricks or clay. Concrete itself can store a large amount of heat, though it has a high conductance and so requires a large amount of insulation to keep the heat within it. Concrete also tends to be very bulky, requiring a large quantity of heat to warm it up. Bricks and clay are less conductive than concrete, and, while insulation is also required to contain the heat within them, the heat will move at a slower rate that with concrete. Timber has a high Specific Heat and is a bad conductor. This means that it can hold a large amount of heat and not carry this away too rapidly. The denser the timber, the greater its heatstorage capacity will be. Timber is, without doubt, the warmest natural material available for building purposes. The actual amount of heat that thermal mass materials can hold is calculated according to the density, volume and specific heat of the materials *fig. 41.*

The maximum effective thickness for a heatstore wall or floor is 150mm. This might seem very small and not at all 'massive' as the words 'thermal mass'

suggest. It should be remembered that too much thermal mass will require too much heat to warm it up to the correct temperature. Where solar heat is being collected, the thickness of the Trombe, or sunspace wall, can be slightly thicker, at 250mm.

Density x Volume x Specific Heat = Heat storage capacity				
Heat storage capacity of 1m³ of:				
Water	1000 x 1 x 1.16	=	1160
Clay	1900 x 1 x 0.255	=	484.5
Timber	650 x 1 x 0.488	=	317.2
Medium concrete blockwork	1400 x 1 x 0.23	=	322
All values in Wh/ºC				

Material	Density Kg/m³	Specific Heat Wh/Kg/ºC
Brick	1700	0.23
Glass fibre	25	0.22
Plywood	650	0.335
Timber	650	0.488
Water	1000	1.16
Clay	1900	0.255
Dense concrete	2100	0.23
Heavy concrete block	2300	0.23
Medium concrete block	1400	0.23
Light concrete block	600	0.23

fig. 41. Density and specific heat of various materials. Heat storage capacity is calculated by multiplying the volume of a material by its specific heat and its density.

Even if a material has a tremendous heatstorage capacity and performs well as part of the building fabric, the heat within it will try to escape to any cold area that it can. Whereas this escape of heat is desirable when it is heating up a room and the people in it, it is often the case that the outside of the building will place the greatest demand on the heat to move and so it will be lost. To prevent this potential loss of heat from heatstore materials, insulation must be used. Insulators are materials of low density that are very poor conductors of heat.

Insulation

In order to contain the heat that has been gathered into heatstore materials and prevent it from escaping to the outside of the building, insulation must be used *fig. 42*. Insulation works by 'insulating' the heatstore material on its potentially cold side. In the case of a wall, this would be the outside and possibly also the ground that the wall is rising out of. In the case of a concrete floor, the potentially cold side would be the side that was resting on the ground. In the case of a roof, it would be, of course, the outside also.

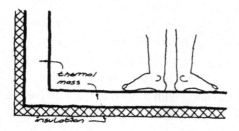

fig. 42: In order to contain the heat that has been gathered into heatstore materials and prevent it from escaping to the outside of the building, insulation must be used.

Insulation can be imagined as a wrapping for heatstore materials. This wrapping should have no holes or gaps in it, in other words, it should be continuous. If this is the case, very little of the stored heat will be able to get through the insulation and be lost. If gaps or holes are left in the insulation, however the heat will escape through these, much as air would escape from a punctured tyre.

Insulating materials have a very low density and are very poor conductors of heat. Fibreglass, Styrofoam and cork are frequently used insulating materials. Anybody who has ever stuffed newspaper inside their clothes will be aware of the insulating ability of paper. Feathers and hair keep animals warm by trapping a layer of warm air within themselves. Corrugated cardboard is also a good insulator, though, like paper, cardboard has difficulty in dealing with moist air. Fibreglass also suffers in this respect. Straw, reeds and rushes are good insulators. Vermiculite, a natural material derived from volcanic ash, is also good.

Whatever insulation is selected, due regard needs to be paid to the health aspects of its use and to the fact that the insulation needs to fully enclose the heatstorage material.

Design Temperatures

The achievement of a satisfactory internal temperature within a building depends on the amount of heat provided by the heating system and by solar and other heat gains. This must be balanced against the amount of heat lost by ventilation and by passing through the fabric of the building. It is possible to make a calculation of heat losses, due to ventilation and building fabric losses, that will allow you to estimate the size of the heating unit that will be providing the heat.

In general, the colder the outside air the more heat you will need to produce inside the building to maintain an acceptable temperature. What this means, in practice, is that your heating unit must be able to provide enough heat for the coldest weather there is likely to be. What this temperature is will depend on the location of your building, though a base temperature of 0^0 C is normally used. Similarly, an internal air temperature of $18-24^0$ C and an internal surface temperature of 20^0 C can be used for calculation purposes, as these will provide a suitable range of comfort.

Heating Measurements

In order to properly design a H&V system, the effects of convection, evaporation, radiation and conduction heat movements have to be quantifiable. Also, optimum internal temperatures have to be expressed numerically, as does the acceptable amount of water vapour that should be present in the air. Similarly, the quantity of fresh air required to maintain a balanced internal environment must be expressed in numbers.

Temperatures are measured in 'degrees Centigrade' and are sometimes written as '^{0} C', or simply 'K'. The freezing point of water is 0^0 C and its boiling point is 100^0 C. Normal internal human body temperature is 37^0 C, with a surface body temperature of $18^0–20^0$ C. An acceptable internal surface temperature for a building is 20^0 C. The temperature of the internal air of a building can range from $18^0–24^0$ C. Hot water for washing should be around 60^0 C. Hot water circulating in a central heating system is normally at around 80^0 C. For heating thermal mass, water can be at 35^0 C.

The amount of heat energy released when fuel is burned is measured in Watts per hour. The heat energy that is produced when a light bulb is 'burned' is

Pages 239-250 of the *Heating & Ventilation* chapter set out the detail of heating measurements; an explanation of what 'U-values' are; how to calculate these and how to calculate the overall Heat Losses from a building. Again, it is the principles involved that you need to grasp at this stage.

For those with an appetite for numbers a *H&V Calculations Worksheet* is provided to speed up the calculations detailed on those pages. Generally, what such calculations clearly reveal is that in cold climates there will be a need to provide heat within a building; a need to insulate the entire building fabric against the loss of this heat; the desirability of having a naturally warm inner layer to a building; a need to properly ventilate, and, an acceptance of the inevitable loss of the heat contained in such ventilated air. In hot climates it will be found necessary to exclude solar energy from entering a building along with a need to insulate the entire building fabric against the penetration of any heat from outside. The desirability of having a naturally cool inner layer to a building will also become clear along with a need to properly ventilate any interior to promote heat loss in the ventilated air.

Even where a building in a cold climate is designed to collect Solar Energy a *H&V* system must be designed on the assumption that at times no such energy will be available and that the system will be required to do all the work in terms of providing the necessary heat.

The choice of any *H&V* system must take account of the operation of the system. This will relate to the lifestyle of the occupants - do you want the system to 'kick in' as you make your way home from work, or, before you rise from your bed in the mornings? If so, you will be led down the road which, inevitably, will lead to the use of unsustainable methods. This is why it is important to understand the importance of a *H&V* at this early stage of the design process.

If you venture to use the *H&V Calculations Worksheet* you will need dimensional information for each *Space*. This can be arrived at by following item **SDP13** on page 101. Also, computer modelling can be used to determine the likely performance of particular combinations of building elements. Usually applications for building permits or planning permission will require a detailed computer-generated evaluation of likely building performance, so it can be worthwhile to begin working with a qualified assessor at an early stage of a project - and get them to do the calculations!

If you are working with an existing building calculating its heat losses will be important. Using information gathered from your Survey it should be possible to calculate the U-values of walls, floors and roof and from these to estimate the likely heat losses. However this can be difficult, if not impossible! In many ways the human body is the best means of assessing hot, cold and draughty spots.

Next: SDP25 - Passive Solar Design, page 252

also measured in Watts per hour – for example a 100W light bulb will produce 100 Watts of heat for every hour that the light is left switched on. The total amount of heat that a building needs every hour to make it warm is measured in Watts or Kilowatts. A Kilowatt is 1000W.

The amount of heat that a material can hold within itself is measured in Watts per kilogram per ^{0}C. What this means, in the case of a material such as brick, is that for each kilo of that material and for each degree of its temperature there will be a certain number of Watts of heat stored within the material.

The amount of heat that a material can conduct through itself is measured in Watts per meter per ^{0}C. What this means is that for every meter thickness of a material, and for every degree of temperature difference between one side of the material and the other a certain number of Watts of heat energy will be conducted through it every hour. For example, a concrete block wall with a temperature of 20^0 C on one side of it and 0^0 C on the other, will conduct more heat than if the temperature on both sides of it were the same. This makes the temperature difference between the inside of a building and the outside very critical when calculating the amount of heat that is likely to be conducted through the fabric of the building. Some materials, such as metals, can conduct large amounts of heat, while insulation materials conduct very little.

Where several different materials are used to make a wall or a roof in a building, the ability of the wall or roof to conduct heat is measured in Watts per square meter per ^{0}C. This means that for every square meter of, say, an insulated concrete block cavity wall and for every ^{0}C difference in the temperature on either side of that wall, a certain number of Watts of heat energy will pass through that square metre of wall every hour. This measurement is normally referred to as the 'U-value' *fig. 43*. U-values can be applied to walls, floors, windows and roofs of a building, allowing calculations to be made as to the amount of heat likely to pass through these under certain temperature conditions. These temperature conditions are usually based on a 20^0 C temperature difference between the interior of a building and the outside air.

The amount of fresh air needed within a building to maintain comfort levels is expressed in Air Changes per Hour. This is a measure of the number of times the air within a building will be changed every hour. Fresh air requirements can also be

expressed in litres/hour. Exactly how much air will pass through a building through inlets and outlets will depend on the size and location of these openings, on the temperature of the air and on wind speed. Inlet and outlet sizes are measured in square meters or square millimeters. Wind speed is measured in miles or kilometers per hour.

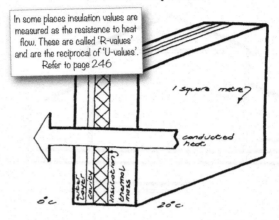

In some places insulation values are measured as the resistance to heat flow. These are called 'R-values' and are the reciprocal of 'U-values'. Refer to page 246

fig. 43: Where several different materials are used to make a wall or a roof in a building, the ability of the wall or roof to conduct heat is measured in Watts per square meter per ^{0}C. This measurement is normally referred to as the 'U-value' of the construction.

U-Values

It is common to quote what are called U-values for the external wall, floor and roof construction of new buildings. Windows also have U-values ascribed to them. U-values are mathematical calculations that indicate how much heat is likely to be conducted through these elements, under certain conditions. These calculations are based on the ability of the materials making up these building elements to conduct heat. A wall, for example, that will conduct a lot of heat will have a high U-value. One that will not conduct a lot of heat will have a low U-value. The same applies to floors and roofs.

Building Regulations stipulate certain U-values for various building elements in new buildings and in extensions to existing buildings that are greater than $6.5m^2$ in floor area. This is done in an effort to reduce energy consumption . For exposed building elements, the following values must be achieved:

Floor – 0.45; Wall – 0.45; Roof – 0.25.

For semi-exposed building elements the following values must be achieved:

Floor – 0.6; Wall – 0.6; Roof – 0.35.

241

A semi-exposed building element means an element such as a floor, wall or roof, separating part of a building from an enclosed unheated space to which the regulations do not apply. A garage, fuel store or workshop for example *fig. 44.*

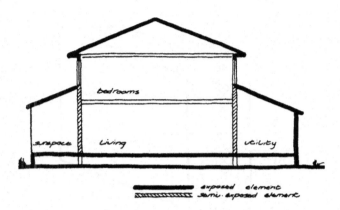

fig. 44: Exposed and semi-exposed building elements.

In the case of material alterations or change of use of existing buildings, the following U-values must be achieved:

Exposed wall – 0.6; Exposed floor – 0.6;

Exposed roof – 0.35; Semi-exposed wall – 0.6;

Semi-exposed floor - 0.6; Semi-exposed roof – 0.6.

The appropriate U-values for the design exercise you are undertaking should be entered into the H&V file at this stage.

U-values are a measure of the number of Watts of heat energy that will flow through a square meter of a particular construction every hour, for every ^{0}C difference in temperature between one side of the construction and the other. A 215mm solid concrete block wall with a 20mm sand/cement render on the outside of it and 16mm of dense plaster on the inside will allow over 2.5 Watts of heat energy to escape from each square meter of its surface area for every degree difference in temperature between the inside and outside of the wall. In contrast, a cavity wall constructed from two 100mm concrete block leaves with 50mm of insulation and a 50mm cavity, plastered and rendered as above, will conduct about 0.5 Watts of heat energy through every square meter of its surface under the same conditions.

U-values play an important role in estimating the likely heat loss from a building. These losses will be verifiable in practice, as heat will definitely leave the building by being conducted through the walls, floor and roof. The calculations however will, by necessity, be an artificial view of what will physically be happening as heat makes its way through the building fabric to the cold outside air. For example, a wall might have an excellent U-value based on calculations which assume that heat will flow horizontally through it to the cold outside. In reality such a wall might be rising up out of the ground and consequently be subjected to a strong vertical flow of heat making its way down to the cold earth *fig. 45.* If it is considered that the temperature of the ground in winter can be very low, a constant flow of heat will occur downwards through the wall. It is very difficult to insulate the bottom of such a wall to prevent heat flowing out of it. Rather, such a heat loss must be accepted as being greater than that reflected in the calculations. As a result of this, more heat would be required to be supplied to the building than is necessary if the building was to be protected from losing heat downwards into the ground. This drain on the heat resources of the building will not be properly reflected in the U-value calculations for the wall, because it will only take into account the flow of heat directly through the wall, including the insulating material. This will give a higher U-value to the wall construction than is in fact realisable.

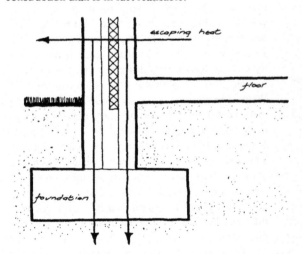

fig 45: U-value calculations assume that heat flows horizontally. In reality, a wall, for example, might be subject to a strong vertical flow of heat making its way down to the cold earth.

What this means is that it is not enough to simply choose a construction with a high U-value. Care must be taken to ensure that there is no major escape route for heat to follow, by-passing the insulation. In principle, insulation needs to be continuous to properly function in stemming heat loss in buildings *fig. 46*. If any part of the building protrudes through the insulation, heat will be conducted away, irrespective of the quality or thickness of the insulating material surrounding the remainder of the construction. Such would be the case with an insulated cavity wall sitting on a concrete foundation. The insulation in the wall would not be continuous with the insulation under the floor and so the wall, protruding through the insulation, would provide an easy path for heat to escape through.

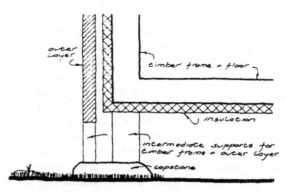

fig. 47: To properly insulate the bottom of a building some form of frame should be used to make the structure.

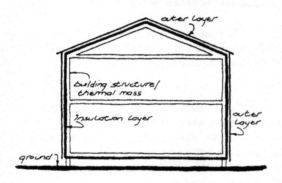

fig. 46: Insulation needs to be continuous to properly stem heat losses in buildings.

While it is impossible to entirely wrap with insulation any building that must by necessity sit on the ground, it is possible to reduce the number of places that the continuity of the insulation is breached to an absolute minimum. Such breaches must inevitably occur where the building structure must touch the ground to channel the building loads into the earth. If these portions of the building structure – its 'legs' for all intents and purposes – are made from a material such as timber, which is not a very good conductor of heat, the heat loss will be reduced to an absolute minimum. This requires that some form of frame be used to make the main building structure *fig. 47*. If concrete or stone piers are used instead of timber uprights, a timber beam can span between these. Such a beam will reduce the flow of heat from the building into the solid piers.

It is far easier to properly insulate a frame building, in contrast to a loadbearing one. This is because loadbearing construction requires more or less continuous support under walls. This requirement effectively breaches the insulation and provides a ready made path for the heat to flow unimpeded down into the ground. A system of piers and beams supporting solid walls used in conjunction with a suspended timber floor will allow a reasonable insulating job to be done on a loadbearing structure *fig. 48*. The elimination of concrete ground floor slabs is vital to this exercise.

The junction between any building and the ground it rests on is the one place where potential cold paths can very easily be created. At the junction of the wall and roof, it is far easier to make the insulation continuous and avoid the creation of cold paths.

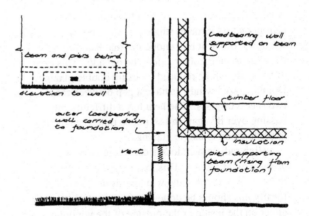

fig 48: A system of piers and beams supporting solid walls used in conjunction with a suspended timber floor will allow a reasonable insulating job to be done on a loadbearing structure.

In effect, it is very important to view U-values of constructions along with the cross section of those constructions to ensure that no permanent cold paths are being created which will seriously increase heat losses. These losses will in reality be greater than those reflected in the heat loss calculations based on the U-values. In other words, if you select the capacity of your heating unit by calculating building heat losses based on U-values, you may underestimate the actual amount of heat you will need to generate to keep your building warm. This would manifest itself in larger than expected fuel usage and, consequently, added expense.

Overall building heat loss calculations are made not only by taking U-values into account, but also by calculating the heat losses due to ventilation and adding these to the fabric heat losses. In regard to the Building Regulations, the requirements are simply to show that the walls, floors, roof and windows of a building achieve a sufficiently high U-value. This is done by calculating the U-values for these particular elements. Heat losses due to ventilation are not required to be quantified for the regulations.

U-values do not actually reflect the thermal mass capacity of a building. The heat storage capacity of thermal mass materials relates to the density and to the specific heat of these materials. The ability of the materials to retain their heat will depend on such materials being properly insulated.

Windows and Glazed Areas

A large degree of heat loss in a building can be caused by loss through single glazed windows. Such windows lose heat by conducting that heat through the glass to their colder side – the outside. This type of heat loss can be reduced by using double glazing. Double glazed windows have a gap between their two sheets of glass. The heat has a difficult time passing over this gap and so not so much heat is lost in comparison to single glazing.

High radiant heat losses can occur from windows at night *fig. 49*. This loss can be considerably reduced by screening the window from the night sky. Ideally this should be done using an insulated shutter either on the inside or the outside of the window. If a shutter is not used, some form of curtain or blind will work. Special coatings can also be applied to glass to reduce the amount of heat radiated to the dark night sky.

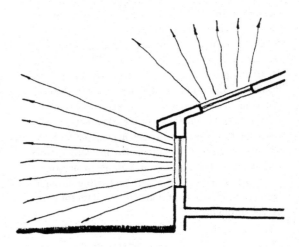

fig. 49: High radiant heat losses can occur from windows, especially at night. Shutters, curtains or blinds should be used to prevent this.

Typical U-values for windows are 5 and 5.7 respectively for wood and metal framed, single glazed windows. For framed double glazed windows the values are 2.9 and 3.3 for wood and metal respectively. These values are measured in Watts/m²/°C and apply to vertical glazing.

U-values for sloping or roof glazing are considerably higher than for normal windows. Typical values are 6.6 for a single glazed skylight with a metal frame. Such glazing is prone to very high radiant heat losses, because they face the cold night sky which draws heat away very quickly. It is very difficult to put shutters on roof glazing and care should be taken when proposing the use of such windows in any building design.

If the total area of glazing in a building exceeds 20% of the floor area, the Building Regulations require that such windows be double glazed and achieve a U-value of 3.6. Glazed areas in external doors have such glazing regarded as window.

If the total area of glazing is less than 12% of the floor area, single glazing can be used throughout. Glazed areas of 14, 16 and 18% of the floor area must have 25, 50 and 75%, respectively, of such windows double glazed to meet the regulations. Building Regulations allow that solar heat gain through windows be taken into account when heat loss calculations are being made.

244

U-Values For Some Typical Constructions

All values are in Watts per square meter per degree Centigrade. (W/m²/°C)

Walls:

19mm sand/cement render; 100mm heavyweight concrete block external leaf; cavity; 50mm polystyrene insulation; 100mm heavyweight concrete block inner leaf; 12mm dense plaster: **0.52**

As above, but with lightweight concrete blocks and aluminium foil lining in cavity: **0.33**

19mm sand/cement render; 100mm lightweight concrete block outer leaf; cavity; 150mm mineral wool insulation;100mm brick inner leaf; 12mm lightweight plaster: **0.28**

19mm sand/cement render; 100mm lightweight concrete block outer leaf; cavity; 8mm plywood sheeting; 100mm fibreglass insulation in depth of timber wall framing; 12mm lightweight plasterboard: **0.25**

As above, but with 12mm timber sheeting internally and aluminium foil lining in cavity: **0.24**

25mm timber weatherboarding; cavity with aluminium foil lining; 100mm mineral wool insulation; 8mm plywood sheeting; 100mm timber within thickness of 100mm timber wall framing; 12mm lightweight plasterboard: **0.23**

Floors:

25mm boarding; 100mm floor joists; 12mm plywood sheeting under joists; 100mm mineral fibre insulation: **0.25**

25mm boarding; 100mm floor joists; 12mm plywood sheeting under joists with aluminium foil lining; 50mm mineral fibre insulation: **0.45**

50mm sand/cement screed; 100mm concrete; 100mm polystyrene insulation: **0.31**

25mm boarding; 100mm brick within thickness of 100mm floor joists; 12mm plywood sheeting; 100mm fibreglass insulation: **0.29**

Roofs:

Clay tiles; rafters; 150mm fibreglass insulation; free attic space; 12mm lightweight plasterboard with aluminium foil lining under ceiling joists: **0.20**

Fibre cement slates; cavity; 150mm mineral fibre insulation; 8mm plywood sheeting; rafters; 12mm timber sheeting: **0.20**

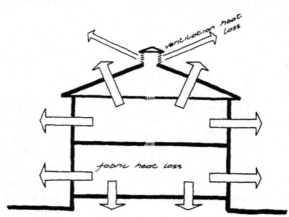

Calculating U-Values

It is possible to calculate the U-value for a particular wall, floor or roof construction by considering the resistance of the individual materials making up the construction, to the flow of heat through them.

A material with a strong resistance to heat passing through it, like insulation for example, has a low conductance value. Similarly, a material such as metal, with a low resistance to heat movement through it, will have a high conductance value. Resistance and conductance, when expressed mathematically, are said to be in inverse proportion to one another. The two conditions are, in fact, opposites. This means that the conductance value of a material is equal to the resistance value divided into 1 *fig. 50*.

$$\text{Conductance value of timber} = \frac{1}{\text{resistance value}}$$

In some places insulation values are measured as the resistance to heat flow and are called 'R-values' and are the reciprocal of 'U-values'.

$$= \frac{1}{6.93}$$

$$= 0.1443 \text{ W/m/}^{o}\text{C}$$

Material	Resistance (m^{o}C/W)	Conductance (W/m/^{o}C)
Glass fibre	28.6	0.035
Expanded polystyrene	28.57	0.035
Urea formaldehyde	25	0.040
Mineral wool	28.57	0.035
Fibreboard	16	0.06
Compressed strawboard	10	0.1
Woodwool slab	10	0.1
Weatherboarding	7.1	0.14
Timber	6.93	0.144
Plywood	6.93	0.144
Hardboard	6.93	0.144
Plasterboard	6.24	0.16
Roofing felt	5.3	0.19
Heavy concrete blocks	0.61	1.63
Medium concrete blocks	1.96	0.51
Light concrete blocks	5.26	0.19
Dense plaster	2.0	0.5
Light plaster	6.25	0.16
Brickwork inner leaf	1.61	0.62
Brickwork outer leaf	1.19	0.84
Clay tiles	1.2	0.84
Window glass	0.95	1.05
Sand/cement render	0.83	1.2
Sandstone	0.77	1.30
Cast concrete dense	0.71	1.40
Limestone	0.65	1.53
Granite	0.34	2.92

fig. 50: Resistance and conductance values of various materials.

U-value calculations for particular constructions begin by adding together the individual resistance values of the materials making up the building element. These are first multiplied by the thickness of the material measured in meters. For example, the resistance value of timber is 6.93. Therefore, 100mm thickness of timber will have a resistance to heat flow of 6.93 X 0.1, which gives a value of 0.693 (W/m/^{o}C). If this figure is divided into 1, a value for the conductance or U-value of the 100mm of timber will be arrived at: 1.443 (W/m/^{o}C). Where several different materials are involved, the resistances are added together before they are divided into 1 to arrive at the U-value. Resistance values for the exposed surfaces of materials within the construction are added into the equation before this is done. In reality, the resistance to heat flow that will occur at the surface of a material will be due to the air surrounding it. If cavities exist within the construction, these will also offer resistance to the flow of heat through the construction and this must be taken into account in the calculations *fig. 51*.

Exposed walls	Outside surface	0.06
	Inside surface	0.12
	Cavity	0.18
	Do. with aluminium foil surface	0.35
Roofs	Outside surface	0.04
	Inside surface	0.10
	Roof space (pitched)	0.18
	Roof space (flat)	0.17
Exposed floors	Outside surface	0.04
	Inside surface	0.14
Values in m^2 ^{o}C/W		

fig. 51: Various surface resistance values.

For a construction such as a cavity wall, the resistances of all the materials making up the wall, adjusted according to the thickness of the materials, are added together along with a value for the resistances of the exposed surfaces and for the cavity. The resulting total resistance is divided into one to give a value for the conductance, or U-value, of the wall.

For example, the U-value of a cavity wall with 105mm brick outer leaf, 100mm lightweight concrete block inner leaf, 50mm fibreglass insulation in a 100mm cavity and with 16mm dense plaster on the inside face is calculated by adding together the resistance values for the internal wall surface, the plaster, the concrete blockwork, the cavity, the brickwork and the outside surface resistance. The total of these is then divided into 1 to give the U-value for the wall *fig. 52*.

Such calculations can be made for all the major elements of the building – the walls, floors and roof – allowing an estimation of the overall heat losses through the fabric of the building to be made. These estimates, along with the U-values for the windows, are then used to estimate the overall building fabric heat losses.

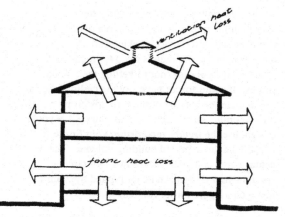

fig. 53: The total heat loss from any building is composed of two parts – ventilation heat losses and fabric heat losses. Ventilation heat losses occur when warm air exits from the building, carrying heat with it. Fabric heat losses occur when heat is conducted through the walls, floor and roof of the building.

Building element	Resistance value m °C/W	Thickness (m)	Total resistance m² °C/W
Brick outer leaf	1.19	0.1	0.119
Light block inner leaf	5.26	0.1	0.526
Fibreglass	28.6	0.05	1.43
Plaster	2	0.016	0.032
Outside surface	—	—	0.06
Inside surface	—	—	0.12
Cavity	—	—	0.18
		Total	**2.467**

$$\text{U-Value} = \frac{1}{\text{Total resistance}} = \frac{1}{2.467} = 0.4053 \text{ W/m}^2/°C$$

fig. 52 Typical U value calculation.

Preliminary Heat Loss Calculations

The total heat loss from any building is composed of two parts – ventilation heat losses and fabric heat losses. Ventilation heat losses occur when warm air exits from the building, carrying heat with it. Fabric heat losses occur when heat is conducted through the walls, floor, windows and roof of the building *fig. 53*. Total heat loss calculations are made in order to estimate the size of the heating unit required to heat your building. These calculations relate to the coldest time of the year and to the desired internal temperature and so allow the heating unit to be sized according to the maximum demand it is likely to be subjected to.

It has become the norm in many places that calculations of the insulation value of new construction work must meet set criteria before construction can take place. Such calculations are normally carried out by approved agents. It is worthwhile working directly with such an approved agents while a system design is being develpoped.

Building Regulations only require that the U-values for the elements making up the building fabric achieve a certain standard. It is not required that the overall building heat losses resulting from the combined fabric and ventilation losses be calculated. Such a calculation however is necessary to properly estimate the size of the heating unit needed to provide the desired temperatures within the building.

Estimating the amount of heat that will be lost through ventilation in a building is a matter of measuring the volume of the building and deciding on the number of air changes per hour that you require in your internal environment. If the volume of the building is multiplied by the required number of air changes per hour, a figure will be arrived at for the amount of air that must be heated every hour to maintain the desired internal air temperature. For example, if the volume of your building is 500 cubic meters and you want to have one air change per hour, you will have to heat up 500 cubic meters of fresh air every hour. How much you will have to heat this air will depend on how cold it is to begin with. If the lowest temperature that is likely to occur is 0° C and you want to maintain an internal air temperature of 18° C, then the incoming air will need to be heated by 18° C.

To calculate the number of cubic meters of air in your building, multiply the floor area of each space by the height of the space, making sure that all your measurements are in meters *fig. 54*. Include all the spaces in the building, not forgetting the circulation spaces. If some spaces have sloping ceilings, be sure to calculate the volume of these rooms properly. To make a preliminary calculation as you evolve your design, use the figures recorded in your Space files to estimate the expected building volume. The percentage area that you have allowed for circulation space in your design can be multiplied by 2.5m to give you a figure for its volume.

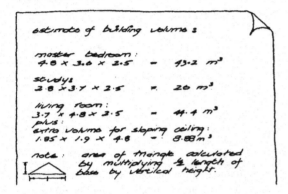

fig. 54: Calculate the volume of your building.

If there are 500 cubic meters of air within a particular building, every cubic meter of that air will require 0.34 Watts of heat energy to raise its temperature by 1°C. For 500 m³ of air that will need to be at 18°C, 500 X 0.34 X 18 Watts of heat energy will be required every hour – 3060 Watts, or 3.06 kW. If two air changes per hour are required, 3.06 X 2 kW, or 6.12 kW – will be required to heat this air every hour.

If 'cold' non-breathable construction is being used, the warm air that rises out of the building will carry away heat and this will be lost to the outside air. If breathable construction is used, however, some of this warm air will pass through the building fabric, surrendering its heat as it goes. This warming of the building fabric will not be reflected in the U-values, which will consider the construction to be 'cold'. In such a situation, the ventilation heat loss calculation will reflect the maximum loss that will occur if the heat in the air is completely lost by being ventilated away at high level.

It should be remembered that estimates of heat loss due to ventilation are in fact maximum values. In reality, an unoccupied building will not need as much fresh air as an occupied one. For the purpose of estimating the size of the heating unit, however, the maximum capacity of this must be calculated.

To the figure for ventilation heat loss must be added a figure for fabric heat loss. Fabric heat loss calculations are based on the U-values of the various constructions the heat is likely to escape through – the walls, windows, doors, floors and the roof. What you must first do is to calculate the surface area of these various building elements. The floor area will, in most cases, be already available to you. This will be listed in your Space files.

To calculate external wall and window areas, you will need cross section drawings of the various spaces in your preliminary design *fig. 55*. Again, these will be available in your Space files. These will show the length and heights of the walls making up the spaces. You should choose the largest side of each room and designate this as an 'external wall' for the purpose of making an early estimate of heat loss. In reality, corner rooms will have two external walls, but until a final layout has been arrived at, there is no way of knowing exactly which walls these will be.

By right, the area of these walls that have been designated 'external walls' should have a reduction made to them to take account of the windows and doors that will be located in them. Walls, windows and doors, having different U-values, need separate calculations to assess their potential heat losses. A figure of 20% of the wall area can be used for this. In other words, your calculation of external wall area should consider that 80% of it is solid wall and 20% of it is window and door area. As the circulation space is unlikely to contain an external wall, no account need be made of this space when calculating external wall area. While these areas are necessarily rough, they will provide sufficiently accurate information for preliminary heat loss estimates to be made on a design that is in the process of development.

When the final total heat loss calculations are being made, you will be working from a completed layout and you will have available to you accurate dimensional information in respect of door and window sizes and external wall areas. In a preliminary design exercise, the roof area can be taken as being equal to the floor area.

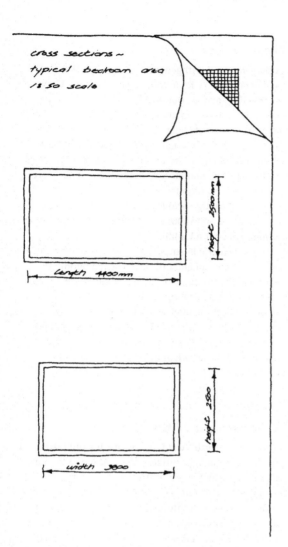

cross sections ~
typical bedroom area
/: 50 scale

height 2500 mm

length 4400mm

height 2500

width 3800

fig. 55: To calculate external wall and window areas in a preliminary design, cross section drawings of the various spaces will be needed.

When the areas of the various parts of the building have been calculated, the estimation of the heat losses through them is very straightforward. Again, this is based on the worst possible scenario, temperature wise – an external temperature of 0° C, for example, and an internal temperature of 20° C.

As you are only at a preliminary design stage, you have not finalised the details of your building's construction and so will not have definite U-values to work with. The U-values specified by the Building Regulations are therefore used at this point.

For example, to calculate the heat loss for an external wall of 180 m², with a U-value of 0.45, you multiply the wall area by the U-value – 180 X 0.45. This will give a figure – 81 Watts – for the heat loss through the wall if there is a 1° C difference in temperature between the inside and the outside. In the case of a 20 °C difference in temperature, this figure of 81 Watts must be multiplied by 20, giving a total of 1620 Watts, or 1.62kW, heat loss through the external wall every hour.

The procedure is the same for window, door and roof heat loss calculations. In the case of windows and doors, where the area involved is 45m² and the U-value is 3, the heat loss estimate will be 45 x 3 x 20 = 2700 Watts, or 2.7kW. In the final calculations, an adjustment can be made to this figure to take account of the solar gain through the windows.

For a roof with an area of 180m² and a U-value of 0.25, the heat loss through it at a design temperature of 20° C will be 180 X 0.25 X 20, which is 900 Watts or 0.9kW every hour. For a floor with an area of 180m², a U-value of 0.45 and a design temperature of 20° C, the heat loss will be 1620 Watts every hour, or 1.62kW. This gives a total fabric loss of 6.84kW.

Ventilation and fabric heat losses are then added together to give a total figure for building heat losses. In the case of the above example, in a building of 500 cubic meters volume requiring two air changes per hour, the total losses would add up to 12.96kW every hour. This, it should be remembered, is a mathematical exercise and based on assumptions about how the heat will perform in trying to leave your building. The constant opening of an external door allowing in gusts of cold air, for example, will greatly increase ventilation heat losses and this will not be reflected in the calculations. Similarly, an open window will also allow more cold air into the building than is strictly necessary for comfort.

In a highly energy efficient building, total building fabric and ventilation losses should be between 1.5 to 2W for every ° C of the design temperature, for every square meter of floor area. For a building of 180 square meters and a design temperature of 20° C, the total heat loss should be between 5400W and 7200W, or between 5.4 and 7.2kW every hour. In the above example, we have exceeded this by almost 5kW. This can be rectified by an increase in the proposed U-values for the various constructions. Considerable improvement in the U-value for the windows can be made simply by assuming that they will be enclosed by shutters at night.

Also, if it is considered that the proposed building might in fact be a two storey building, and not a single storey one as we have calculated for, a considerable reduction in the fabric heat loss can be made. In a two storey building of 180m² floor area, only 90m² of this area would be subject to heat losses to the outside. The roof of such a building would only need to be 90m², or half the size of its single storey counterpart. This reduction in external fabric area will improve the overall heat loss calculations as follows:

Floor: 90 x 0.45 x 20 = 810
Roof: 90 x 0.25 x 20 = 450
Total = 1260 (1.26kW)

This represents a reduction of 1.26kW in heat losses every hour, if the building is constructed on two floors rather than on one. Preliminary calculations of this nature will immediately make one realise that heat will leave a building in considerable amounts, even if the regulation U-values are used. The figures for overall heat loss will in fact reflect the capacity the installed heating unit must have to provide the specified design temperatures. This capacity is in fact the maximum required, and the heating unit would not have to produce this amount of heat all the time. In reality, the degree of heat production reflected in the calculations represents the heat requirement in the worst possible conditions – when it is freezing outside.

If the number of air changes per hour is also kept to a minimum, a considerable reduction in the overall heat losses can be achieved on paper. For example, changing the air twice every hour in bedrooms is really only necessary during the occupation of those rooms. Similarly, if the building is unoccupied during the day, the fresh air requirements in living areas will decrease. Also, if reasonable thermal mass capacity is installed, this will in fact contribute towards heating the air.

It must be remembered that calculations of this nature are theoretical and so are not wholly real. The proper sizing of the heating unit, however, is a critical aspect of the overall building design. As the design exercise progresses, considerable refinement can be made, both to U-values and to overall building heat losses. This will involve the careful selection of materials and construction, as well as the careful planning of the building. Reductions in overall heat requirements can also be achieved by taking advantage of available solar gains.

Heat Gains

A person at rest will generate around 115 Watts of heat energy every hour while a person doing heavy work will generate over 400 Watts. Lights, fridges, televisions, ovens, motors and many other household items also generate heat. Such heat is normally carried away on the internal air of a building. If heat absorbing materials are located close to the source of such heat – thermal mass – this heat can make a significant contribution to the overall heating needs of a building. Strictly speaking, such heat gains should be calculated and subtracted from the overall heating requirements of a building.

A considerable amount of heat can also be gathered from the sun and utilised to heat a building. Any solar heating system however cannot be relied upon to provide heating at all times. This means that a conventional heating unit will also have to be installed. The sizing of this follows the normal procedure though in practice the use such a unit will be restricted to times when insufficient solar heat is available.

Choosing a H&V System

The word 'hearth', used to describe the old fashioned open fire, is an appropriate way to describe the function of any H&V system. Heat is necessary in a building to warm the air and/or the internal fabric in order to make it comfortable for human occupation as well as removing stale air and so on. The source of such heat and the way in which it is distributed can take many forms. In essence, such a heat source is the 'hearth' of the building.

The choice of a particular system will depend not only on its ability to provide efficient and economical heating and ventilation, but also on health and psychological factors. For example, the open fire which can easily be dismissed on grounds of inefficiency is unrivaled as a source of psychological comfort or as a focus for a gathering *fig. 56*. On health grounds, the open fire is also beneficial, providing a source of negatively charged air particles, or ions, which are essential to a feeling of well being. An open fire will also draw fresh air into the dwelling. Because of this it may be decided to incorporate an open fire into a house design not as a primary source of heat but as a source of occasional comfort and enjoyment.

fig. 56: The open fire is unrivalled as a source of psychological comfort, or as a focus for a gathering.

The choice of a main heating unit has to be made in relation to the type of internal environment that is to be created, and with proper regard being paid to the construction and insulation of the building fabric. The heating system is a component part of the overall building concept and, as such, the choice of type can only be made by considering all aspects of the building in relationship to each other. This choice can radically affect the layout of the building, its construction, insulation and so on. For example, a choice to exploit solar energy for heating purposes will strongly influence the orientation and the planning of the building. Similarly, a two storey design might be chosen to minimise fabric heat losses.

Environmental factors also come into play in choosing a heating unit. Oil fired boilers, burning coal and even wood can be sources of air pollution. The increasing expense of fossil fuels, and the dependence on outside sources for their production, are also serious considerations in making a wise choice. Convenience, of course, is also important. A heating system should be easy to operate and to fuel and should be able to provide heat when it is needed without too much hard work being involved. Generally speaking, H&V systems can be divided into two broad types – systems that heat the air and systems that heat the fabric of the building. Air heating systems require relatively high temperatures and can suffer from high degrees of heat loss through ventilation. Radiant systems which rely on heating the fabric of the building work at lower tempera-

tures, are less prone to heat losses and allow for better control of the internal environment.

The heat output from a heating unit is measured in Kilowatts. The size of heating unit required in a building will relate to the amount of heat loss from that building. Such losses will occur through the fabric of the building – the walls, floors, windows, doors and roof. Further losses will occur through ventilation. The preliminary calculations of heat loss can be used to estimate the capacity of the heating unit you will require.

Your 'Heating and Ventilation' file should now contain information on all aspects of the subject fig. 57. This will include brochures, articles, newspaper clippings, as well as your preliminary calculations. It is important to become aware of the various systems that are available especially in relation to their potential problems in use. If careful preparatory work is done, the eventual choice of system will be reasonably straightforward. It is very important to begin investigations into the various systems, and to make an estimation of the heating needs of your design, before the house plan begins to take a definite shape. A decision in principle as to the general type of heating system that is required should be made as early in the design process as possible. It must be realised that the type of construction, as well as the layout of any building, is closely connected to the type of H&V system used to heat and ventilate that building. These items must be carefully considered in relationship to each other and not as separate subjects.

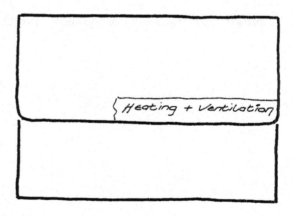

fig. 57: Information on all aspects of H&V should be collected in a file.

Pages 253-257 of the *Heating & Ventilation* chapter concern themselves with passive solar energy. Exercising the option to gather solar energy will have a profound effect on the layout of your building, its siting and orientation and on the materials used to construct it. There are also lifestyle issues involved.

If this is an option which you wish exercise the choice of site will become of critical importance - both for obvious reasons as well as for more obscure ones. The latter has to do with Planning - the use of large the area of glazing required, where this might front onto the public road, will oftentimes not accord with the Local Authority guidelines which generally prefer traditional-style 'front' elevations. A site with road frontage to the north (south if you are in the southern hemisphere) is therefore preferable, allowing the south elevation to face away from the road. If you wish to incorporate the gathering of Solar Energy in your design you should declare this preference now, entering this decision into the *H&V System Worksheet*.

If you are designing for a hot climate or a climate with hot summers/cold winters the building fabric will have to be versatile enough to cope with the extreme conditions. This can be achieved with roof overhangs, temporary shutters, adjustable ventilation and so on. Obtain information on the relevant solar angles at your location and store these in your *H&V* file.

If you are working with an existing building your options for gathering solar energy might be limited by the orientation of the existing structure. You can ascertain the orientation from your Survey information. Any changes to the use of existing *Spaces* wrought by the desire to bring solar energy into the building should be noted on the relevant *Space Analysis Sheets*.

Next: SDP26 - Fuels & Systems, page 258

Passive Solar Heating

The radiant heat energy of the sun can be utilised to contribute to the heating needs of a building. This is done by using glass, or some other translucent material, to trap the available radiation within a solar collector – the same principle as the glasshouse. Passive solar heating is based on the principle of capturing, storing and distributing solar heat, by natural means. In effect, this means holding the heat within some thermal mass/heatstore material. No fans, pumps, or other artificial methods are used to distribute the solar heat to the interior of the building. Rather, natural convective currents and radiation are utilised. The plan of a building must be organised to accommodate the use of a passive solar heating system.

The operation of a such a system requires that some type of collector is used to trap the available solar radiation *fig. 58*. Glass and certain types of plastics that enclose the heatstore materials are used to do this. When solar radiation passes through such a collecting surface – a window, for all intents and purposes – and then strikes the thermal mass behind it, the wavelength of the radiation is changed and heat is released in the process. The thermal mass/heatstore materials soak this up, rather like a sponge gathers up water, slowly warming up during daylight hours. The stored heat is then released naturally to the interior of the building.

A solar collector is, in fact, a glass wall through which solar radiation can pass. The other side of the glass wall is made from materials that have a high

heat capacity, that is, materials that can absorb large amounts of heat without getting too hot to touch. Brick, stone, concrete, water and even timber are suitable heatstore materials. The amount of heat energy that is absorbed depends on the amount of solar radiation available, and on the colour of the heatstore material. If the material is black, approximately 90% of the energy will be absorbed and stored in the form of heat.

It is important to have storage materials with low thermal resistances and high heat capacities to induce the heat to remain within the storage medium and to reduce the surface temperature rise. If this can be achieved, then the air within the collector will remain at a fairly constant temperature and overheating will be avoided. The object of thermal mass is to maintain a low surface temperature, as well as to store heat. To be effective, the thermal mass/heatstore material needs to have the sun shining on it for the best part of a winter's day. The large amount of glazing needed to gather solar radiation can cause problems of night time heat losses, unless they are properly screened by shutters or curtains during the hours of darkness.

The simplest type of solar collector is an arrangement whereby sunlight falls through a large south facing window and directly heats up the materials making up the floor and walls of a sunspace or solarium *fig. 59*. This space can form part of the usable accommodation in any home and can be used for a variety of purposes, from entrance hallways to hot tub rooms. The cross section proportions of such a space need to be carefully considered in order to be effective during the winter. The height of the collector surface and the width of the space will need to be made equal, to achieve the best overall results. Such a passive solar heating system is known as a 'direct gain' system.

The Mass Trombe Wall is another passive solar collector, named after Dr. Felix Trombe, a solar energy researcher. This comprises a dark coloured thermal mass wall, placed directly behind south facing glazing *fig. 60*. Such a wall would form part of the enclosure of a space or room within the building. It takes several hours for energy falling on such a wall to be transmitted as heat to the room behind. This time lag depends on the conductivity of the wall material and varies with thickness and construction. In general, a thickness of 250mm will be found to be the most effective for a Trombe Wall.

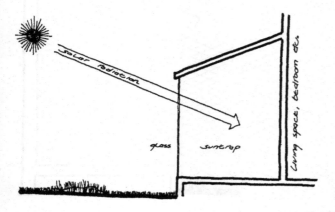

fig. 58: The operation of a passive solar heating system requires that some type of collector be used to trap the available solar radiation.

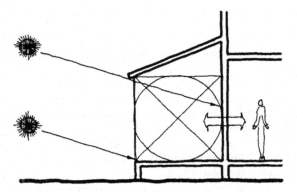

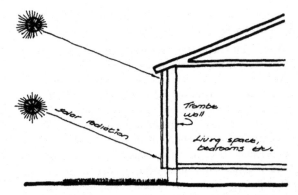

fig. 59: The simplest type of solar collector is an arrangement whereby sunlight falls through a large south facing window and directly heats up the materials making up the floor and walls of a sunspace or solarium. The cross section proportions of such a space need to be carefully considered, in order to be effective during the winter.

fig. 60: The Mass Trombe Wall is another passive solar collector. This comprises a dark coloured thermal mass wall placed directly behind south facing glazing.

Substitute locally relevant data for solar orientation - for example, in the southern hemisphere the sun is due north at local noon.

The glazing used in any collector surface will have a bearing on the amount of solar radiation trapped in the sunspace or Trombe Wall. Certain plastics perform better than glass – glass with a low iron content, for example, or glass that has been coated to reflect back infrared radiation originating within the collector itself. In any event, any glazing must be kept clean in order to be effective.

If special diffusing glass is used in a sunspace, and a light coloured ceiling is used to reflect radi-

ation onto the heatstore materials, the even distribution of energy resulting from this gives lower surface temperatures to the thermal mass and reduced temperature variations within the space.

The amount of solar radiation that can be collected into a sunspace or Trombe Wall can be considerably increased by the use of a reflecting pond in front of the collecting surface. This will reflect solar radiation towards the collector surface, especially during winter months when the angle of the sun is very low fig. 61.

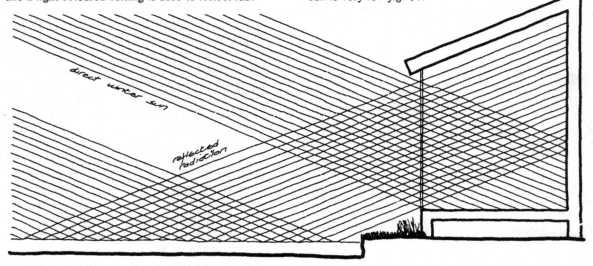

fig. 61: The amount of solar radiation that can be collected into a sunspace or Trombe Wall can be considerably increased by the use of a reflecting pond in front of the collecting surface. This will reflect solar radiation towards the collector surface, especially during winter months when the angle of the sun is very low.

Heating, using the Trombe Wall, is provided by opening vents at the top and bottom of the wall. Warmed air, in the space between glazing and wall, rises, drawing cool room air in through the bottom vent, thus setting up convective warm air currents. The warm surface of the wall will also provide radiant heat to the room behind it. In the case of a sunspace, a similar arrangement can be made *fig. 62*. It is important that any door leading from a sunspace to the outside of the building has a draught lobby fitted to it. This will prevent the loss of heat that would occur if the sunspace were suddenly to be opened directly to the outside.

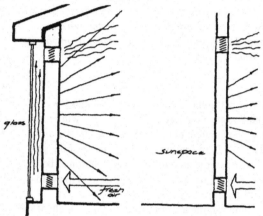

fig. 62: Heating, using the Trombe Wall, is provided by opening vents at the top and bottom of the wall. Warmed air, in the space between glazing and wall, rises, drawing cool room air in through the bottom vent ,thus setting up convective warm air currents. The warm surface of the wall will also provide radiant heat to the room behind it. In the case of a sunspace, a similar arrangement can be made.

In many ways the Trombe Wall system is inflexible. It is also less efficient than direct gain sunspace systems, because the storage of energy takes place with high temperature fluctuations – in other words, one side of the Trombe Wall gets very hot. This can cause a severe problem of radiant cooling to the dark night sky. The only way this can be prevented is by screening the glazing at night, which is difficult, unless the shutters are placed on the outside of the collector surface. The windows of a sunspace also need to be screened at night by shutters or curtains. These can easily be placed within the space and so are easier to operate.

Solar radiation reaches its peak intensity when the sun shines, though a passive solar heating system does not depend on the sun shining in order to work. Diffused radiation will travel through cloud cover to deliver radiation and heat to a building, even on an overcast day. When the sun does shine, however, the amount of solar radiation increases and may lead to a situation of too much heat being gathered! Such a situation is controlled by ventilation – using air to cool off the heatstore.

In summertime, to moderate possible excessive heat gains, a sunspace or Trombe Wall can be used to induce ventilation. To do this, solar heated air is allowed to escape at high level and cool air is drawn in from a cool source – a buried duct or from over a pond located on the shaded north side of the building *fig. 63*.

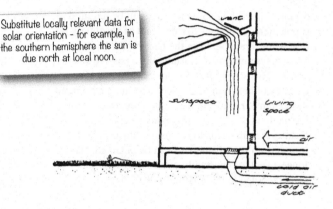

Substitute locally relevant data for solar orientation - for example, in the southern hemisphere the sun is due north at local noon.

fig. 63: In summertime, to moderate possible excessive heat gains, a sunspace or Trombe Wall can be used to induce ventilation. To do this, solar heated air is allowed to escape at high level and cool air is drawn in from a cool source – a buried duct or pond for example, possibly located on the north side of the building.

At all points in the procedure of gathering solar radiation, the aim is to have a gradual heating up of the thermal mass. If too much radiation is gathered up too quickly, the effect will be similar to what happens when a car is allowed to stand in the sun with all its windows closed – too much radiation will be trapped and the interior will overheat. The most likely time for this to happen is during the summer months.

It should be understood, when speaking about passive solar energy, that the temperatures generated in the heatstore during the heating season are, ideally, relatively low temperatures. The aim is to gently warm the thermal mass and to deliver the stored heat by radiation and convection to the interior of the building. This radiation, which is emitted at around body surface temperature, will not heat the air directly, but will release its heat when it falls on an absorbent surface. For example, the surfaces of soft furnishings of low thermal capacity will heat up quickly when struck by radiation from a heat store, and will, in turn, gently heat the room air by convection. In other words, the interior surfaces are brought into balance with body temperatures, ensuring a pleasant internal environment.

On its own, solar heating will not usually be enough to heat an entire house, and some other means of providing space heating will be required to supplement it. In the extreme event of absolutely no heat being available from the heatstore, a back-up heating system must be installed in a passive solar house. This should be sized to provide whatever quantity of heat will be needed to create the required design temperatures, in the coldest conditions that are likely to occur. In other words, a conventional heating system needs to be sized in the normal fashion, as if no solar heat gains can be obtained. The longest spell of constantly overcast weather that has been recorded in these latitudes is 30 days.

Orientation

The orientation of any solar collector should be as close to due south as possible, though any variation in this up to 30% will not unduly impair its performance *fig. 64*. The angle of the collecting surface – the glass – is also important.

Large windows on the east or west elevations of a sunspace will cause summer overheating. Such windows should only be installed in such a way that they can be screened in the summer and exposed in the winter, to benefit from the solar energy that they will collect. Inclined glazing will also create a summer overheating problem. In addition to this, excessive radiation losses will occur during the hours of darkness from such glazing. For these reasons, such inclined glazing should be avoided. Generally speaking, tall vertical glazing will give the best results.

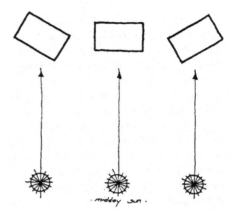

fig. 64: The orientation of any solar collector should be as close to due south as possible, though any variation in this up to 30% will not unduly impair its performance.

Vertical south facing glazing is, in many ways, the ideal collecting surface, allowing the winter sun to fully penetrate into the collector, especially a sunspace *fig. 65*. In summer, the high angle of the sun will cause a large amount of solar radiation to be reflected back from the glazing, and so help avoid overheating.

There is quite a large variation in the angle of the sun from its lowest position at mid-winter to its highest position in the sky on June 21st. These angles are approximately 15° and 61° respectively, and are caused by the tilt of the earth, relative to the sun. This inclination causes the seasonal changes.

Substitute locally relevant data for solar orientation - for example, in the southern hemisphere the sun is due north at local noon.

fig. 65: Vertical south facing glazing is the ideal collecting surface, allowing the winter sun to fully penetrate into the collector, especially a sunspace. In summer, the high angle of the sun will cause a large amount of solar radiation to be reflected back from the glazing, and so help avoid overheating.

Solar Heat Gains

Approximately 1000 kilowatts of solar heat energy falls annually on every square meter of the earth's surface at 52° latitude. If this heat is collected and held in a heatstore, it can contribute a considerable amount of the heat required in any building.

The amount of solar heat that is likely to be collected by a sunspace or Trombe Wall is calculated by multiplying the value of the solar radiation falling on each square meter of a vertical collecting surface by the area of the solar collector glazing. This figure is then modified to take account of the ability of the internal heatstore surfaces to absorb heat. For dark surfaces, a multiplying factor of 0.9 is used.

The amount of radiation that falls on each square meter of a collector surface will vary according to the time of year, and with location fig. 66. In the case of a collector surface of 12.5 m², in the month of December, with dark heatstore surfaces, 12.5 x 29 x 0.9 kWh of heat can be captured. This amounts to 326 kWh for the month.

Substitute locally relevant data for solar angles, solar intensity, etc.

Solar radiation falling monthly on vertical south facing glazing at 52° N. Values in kWh/m²					
Jan 37.32	Feb 61.15	Mar 80.72	Apr 78.97	May 78.74	Jun 64.90
Jul 68.08	Aug 78.37	Sep 75.00	Oct 64.71	Nov 43.20	Dec 29.00

fig. 66: The amount of radiation that falls on each square meter of a collector surface will vary according to the time of year, and with location.

A rule of thumb for sizing the area of the collector surface is to allow one third of the floor area of the building for this purpose. For example, a building of 150 square meters would have a collector surface area of 50 square meters. If this were to be made 4m high, it would then need to be 12.5m long. The incorporation of passive solar heating into any building design will have a strong impact on the plan of the building, as well as affecting the selection of materials and the outward appearance of the building. Because such large areas of glazing are involved, double glazing will have to be used throughout the building to meet the regulations.

Fuels

Any conventional heating unit that will provide heat to your building will require some fuel to burn. Coal, gas, wood and turf are all common fuels. In terms of their heat value per kilogram, gas has the highest value and wood the lowest. Oil comes somewhere in between and turf is similar in value to wood. Coal has a higher value than either turf or wood, but considerably less than oil fig. 67.

Your choice of fuel will have to be burned to release the heat held in it and this will require some form of boiler or grate. The capturing of the heat from the decay process of wood would be an exception to this, as there is no burning involved.

Oil and gas, being fluid, require no handling to take them from storage to the boiler. They are usually delivered by tanker truck and are fed directly to storage tanks, and so require no handling. Such tanks are connected directly to the boiler. Gas can also be stored in cylinders, which can be manhandled fig. 68. Wood, turf and coal must be brought to the

Fuel	Calorific value W/kg	Sulphur content %
Natural gas	14.76	0.03
Propane	13.9	0.02
Butane	13.76	0.02
Gas oil	12.64	1.0
Paraffin/kerosene	12.23	0.1
Light fuel oil	12.0	63.2
Medium fuel oil	11.9	23.5
Heavy fuel oil	11.81	3.8
Town gas	9.11	0.003
Coke	8.99	—
Anthracite	8.42	1.0
Coal	7.42	1.7
Turf	6.12	—
Dry Wood	5.56	—

Bulk of solid fuels		
Fuel:	Cubic meter/tonne	kg/cu. m
Turf	3.25	400
Wood	3	384
Coal	1.4	800

fig. 67: Calorific values of various fuels.

26 Sheltermaker Design Programme
Fuels & Systems

At the end of the day using the information contained in the *Heating & Ventilation* chapter will lead to a choice of heating system. Pages 257-269 detail the various options for doing this.

Usually a choice of *H&V* systems will be made on the basis of money. While this is understandable other considerations should not be ignored - the long term availability and cost of a chosen fuel; the environmental consequences of burning fossil fuels and the maintenance of complex plumbing systems, to name but a few. As a general rule, a high level of insulation is the best choice, combined with the capturing of solar energy, a storage capacity for this and the installation of a slow-combustion wood-burning stove distributing heat to where it is wanted by natural air circulation, possibly assisted by ceiling-mounted fans. The fuel for such a system should preferably be grown on-site.

It should be borne in mind that the normal practice of imagining houses as being collections of isolated rooms will be challenged by requirements of an ideal *H&V* system. Remember, all *H&V* systems owe their origins to the campfire and to the sense of togetherness engendered by sitting around one. This invites the planning of spaces which can on occasions be opened up to each other via sliding screens to allow heat from a central source to freely circulate.

If you are designing for a hot climate you may not need a heating system at all! However, at some such locations cold nights can be encountered requiring that solar heat be gathered and stored during the day then slowly released to the interior at night.

In the case of upgrading or extending an existing building there is no ideal system. However well thought out comprimises of the principles articulated in this chapter will be found to be adequate to cope with most situations.

Outline your preference as to fuels & system on the *H&V System Worksheet*. Gather information on slow-combustion wood-burning stoves, etc. Refer to the information on *H&V* available from other sources. Store all this material in your *H&V* File.

Next: SDP27 - Reviewing Your Work, page 270

boiler or grate by hand, in order to burn them. Being heavy, this is quite a laborious operation. With coal and, to a certain degree, turf and wood, this is also a dirt producing activity. Certainly, for all these 'solid' fuels, the removal of ash is a regular necessity. This activity is dirt producing and can severely affect the internal environment, contaminating it with dust.

The likely consumption of fuel will be based on the capacity of the selected heating unit and on its efficiency, as well as on the calorific value of the fuel used. This consumption can be directly related to cost. The effect of gathering solar heat on heating costs will be a reduction in the time the unit needs to be operated to produce the desired temperature.

Wood For Burning

Wood should be seasoned for a minimum of six months before burning. All wood contains moisture when it is cut. Moisture content is a measure of the amount of water present in the wood. At cutting beech can have a moisture content of 47%, oak 47%, ash 32%, sycamore 41%, birch 43%, elm 58%, sitka spruce 62%, Norway spruce 65%, lodgepole pine 59%, Scots pine 60% and Douglas fir 51%. When the wood is ready to burn it will make a 'bonking' sound, and the surface of the wood is likely to be cracked from the drying process. Wood for burning can be air dried, as long it is protected from getting wet. Drying times will vary from wood to wood, but at least six months will be needed in most cases. A simple solar dryer can be made from polyethylene and this will speed up the drying process. This should face south and be well ventilated *fig. 69*. A drying wood stack will also make a good insulating coat on the north side of a house.

fig. 68: *Oil and gas, being fluid, require no handling to take them from storage to the boiler. Gas can also be stored in cylinders, which can be manhandled. Wood, turf and coal must be brought to the boiler or grate by hand, in order to burn them.*

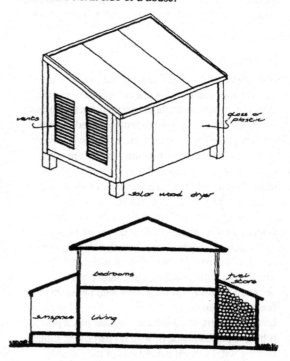

fig. 69: *A simple solar dryer can be made to season firewood. A drying wood or turf stack will also make a good insulating coat on the north side of a house.*

Wood with high heat values are beech, hornbeam, yew, oak, ash, birch, hawthorn, hazel or plane.

Wood with medium heat values are elm, cherry, sycamore, cedar and Douglas fir.

Wood with low heat values are poplar, spruce, alder and Corsican or Scots pine.

Fruit woods such as apple or pear have high heat values and a pleasant aroma. Ash and beech can be burned green, that is, unseasoned.

Beech, ash, laurel and hawthorn have always been favoured for burning. Green ash has a very low moisture content. Beech is easily split. Laurel and hawthorn are very dense timbers and will last longer on the fire.

If a system of coppicing is used, an area of 2-3 hectares will provide a continuous supply of wood to a household. A coppice is a wood or plantation which is regularly cut for firewood. New growth is produced from the stump. Most temperate-zone broadleaf trees are capable of coppicing. Conifers are not suitable for this purpose. Poplar, nothofagus, eucalyptus, alders and willow are all suitable species.

Biomass

One system of domestic heating that involves no burning and, indeed, no work or constant expense, works by capturing the heat from the decay process in wood. In this system a mound of shredded wood chips is soaked with water which sets the decay process in motion. Forest thinnings and trimmings, shredded into chips about 4mm thick are used to make the mound. Pine wood can be used on its own or a mixture of pine, birch and beech.

A large mound of around 50 tonnes of the chips is made near to where the heat is required fig. 70. This can be located on the northern side of a building or indeed in any convenient place within the site. The mound, which will be quite large, can be screened from view if necessary with trees, shrubs or fencing. When the mound is being formed several hundred meters of 30-40mm diameter black plastic tubing is placed inside it, with no part of the tubing coming within 1m of the outside of the mound. When the mound is complete, it is thoroughly soaked with water, which initiates the decay process.

Within 14 days, the wood chips heat up to around 70° C. This settles back to between 58-60° C within a short time. When water is circulated within the plastic tubing it picks up the heat of decomposition. This heat can then be used to heat the interior of a dwelling, using a system of radiators, or it can be used to warm the thermal mass of the building to an agreeable temperature. A simple heat exchanger can be employed to transfer the heat from the mound circuit to the heating circuit itself. The convection currents set up within the mound circuit will allow the water to circulate, without the need for a pump.

Each tonne of wood chips utilised will produce 322 Watts of heat per hour. For a 50 tonne mound, this would represent an output of 16kW per hour, more than sufficient for any domestic situation. The wood chips will remain active for eighteen months to two years. When its useful life is over, the resulting residual material makes an excellent fertilizer/soil improver.

The benefits of such a system are obvious. No work is involved, no emissions result from the heat production, the system is self-regulating and a useful by-product is created. When the useful life of the mound has been reached, it can be replaced with another.

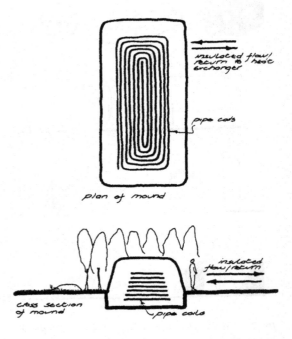

fig. 70: One system of domestic heating that involves no burning and, indeed, no work or constant expense, works by capturing the heat from the decay process in wood.

The Open Fire

The open fire is probably the oldest type of domestic heating system. Traditionally placed in the centre of the dwelling, the open fire provides both focus and warmth to the home. Heat is provided by convection and by radiation, though the convection currents mostly carry the heat away up the chimney! Because of this, an open fire is certainly not a good way of heating your entire house, and it certainly can contribute to air pollution if coal is burned.

While an open fire might be discounted on the basis of its inefficiency, its therapeutic value should be remembered. From this point of view, an open fire might be installed in a building, to allow an occasional wood fire to be lit and enjoyed. The chimney or flue of such an appliance should have an efficient damper, to allow the flow of air through the chimney to be shut off when the fireplace is not in use. This will slow down or eliminate completely the 'draught' on the chimney.

Building Regulations often require that fireplaces have masonry chimneys of a certain thickness, containing fireclay flue liners. In a timber framed building, such a construction would have to be carried through the floor and down to a foundation. A stone chimney, or a chimney faced with brick, will capture some of the heat being carried up the chimney and will provide a warm radiating surface, if it is left exposed to the interior *fig. 71*. Alternatively, a cast iron fireplace and a metal flue can be considered for use.

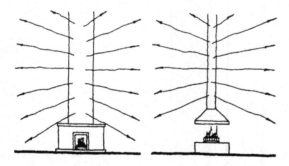

fig. 71: A stone chimney, or a chimney faced with brick, will capture some of the heat being carried up the chimney and will provide a warm radiating surface, if it is left exposed to the interior of the dwelling.

The 'father' of the modern chimney is a gentleman by the name of Count Rumford, who, in 1796, published his book, *'Chimney Fireplaces'*. In it, the Count showed how a chimney should be made to avoid smoking and excessive waste of fuel. The distance between the top of the fire and the entrance to the flue were the crucial factors, he discovered. If the gap were too great, the hot combustion gases rising from the fire would be over-cooled and the updraught would be sluggish. If the distance were too small, the hot gases would rush into the flue, wasting heat up the chimney and causing the fire to burn too fast. Count Rumford found that a distance of 360-510mm between the top of the grate and the flue gave the best results. Another useful suggestion was the introduction of a 'throat' to improve the flow of chimney gases. This, he suggested, should be limited to a depth of 100mm, extending across the width of the fireplace. Also, the grate should be brought as far forward as possible, while still keeping it directly below the throat of the chimney. The Count also introduced the splayed fireplace, which was wider at the front than at the back. The recommendations of Count Rumford, found effective in practice, apply to this day.

The location of an open fire should be carefully considered in relation to the house plan and to the type of use the fire is likely to get. If you refer back to your Brief, you should be able to tell the best place to locate the fire. A central location will be the most sensible.

Fuel for any open fire should be carefully considered – its type and where it is to be stored for use. How the fuel is to arrive at the dwelling is also important. The cost of the fuel should be considered too. How the fuel will get from the fuel store to the fireplace should also be given serious thought.

In many ways, the most important consideration to make in opting for an open fire is the removal of ash and the cleaning of the chimney. Both operations are dirt producing, as well as being time consuming.

The efficiency of an open fire can be as little as 20%. In other words, only one fifth of the heat available from the fuel that is being burned can be made useful to heat the building and its occupants.

Central Heating

Central heating systems distribute heat throughout a building, using pipes and hot water. The origins of central heating stretch back to Victorian times, when the need to heat glasshouses was important in order to grow tropical plants. The system of piping hot water, or even steam, through pipes was adopted from this use for the heating of factories and homes. An even earlier system of domestic central heating used domesticated animals to keep people warm!

Modern domestic central heating systems are based on the use of a heat producing unit that burns coal, oil, gas or wood. Such a unit heats water, which is then piped to a series of radiators fig. 72. Water is very useful as a means of storing and moving heat, because it can be moved easily from place to place and can also hold a considerable amount of heat.

The hot water within radiators sets up convection currents in the air, which distribute the heat. Such warm air, though, because it rises naturally, tends to get trapped under ceilings, leaving a layer of cooler air surrounding the occupants. Slow moving ceiling fans can help to distribute such heat more evenly. However, because the warm air is moving when it leaves the radiator surface, it can, in fact, carry heat away from the occupants, cooling them. To counteract this, central heating systems are oftentimes set to run at a high temperature, which results in stuffiness in the internal environment, as well as high heat losses.

Unless the warm air generated by radiators can heat the actual surfaces of the interior spaces, much of the heat will not be of much benefit, because it will be carried away. Sealing up the house to prevent this only leads to the internal air becoming stale and moisture laden. This can lead to severe problems with condensation, mould growth and even illness.

To properly benefit from the heat produced by radiators, the interior surfaces of a building, especially the walls, need to be made from materials that have a capacity to store heat. Brick, for example, works well in this capacity, as does timber. Such materials need to be insulated to assist in the storing of this heat and to ensure that it is not lost to the cold exterior of the building. If the system of heat distribution is not carefully arranged – the pipework and radiators – the internal surfaces will not in fact heat up very well, but remain relatively cold. If this happens, the warming of the internal air will be relied upon to keep the occupants warm. The potential difficulties with this – condensation, high relative humidity and possible unhealthy conditions – are considerable. Unless the building fabric is very carefully designed, heavy losses due to conduction can occur. This is especially true in loadbearing structures.

In timber frame construction, the placing of insulation immediately behind the surface of the interior walls has the effect of trapping the warm air produced by radiators, and preventing excessive losses through the building fabric fig. 73.

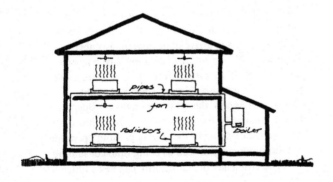

fig. 72: Modern domestic central heating systems are based on the use of a heat producing unit that burns coal, oil, gas or wood. Such a unit heats water which is then piped to a series of radiators. Slow moving ceiling fans can help to distribute the heat produced by radiators evenly within a space.

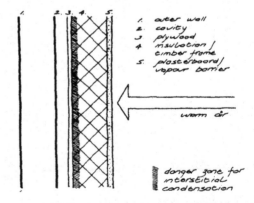

fig. 73: In timber frame construction, the placing of insulation immediately behind the surface of the interior walls has the effect of trapping the warm air produced by radiators, and preventing excessive losses through the building fabric.

There are potential difficulties with this arrangement, however, mainly due to the possibly high moisture content of the air that is carrying the heat. When this warm, moist air has progressed through the insulation and reached an area that is cold, there is a definite possibility of condensation occurring. Such internal, or interstitial condensation, must be avoided at all costs. One common solution to the problems of interstitial condensation is the use of vapour barriers.

Vapour barriers are in fact waterproof layers that halt the passage of moist air through the constructions containing them. The theory behind their use relies on this waterproofing ability to prevent warm, moist air from passing through walls and possibly condensing in the cold regions behind the insulation. While this theory is workable in practice, the dangers of using such vapour barriers is to cause a build up of moist air in the interiors of buildings that employ them. Unless this air can be ventilated to the outside of the building, the resulting high relative humidity will cause problems in the internal environment. Such barriers are commonly used in timber frame construction. To rid the interior of a building of the moist, stale air that cannot escape through the building fabric, a high degree of ventilation is needed. As this air will have been warmed up by the central heating system, the resulting loss of heat will be very severe. The use of vapour barriers can, in some ways, be likened to the suffocating effects of a plastic bag placed over the head.

The elimination of vapour barriers from timber framed buildings requires that the layers of the building fabric be rearranged to avoid the danger of interstitial condensation, by using a breathable construction and possibly some thermal mass *fig. 74.*

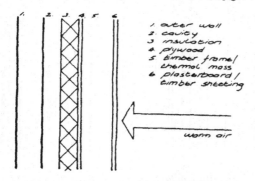

fig. 74: The elimination of vapour barriers from conventional timber framed constructions requires careful arrangement of insulation and thermal mass.

Thermal mass, to store some of the heat produced by radiators, is a very important aspect of making a workable central heating system. Similarly, proper ventilation is essential. The location of radiators will depend on the location of the thermal mass. These radiators can be thermostatically controlled, which means that each individual radiator can be set to a particular degree of warmth. It is usual for the water in a central heating circuit to be circulated by electrical pump.

Normally, central heating systems are designed to run at quite high temperatures and are intended to heat the air in a dwelling. To properly heat thermal mass/heatstore materials, low temperatures are best and the heat should ideally be applied to these materials from within.

The final layout of the heating system is covered in the chapter entitled *'Plumbing'* in Volume 2. Hot water systems are also covered in that chapter.

Radiators

Radiators are metal panels containing hot water, which cause convective currents in the air surrounding them. The 'output' of radiators is measured in kilowatts and radiator sizes are chosen according to location and the size of the space they are intended to heat. Traditionally, radiators are placed under windows to ensure that they have a supply of air, though this is not necessarily the most efficient place in which to locate them. Radiators can be bulky as well as unsightly, disturbing the clean lines of a room. Enclosures can be made to house radiators, though these cut down on the efficiency of the units.

Skirting radiators, placed under walls containing heatstore materials such as brick or wood, will produce a gentle flow of heat up into the wall, allowing some of the heat to be absorbed, as well as providing some convective heating *fig. 75.*

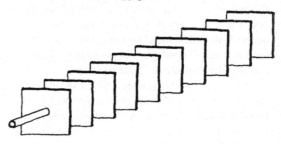

fig. 75: Skirting radiator.

All piping to and from the boiler to the individual radiators should be properly insulated. Radiators can be fitted with thermostatic controls, ensuring that a particular unit runs at a specific temperature. It should be remembered that radiators work by convection, and not by radiation, as their name suggests.

Radiant Surface Heating

Floors, walls and even ceilings can be organised to be warmed up by circulating low temperature hot water within them. This allows such surfaces to be brought into balance with the natural surface temperature of the building's occupants and so eliminate radiant heat losses from them. The temperatures at which such systems operate is far lower than for central heating systems using conventional radiators. Typically, a water temperature of 32-37° C is used, as opposed to around 80° C for radiator systems. The use of such low temperatures produces a gentle heating of the interior of a building and allows the internal air temperature to be kept quite low, thereby allowing for a pleasant and healthy internal environment to be maintained.

Commonly, underfloor heating uses spirals of 16mm black plastic pipe to transfer heat into a concrete slab, producing a surface temperature of 20° C, or slightly higher. A suspended floor arrangement using bricks or hollow clay units, will give better results. This will be easier to insulate and to protect from moisture penetration *fig. 76*. Approximately 55% of the heat of a radiant floor is given off by radiation and the remaining 45% by convection. A hard surface finish, such as ceramic tiles, will be found to give the best results, though wood block timber flooring could also be used successfully.

A concrete slab functioning as a heating unit must be very well insulated to prevent the loss of heat into the cold earth below it. Damp-proofing must also be very well taken care of. A concrete radiant floor will have a very slow warm up time. In use, any radiant floor will be found to create a very pleasant environment. It is perhaps the only situation where a concrete slab should be considered for use.

Walls can also be warmed up by inserting piping within them. Brick and even timber will be found to be ideal for this. Alternatively, pipes can be embedded in plaster over a core of brick *fig. 77*. The effect is not dissimilar to the use of a Trombe or sunspace wall, where walls are heated up from

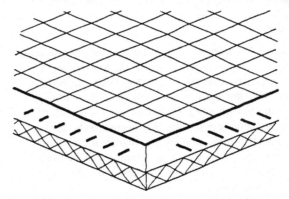

fig. 76: Commonly, underfloor heating uses spirals of 16mm black plastic pipe to transfer heat into a concrete slab.

the heat of the sun. Typically, a warm radiant wall will radiate out 65% of its heat and supply 35% of its heat by convection.

The use of radiant wall heating will require the careful placement of furniture in the dwelling, as well as the careful organisation of the plan. As with radiant floor heating, the effect of such a heating system on the internal environment is extremely pleasant. As with the floor heating the warm up time for radiant systems can be quite slow, though an arrangement could be arrived at allowing convective currents to circulate at the beginning of the heating period to rapidly heat the internal air. When sufficient heat has been generated, the system can revert back to slowly heating the thermal mass. Back boilers, furnaces, oil and gas boilers can all be used to heat thermal mass materials.

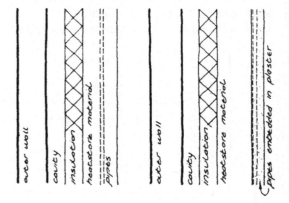

fig. 77 Walls can be warmed up by inserting piping within them. Brick and even timber will be found to be ideal for this. Alternatively, pipes can be embedded in plaster over a core of brick.

Back-Boilers

An open fireplace can be fitted with a device known as a back boiler. A back boiler is a jacket filled with water that heats up when the fire is alight. Such a device will considerably increase the efficiency of the fireplace. What this means is that a lot more of the heat of the fuel will be captured than would be in a normal open fire.

Such systems can work quite well, but usually they require that a fuel such as coal be burned in order to produce the quantities of heat necessary for efficiency, especially if a large number of radiators are used. There are two problems with having to burn coal in an open fire. The first is the question of the air pollution generated, and the second is the question of bringing fuel to the fire and removing the ash from it. Both tasks are dirty and time consuming. Removing ash from an internal fireplace will produce dust that will be impossible to remove from the internal environment. Also, regular cleaning of the chimney will be required.

In a building with proper ventilation inlets, the air needed for the fire to 'draw', or burn, will be supplied from these inlets. If breathable construction is used, some air will also be drawn in through the fabric of the building for this purpose.

The hot water produced from a back boiler can be piped to a hot water tank to provide hot water to supply the hot taps in the house. The water can also be piped to radiators, where convective air currents will carry the heat away. Alternatively, the hot water produced can be used for the heating of radiant walls or floors.

The efficiency of back boilers is 35-55%.

Ranges and Stoves

A variation on the open fire/back boiler arrangement is the range or stove. Such devices, normally made from cast iron, contain a firebox in which solid fuel is burned to produce heat. An oven and hotplates can also be incorporated. It is also normal for a back boiler to be included.

As with the open fire, the fuelling of a range or stove can be difficult and time consuming. Similarly, the removal of ash and soot is problematic. Some ranges are oil or gas fired, and so are automatically fuelled.

A range, or stove, will adequately heat the room it is in by convection currents, as well as by radiation.

Some thermal mass can be incorporated to capture this. A location in the centre of a building and an enclosing brick wall – thermal mass – will best exploit the heating potential of a range or stove, allowing other rooms to benefit directly from the heat fig. 78.

Because they oftentimes operate at low temperatures, and so produce low temperature hot water, ranges and stoves can be utilised for heating thermal mass, rather than conventional radiators.

The efficiency of ranges and stoves is 45-60%.

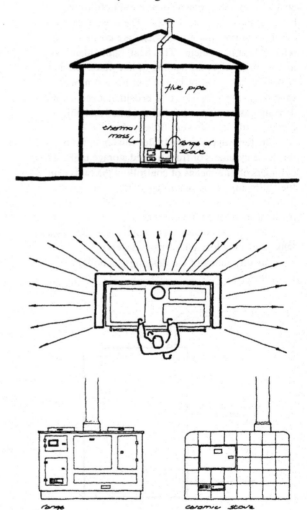

fig. 78: A location in the centre of a building and an enclosing brick wall, to provide some thermal mass, will best exploit the heating potential of a range or stove.

Condensing Gas Boilers

If a solid fuel system is not being used to heat the house, a central heating boiler might be used. Such a boiler will heat hot water both for domestic use and for radiators. A condensing gas boiler is the most efficient and least polluting type of central heating boiler. Suitable for LPG and natural gas, these heaters burn gas very efficiently. Efficiencies as high as 96% have been achieved. What this means is that 96% of the heat in the fuel can be extracted by burning it.

Condensing gas boilers do not require chimneys or flues, but only a plastic pipe running from the boiler to the outside air *fig. 79*. The reason for this is because the hot combustion gases are condensed to remove heat from them. This heat, rather than being lost, contributes to the heating of hot water. Such a boiler can easily be located in a utility room, workshop or garage. The size of a bedside locker, a condensing gas boiler can be wall mounted and will consequently take up very little space.

The fuel supply to the boiler can come from refillable cylinders or from a fixed storage tank. The cylinders offer a means of controlling the outlay on fuel, allowing small quantities of gas to be bought. The fixed cylinders require a special delivery to be made, usually of a minimum quantity.

Care should be taken when cylinders and storage tanks are being located to ensure safety.

The efficiency of condensing gas boilers is 90-96%.

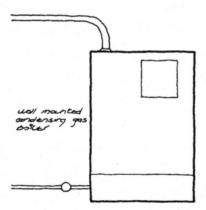

wall mounted condensing gas boiler

fig. 79: Condensing gas boilers do not require chimneys or flues, but only a plastic pipe running from the boiler to the outside air. The reason for this is because the hot combustion gases are condensed to remove heat from them.

Wood Burning Stoves

A benign alternative to the open fire is the wood burning stove. A wood burning stove will provide heat by radiation and by convection, as well as being able to heat water for distribution to radiators in other parts of the building. Such a stove should be centrally placed in the building with its insulated metal flue carried straight up through the building *fig. 80*.

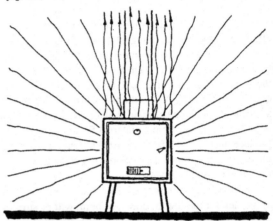

fig. 80: A benign alternative to the open fire is the wood burning stove. A wood burning stove will provide heat by radiation and by convection, as well as being able to heat water for distribution to other parts of the building.

The work of feeding a wood burning stove is less arduous than with the open fire. A stack of dry wood beside the stove will have a far more pleasant appearance than a pile of coal! Ash removal, however, can be tricky, and care should be taken when doing this to avoid releasing the ash into the building.

A wood burning stove, fitted with a back boiler, will heat hot water for domestic use, and such a boiler will also heat radiators located some way from the primary heat source. Alternatively, the heat can be used for the heating of radiant walls or for supply to skirting radiators.

The wood that is burned in a wood burning stove should be dry. This is very important, otherwise the stove will not work efficiently and you will have to burn more wood than is really necessary. Unseasoned wood has a lot of water in it. If unseasoned wood is burned, the water in it has to be boiled off and this can cause condensation in the flue pipe and a build up of creosote.

The rate of burning of a wood stove can be controlled, allowing adjustments to be made to the amount of heat being produced. The door can also be left open to allow a glimpse of the flames for those times when you want to sit and look into the fire.

One of the great advantages of a wood burning stove is that it allows you to stay warm in almost any circumstances. Fuel can usually be found, oftentimes at no cost other than the labour involved in gathering wood and cutting it.

A wood burning stove can be located in a well insulated room below the living areas of a house and its heat allowed to rise up naturally into the dwelling. No pump will be needed to circulate the hot water in the heating circuit if this is done. This same principle applies to back boilers. Also, such an arrangement allows for fuel and ash to be handled without disturbing the internal environment. There might, however, be a considerable amount of walking up and down stairs!

The efficiency of wood burning stoves is 60-70%.

The Finnish Fireplace and The Ceramic Stove

A Finnish fireplace is a massive masonry heater in which a wood fire is burned. This fire is burned intensely for several hours and the flue gases from the fire are directed through the fireplace, so that they can release their heat to the masonry or brick. When the flue gases have cooled, they are carried into an ordinary chimney, which delivers them outside. Such a fireplace is in fact a self-heating thermal mass *fig. 81*.

Once the burn is completed, dampers in the chimney flue are shut and the entire mass radiates heat for the next 12-24 hours. Masonry stoves require a solid foundation under them and are quite large. They work on the principle of thermal mass – holding heat and releasing it slowly to the surroundings.

To incorporate such a heating unit within a dwelling requires that the plan be made to accommodate it. As with all forms of solid fuel heating, the storage and movement of fuel is important to consider at an early stage of the project. The method of ash removal is also critical to the easy operation of the unit.

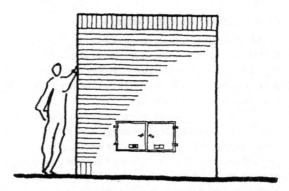

fig. 81: A Finnish fireplace is a massive masonry heater in which a wood fire is burned for several hours. The flue gases from the fire are directed through the masonry in the stove so that they can release their heat to the masonry or brick. Such a fireplace is in fact a self-heating thermal mass.

Ceramic stoves, which are smaller than Finnish fireplaces, operate on the principle of being self-warming thermal masses. Their name derives from the fact that they are oftentimes faced with ceramic tiles *fig. 82*. As opposed to the larger fireplace, the ceramic stove is left burning for long periods. Wood is the preferred fuel for such devices. A ceramic stove should be centrally located and the flue carried up through the interior of the dwelling.

The efficiencies of Finnish fireplaces and ceramic stoves is up to 90%.

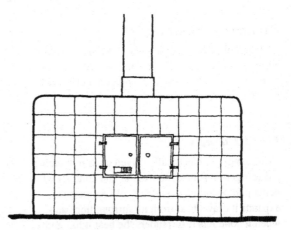

fig. 82: Ceramic stoves operate on the principle of being self-warming thermal masses. Their name derives from the fact that they are oftentimes faced with ceramic tiles.

Radiant Heating Panels

Radiant heating panels are made of marble. They are heated electrically. When warm, they radiate out their heat to the colder surfaces surrounding them. Radiant heating panels are in fact thermal mass that is heated directly by electricity.

Electricity production, when carried on commercially, can be wasteful and polluting. This makes the use of these panels, and all forms of electrical heating, difficult to justify. It takes approximately twice as much fuel – oil, gas or turf – to produce 1kW of electricity than it does to produce the same amount of heat by burning the fuel yourself. So, even though electrical heaters can be said to be 100% efficient, the plants that produce that electricity are not at all efficient.

Wind or water power could, however, be used to produce electricity for such panels.

Oil-fired Boilers

Oil-fired central heating boilers are used to heat water for use in radiators. These types of boilers are polluting, inefficient and are not to be recommended for installation. Apart from any other consideration, the future supply of fuel to such units is uncertain. Some types of condensing gas boilers are now available. These display greater efficiency as they can reclaim heat from the flue gases.

The efficiency of oil-fired boilers is 55-70%.

Electrical Heating

All types of electrical storage and convector heaters, while being 'clean' and efficient, can only be chosen by disregarding the facts of commercial electrical production.

Heat Pumps

Heat pumps are electrically driven units in which a gas refrigerant is made to expand and contract while being pumped around a circuit. When the gas expands it draws heat from its surroundings and when it contracts it surrenders the heat it has gathered. This process is repeated over and over again. The heat that is gathered in this process is usually 'low grade heat' and is oftentimes gathered from flowing water or even from the air. The heat pro-

duced in this manner can be used to heat water for use in a normal central heating system *fig. 83*.

An additional use of heat pumps is to cool a particular room or space by drawing heat from it for use somewhere else in the building. In this way, a cold-room or walk-in refrigerator could be created within a building.

Heat pumps rely on CFCs to work efficiently. While the energy input into heat pumps is far out-weighed by the energy they produce, it is necessary to take into account the inefficiencies of electricity generation to make these equations more realistic. Gas fired heat pumps are also becoming available.

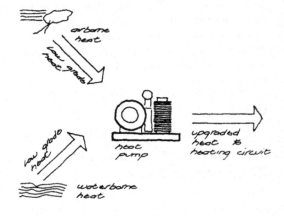

fig. 83: Heat pumps gather 'low grade heat' and upgrade this to a higher temperature.

Chimneys & Flues

Building Regulations require that heat producing appliances be installed so as to ensure an adequate supply of fresh air to the appliance, to allow for the efficient operation of the flue pipe or chimney. In effect, this means that the appliance must be contained within a space which has a permanent ventilation opening. This opening can either connect directly to the outside air, or be an opening to a space which contains a permanent opening direct to the outside air. For example, a wood burning stove contained within a central hallway must have a permanent ventilation opening to an adjoining space containing an opening directly to the outside air. Such an adjoining space could be a front porch or even a living space. A ventilator providing fresh air to the occupants would in fact also feed the appliance.

268

For solid fuel burning appliances, the area of the ventilation opening supplying it with fresh air must be at least 50% of the appliance throat area. For other appliances, ventilation openings with a total free area of at least 550mm^2 per kW of rated output above 5kW must be provided. Where a flue draught stabiliser is used, the total free area of the openings should be increased by 300mm^2 for each kW of rated output. Throat areas of appliances are available from manufacturers trade literature.

In any building containing an extract fan or fans, the heat producing appliance and flue should be able to operate effectively whether or not the fan or fans are running. This requirement can be met by providing adjustable ventilation inlets.

Building Regulations also require that there be adequate provision made for the discharge of the products of combustion to the outside air. In other words, a properly designed flue or chimney must be installed, connecting the appliance to the outside air. Low level or balanced flues, as well as flue pipes and chimneys, once they are properly designed, will all meet this requirement. Details of the type of chimney or flue any particular appliance needs will be contained in the manufacturer's trade literature. Condensing gas boilers, because they extract heat from the exhaust gases, require only a small plastic pipe connected to the outside air.

Chimneys and flue pipes must be designed, installed and constructed so as to reduce to a reasonable level the risk of the building catching fire in consequence of its use. Details of how to meet this requirement are contained in the chapter entitled 'Construction' in Volume 2.

Control Systems

Building Regulations require that any heating unit capable of automatic on/off operation should be connected to sensing devices and time switches to regulate their operation. Sensing devices in the form of thermostats can be installed within rooms, or incorporated into individual radiators. These accurately gauge temperature and trigger the operation of the heating unit when the temperature falls below a certain set level. The regulations also require that a weather compensation control unit be installed externally. This gauges the outside temperature and so regulates the generation of heat by the heating unit. Time switches allow the heating unit to come into

operation at particular times of the day or night. The output from solid fuel heating systems can only be controlled manually.

Ceramic, or, masonry stove

Summary

Heat moves in several different ways – by convection, conduction, radiation and evaporation. Our bodies produce more heat than they need to survive.

Because air plays such a vital part in maintaining an even body temperature, heating and ventilation are considered as a single question in building design.

The design of any H&V system needs to be based on the way in which the human body functions and is clothed.

Heat is lost from a building in the same way that it is lost from our bodies – by convection, conduction, radiation and evaporation. These losses need to be controlled to minimise energy usage. Convection heat losses also help to cleanse the air within a building.

The sun, wood, oil, coal, gas, turf and electricity can all be used to supply heat to the interior of a building.

Make preliminary calculations of overall heat loss from your building.

Decide in principle the type of H&V system and fuel you wish to use.

27 Sheltermaker Design Programme
Reviewing Your Work

At this point a clear idea of the kind of home you wish to make will have emerged. Before the job of selecting *Materials, Products* and a *Construction System* begins, it might be wise to comb through your files discarding irrelevant items, filling in gaps etc. Also, you might want to make revisions to your *List of Spaces, Space Analysis, Floor Area, Budget Worksheets* and so on, to bring them in line with your recent decisions.

Design is a process - it is not linear but rather is made up of a series of interconnected strands that must be continually adjusted to satisfy the varied requirements generated by you, the world, by cost, expectation, environment, regulations and so on. These adjustments are ongoing and gradually reduce in scale until the design can said to be 'complete.'

You will now be a different person from the one who embarked on this design exercise in the first place. Keep this in mind and allow such changes to penetrate your sub-conscious where they can influence your dreams. Take careful note of these!

The focus is now going to turn to the materials and products with which to construct your design. The invisible aspects of the design as expressed by you in your *Worksheets* are now going to be translated into physical reality. It is critical therefore that these invisible aspects truly reflect the life you wish to live.

If you have skipped the *Space Mock-Up* exercises and consequently avoided calculating the Heat Losses from your building, you will have to tackle this work before embarking on item *42 - Developing A Layout*. In many ways this is the desirable approach - to grasp the principles of *H&V* and the other critical 'ingredients' of the design - before putting your 'recipe' together.

Next: SDP28 - Understanding Timber, page 3, Volume 2

Index

A

B

C

I

K

L

P

T

U

Volume 2 Contents

LIVING ARCHITECTURE CENTRE.COM

The Living Architecture Centre is an internet-based school of vernacular architecture, founded and directed by Peter Cowman who was born in Ireland. He is an architect, eco-builder, writer and teacher delivering Courses & Workshops internationally on the subject of sustainable house design and construction. He has a special interest in the creation of affordable, low-impact buildings.

The Living Architecture Centre offers a wide range of resources on all aspects of the role of eco-architecture in the achievement of a sustainably way of life – Articles, Sheltermaker Magazine, LIVE & Distance Learning Courses, Talks, Workshops, Sheltermaker Theatre presentations as well as Consultancy & Mentoring Services.

Mentoring for users of *The Sheltermaking Manual*

Students can submit *Assignments* and receive written *Feedback* and *LIVE Video Consultation* on their projects. Further details available from livingarchitecturecentre.com

EconoSpaceMaking Course

Sustainability begins in your own backyard - that is the compelling argument put forward on this dynamic combination of text, drawings, photographs and video information which is supplied on a DVD.

By learning how to create a small sustainable shelter - with no need to first obtain planning permission - you are offered the opportunity to regain territory lost to an economic system which depends on mortgage debt to satisfy its insatiable appetite and growth.

From drawing to modelmaking, from concept to built reality, EconoSpaceMaking provides you with the means to create your own living architecture and to discover, in the process, who you really are.

EconoSpaceMakers can also participate in a dedicated online Forum where they can exchange ideas and information as well as keeping up with the latest developments.

See page 286, *Vol. 1* for further details or go to livingarchitecturecentre.com

Living Architecture PRIMER

Not certain if the Living Architecture is for you? Then try the Living Architecture PRIMER. This is a disc-based compilation of published *Articles, Course Handouts, Films* and *TV* documentaries, plus *Sheltermaking Manual* and *EconoSpaceMaking Course* material, all of which will serve as an excellent introduction to the subject of *Living Architecture*. The budget-priced PRIMER includes a discount voucher redeemable against the cost of the full *EconoSpaceMaking Course* when you are ready to upgrade. To order or to obtain further details go to livingarchitecturecentre.com

The EconoSpace

The EconoSpace first came to life as an idea - the idea that it should be possible to construct a small habitable building with very little in the way of money. The realisation of this idea took some time for a variety of reasons. Students who attended early 'Be Your Own Architect' Courses - where I was promoting the idea - were more interested in creating better houses for themselves than in escaping the tyranny of the mortgage. This skewed my attention in favor of developing a viable house design strategy which in turn led to the concept of 'living' architecture, to the development of the Actual House and to the writing of what has now evolved into The Sheltermaker's Manual. Much was learned on this journey which, when time allowed, proved useful in the pursuit of my original objective - how to design and construct a small habitable building with very little in the way of money, and, possibly, building skills.

On this quest it became clear that control of building development by means of planning laws, combined with the ruthless exploitation of people's need for shelter through mortgage debt, is the system responsible not only for environmental destruction but also for the psychological crisis infecting large numbers of people as they strived to define the meaning of their lives within the context of modern society. While this understanding lent urgency to the quest to develop an affordable architecture more closely related to our true nature as human beings, it also highlighted the threat to the economic system if people regained control over their own housing needs.

As I worked on the first EconoSpace design the issues which needed most attention were not physical at all but concerned themselves with where one might locate such a building. This 'land' issue was dealt with by working within the parameters of 'Exempted Development'. Under this regulation, in Ireland, you are allowed to construct a 25sqm 'shed' in the back garden of an existing house without the need to apply for planning permission.

The physical issues involved in the first EconoSpace design were myriad - how to develop a versatile construction system suited to the 'time poor'. How to teach unskilled people the

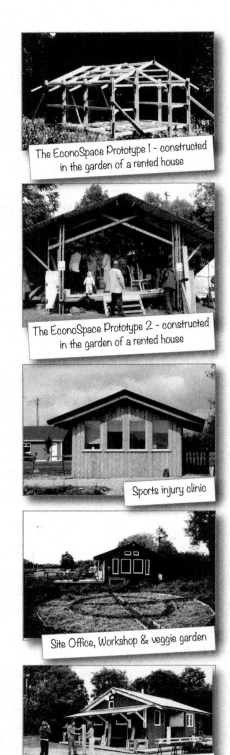

The EconoSpace Prototype 1 - constructed in the garden of a rented house

The EconoSpace Prototype 2 - constructed in the garden of a rented house

Sports injury clinic

Site Office, Workshop & veggie garden

Site Office & Workshop

rudiments of construction. How to find suitable and affordable materials locally. How to keep costs down and standards up.

The economic meltdown of 2008, triggered by the sub-prime mortgage crisis, has now proven beyond doubt that mortgage debt fuels economic growth and perpetuates the endless cycle of exploitation and destruction that bedevils the world. This clarity has added urgency to the need for people to reconnect with their sheltermaking instincts - to simply get out there and start building affordable architecture for themselves! When people do this, they enter a new world where the hidden dimensions of life can be experienced to the full!

The EconoSpace design and construction process has been configured to be practical and realistic in respect of the skills, time and resources most people have available to them. It offers few excuses as to why we cannot construct the future according to our oft expressed desire to embrace a sustainable way of life.

Economical, versatile and adaptable, EconoSpaces are an ideal 'starter building' for those wishing to explore the world of 'self-building'. They will also appeal to people needing additional space for guests, creativity, home offices, etc.

Some of the many uses to which an EconoSpace can be put:

Art Studio   Bath House
Unit of Dwelling   Garden Building
Playhouse   Computer Room
Storage Room   Site Office
Meditation Space   Writers Retreat
Home Office   Love Shack

The EconoSpace has been featured in various magazines - Owner Builder; Permaculture UK; Crann & Self-Build - as well as appearing on RTÉ1's 'Nationwide' and TG4's 'Teach Glas'.

Site Office & Workshop

Site Office & Workshop

Mary Kennedy, RTÉ1 'Nationwide'

Site Office & Workshop

The EconoSpaceMaking DVD

Sustainability begins in your own backyard - that is the compelling argument put forward on this dynamic combination of text, drawings, photographs and video information.

By learning how to create a small sustainable shelter - with no need to first obtain planning permission - we are offered the opportunity to regain territory lost to an economic system which depends on mortgage debt to satisfy its insatiable appetite and growth.

From drawing to modelmaking, from concept to built reality, EconoSpaceMaking provides you with the means to create your own living architecture and to discover, in the process, who you really are.

EconoSpaceMakers can also participate in a dedicated online Forum where they can exchange ideas and information as well as keeping up with the latest developments.

WHAT'S ON THE DVD

• A 63 page A4 fully illustrated Manual detailing how to design and construct your unique, low-cost EconoSpace.

• Over 2 hours of Video Instruction offering invaluable insights into the design and construction processes

• Model Templates, allowing you to design and assemble your EconoSpace in miniature before constructing it full size.

• Working drawings for 10sqm and 25sqm EconoSpaces – all the information you need to create your unique building, plus supplementary texts.

• EconoSpaceMakers can also participate in a dedicated online Forum where they can exchange ideas and information and help each other make their EconoSpaces happen.

The EconoSpaceMaking DVD is available exclusively from the Living Architecture Centre:

LIVING ARCHITECTURE CENTRE.COM

Film editing studio

Art studio model

Art studio under construction

Art studio under construction

Art Studio

EconoSpace Gallery

The Round Hut

The Round Hut emerged from a dream. A client had asked me to look at a site where he proposed to build a house. He mentioned that there was a Stone Age carving at one end of the land which I examined when I visited there. It was after that I had the dream - a vision of the house for the site. It was a round hut to shelter the guardian of the carved rock. I sketched out the plan and drew some impressions of how it might look.

The client was from a theatrical background and so appreciated my dream and the embryonic design. However, he had five daughters who were determined to have the design conform to their dreams! So the lovely round hut nestled inside me, occasionally inspiring a sketch or a model to be made, enticing me to gently probe its mysteries.

The HeadSpace

The HeadSpace evolved from the making and using of scale models as part of the design process. These were useful in allowing one to examine the 3-dimensional proportions of a building, particularly a buildings' external appearance. However, as far as examining the proportions of internal space the models were limited. One could peer through window or door openings to gain a sense of the internal space being enclosed but this offered only a limited view that was far from satisfactory.

I though that if I cut a hole in the floor of a model I could use a small periscope to view the inside space it would solve this problem. But alas, the images appeared upside down and were totally confusing!

I thought, *'if only I could get my head inside the model ...'* This inspired a radical approach - to make a large scale model with an opening in the floor big enough to accommodate my head. I thought of this as a 'HeadSpace'.

The making of the TV documentary *Building On the Edge** offered the perfect opportunity to make and experience a HeadSpace. I based this on the Actual House (see page 292, *Volume* 1), a design which had come to me in a dream. At a scale of 1:8, the floor of the model measured 2mX2m with the external walls standing over 300mm high. The entire structure was mounted on legs to facilitate easy viewing.

The effect of viewing the model from within, as it were, was spectacular! One was *inside* the space, despite the fact the bulk of one's body remained outside! With the model erected in the exact location where I planned to build myself an Actual House it was possible to assess the views in all directions and to get a real sense of how the completed space would be!

Generally, when people experience the HeadSpace their first reaction is always the same - a broad smile crosses their face!

**Building On the Edge*
Bandit Films 2006, directed by Johnny Gogan
This documentary can be viewed at:
LIVING ARCHITECTURE CENTRE.COM

THE ACTUAL HOUSE

The Actual House concept grew out of the original Be Your Own Architect Course, first staged in 1989. Many people were inspired in these Courses by the idea of the different kind of house that I spoke of. Because they could not 'actually see' one of these houses they felt a little at a loss. Things were still at an early stage. No designs had yet been constructed.

I decided to design an 'actual' house that people could see and experience. I saw this as a versatile framework which could be adpated to individual circumstance and need. I followed the strategy developed in the Courses for the initial design development. This was quite difficult as this strategy was geared to the creation of totally individual design solutions — the shaping of the architecture specifically to suit the lives of those who would live within. The Actual House concept somewhat contradicted this idea of a totally individual design solution for each Course participant. I seemed to be embarking on the creation of a standard box into which anyone could fit! This contradiction seemed worth exploring however as many other issues were arising in the Courses which needed to be addressed — the time people had available to develop totally individual designs; the preparation of the necessary drawings; questions of building economics and planning issues – to name but a few.

In resolving these issues The Actual House Design began to evolve into a standard framework that could support a complete range of individual needs from common necessities such as Bathrooms, Entrance Lobbies, Bedrooms and Kitchen/Dining/Living Areas, to more specialised requirements such as Offices, Workshops, Sunspaces and so on. Coupled with the evolving versatility in providing for a complete range of individual accommodation needs, the design began to embrace wider issues such as economy of construction; healthiness; buildability; passive solar energy usage; planning ; interior flexibility and expandability.

Two versions of the Actual House evolved from this – a single storey 100sm/1000sqft version and a 'loft' version capable of providing up to 150sqm/1500sqft of versatile floorspace. With both versions utilising a similar ground floor

Actual House –
Loft version

292

'footprint' this granted immense flexibility in the creation of individual plans and further allowed for these plans, once built, to be changed with a minimum of disruption. Featuring highly insulated suspended timber ground floors and passive solar capability, the timber frame structures could be married to a variety of insulating and finishing materials and the entire building could be self-built with a minimum of previous experience.

Soon, the focus of attention began to turn to the creation of a full size version of the Actual House. Naively, I thought it possible to access some of the European Structural Funds flowing about to construct the initial prototype! The extent of my naivety only manifest itself after a series of rebuttals. The inevitable analysis that I had to bring to bear on these blockages yielded some interesting truths – there is no support for solutions that promote lower expenditure in the housing field; the construction industry is a law onto itself; modern economics are based on borrowings using Bricks & Mortar as security; the politics of growth depend on the creation of bigger and more expensive houses and constantly increasing consumerism; alternative housing solutions are a threat to established property values; fear is the primary tool used in maintaining this status quo. Within this web, the frustration that many people feel about mortgages and dreary houses abounds.

Once these blockages were identified they could be circumvented and the development of the Actual House design could proceed. Creative energy was lavished on realising the goal of building the first one. This began by developing a set of technical drawings, securing the rights to the design and then subjecting several different versions of the Actual House the rigours of the Planning System — which it passed with flying colours!

The first Actual House - a loft version - was constructed in Co. Wicklow by myself working with unskilled labour on a shoestring budget.

3 Actual Houses have now been completed with a total of 5 Planning Permissions granted.

Individual versions of the Actual House can be developed through the Living Architecture Centre.

Actual House - Single storey version

293

Coimisiún na Scrúduithe Stáit
State Examinations Commission

Leaving Certificate Examination, 2003

Construction Studies

Theory - Higher Level

Wednesday 18 June
Afternoon, 2.00 to 5.00

M.76

Success!
Embraced by The System!

10. A detached single-storey house is situated adjacent to a main road on the outskirts of a large town and is within easy reach of the town centre. Planning permission is being sought to demolish this house and to erect a four-storey apartment block on the site.

  (a) What arguments might be presented:

  (i) In support of the erection of the apartment block;

  (ii) In support of the retention of the existing house?

  (b) Make a recommendation to the planning authority on this proposal and give **three** reasons in support of your recommendation.

OR

"Vernacular styles of buildings exist all over the world. These styles are characterised by their simplicity, by their use of local materials and by the ease with which they can be constructed. The knowledge required for the creation of such buildings was long regarded as common knowledge and freely available to all. The decline of the vernacular tradition with its simple forms and its accessibility to people has resulted in the loss of the knowledge and skills needed to design and construct small buildings, especially the buildings in which people live – their homes."

Be Your Own Architect (1992) : Peter Cowman.

Discuss.

At the premiere of the documentary 'Sheltermaker' with Justin Leijon, director.

Australian Centre For The Moving Image
Melbourne   December 2012

PETER COWMAN
建筑艺术 筑起能量屋

彼得总是给人善良及洒脱的印象，是个生态与生活建筑的快乐哲人。他思维系统的构造似乎没有现代人普遍的复杂。我们一般所认知的建筑师，是个设计建筑物构造的人；而生活建筑艺术的重要性，在于考量内在并存的时间与空间。正如彼得所说，我们需要的是一个"泊巢"的居所，而非有着奢华躯壳却缺乏内涵的房子。

Text : 郑彩清 Photo : 受访者提供

记 记者 凌 彼得

记：你的《生活建筑》理念是从何开始的？
彼：当年毕业后我曾经在建筑领域工作3年，然后再人销售领域做了一阵子银行的销售及游说工作近10年，我不断试种事。我是个建筑师，我有能力建造自己的房子，于是我找到一个"泊巢村庄"里去生活，也纳入知道我是建筑师。

It's all Chinese to me!
Living Architecture featured in Malaysian wholistic living magazine

acmi
AUSTRALIAN CENTRE FOR THE MOVING IMAGE

294

PYTHON PRESS BOOKS
Books on sensitive and sustainable living, esoteric agriculture and
awareness of the spiritual dimensions of life and planet
Available at bookstores around the world or buy directly from:
Python Press PO Box 929, Castlemaine, Vic 3450, Australia

www.pythonpress.com

pythonpress@gmail.com

Sensitive Permaculture
- cultivating the way of the sacred Earth

by Alanna Moore

This 2009 book explores the living energies of the land and how to sensitively connect with them. Positive and joyful, it draws on the indigenous wisdom of Australasia, Ireland and elsewhere, combining the insights of geomancy and geobiology with eco-smart permaculture design to offer an exciting new paradigm for sustainable living. It includes the authors experiences of negotiating with the local fairy beings over land use in Australia and Ireland.

Readers say:

"A delight to read" Callie

"You make permaculture so easy and alive---and sweet" Joy, Taiwan

"...Hard to put down" Celia, Permaculture Association of Tasmania

Reviewers comments: *"A very practical and thoughtful guide for the eco-spiritual gardener,*
bringing awareness to the invisible dimensions of our landscape"
Rainbow News, New Zealand

"An adventure in magical and practical Earth awareness"
Nexus magazine

Divining Earth Spirit   by Alanna Moore
An Exploration of Global & Australasian Geomancy

A global look at geomancy and geobiology from an Australasian perspective, from English ley lines and fairy folk, to geopathic stress and the paradigms of the Aboriginal Dreamtime. The environment is alive and conscious!

"This book is a classic for anyone wanting to get involved with Earth healing. It contains information by the bucketload... The research that has gone into this book is incredible and no doubt will stir you into wanting to use it yourself"
Radionics Network Vol. 2 No.6

"Excellent reference book" Don McLeod, Silver Wheel

"Love of the topic clearly shows, as Moore brings clarity and a sense of the necessity of personal involvement and engagement with the Earth. The great advantage of Moore's book is in its detailing all the salient aspects of Earth Spirit phenomena....all covered succinctly and with precision... the perfect introduction to the topic." Esoterica magazine, No. 4, 1995

Backyard Poultry - Naturally   by Alanna Moore

From housing to feeding, from selection to breeding, from pets to production and from the best lookers to the best layers, this book covers everything the backyard farmer needs to know about poultry husbandry - including preventative and curative herbal medicines and homeopathics, plus permaculture design for productive poultry pens. It has long been Australia's best-selling 'chook' book!

The Reviews:

"A wonderful resource! Alanna Moore has provided poultry enthusiasts with all the information they need to raise healthy poultry without using harmful chemicals."
Megg Miller, Grass Roots magazine.

"The poultry health section is the best I've seen."
Eve Sinton, Permaculture International Journal.

"An interesting and worthwhile book that will no doubt have a lot of appeal for the amateur or part-time farmer."
Kerry Lonergan, Landline, ABC TV.

Stone Age Farming - tapping nature's energies for your farm or garden
(2nd edition, 2012)   by Alanna Moore

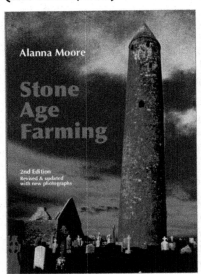

From Irish Round Towers to modern Towers of Power for enhancing plant growth. In this book ancient and modern ideas about the energies of rocks and landscapes are explored for practical use in the garden, including the application of dowsing, Earth wisdom and geomantic understandings.

What reviewers have said of the 1st edition (2001):
"Simply fabulous!"
Maurice Finkel, Health and Healing.

"Quite fantastic."
Roberta Britt, Canadian Quester Journal.

"Clear, lucid and practical" Tom Graves

"A classic"   Radionics Network.

"Will change your perception of the world"
Conscious Living magazine.

A Geomantic Guidebook to

Touchstones for Today
- designing for Earth harmony with stone arrangements and subtle energy dowsing
by Alanna Moore, 2013

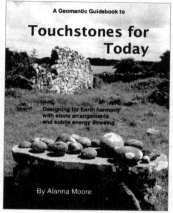

Ancient and enigmatic, the standing stones, labyrinths and stone circles that still haunt various corners of the world have often been subject to systematic destruction. But yet, in some form, they have survived over several millennia. Their enduring presences beg so many questions. How did the ancients manage to erect the huge megalithic monuments, when it is a struggle to replicate them today? For what purposes were they made? They must have been highly significant, given the enormous amount of effort involved. Science and folklore can provide clues. But personal experience of sites and energies detected at sacred stones can be much more revealing and rewarding than bland facts.

Today, sensitive people find that the ancient standing stones, both natural and intentionally placed, can act as transmitters of beneficial Earth energies, providing anchor points for the power and spirit of the land. Not surprisingly, old traditions of healing, divination, wish fulfillment and fertility associated with certain sacred stones continue to find currency today. And anyone may potentially tune in to the sacred stones by taking up the ancient art of dowsing (also known as divining), or other forms of psychic attunement. It can be personally most enriching!

This Guidebook encourages people to discover for themselves the magical and transforming energies associated with both ancient megalithic sites and modern stones of power; and to be inspired to create one's own energetic stone arrangements, as Touchstones of interaction with the Sacred Earth.

144 pages, with 90 black & white illustrations

About the Author

Alanna Moore was a co-founder of the New South Wales Dowsing Society 1984. A professional dowser, she is internationally known for her writing and teaching of dowsing and geomancy. She lectures worldwide and also makes films. A permaculture farmer and teacher as well, her writings are archived at www.geomantica.com as well as at Australia's National Library.

Diary of A Sheltermaker   by Peter Cowman

COMING SOON!

When architect Peter Cowman opts to follow his own 'living' architecture philosophy he's in for a few surprises. After 30 years of itinerant life, the lure of the acre of boggy meadow in Ireland's northwest is compelling.

Juggling work commitments alongside construction of his low-cost, low-impact, mortgage-free cabin, his adventures are both amusing as well as hair-raising.

True to his own predictions, the issues which the design and construction process raise track to the very core of his being, challenging his grasp on reality.

Rooted in the here and now, his timepieces are the sun, the moon and his commitment to unravelling the mysteries of sheltermaking.

Living off the grid and off his wits, surprises appear out of nowhere, demanding time and attention.

Nestled by the warm stove of his imagining, absorbed within the gentle beauty of the ancient land, the dreams which sustain him have an agenda of their own.

When sheltermaking activities hit a blockage, despite having willing volunteers and materials on hand, Peter has to call a halt to further progress.

In an instant his plans are turned on their head and he suddenly finds himself on the other side of the planet!

This resumption of his itinerant life leads to unexpected discoveries.

Piecing together shards of the past, the picture he has long imagined is suddenly complete!

So, the mystery unfolds and the reluctant hero finds solace in the realisation of his freedom to act out his sheltermaking dreams wherever he happens to be.

GEOMANTICA

Correspondence Course
Diploma of Dowsing for Harmony

This correspondence Course imparts techniques and applications of pendulum dowsing that will help you to create a more energetically harmonious world and to potentially have a career doing this work. Originally written in 1989, many hundreds of students from around the world have enjoyed this opportunity for distant study. It has been revised and updated over the years. The Course can be bought in ten parts or all at once.

The Course includes comprehensive notes, dowsing charts and lists, practical exercises and personal Assessments from Course originator and internationally acclaimed tutor Alanna Moore, who has over 30 years dowsing and teaching of dowsing experience. You can start now or anytime and complete it in your own time, although generally it is usually undertaken over one or two years. No obligation when to finish. (It has also just recently been made available to a wider audience, for people who don't want to achieve a Diploma.) See www.geomantica.com/dowsing-correspondence-course

The 10 Units of in-depth study are these:

Unit One: The Basics of Dowsing - Theories that help to explain dowsing. Clear, simple techniques and useful exercises.

Unit Two: Wholistic Diagnosis – The philosophical basis of holistic health and harmony, the importance of seeking balance of the mind, body, emotions, spirit and environment. Dowsing the levels of being and divining peoples' esoteric psychology with the Seven Rays.

Unit Three: Body Systems – An integrated approach to anatomy and physiology – from the physical to the energetic in global traditions, including Chinese medical philosophy.

Unit Four: Analytic Dowsing – Dowsing for causative factors in disease, diet selection, food and water testing, allergen detection. The problem of pesticides, additives and pollutants in food and water and how to test for them. Using samples for analysis.

Unit Five: Dowsing for Solutions – Selecting remedies and therapies by pendulum and Seven Ray analysis. Working with vibrational remedies made from flowers, gems, shells etc. Dowsing for homeopathic remedies.

Unit Six: Distant Dowsing and Healing – Remote health analysis and energy balancing techniques. Using symbolic patterns plus crystals and gems for remote healing work. Chakra balancing with the pendulum and more.

Unit Seven: Earth Energies and Health – How underground streams, geological faults and the like can cause geopathic stress. How to create and maintain harmony with geomancy and feng shui. Working with the devic dimensions – the nature spirits.

Unit Eight: Building Biology – Our homes are our third skin, and should protect us to some degree. Unhealthy homes can poison or irritate us with their toxic building materials and electro-magnetic fields etc. How to check for sick building syndrome and find healthier alternatives.

Unit Nine: Map Dowsing and Environmental Remedies – Distant dowsing by map to seek out harmful zones in the home and environment. Geomantic cures such as Earth acupuncture methods using copper pipes, crystals, etc to neutralise noxious zones.

Unit Ten: Towers of Power & The Professional Dowser - How to locate and make Towers of Power for environmental energising and harmonising. Professionalism in dowsing.

Geomantica Films
by Alanna Moore
Only available from www.Geomantica.com

(See extracts of Geomantica Films on You Tube.)

* The ART of DOWSING & GEOMANCY
140 minutes of dowsing and geomancy training sessions with Alanna Moore and her students, ideal for beginners.

* DOWSERS DOWNUNDER
102 minutes of interviews and demonstrations with a diverse range of amazing dowsers filmed around Australia.

Three film series (with each film around half an hour):

* EARTH CARE, EARTH REPAIR (8 films)
Dowsing, Greening & Crystal Farming (including interview with broadscale wheat farmers about crystal farming). *Eco-Gardeners Down-Under* (featuring Bill Mollison and David Holmgren). *Grassroots Solutions to Soil Salinity* (with dowsers saving landscapes from dryland salinity). *Growing & Gauging Sustainability* (using Universal Knowledge to Brix meters). *Remineralising the Soil* (the value of paramagnetic rock dust and dowsing its qualities). *Making Power Towers* (shows the construction of a paramagnetic antenna, or Power Tower). *Agnihotra / Homa Farming* (an ancient Indian fire ritual that has marvellous effects on plant growth).

* GEOMANCY TODAY (5 films)
Megalithomania (stone circles and the like from Europe to Australasia). *Divining Earth Harmony* (5 geomancers talk about their diverse approaches.) *Discovering the Devas* (yes, they are out here and you can dowse for them!) *Helping the Devas* (interview with Swedish dowsers who work with the devic kingdoms). *The Sacred World of Water* (from mythology to a geomantic appreciation of water in the landscape).

* STATE of PILGRIMAGE (6 films)
Glastonbell Dreaming (interview with Australia's first white geomancer). *Pilgrimage to Central Australia* (exploring Aboriginal sites and culture). *A Thirst for Ireland* (indigenous geo-mythos). *Bali – geomantic journeying in paradise. South Australian Sojourn.*

Lightning Source UK Ltd.
Milton Keynes UK
UKOW04f0622050717

9 780975 778265